PRAISE FOR

MY LIFELONG FIGHT AGAINST DISEASE

"The world needs more thinkers, people full of novel thoughts who consistently create and add to our fund of knowledge—people like Bill Haseltine. While the world knows him as a prominent molecular biologist, biotechnology entrepreneur and global health author, Dr. Haseltine has also navigated the halls of Congress, the news media and Wall Street. He has touched and changed so many different sectors of our society, and we are all better because of it. If you are considering a career in science, or know a young person who should be, place this book at the top of your list. You will be inspired to make an impact on the world, with a remarkable guide to help show you the path."

—Sanjay Gupta, MD
Associate Professor of Neurosurgery, Emory University;
Chief Medical Correspondent, CNN

"William Haseltine's life story offers a unique perspective on science: science as a powerful tool to radically improve human health and well being across the planet. Readers will be swept along by the excitement of discovery, the urgency of breakthrough treatment, the impact of policy and the thrill of success. I can well imagine future leaders in health science looking back on this book as formative to their own journeys."

—Brian Greene
Professor of Physics and Mathematics, Columbia University;
Co-founder and Chairman, World Science Festival

"William Haseltine's expertise and career as a scientist, educator, philanthropist, entrepreneur and advisor in global health are as rich and varied as his contributions to biomedical research, biotechnology, drug discovery and public policy. He makes another valuable contribution to the field with his autobiography, sharing a lifetime of knowledge, lessons and unique experiences. Against the backdrop of some of the greatest health threats we have known—HIV/AIDS, cancer, polio, diabetes, anthrax and now COVID-19—this compelling personal and professional story offers a superbly insightful analysis of what it will take for humanity to keep combatting increasingly complex health challenges and their devastating impacts. This book makes a strong case for the paramount importance of science, scientific innovation and effective communication of scientific knowledge to address the most difficult societal problems. A life and career guided by a purpose to improve the health and well being of people everywhere is a legacy that gives hope."

—Michelle Williams
Dean of the Faculty, Harvard T.H. Chan School of Public Health

"Bill Haseltine is a creator of knowledge, a communicator of science and humanities and a powerful policy influencer. Here, he tells his compelling personal story, revealing the fascinating backstories that led to his extraordinary success. Enthusiasm in embracing the public context of science—including the political context—is all too rare in the science community. Bill models this in a joyful way, inspiring others to relish science and public engagement. It's an instant classic!"

—Mary Woolley
President and CEO, Research!America

"Few individuals make positive global impacts. Bill Haseltine is one of these rare human beings!"

—Hans Wigzell
Professor Emeritus, Karolinska Institute

"Haseltine has had an extraordinary life, and has produced a timely, moving and inspirational account of the difference that a curious man can make in the world. He has spent his life battling disease, often in the face of considerable odds, and he tells his tale with passion. He combines his powerful personal story with easy-to-read explanations of his tussles with medical science, and thrilling accounts of the political battles he faced."

—**Gillian Tett**
Chair Editorial Board and Editor-at-Large, *The Financial Times*

"I first met Bill in the early 1970s at Harvard. He was already a brilliant scientist and effective teacher, but he was just beginning his journey to become the biotech entrepreneur, global health philanthropist and major leader in the fight against infectious diseases whom we recognize today. He has devoted his career to using science to improve the human condition. Early on, Bill's major contributions to understanding HIV advanced our ability to combat its devastation. He went on to help revolutionize biomedical research through his work in genomics, strengthening health systems in many countries across the world and, today, helping us contain a new global threat, COVID-19. Bill possesses a remarkable combination of intellect, curiosity, compassion and communication skills that enable him to make a powerful difference wherever he goes."

—**Margaret (Peggy) Hamburg**
Former Commissioner of the U.S. Food and Drug Administration;
Former President, American Association for the Advancement of Science

"Searching for meaning in life, William Haseltine discovers the transformational power of science. *My Lifelong Fight Against Disease* is an appealing invitation to basic, clinical and policy research as a critical instrument for improving the human condition."

—**Julio Frenk, MD, PhD**
President, the University of Miami

"This gripping autobiography is at once a study in the development of a scientific mind infused with humanist commitment and a candid revelation of a complex and many sided personality. The arc of Bill's work, from central contributions to addressing the HIV/AIDS pandemic in the 1980s to his current role vis-a-vis COVID-19, is stunning. Readers will get to know great scientists like James Watson and Anthony Fauci, political figures from George W. Bush to Richard Holbrooke, AIDS activists such as Elizabeth Taylor and above all the author himself, whose careers in molecular biology research and biopharmaceutical entrepreneurship have been of immense benefit to humankind."

—**Leo J. O'Donovan, S.J.**
President Emeritus, Georgetown University

"Even around Harvard, Bill was recognized as one of the brightest. His vision and energy are extremely impressive. His career accomplishments should provide inspiration for the next generation of medical scientists."

—**Max Essex**
Mary Woodard Lasker Professor of Health Sciences,
Harvard T.H. Chan School of Public Health AIDS Initiative;
Chair, Harvard T.H. Chan School of Public Health AIDS Initiative

"A fascinating tale of growth and discovery of a medical scientist who thinks both deeply and broadly. Bill Haseltine's commitment to global health brings Pasteur's famous pledge to bringing discoveries from 'the bench to the bush' full circle, by disseminating successes achieved in lower income countries back home in the United States."

—**Alfred Sommer, MD**
Dean Emeritus and Professor, Johns Hopkins Bloomberg School of Public Health

My Lifelong Fight
Against Disease
FROM POLIO AND AIDS TO COVID-19

WILLIAM A. HASELTINE, PhD

amplifypublishing.com

My Lifelong Fight Against Disease: From Polio and AIDS to COVID-19

©2020 William A. Haseltine, PhD. All Rights Reserved. No part of this publication may be reproduced, stored in a retrieval system or transmitted in any form by any means electronic, mechanical, or photocopying, recording or otherwise without the permission of the author.

The conversations and events described in this book come primarily from the author's recollections and extensive archives. The author and publisher have made every effort to ensure that the information and re-creation of events included in the book are correct but assume no liability to any party for any loss, damage, or disruption caused by errors or omissions.

For more information, please contact:
Amplify Publishing, an imprint of Mascot Books
620 Herndon Parkway, Suite 320
Herndon, VA 20170
info@amplifypublishing.com

Library of Congress Control Number: 2020919112

CPSIA Code: PRV1120A
ISBN-13: 978-1-64543-826-7

Printed in the United States

*For all those who fight for health with
science, medicine and public policy*

A NOTE TO THE READER

As I closed out writing my autobiography in the last days of August 2020, I found myself in the midst of yet another pandemic, COVID-19. After more than two years researching, writing and editing this book, I had not expected to be working eighteen hours a day to vanquish a new global biothreat.

However, scientists, companies, governments and media outlets from all over the world sought my advice on how to monitor and interpret COVID-19 related research, drug and vaccine development, public policy and news reports. I am using a lifetime of knowledge of fundamental science, drug and vaccine development, public health systems and public communication to push back against this new disease.

In these pages, you will learn about my life's calling: to heal the ill no matter what their age or where they live. My goal is to give you the clearest view possible of how I acquired the skills, experience and know-how that equipped me to play the unique role of independent advisor to so many at the forefront of what I am certain ultimately will be the successful conquest of a deadly scourge.

It is not a role I imagined for myself in my mid-seventies, but it is a role, as evidenced in these pages, for which I am prepared.

WILLIAM A. HASELTINE
MANHATTAN, 2020

CONTENTS

INTRODUCTION

THIS IS THE STORY OF MY LIFE. I write it in hopes it will help you, the young reader, find a path in yours. In this time of plague, I also write for every one of us at every age. There is a desperate need to understand science as a tool to address our most pressing societal problems and, most urgently, to end COVID-19!

I knew early on that a life of healing was for me. As a four year old standing next to my mother's sickbed, terrified she might die from sepsis, my purpose began to form: to make a difference to human health. I thought my destiny was to be a doctor, to heal the sick. But in my early twenties, I discovered I could make an even bigger difference to health through a career in medical science.

I want the young to know that science offers a unique opportunity for one person to influence human life for all time. A single person can unravel a mystery that may improve people's lives everywhere. No matter your age or eminence, if you have good reason to hold a contrary opinion to a popular assumption, science compels you to hold your ground—as I have and still do—regardless of opposing politics or power.

Science opens a pathway to a wonderful life: a life of meaning, of world travel, of wonderful friends and like-minded colleagues, of business and philanthropy and of political impact. Science is a path of upward mobility for students from any background. Creating and communicating knowledge is an endless adventure.

I have had a fantastic life, one I could not have imagined in my most optimistic daydreams. I have created and contributed to new cures for cancer, HIV/AIDS, anthrax, lupus and diabetes, and, by applying genomics to drug discovery, speeded the discoveries of countless other cures. I have created more than a dozen biotechnology companies and influenced public policy at the highest levels. Over the past fifteen years, I have created two foundations with wealth from my business ventures, one to foster collaboration between the arts and science and another to advise governments around the world on how to bring high-quality, affordable healthcare to all their people.

Along the way, I have had the privilege of forming lifelong friendships with world-renowned actors, artists, musicians, writers, economists, business titans, military men and women and politicians, and have had a richly rewarding personal and family life.

The book is organized into seven parts:

- My family life and formative years in China Lake, California, at the western edge of the Mojave Desert.

- Explorations into biochemistry, other sciences and humanities, and immersion in the Free Speech Movement and campus politics at the University of California, Berkeley.

- A thrilling education with three Nobel Prize winners, including James D. Watson, co-discoverer of the DNA double helix, at Harvard and the Massachusetts Institute of Technology (MIT), while at the same time working as a journalist and activist against the Vietnam War.

- Establishing research laboratories at Harvard's Dana-Farber Cancer Institute and the Harvard School of Public Health to combat cancer and the HIV/AIDS pandemic.

- Creating biotechnology companies, bringing new cures to the market and raising billions of dollars on Wall Street.

- Building ACCESS Health International, a think tank and advisory group, to improve access to high-quality, affordable healthcare for all, no matter their age or where they live.

- Using my accumulated knowledge to combat COVID-19 through research, communication, public health and international cooperation.

I hope many younger readers will be enthralled by these stories and moved to pursue a life in science for themselves and for the contributions they could make to improve human life. I also hope readers who may have regarded science as removed from our collective drama will see the pursuit of scientific knowledge as intimately connected to realizing all that we hold valuable in life.

PART I

1

1985: RACING TO FUND
THE AIDS FIGHT

In July 1985, I was vacationing with my family on Mount Desert Island just off the coast of Maine. Despite our pristine surroundings, I was anything but relaxed. In fact, I was increasingly desperate, living a waking nightmare.

A professor in medical sciences at Harvard Medical School and director of two research laboratories at the Dana-Farber Cancer Institute, I was one of the world's very few experts on the AIDS virus, HIV. I knew a tidal wave of lethal disease was descending on an unprotected world, and that very little was being done to avert disaster.

The primary problem was money—money to further research on the startlingly evasive biochemistry of HIV and its vulnerabilities, money to design new drugs to contain and attack HIV, money to provide social services for legions of Americans infected with AIDS. With enough money I knew we could harness the best resources in science and medicine to avert the worst. Yet that money was nowhere on the horizon.

At the time, AIDS infection almost uniformly, over time, triggered a descent into terrible death, the immune system deteriorating as cancers, viral hepatitis, cardio vascular disease or other lethal ailments preyed more aggressively upon vital organs. No drugs to treat or prevent the AIDS virus existed. Meanwhile, epidemiologists estimated at least half a million Americans already were infected.

"WE ARE NOT HELPLESS"

For more than a year, I had been warning anyone who would listen:

"Don't think you can control the epidemic in the near term by asking people to change their sexual behavior. It took decades of constant messaging to reduce smoking. Sex is an even stronger human urge. Don't pin your hopes on a vaccine against the virus working anytime soon. Our data show that this virus evades every trick in our immune repertoire. Our experiments show that once the virus is in the body the story is over. The immune system can't stop it.

"We are not helpless. We have the complete blueprint of the virus. I see the chinks in its armor as clear as day. I count seven enzymes the virus cannot live without. Stop anyone of these and you will stop the virus and stop AIDS. Discovering antiviral drugs is easy compared to the discovery of new anticancer drugs. Why? Cancer is us, our own cells. The virus is not. Given the money I am certain that our scientists and the biopharma industry can come up with the drugs and do it fast."

Hardly anyone in government, business or academic research believed me. Many argued that AIDS would be confined to homosexuals and would never reach pandemic proportions. I came to understand the curse of Cassandra: listened to, not believed. People listened to me because I was an eminent scientist, but they did not believe my warnings. Of twenty scientists and public health officials surveyed by *Discover Magazine* in 1985, I was the only one to accurately predict the future.[1]

Then came stunning news. Hollywood film star Rock Hudson was on a chartered 747 flying from Paris to Los Angeles, critically ill with AIDS. One of America's most popular actors, Hudson, fifty nine years old, was returning to the United States after a questionable eleventh-hour treatment in France had failed.

Rock Hudson's tragedy pulled AIDS from the shadows. I felt sad for him, dismayed that he had put his health in even greater danger by flying to France for this experimental drug, a drug that I knew would fail. (My experiments at Dana-Farber had already showed the drug did not stop the virus).

I was also energized. "This is it," I said to my friends in Washington. "This is one of those once in a lifetime chances to capture America's attention, to be heard, to push Congress hard for serious money to develop the drugs we need to control the epidemic."

I proposed a clear, simple message:

Why does an American icon have to risk his life to go abroad for treatment? What is wrong with American science and medicine? Why can't we help our own? What do we need to do to protect ourselves and those we love?

"You guys stay here," I told my family in our Maine island hideaway. "I need to go back and get to work on this right away."

Driving to Boston, my mind racing, I pieced together a strategy:

"The country needs a War on AIDS, a massive institutional response mirroring the War on Cancer. Leadership from the top, nationwide health messaging, social support, physician, nurse and social work training and above all funds for research. That is what it will take. A full court press. If we can capture the public's interest around Rock Hudson and AIDS before it fades, we can begin to solve the problem. I will call everyone I know who might make a difference. Surely they will be interested now."

And they were interested. AIDS became front page news. *TIME Magazine*, *Newsweek*, *USA Today* all were eager for interviews. Live appearances followed on NBC's *Today Show* and ABC's *Good Morning America*. My name and face quickly became associated with a public warning, pleas for stronger government action.

THE ESSENTIAL ELIZABETH TAYLOR

This was the time to ask Congress for more AIDS research money. The Reagan administration had asked only for an additional one million dollars in the fiscal 1986 budget to fund AIDS research. How pathetic, I thought. A million dollars is not enough to fund even one lab with eight researchers! We must do better. Perhaps Elizabeth Taylor might be willing help.

I had become friends with the radiant Hollywood star in recent months, collaborating to push awareness of the AIDS crisis into the mainstream, turn public opinion and promote private funding for a cure. As I'll describe in more detail later, Elizabeth chaired a new philanthropy for that purpose, the American Foundation for AIDS Research, or amfAR. I led the foundation's team of scientific and medical advisors.

When we connected by phone the next day, she responded immediately.

"Rock is a dear, dear friend of mine. I am devastated. I will do whatever I can to help end this terrible disease."

"Would you be willing to come to D.C. to lobby Congress with me for more money next week?"

"You tell me where and when and I'll be there."

My next call was to Terry Lierman. Terry was the top lobbyist for what since the 1950s had been the most effective advocacy group in Washington for science research, the Albert and Mary Lasker Foundation. I met him while serving on the Lasker jury that confers what is considered to be the American Nobel Prize in medicine, the Lasker Awards. The Lasker Foundation was renowned, vital in winning major government funding for biomedical research, especially for cancer and heart disease. Terry was the political wingman behind the scenes, a master at the nuts and bolts of health research legislation.

"You are right. Now is the time to move," he told me. "But we don't have much time. The 1986 budget is almost final. The window for supplemental appropriations closes in six weeks. If we move fast, we can make it. We will need support from across the aisle. I know the Democrats well, but you'll have to come up with the Republicans."

"I am great friends with Katherine and Ted Stevens," I reassured him. "Ted is Republican Whip of the Senate and chair of the Armed Services

Committee. Elizabeth Taylor also is a good friend. She was married to Senator John Warner, remember? He is a Republican too. I know they will help. When can we start?"

"Right away. If you are here Monday I will introduce you to top staff members in Ted Kennedy's and Henry Waxman's offices. Those two are key to getting the Democrats."

"Super. Elizabeth says she can be here next week. Let's get started."

Within two weeks, we secured great support from Kennedy, Waxman and their staffs. They proposed two hundred and sixty million for the fiscal 1986 budget bill, a supplemental appropriation to support AIDS research within the National Institutes of Health budget. But what about the Republicans?

Elizabeth was confident that John Warner would open the right doors. "I will ask John to pull together a lunch of the most senior and influential senators, the so called old bulls. I know them all and they like me. I am sure we can get them on our side."

FOUR QUESTIONS

Elizabeth was trim, sparkling and full of energy in a pink Chanel suit trimmed with a gold chain link belt a few days later as we walked into the Hart Senate Office Building. "Do I need to take off my belt?" she asked, smiling at two security guards. She was about to step through the metal detector. They nodded, she complied, and we proceeded toward Senator Warner's office.

Just before I opened the door to the senator's private dining room, she paused, suddenly serious, with a directive for me. In a low voice, she said, "You've got to do something, Bill. When I ask you a question during the lunch, the answer has got to be yes. Remember, yes to all my questions! Will you promise me?"

"If you think it is important, I promise."

On the other side of the door, we were greeted by John Warner and a collection of the most iconic Washington conservatives of the time: Republicans Jesse Helms and Barry Goldwater, and Democrat Daniel Inouye.

After we finished eating, Elizabeth shifted from what had been an informal, polite conversation to the business of the hour.

"We are here to ask you to add more to the budget to support AIDS research," she began, then turned to me. *"Now, doctor, I want to talk about AIDS. AIDS is a serious problem, right?"*

"Oh, yes, it is a serious problem."

"And it is a sexually transmitted disease, isn't it?"

"Yes, it is."

"I also heard you can catch AIDS from having sex with a man or a woman. Is that true?"

"Yes it is."

"Doctor, you can get AIDS from a blowjob, isn't that also true?"

The answer to that entirely unanticipated question, then as now, is no. Not that it might not happen but in all the time we have studied AIDS it has never been known to happen. But I had been instructed on how to reply, and I kept my word, unflinchingly, even though I was about to violate a sacred principle of science: stick to the known facts.

"Yes," I answered.

Suddenly, each of the senators, some of whom seemed to have drifted off, snapped to attention. I assumed they thought oral sex was safe sex. Most men do. But that day, with that group and what was a stake, my unscientific "yes" might have been worth the two hundred and sixty million dollars these senators agreed to support. Ted Stevens soon added another sixty million dollars, transferring funds within the Pentagon budget, and increasing proposed new funding for AIDS research to three hundred and twenty million dollars.

"THE SCIENCE IMPERATIVE"

Days before the vote on the supplemental budget, I laid out the full scope of the AIDS threat in testimony for more than an hour in the Senate chamber in the Capitol. The policy climate around AIDS was colored by a tremendous wave of opposition. Part of this reaction, beyond politics, reflected a deep instinct of human nature. We do not want to be threatened by some new danger. We want to minimize it, deny it and ignore it, until we ourselves are in obvious danger. I made the case as powerfully as I could that we had to go against our instincts and take a bold new direction to fund the science imperative to fight AIDS.

"We see this wave of devastating disease approaching. The magnitude and nature of the problem is crystal clear. As the disease continues to spread, the magnitude of the problem must increase. I urge you to begin planning now for the inevitable.

"AIDS has the potential to devastate our young adults, their children, their grandchildren. The crisis is already denting the nation's economy. The accumulated costs from hospital bills, lost wages, and benefits exceeds five billion dollars and within a few years could surge towards fifty billion. At least a half million Americans, and perhaps as many as one million, are already infected with the AIDS virus.

"The discovery of the AIDS virus would not have been possible without strong federal support of cancer research. The prevailing view that the AIDS virus was transmitted mostly among homosexual is misplaced. Studies by Robert R. Redfield, head physician at Walter Reed Army Medical Center,[2] document worrisome rates of heterosexual transmission between couples in the military, transmission from men to women and from women to men. In West Germany, a study showed twenty percent of female sex workers were infected. Intravenous drug users who shared needles are at even greater risk of infection."

Framing the research challenges, I said, "We have now progressed into the broad seas of the unknown... We confront problems never before encountered. The solution to these problems will require great ingenuity." I envisioned three interlocking paths for AIDS virus research: "We must understand the workings of this new virus... We must also learn how this virus lives with and/or kills cells that it infects... We must understand the body's immune reactions to the virus."

Finally, I bluntly confronted the Reagan administration. Its proposed one million dollar increase, requested by the Department of Health and Human Services, "is the functional equivalent of ignoring the problem entirely.

"The current situation is intolerable. We have the best biomedical apparatus in the world. Much of it is lying idle with respect to the AIDS problem as a result of inadequate funding and shortsighted programmatic efforts... But AIDS is a problem that will not go away. Every time that we look, it looms larger so that now the shadow of the disease has begun to darken all our lives."

A few days later, success. Congress voted to add the Kennedy-Stevens supplemental bill to the fiscal 1986 federal budget.

TWO HUNDRED MILLION LIVES SAVED?

That moment in the late summer of 1985 marked the beginning of an effective, coordinated commitment to combat AIDS that continues today. Without that initial surge in federal funding we would have lost a crucial year, and possibly more. Over the years, federal funding for AIDS research has continued to grow from that three hundred and twenty million in fiscal 1986 to more than $2.5 billion in 2020.

Thanks to that continued funding, as I'll explain in Part IV, we developed the knowledge and drugs, prescribed in myriad combinations for effective treatments, that enable most people infected with HIV to live long and productive lives. More than twenty million people around the world were treated with these antiretroviral drugs to contain HIV and protect their immune systems in 2020.

My guess is that the courageous decision by Congress in 1985 has saved as many as two hundred million lives around the world. I am hedging here only because the majority of those in my estimate of two hundred million *never were infected*. Scientific and related pharmaceutical discoveries, built upon the surge of federal research support in those early days, have made it possible since the early 1990s to control the epidemic in many parts of the world.

| 2 |

A PASSION FOR HEALING

I MUST HAVE BEEN NOT QUITE FOUR YEARS OLD, standing next to my mother's bed. Her arm was draped over the side next to me, her hand dipped into a steaming pan. An intense purple-red line ran from her wrist to her elbow. If the infection rose much higher, she would die.

I felt helpless, dreading those hours as the purple-red line of psoriasis infection advanced. With all my might I willed that line to fall back down her arm and disappear.

Why is she suffering? Will she die? What can I do to help?

My mother suffered multiple illnesses, some of which I was aware of and understood as a boy, others not at all until I was a teenager. This first, psoriasis, is an itchy, scaling inflammation of the skin related to bouts of anxiety. Inflammations can turn deadly through infection.

The purple-red line appeared again when I was six, yet again when I was seven. Each time I kept vigil at her bedside, besieged with the fear. *Would she die this time? If not now, what about the next time? Would there be a next time?* The psoriasis infection always stopped its advance, then retreated down her arm. My terrors abated, but never vanished.

My mother was diagnosed with a detached retina when I was still seven. I remember her fear as she described to me a black curtain descending over her vision. Again, I was anxious, frightened. A doctor warned she could lose her sight if the detached retina were not repaired immediately. The treatment required severing muscles that move the eye, gently lifting the eye from the socket, cauterizing the retina to the back of the eye, stitching together the muscles and replacing the eyeball back in the socket. (The procedure now is much simpler: lasers aimed through the pupil tack the retina in place.)

Again, the questions: *Why is she suffering? Will she go blind? What can I do to help?*

Recovery was brutal. Lie flat on your back in hospital for the next two weeks, head stabilized with sandbags to prevent any movement. Back at home my mother wore glasses with tiny pinholes to prevent her eyes from moving too much. The muscles needed time to heal. Doctors widened the aperture slightly more each month.

This delicate recovery went on for nine months. My mother was terrified; the slightest bump on the head or any sudden movement would free the loosely attached retina. She could not lift any weight, do the dishes or shop by herself. Two years later, the same ordeal repeated: two weeks in the hospital, nine months' recovery.

Another year to carry my fears about her health. *Why is she suffering? This is not fair! Will she go blind?* I did what I could. Open doors, carry groceries, clean the house. I wanted to do more, to make the suffering pass. Although I knew I had little to offer then, I was determined to find a way to help her and others.

TRAUMA ON A SUNDAY AFTERNOON

"Billy! Get your younger sister and brother out of the house, now!" My dad was screaming. "Take them where they won't see what is happening. NOW!" It had been a quiet Sunday afternoon. Dad had been napping. I was eleven, starting junior high. My sister Florence had just discovered my mother, barely conscious, in the master bathroom, her wrists and throat slashed, bleeding into the sink and tub.

Racing out into the backyard, my two siblings in hand, I saw an ambulance pull up to the house, sirens blaring. Two medics with a stretcher rushed in. The three of us kept moving, hurrying away to a quiet spot surrounded by poplars two blocks away. After a long, nerve wracking interlude, the sirens faded into the distance, and we slowly returned home, riddled with confusion and anxiety. This time, my mother was in hospital for two months. *Why had she done this to herself? Could I have done anything to help?* One more spur toward a purpose, a determination. When I could, I kept thinking, I would learn whatever skills I needed to help her and help others.

Two years later, the summer before I entered high school. Another health crisis. Another ambulance. An even longer absence.

Mom had been acting strange for a few weeks. Pacing anxiously in the house, peering out windows. Convinced neighbors were circling the house, scheming to hurt us all. She was losing touch with reality, my dad explained. "Your mother has a mental disease called manic depression," he said. "She can't help herself. Her brain acts up and controls what she feels and thinks. She is now in a manic state. She has irrational fears. It will pass, but she needs to be in a hospital for a while."

Several months later she returned from a sanatorium, but it was clear she remained unwell, catatonic. No speech or reaction to anything happening around her. Again, my dad explained. "Your mother is now on the down cycle of the disease. She is depressed. She will be in the hospital again but will come back better." Fortunately, as Dad predicted, she returned a few months later, stable and lucid.

The way she described for me what she had gone through is etched deeply in my memory.

"I was in so much pain I could not speak," she said. "As if I was living exposed, with no skin, flayed alive. Even the slightest breeze burned like fire. A wall of blinding pain obscured everything around me." Catatonia, she went on, "is not the absence of feeling. Just the opposite! It is constant blinding pain, pain that can drive you to suicide."

Many years later those exact words jumped from the page when I read William Styron's description of his own depression in *Darkness Visible*.

PENICILLIN SAVED MY INFANT LIFE

My mother's struggle with mental illness further sharpened my thoughts about a career in medicine. I would become a doctor, then a psychiatrist.

I will find new ways to spare others the suffering I witnessed in the person I love most.

To be honest, my own struggles with disease and recoveries aided by modern medicine certainly contributed to my thinking. I knew antibiotics were wonder drugs of the 1950s. It must be possible, I convinced myself, to discover wonder drugs on my own to heal people around me.

My mother told me how my life was saved early on, when I was an infant. It was January 1945. Dad was with the army in Europe, and Mom was living at Jefferson Barracks in St. Louis, caring for two small children. With me lying gravely ill in her arms, Mom begged army doctors to treat me with the new miracle drug, penicillin. Penicillin was uncompromisingly restricted for military use only.[3] Nonetheless, she prevailed. I became one of the very first non-combatants to be saved by penicillin. Without the miracle drug, and my mother's frantic efforts to save me, my story would have ended before it began.

Despite her battles with debilitating disease my mother carried on. When she was well, she was an engaged, loving and vibrant parent. Her enjoyment with life was immediate, infectious. Her rapturous exclamations—seeing a beautiful sunrise, hearing a great singer or eating a delicious dish—endure as joyful memories for me.

My mother struggled for the rest of her life with the mental anguish she described to me that day. She died by suicide twenty five years later. After the memorial service, Mom's best friend pulled me aside. "She fought for life so long, in such pain," she told me, with affection and genuine admiration for my mother that I found uplifting. "Your mother was a hero."

When I received that terrible midnight call, I was already a professor at Harvard Medical School fully engaged in the fight against a new enemy, AIDS, applying all my intellect to defeat it.

I know my mother would have been gratified to know that her courageous battles against illness inspired her son toward a path that would help millions resist HIV infection, recover and live, and would benefit millions more through discoveries in cancer and genomics research.

3

A LOVE FOR SCIENCE

I CAN STILL FEEL THE SHAME, Mrs. Whistler hauling me into the punishment corner of our fourth grade classroom. Her bright red fingernails pierced my neck, her inflamed words and visage shook my vulnerable psyche.

"Not only do you misbehave, you are flunking," she said. "I may have to hold you back a grade. If you pass into fifth grade it will be by the skin of your teeth!"

I know how it feels to believe you are failing, to be mentally dull. You are confused. You do not understand what is happening around you or why. You fail to understand even simple instructions. You show up at the wrong place at the wrong time. You walk alone home from school because classmates avoid you. You feel bad about yourself.

But even with Mrs. Whistler's words ringing in my ears, I knew that was not my whole story. Walking home that afternoon, I asked myself over and over, "Why are you doing so much worse than the other girls and boys? You know you are not that stupid. Sometimes you understand things much better than they do. *What is wrong with you?*"

I was definitely off to a slow start. Looking back I now realize that I was clinically depressed, upset about my mother's illness and alienated from my father—a man with a brilliant mind yet unable to relate emotionally to anyone, including his children. The only emotion I ever saw him express was anger. He was ill prepared to help any of his four children through that troubled time.

In some ways I consider my unhappy years a perverse gift. Knowing unhappiness as I do, I also know what true happiness is. I know how to enjoy a moment and how to enjoy success. I take nothing for granted. As a child I did not expect life to be a joyous voyage filled with wonder, beauty and happiness. But so it has been. I know what it means to be unhappy and happy. And I am very happy.

May this be a lesson for those who suffer as I did: slow to start does not mean slow to finish!

AWAKENING

The simple truth about reading books hit me one day like a bolt from the blue.

"I don't have to be here anymore. I can be riding a wild stallion on a deserted island. I can jockey my horse to a championship finish. I can communicate my deepest feeling by telepathy. I can save the world from invading aliens in my homemade rocket ship."

It was the first months of fifth grade (I did make it). I had discovered reading. My first book was *The Black Stallion* by Walter Farley. I read it in one gulp, hiding a light under the covers to finish. The next day I raced to the library to take home all of Farley's sequels, then every Hardy Boys and Nancy Drew mystery, and over time A.E. Van Vogt's Slan novels, Isaac Asimov's Foundation series, Erle Stanley Gardner's Perry Mason, Rex Stout's orchid loving Montenegrin genius Nero Wolfe and Sir Arthur Conan Doyle's Sherlock Holmes, the Sir Walter Scott adventures and Charles Dickens.

Reading saved me. A fifth grade friend, Bobby Ellison, and I escaped into the world of books. We shared notes and challenged each other. Who could read the most books per week? On a good week we read five each. At last I was good at *something*. Our teacher awarded a gold star for every book we read. Bobby and I led the pack by a mile. At home, when trouble brewed, I retreated to my room, shut the door and focused my imagination on a new and better place.

Reading opened my mind to the richness of the world. The feeling was akin to putting on glasses for the first time. The world suddenly looks different. Trees are no longer green blobs; they have individual leaves. Distant mountains aren't uniformly grey; they have color and texture. So too within my mental world. My confidence took off, grades improved, and I began to have friends who shared similar thoughts and feelings. By seventh grade I was at the top of my class.

I have never lost the reading habit. Kindle tells me that I have read a book each of the past four hundred and twenty weeks. When waiting for a plane or stuck in a line, all I need do is open Kindle on my phone and away I go!

SANCTUARY FOR WEAPONS RESEARCH

I lived almost my entire youth on a naval weapons research base in southern California's Western Mojave Desert. The War Department[4] established this vast expanse (a million acres, bigger than the state of Rhode Island) in 1943, between the highest and lowest spots in the continental United States, Mount Whitney and Death Valley.

The mission for the Naval Ordnance Testing Station at China Lake[5] was to design and test new rockets, missiles and other airborne weapon systems—air to air, ground to air and air to ground. The Sidewinder, Shrike, Walleye and Tomahawk, submarine-based Polaris and Poseidon[6] missile systems and more would be emblematic of U.S. military prowess for the next half century, in Korea, Vietnam, the Middle East and the Cold War with the Soviet Union. Put simply, China Lake was one of the world's most formidable centers for advanced weapons research.

It was a remote, compact community, a mix of stellar scientists and daredevil aces who had battled Russian and Chinese pilots in the Korean War. Many of my friends' scientist fathers, as well as mine, were inveterate garage tinkerers. They had amazing hobbies: building beautiful glider planes, devising new scuba diving techniques, growing orchids, experimenting with new mechanical designs. Generous with weekend or evening hours, unassuming, many of these men explained their garage works, told amazing stories, tutored us in math and science and coached science fairs.[7]

Think of a non-nuclear Los Alamos National Laboratory, add the glamour of *The Right Stuff* and *Top Gun*. Two Korean War aces were fathers of my buddies living across the street, Tommy Amen and Sean Callahan. When these pilots' flight tests arced high above our neighborhood, they would tip the wings of their deep blue Panther or Cougar jets, a "hello gang!" salute as we scurried outside to send up a cheer and wave. Wally Schirra, another Korean War ace and Navy test pilot, was a neighbor. In 1959 NASA made him one the seven original Project Mercury "Right Stuff" astronauts; nine years later, he commanded the first Apollo manned mission, Apollo 7.

From our classroom desks, we could track the aces' takeoffs and landings, often in experimental aircraft, prototypes. An intense Cold War urgency in Washington pushed the limits of weapons development and training. Test pilots had incredibly dangerous jobs. I will never forget the times—there were more than a few—when planes splintered in midair or plummeted from near vertical climbs straight into the desert floor. Haunting tragedies.

Those pilots' families occasionally included kids I played or studied with. A few months after a fatal crash, they moved away. To where? Who knows? Just, gone. What moral was I supposed to draw? What would I do if I lost a parent? Would my friends be okay? I would never see them again.

Everybody at China Lake was more or less middle class, living on modest government salaries. Houses were assigned according to civilian or military rank. You earned a promotion? More living space for you and your family. The Haseltine family of six lived in four locations: the first three were duplexes with one, two, then three bedrooms. The fourth, my home from the mid-'50s until my 1962 high school graduation, was a four-bedroom house on the same street, Lexington Street, with senior Navy officers. The entire base community was government funded.

We had excellent public school teachers. (A federal subsidy paid more than average wages to entice quality teachers to isolated military bases.) For example, a young woman just starting her teaching career, Ann Cierley, coached me on the first Burroughs High debate team.[8] Mr. Brubaker described on freshman biology outings how we could be more aware of the myriad ways animals, plants and insects adapted to the harsh high desert. An expert on small desert rodents, he had a marvelous collection of skulls. Mr. Reisser, contemporary history instructor and World War II veteran, explained battles of the war in detail.[9] Those Reisser lectures were more than an academic exercise. Many scientists, their staff and military personnel we knew fought in the war.

SCIENCE FAIR

The little stage was set. A large jar containing a dozen preserved *Rana pipiens*, common leopard frogs, was at my elbow. The dissecting tray was ready. Our seventh grade science fair was about to begin. The week before I had asked our science teacher, "Can I dissect frogs during the fair?" "Sure," he said. "How many do you need?" "About a dozen, two an hour if I am there all day," I replied.

"The frog is very different from us on the outside but inside it looks like us," I explained to each new group. Pointing with one hand and separating tissue in each frog with a small scalpel in the other, I would continue, "Here is the heart, lungs, liver, intestines, kidneys and spleen. All pretty much in the same place as ours." The adults were genuinely interested; the kids, fascinated. I was teaching something immediately relevant to them, the anatomy of their own bodies. "Look at the leg muscles. Feel your own. Don't they seem to be in the same place? Can you jump?" I stayed at my table all afternoon, until the jar was empty. That night I went to bed happy, happy to have shared my knowledge.

FIRST EXPERIMENTS

My very first independent experiments were with explosives, a natural for a kid growing up by a rocket and flight test field. On any given day, we could witness from our elementary classrooms fearsome tests of jet fighter and rocket warfare.

I read up on the ingredients of gunpowder, then bought saltpeter and sulfur flower from the local pharmacy. I made my own charcoal, and ground ingredients in different ratios, looking for the perfect mix. It was not long before I was blowing up everything within reach.

My work bench was my bedroom desk. This all ended badly when a spark from a test mix ignited the main cache. My desk went up in flames instantly. Were it not for a handy fire extinguisher wielded by a very angry dad, the entire house might have as well.

Okay, no gunpowder, but what about homemade rockets? The rocket of choice: an empty CO_2 cylinder of the type used to make fizzy drinks. The fuel: match head shavings ground to a fine powder. The launcher: a three foot long L shaped length of iron. The result: several holes punched though our one inch thick concrete garage wall. The reward: a month of weekend chores.

My father, William Reed Haseltine, understood weapons extremely well because he helped to create them and to keep their flight paths true. A gifted physicist, with undergraduate and PhD degrees from MIT, he had perfect recall, an encyclopedic knowledge of physical sciences and numerous other subjects (as we will see in the next chapter). He was part of an elite team of designers and engineers that for three decades invented and developed airborne U.S. Navy weapons. When the group was stumped by something, especially a physics problem, they went to my father. "Duke, we have a problem." Everybody called him Duke. And Duke would solve the problem.

WORLD OF MICROBES

I loved freshman biology. I was fascinated by bacteria. "Is it true that these invisible organisms live everywhere?" I wondered. "Is it true that they cause disease? Is it true that to cure a bacterial infection you need to pair the right antibiotic to the right type of bacteria?" I decided to find out.

I swabbed every surface I could find—walls, tires, snake skin, even soap. To my delight each swab produced small mounds of bacteria, each with different color and texture on plates I made in the kitchen by adding beef or chicken bouillon to agar. Yes, bacteria were everywhere—on doorknobs, windows, skin, lizards, tarantulas and even soap! Under the microscope each had distinct shapes; rods, spheres, beads on a string and tightly connected hemispheres.

Were any bacteria dangerous? My buddy since kindergarten, Jeffrey Besser, and I planned a test of Koch's postulates on that question for our sophomore science fair. We isolated bacteria from my throat, one yellow, one white. Rats we injected with the yellow bacteria but not the white bacteria developed severe boils. Antibiotics that killed the yellow bacteria on our petri dishes cured the boils; those that had no effect in the petri dish had no effect on the rats either. Our winning project's name, "Bacteria: Dangerous or Not?"

I soon learned, distressingly, that my part of the science project might have unleashed some potentially dangerous molecules in the bacteria. My dad came down with a high persistent fever. He was rushed to the hospital one afternoon with a fever of one hundred and five degrees. The bacteria I had stored in the family fridge were prime suspects. My dad recovered—after ten days—but my home brewed studies of bacteria were over for good.

PHOTOCHEMISTRY INTERN

Scientists like to recruit young scientists. That is why there was a special program for promising high school students at the weapons lab. When they asked for volunteers I jumped at the chance. Carl Heller, a chemist who was also on the mountain rescue team, was my assigned mentor. When I showed up, proudly wearing the official laboratory pass around my neck, he said:

"I am happy to have you here. I have some measurements I want you to make. I am working on a new type of chemical that will change color when exposed to sun light and then change back again in the dark. I have made ten different members of this family. They are called benzo(a)pyrene spirans. Your job is to measure how fast they become dark in bright sunlight and how fast they become clear again. After that I want you to determine what type of light works best to cause the color change."

I spent many afternoons in Carl's lab that school year, learning how to use different light sources and instruments for measuring color density.[10] One day I asked Carl, "Why did you make these molecules? What will they be used for?" Before he could answer, I added, "Can we publish our results?" He replied, "Sorry. The research is classified. We can't publish." Years later I learned that our labors in Carl's lab had helped pave the way for a manufacturing process that turns clear glass or plastic dark when exposed to the sun, then clear again in the shade. Sound familiar? You might even own a pair of photochromic sunglasses.

FLORENCE

There must have been something in our family experience and the China Lake environment that conditioned inordinate success in science.

My older sister Florence has had a spectacular career. After graduating with honors in biophysics from UC Berkeley two years before me, she became one of the first women to receive a PhD in molecular biology at MIT. She built on that lofty foundation, earning a medical degree from the Albert Einstein College of Medicine, then rising to chief resident in obstetrics and gynecology at Harvard's Boston Lying-in Hospital.

On the Yale Medical School faculty, she trained a generation of doctors in techniques of in vitro fertilization, then transitioned to government, leading extramural funding for the National Institute of Child Health and Human Development at the National Institutes of Health. She directed that federal agency's Center for Population Research for nearly thirty years, to 2012, championing and ultimately introducing a policy to include women in clinical trials. She was founding editor of the *Journal for Women's Health*, and later founded the Society for the Advancement of Women's Health Research. She holds several patents on inventions and organized a company to improve the mobility of wheelchairs. Her coauthored novel, *Woman Doctor*, is a journey—descent might be the better word—into gender bias against women in the medical professions in the 1960s and 1970s.

Florence tried to retire in her early '70s, but it turned out to be just a pause. In 2019, she added another role model laurel, this time for aging baby boomers and following generations. At age seventy six, she became a distinguished professor with tenure, teaching graduate nursing courses at the University of Texas at Arlington. The takeaway? We should plan for at least three or four careers in our extended lifetimes, into our 80s.

ERIC

My younger brother Eric also has had a wonderful career. After studying economics and psychology at UC Berkeley, he received a PhD in neuroscience (physiological psychology) at Indiana University, then became a manager and later engineering director at Hughes Aircraft, creating flight simulators to train pilots for advanced fighter planes.

At famed Walt Disney Imagineering, he used his skills in virtual reality and human machine interface, creating large scale virtual reality experiences. In time he was promoted to chief technical officer of the entire corporation, responsible for technical aspects of all Disney ventures including theme parks and the ABC television network.

Following the 9/11 attacks, the government recruited Eric to become head of research at the National Security Agency. He later led the technical side of all our nation's intelligence services in the Office of the Director of National Intelligence. Eric now consults for Disney, designing the first successful augmented reality toys, and for our intelligence services. He is author of a growing list of titles on topics as diverse as his interests, and chairs the U.S. Technology Leadership Council.

Our sister Susan, also brilliant, has chosen a much quieter life.

I am often asked what was in the water when we were growing up in China Lake that hyper charged the three of us. My answer, half in jest, "Our parents wound us up so tight we are still unwinding."

SPUTNIK

Science was playing an important role in our national dialog in the late 1950s and early 1960s just as I was deciding upon a career. We were reacting to the launch of Sputnik in 1957. Americans were traumatized. Were the Russians ahead of us in science? Would their missiles rain down on us unprotected? Would they dominate space? President Eisenhower and Congress and later President Kennedy initiated a surge in federal funding for science and science education.[11] New energy and enthusiasm for science and technology programs fed rapidly into the ranks of me and my peers in high schools and colleges.

Presidential leadership was then and still is a determining force in the career decisions of young men and women. I was incredibly fortunate that, when the time came for me to decide on my future, respect and support for science was at a peak.

My Lifelong Fight Against Disease

4

PARALLAX VISION

My parents had strikingly different personalities and values. Their views of how to best make your way in the world often clashed.

My father's approach was very strict, proudly Puritan: honesty, hard work, self-discipline, play by the rules, merit wins the day. My mother's was an immigrant mindset: The world is harsh, unforgiving. Do not expect any favors. Understand nuances in society to survive. Work hard. Be flexible, adaptive. Understand the other person's point of view. Do not take no for an answer. You will succeed or fail based only on your own efforts.

Trying to decide how to resolve these conflicts was a constant puzzle for me. I was forced to weigh conflicting commands on how to behave and respond in a situation. And struggle to grasp unspoken messages in my parents' behavior as they navigated the routines and caprices of their daily lives. It was enervating, confusing, streams feeding undercurrents of anxiety. I often thought, if my parents are giving me directions for how to behave and think that are so different, they cannot both be right, can they? Should I adopt my father's or my mother's world view? Which is right? Possibly, they are *both wrong*!

From a young age, I coped as best I could—mostly alone. But it was difficult. Often, I was unhappy, and for long periods depressed for that and other reasons. My solution over time came to be questioning everything, to learn from my personal experience, my studies, my reading, my teachers, my friends—and, yes, my parents. Then, make up my own mind.

I discovered by accident through these struggles an unusual way to frame and solve problems, a method beyond reflexive questioning. I refer to this as my parallax vision of the world.

I like the metaphor. For my purposes, the parallax vision enables you to perceive things that most others miss. In later chapters, we will touch on many occasions when the parallax vision led me to significant insights. Some of these upended established theories. Some opened new avenues to treat and cure disease. Others to identify targets for new drugs, tracking down pathogens by rapidly sequencing genomes of cells and proteins.

The parallax view requires you always to be questioning yourself and others, to seek new perspectives, especially when you or others might believe something is beyond question, or impossible to achieve. I view the world from scientific *and* humanitarian perspectives. I analyze the values implicit in each decision I make.

Other factors than my parents certainly contributed to my parallax vision and the ways my mind, my thought processes, appear to work differently. We will get to those shortly. But because of my mom and dad's complex relationship with each other, and with me, it will help to know something about each of my parents and my life growing up in remote, rarefied China Lake. We should begin with them.

Jeanne Ellsberg Haseltine and Duke Haseltine were well matched in their love for knowledge, in any subject. They shared a fascination with the humanities as well as science, exploring as many aspects as they could: art, classical music, history, theatre and literature. This twin presence of humanities and science in my youth was a wonderful influence. Many scientists are interested in science for the sake of science. I would become interested in science for what science could contribute to human progress. This required a broad understanding of the humanities—the flow of human history, of culture, anthropology and the arts. Collectively, they help guide you to what society needs at any point in time.

My parents' love for the humanities in a military community largely dedicated to scientific discovery and innovation was an important influence in forming my parallax vision.

Classic music was always playing in the house, from Los Angeles radio stations or my parents' collection of long playing records, amplified through a prized hi-fi system.[12] Sunday afternoon New York Philharmonic concerts were a shared ritual. Several families on the base including ours sponsored a monthly, aptly named Great Artists program.[13] World famous musicians such as Arthur Rubinstein, Jerome Hines, Patrice Munsel, Yehudi Menuhin and more performed in our small 250-seat auditorium in the middle of the desert.[14]

MOTHER – JEANNE HASELTINE

My mother added a passion to her curiosity that my father lacked. Her enjoyment of all senses was immediate. She had a buoyant sense of aesthetics, bursting with joy at a striking image: a tree, a flower, a dazzling distant panorama. She communicated her sense of the wonder of life, of the earth, of all living things. My father was as equally steeped in his knowledge of the humanities as he was in science. He understood aesthetics. But he had no obvious emotional connection for reasons that might well have been unavoidable, for reasons wired too deeply in his genome.

When my mother was healthy—and, as we saw earlier, for distressing periods lasting months or even years she was not healthy—she was a powerful emotional force: a warm, funny human being with a wide range of pursuits. She danced when she was younger, painted, rode horses and skied. She communicated a sense of wonder about the earth and all living things.

Like so many educated women of that era in America, she poured her creative talents into her home and family. She became a superb cook with a passion for French dishes. She rolled her own phyllo dough—a big task—

and made her cannoli shells. She created delicately painted marzipan fruit baskets. She dipped her own chocolates.[15] She created her own recipes. She baked elaborate wedding cakes for friends and decorated whimsical birthday cakes for us and other kids with rocket ships, trains and clowns. I loved to eat and cook alongside her in the kitchen, and became her sous chef when I was in high school. I still love to cook.

My mother was raised in an East European Jewish family; her mother from Hungary, her father, Belarusian, from Moscow. Discrimination in America was rampant in the '30s and '40s. She had terrifying, distressing experiences. Many hotels, motels and restaurants were "restricted": no Jews, blacks or Asians allowed. She knew Jews were being rounded up and killed in Nazi Germany.

One day an invitation to the bar mitzvah of my friend Jeffrey Besser arrived in the mail. "What's a bar mitzvah?" I asked my mom. Without missing a beat, she explained the Jewish tradition—age thirteen, boys reaching the age of accountability for their actions, ritual readings in the temple surrounded by family and friends. "I know because I was raised in a Jewish family," she said. As far as I had ever considered, our family was descended from the Scottish Puritans my father loved to talk about on his side of the family. I stopped Sunday school after junior high. Religious beliefs were rarely discussed at home. "I converted to Christianity before I married your father," my mom continued, without any prompting. "I did not want any of my children to face the kind of prejudice that I and my friends and family did."[16]

LOS ANGELES EXCURSIONS

When I was about twelve, my mother started driving to Los Angeles every other week to meet with a psychiatrist. It was a long trip, two and a half hours each way, so she always took one of us four kids to keep her company. I was excited when it was my turn. We usually left home before dawn, heading south along Interstate 395, the East Sierra Mountains' splendid granite ridge off to our right. As the pink hue of sunrise slowly descended the white granite mountain ridge, she would quote from Homer's *The Odyssey*.

When rosy fingered Dawn came bright and early...

Soon Dawn appeared and touched the sky with roses...

When early Dawn, the newborn child with rosy hands, appeared...

... she roused the newborn Dawn from Ocean's streams to bring the golden light to those on earth.

After her counseling sessions in L.A., we would visit museums, head to a fine early dinner along La Cienega Boulevard's Restaurant Row, then go to the theatre or a symphony performance. The Bolshoi Ballet, El Greco and Martha Graham dance companies. Arthur Miller's *Death of a Salesman* and William Inge's *Bus Stop*. Visiting opera companies and the Los Angeles Philharmonic. These were exceptional cultural and culinary experiences, capped by overnight stays at a hotel in Beverly Hills. Returning home, I studied catalogs we retrieved from museum exhibits, then, stretching out on our living room floor, lost myself in the images and vibrant colors of my parents' glossy art books. My introduction to the visual arts.

My mother majored in French literature at the University of California, Berkeley, cooking meals for a physics professor to cover room and board expenses. She had transferred from Reed College after two years; her family could not afford Reed's private tuition. She loved French language and culture, and soon I began studying and speaking French with her. She and my father shared a passion for the existential philosophies of Sartre and Camus.

She bought a paperback copy of Camus's *The Fall* as soon as it was published in French in 1957, slicing open the paper leaves before she could begin. (Why, I wondered, did French publishers not cut the pages of their paperbacks?) Camus's allegory examining Nazism, totalitarianism and human nature, *The Plague*, was her favorite. Thirty years later, with unspoken gratitude to my mother, I invoked Camus and *The Plague* in my AIDS funding speech in the chambers of the U.S. Senate:

The natural human response is to hope that we ourselves will be spared from this disease... (Camus) writes that at first people thought the disease was only a problem for rats, then for dirty people who lived across town. Fear came home when death visited next door... I am confident that we will awaken to realize what problem is in our midst, but when? And how late in the day will it be?

FATHER – DUKE HASELTINE

Duke Haseltine had the gift of perfect memory. He remembered every place he went, everything he read from age two onward. Most evenings at home he devoured science books and magazines, sitting in an overstuffed red leather chair, smoking a pipe, feet propped on a matching footstool. He was intensely curious about the world. Before turning ten, he completed the entire *Encyclopedia Britannica* published in 1911, the year he was born.[17]

My father did not talk much around the house about his weapons projects, but the work fascinated him. I asked him when I was very little what he did all day, and he said, "I make rockets fly straight." Weapons decorated our home, a hint of his exhaustive knowledge of the origin and history of countless weapons developed since the Stone Age. A small Indonesian cannon in front of the fireplace. A pair of crossed French rapiers above the mantle, centered on a fearsome Russian dagger. In the dining room, three impressive Kris swords taken from men who attacked my grandfather's friend during the U.S. war in the Philippines.

My dad was a direct descendant of Scottish Puritans who fled religious conflicts for New England in 1637.[18] He proudly informed me when I was little that I was not only the firstborn male of the tenth generation of Haseltines in America, but another eldest son of an eldest son. A family bible handed down for generations featured inscribed names and birthdates of each eldest son on its frontispiece.

Dad enjoyed recounting many highlights in the family legacy. He traced Haseltines all the way to the borderlands of Scotland in 1610, and earlier to

Normandy.[19] Two brothers were founders of Haverhill and Bradford, adjacent towns thirty five miles north of Boston. Haseltines fought in every American war from the French and Indian War (1754–1763) to Korea (1950–1953). (Dad himself was a military scientist in the Cold War fight against the Soviet Union.) In the 19th century, Haseltine engineers helped construct the Erie Canal, then moved west, settling along the west coast of Lake Michigan in Ripon, Wisconsin. That is where my father grew up.

A physics instructor at UC Berkeley before World War II, he met my mother one night when he was a dinner guest in the home of his more senior physics faculty colleague—the same professor whose suppers my mother prepared. They married in 1941. I was born at Jefferson Barracks along the Mississippi River south of St. Louis, in 1944. We moved to China Lake shortly after that base was established in Indian Wells Valley.

Weapons research was a natural for Duke. He could cite overwhelming details of every battle in America's wars. Moreover, his curiosity ranged widely. Einstein's theory of General Relativity. Geology and the emerging field of plate tectonics. Human evolution and debates raging on what was then called the origins of human races. The history of manufacturing. Contemporary fashion, art and politics.

A PENETRATING DIAGNOSIS

My father was not a role model for me. Far from it. He was emotionally distant, exceptionally frugal. We took just two family vacations: one driving cross country to visit the old family home in Ripon, the other to see relatives in Seattle. Years later, my younger brother Eric pieced together a penetrating insight. Already a PhD in neuroscience, Eric had become a licensed clinical psychologist.

One day he tallied twenty of our father's behaviors and sent them to me with a note, "Do any of these sound familiar?" Dislike of change. Loath to make eye contact. Superior intelligence. Intensity for a single subject. Socially awkward. Aloof. Abrupt. And so on. We agreed each one fit Dad perfectly.

The diagnosis? Asperger's Syndrome. Dad listened when we presented this analysis to him later but did not agree or disagree.

We certainly had decades of anecdotal evidence. Once Eric and I were chatting with a younger friend, a brilliant inventor and entrepreneur named Danny Hillis. Danny was famous for pioneering parallel computing and conceptualizing it as a foundation for artificial intelligence. Spectacular innovations. This day he mentioned to us that he was puzzled by some aspect of Einstein's Theory of General Relativity (I do not recall which one). Danny said he consulted every famous physicist he could reach but remained confused. None was helpful. "Why don't you talk to our father?" we suggested.

Immediately, Danny picked up the phone and called Duke Haseltine. He quickly asked his question. For the next twenty minutes, Eric and I watched silently. Every so often Danny would say, "Uh-huh, uh-huh, uh-huh. Yep, yep, yep." Nothing more. After the twenty minutes, Danny asked a second question. Within seconds, he hung up the phone, an astonished look on his face. What happened? "He gave me the answer!" Danny replied.

But, what happened? Why did Danny put down the phone so abruptly? "Well, when I asked that second question, your father shouted, 'If you keep interrupting me, how can I give you the answer?' And then he hung up on me." We quickly realized two things. First, Danny reveled in my father's uncanny insight in answering his first question, whatever that was. Then, Danny was reeling after our father's abrupt dismissal of the second question.

Years later when Eric told me about his Asperger's diagnosis, he and I flashed back to those details of Danny's two question call.

GRANDPA – BILL HASELTINE

My paternal grandfather was the opposite of my father in many ways, a clever, fun-loving character, inventive, energetic, a joy to be around. He stood about five feet six inches, trim, confident, erect in a tweed jacket with his bolo tie. William Ebenezer Haseltine was full of amazing stories of his life, some hair raising, many awe inspiring.

Taking his savings, Grandpa suspended his engineering studies at MIT near the end of the 19th century to travel four thousand miles away into the Canadian Yukon. Among thirty thousand teeming prospectors in the Klondike Gold Rush (1896–1899), he wielded his pickax and panned for nuggets.

But it was dangerous. Murderous claim jumpers ran amok. He soon retreated four hundred miles southward to Skagway, a staging area for Klondike miners near lower Alaska's Pacific Coast. Skagway was a boomtown. Bill Haseltine became a shopkeeper, selling eggs for ten dollars apiece (about *one hundred dollars* today) and other supplies to miners. In lawless Skagway he was a vigilante, too. One famous gunfight he survived unscathed in 1898 killed the notorious swindler and gangster Soapy Smith, and inflicted mortal wounds on his assailant, fellow vigilante and friend Frank Reid. Reid died twelve days later.[20]

Flush with a stash of gold nuggets, and the small fortune it bestowed, Grandpa returned to Cambridge, finished his MIT studies, and married a young woman who attended the Boston Conservatory of Music, my grandmother Florence. A knitting factory he opened back in Ripon prospered until the Depression. He closed it and moved the family for five years to Germany, France and Switzerland, where in Zurich my father studied at an elite technical high school. They repaired to Ripon as World War II storm clouds gathered.[21]

CHINA LAKE VISTAS, WHAT SUSTAINS US

China Lake was a wonderful place to grow up. The Indian Wells Valley was rimmed by towering mountains and volcanic mounds. The Sierra Nevada to the west, White Mountains to the north, Panamint Range to the east and Black Hills to the south. This storied geological terrain formed four million years ago was fabulous for hiking, with mesmerizing varieties of fauna and flora and magnificent vistas.

I started riding horses when I was four. It was perfect country for Cub Scout day trips and extended overnight camping trips for Boy Scouts. We were free to wander into the desert and up into the mountains, rattlesnakes our only worry. Equipped only with a canteen—and snakebite kit—we hunted lizards, tarantulas and snakes to bring home as pets. We climbed peaks, hiked the John Muir Trail and camped beside creeks that streamed down mountain valleys. In high school I would head out alone any afternoon I could, free and clear, on horseback into the trackless deserts and low hills.

The love of beauty, nature and of all that surrounds, sustains and uplifts us as humans is a constant and immediate source of pleasure and joy. Closing my eyes, I can see dark bushes dotting the light sand, a multicolored carpet of desert blooms after a spring rain. I see brilliant sun rises to the east, delicate fast fading colors in sunsets, white mountains turning to pink then deep purple under an evening sky serrated by the mountains' jagged silhouette. Billowing rolls of clouds pile high atop the Sierra, dropping rain to the west then sailing high and dry across our valley. It was this lack of rainfall across the millennia that created the arid landscape of Indian Wells Valley, the opening act of the Great Western Desert.

The setting was remote, isolated, timeless in many ways. Removed from mid-century modernity. Far from coastal population centers. All reasons why military planners at the California Institute of Technology and the War Department selected it. The geography was ideal for developing and testing—in relative secrecy—new rockets, missiles, other airborne weapons and warplanes. These China Lake inventions would become formidable, intimidating assets for the United States on the chessboard of Cold War strategy.

INTERNAL IMMIGRANT

I never rode a bus, used a pay telephone or had any concerns about crime during my entire youth in China Lake. The only thing I believed about business was that it was a dangerous occupation; in high school, a friend's father died of a heart attack trying to start a company selling household cleaning fluids. Why would I ever want to work in a business?

Then, a group trip to the United Nations. Traveling cross country by bus to New York City and back, I spent many days in the summer of 1958 watching farmlands and small towns roll by. An uneasy feeling came over me. My experiences in the world to that point were limited almost entirely to a California desert lined by distant mountains. The routines of daily life, and they were routines, were defined by mores of highly disciplined scientists, jaunty test pilots, war hardened military officers and their spouses. They resided, worked and relaxed, and their children were educated on a no frills base funded almost entirely by the government and encircled by barbed wire chain link fencing. Most young Americans my age in the late 1950s were living very different lives. That feeling made me nervous.

Yes, I was an American, but I worried that I did not understand America. I began to think of myself as an internal immigrant. Immigrants in a strange culture do not know how things work. They do not know appropriate behaviors. They have to figure it out by observing carefully, always questioning what is happening around them and why. When you are an immigrant living in a foreign land, you do not just *have* an experience. You *analyze* the experience. In some respects, this is all very positive. But in others, it is not so positive because you are never not analyzing. You are always seeking another perspective. You are restless. These qualities came natural to me. Always looking for another perspective. Never satisfied accepting what seems obvious to most others.

It is possible this thinking about the world and my role in it at the time was a maturing of something innate. When I was a boy, I often would mark things in my mind to remember for later. When I was eight, I took my dime and headed to Saturday movie matinees. They always opened with Hopalong Cassidy, Gene Autry, Flash Gordon or Batman and Robin in short cliffhangers, then to newsreels often about the Korean War and on to the main feature, usually a cowboy movie. I loved them. But why were no teenagers there? What is wrong with them? Don't they know this is fantastic?!? Maybe teenagers are not supposed to be there.

When I was nine I thought, "You can think as well as any adult. They don't know that. When you are older remember that a nine year old can think as well as you. Treat them with respect." At twelve, I remember asking myself, "Why are all the teenagers making such fools of themselves around girls? Ask yourself that question when you are fifteen and maybe you will find the answer." I did.

China Lake got its name from 19th century Chinese laborers in the area, attracted by the daily wage of one dollar and fifty cents to mine borax deposits in the dry lakebed. The civic center of the military base was a series of Quonset huts, big rounded domes all in a few rows arranged in a T shape. They housed a PX store stocking goods priced at military discount, the officer club swimming pool, a theatre, barbershops, a library, a grocery store, a multi-denomination religious center, with synagogue attached, and a recreation center with our unadorned Great Artists auditorium. Elementary and junior high school buildings were not far away. Everything was inside a tall chain link fence with barbed wire.

Over the years a small service community sprang up just south of the base, Ridgecrest.[22] Only civilians who carried what we called an "ecstasy pass" for XTC (PX, theatre and community housing complex) were waved through by military police at the base gates. The population of Ridgecrest has grown to nearly 30,000. It was the epicenter of two significant earthquakes that rocked southern California in the summer of 2019.[23] At 7.1 and 6.4 on the Richter scale, these quakes were California's biggest in more than twenty years.[24] Impacts on the China Lake military base were potent. The government estimated repairs and reconstruction costs at more than two billion dollars.[25]

BIPOLAR DISORDER

My mother's legacy of battling serious illness might also be a factor in how I think. Her paternal family had a long history of bipolar disorder. More than one third are or were admittedly bipolar, or manic depressive, as it was called in those days. What causes extreme mood swings of bipolar disorder in some people may cause a different type of mental disorder in others. There obviously are compensating genes; I am not bipolar myself. Most people are surprised when they learn that almost all genetic traits that cause the disease do not have a very high penetrance. Penetrance refers to the proportion of people with a genetic predisposition that actually manifest the trait. Sometimes it is only five, ten, or fifteen percent. The reasons for varied penetrance of inherited traits are many.

Most inherited traits are the result of slight variations in the protein products of specific genes. Each protein acts in concert with one or more other proteins, each of which may also vary from person to person. The effect of a specific variant may be influenced by the proteins with which it interacts, amplifying or masking the effect. Factors other than inheritance may also exacerbate or conceal the effect of a specific variant, including the environment in the womb and afterwards. For example, a predisposition to multiple sclerosis is inherited but only those living in temperate zones, not the polar zones, are at significant risk.

TERROR OF POLIO

Each time I came down with a cold my mother would say, "Bill when you grow up, discover a cure to the common cold. You will be a millionaire and have the gratitude of mothers everywhere!" A mother's wisdom is often deeper than we think. Twice in my lifetime the world has been traumatized by a common cold virus gone bad, first polio and now COVID-19. Both are cousins to viruses that cause the common cold.

I vividly remember the terror of polio, another serious disease with immediate consequence in my life that shaped my thoughts about illness, medicine and science. The disease struck suddenly, seemingly at random, paralyzing and killing children during the summer months. Swimming, my favorite relief from the oppressive heat of the Mojave Desert summers, was forbidden. So too were the cool dark theaters where I longed to see the latest Flash Gordon, Batman, Hopalong Cassidy, Roy Rogers and Gene Autry films. We were allowed the company of only one or two friends, no more. Cub Scout and later Boy Scout activities were off the table. Isolating behavior was a primary defense. We waited impatiently for science to save us, for a vaccine to protect us or a drug we might need to cure us. Sound familiar?

Fifty eight thousand polio cases were recorded in 1952, the peak year of the U.S. outbreak. Following mass inoculations with the Salk vaccine, introduced in 1955, cases plummeted by 1961 to one hundred sixty one. The Sabin oral vaccine, introduced in the U.S. in 1962, further simplified inoculation programs.

Years after the fear of polio faded, I would be assigned the same laboratory at Harvard's Jimmy Fund Building (soon to become the Dana-Farber Cancer Institute) where the polio virus was first isolated in the late 1940s by the great John Enders. I sat in his chair. I used the same bio-containment hood in which he grew the first poliomyelitis viruses in various types of tissue cultures. That discovery, for which Enders shared the Nobel Prize in 1954, would enable mass production of the Salk and Sabin vaccines. I was in awe, knowing the terror and disruption polio inflicted when I was a boy, and inspired to understand these viruses and follow in John Enders's footsteps as best I could.

Some twenty to thirty percent of all colds are caused by coronavirus cousins of COVID-19. My mom was right to worry about the "common cold." Had we known more then, it was the uncommon cold we had to fear.

AMBIDEXTROUS

I am ambidextrous, adept at using either hand with almost the same ease. This was uncommon in our extended family. I had an uncle who was also ambidextrous; he wrote with his right hand, shot a pistol with his left. I never developed a dominant side. My teachers repeatedly told me that if I had a choice I should write with my right hand. I took their advice, writing with my right hand, playing most sports with my left except tennis, which I play (poorly) with both hands.

Being ambidextrous may explain my uneven abilities in sports. I excelled at hiking, running and swimming, and in junior high was on the swim and track teams. My first paying job was as a lifeguard. I was never good at sports that required fine motor skills: baseball, basketball or volleyball.

I suspect being ambidextrous is another trait that influenced my parallax vision. Being ambidextrous requires an extra mental checklist, an extra split second reflection: Which hand, arm or leg shall I use for this task? Which is the best approach? I wonder if the left and right functions of my brain are similarly mixed. Might one source of creativity be an admixture of the emotional with the rational, using both halves of the brain for every task?

Looking back, I ask myself, what is it that allowed me to do what I do, what I have done? What is it about my mind that is different? Am I smarter than other people? I do not think so. Smart enough, but other people are smarter. My purpose fueled my curiosity and energy. Asking questions helped me understand the intrinsic properties of my mind. What are my talents? How do I think—literally, or imaginatively? These are fundamental questions anybody should ask themselves.

My instinct is to question everything. I do not accept easy explanations when analyzing anything. I believe the parallax instinct enables me often to perceive things others miss. Critical thinking skills are valuable in any aspect of life, but I think the parallax vision is perfectly suited for achieving breakthroughs in science. I would even go further: it is *required* for breakthroughs in science.

The science life at the highest levels is intensely competitive. Scientists do not like to have their theories questioned, especially elite scientists with celebrated reputations. They hate it when their theories are disproven. But, as we shall see in Part III and Part IV, upending accepted theories with new insights is how knowledge evolves. Parallax vision helped me uncover those insights.

GREAT GIFTS

When I was a boy, I did not expect to be a happy adult. My perception was that I was having a hard childhood and that was how things would be when I was an adult. I think this is how I came to know what happiness is; you know what happiness is from being unhappy. Every day now I am happy, I am really happy.

Many years after leaving China Lake, I came to appreciate what strengths my life in the desert and my family gave me. By then I had taught hundreds of Harvard undergraduates and Harvard Medical School students, many of whom were alumni of elite east coast boarding schools. I could appreciate that the informal education I received at home, coupled with all that I learned from many remarkable high school teachers, prepared me for high level college, graduate and post-graduate studies as well as any east coast private schools would have.

For all of their troubles, and they had lots of troubles, my parents gave me great gifts. The love of science, of music and art, of history and culture, of literature and food. The joy of knowledge, one of life's great treasures. "Ask questions about everything possible," Jeanne and Duke Haseltine urged me. A life devoted to curiosity may have been their greatest gift to me.

Examining questions from different perspectives, creating your own parallax vision, will make you a more disciplined, confident explorer whatever you choose to do. It will help you discover even more of what is going on out there.

PART II

5

OPENING TO THE WORLD

I AM ABOUT TEN YEARS OLD, crouching beside Grandpa. We are scooping river sand into a broad shallow pan. Glittering flakes of gold appear as he gently swirls the pan, separating lighter sand from heavier gold. "I did this for real a long time ago," he whispers, pouring tiny gold flecks into a small bottle.

"I was lucky," he smiles. "I hit it rich."

We were hitting it rich that day, too. Rich in new memories, deepening love and admiration. That little river flowed through Knott's Berry Farm, the southern California amusement park. We were far from the Yukon Territory and Klondike Gold Rush in that moment, time and place, but in our imaginations we were there, together.

"I took all my savings, left college and bought a ticket on the first boat to Alaska I could find," Grandpa says. "Set up camp, staked my claim and began to pan and prospect. But I didn't stay long. It was too dangerous. Several friends with nearby claims were robbed, murdered."

Hopalong Cassidy matinee shorts had nothing on Grandpa's adventures. Better yet, Grandpa's stories were *true*. *My* grandpa. Distant travel. Seeking his fortune. Surviving by his wits. Taking on bad guys. It all was captivating. My wanderlust wakening, literally at my grandpa's knee.

"The town where I opened a dry goods and grocery store was lawless, so several of us formed a group of vigilantes." He pauses, tensing. "One day on the town pier we cornered a claim jumper and notorious bandit, Soapy Smith. My best friend Frank Reid shot and killed Soapy." Downshifting now to a softer, melancholy tone. "But Frank was badly wounded; he died about ten days later." Another pause. "I decided that was enough of Alaska for me, and headed home."

Grandpa retold those stories and more later over the years when we were together. Hunting with Indian tribes in Canada. Driving in the early days of the automobile from Wisconsin to California. Engineering specialist on the World War I staff advising General John J. Pershing, and Army colonel in World War II. Those years during the Depression with his family in Germany, France and Switzerland.

He was a warm, gentle man with a dry sense of humor and twinkle in his eye. We drove down occasionally to visit him when he retired to a home in Corona Del Mar, near Newport Beach. A skilled painter, he immersed himself for months in picturesque settings in Mexico and Central and South America, such as Mazatlán, Lake Titicaca in Peru or a scenic mountain lake somewhere in the Andes. His subjects, in all colors: local people on church steps, fishermen casting nets from butterfly boats.

My grandfather was an inspiration to me for what a man and father should be. I have hung his paintings on the walls of my homes for decades. I wish we could have spent more time together.

JAPAN AND PACIFIC WATERS, 1960

"Okay, young men," an officer on the U.S. Navy ship announces in command voice. A gaggle of thirty American teenagers, all boys, is clustered by real sailors near a footbridge. At fifteen, I am the youngest, awestruck by historic Yokosuka naval base sprawling nearly one square mile before us.

"You are on your own tonight—and tomorrow," he continues. "Go out and have a look around. Groups of three, mandatory. If someone gets hurt, one stays with the hurt guy, the other goes for help. Understand?" Most everyone nods. "Oh, grab a handful of condoms on your way down the gangplank." I am a bit confused. What does he mean?

What am I doing here? The simple answer to the second question is, the Navy League.[26] The organization, of mostly retired naval personnel, sponsored the summer long trip each year. The goal was to recruit young men (no women in those days) to become officers. One lure was sharing life aboard an active duty troop transport ship with rough edged young seamen and their more polished officers on Japan-and-back Pacific crossings. Another was taking in cultural treasures, meeting Japanese people and witnessing realities of post-war life in Japan. But I am getting ahead of the story.

To make it on board, I had to outperform three other students initially selected by our Burroughs High School principal months earlier. With a push from my mother—"Tell him your grades and accomplishments are as good as the others. Insist you be included!"—I was added as contestant number 4 to speak before the local China Lake selection committee. Our topic, "Why Do You Want To Go To Japan?"

I drafted two versions. The first touched on my curiosity about different cultures, and what I hoped to learn about Japan. The second served up my admiration for the Navy, especially the Korean War era fighter pilots I knew, fathers of friends. I stopped short of expressing interest in a Navy career, and mentioned Japan only in passing, but did say I was eager to experience naval life at sea.

The question to my parents, "Should I combine these two or give one or the other?" Stick to the topic, Dad said. "The question they asked is not about the Navy. It is about why you want to visit Japan." Mom countered: "These men love the Navy, not Japan! They fought in the Pacific. They had friends killed by the Japanese!" Dad says this; Mom says that. More Parallax Vision. I took my mother's advice. A good thing in this case. The selection board was delighted by my remarks, and I was chosen.

Traveling to Japan at that impressionable age was an exotic adventure on many levels I never could have imagined, from the prurient to the sublime.

It opened my mind to different cultures and subcultures, to unfamiliar ideas that in time altered my thinking about America's role in the modern world. I began to see what that modern world was like, not through books and stories but from vivid personal experience. Or, as a scientist would put it, through direct observation.

We coasted into Pearl Harbor at dawn, following, of all things, in the wake of a Japanese destroyer, its Rising Sun flag snapping in the southern Oahu wind. That sight made me uneasy moments later. We passed in silence the sunken USS Arizona, oil oozing to the surface (as it does today), a submerged tomb with remains of 1,177 crewmen who perished in the 1941 surprise assault. Most of those young sailors, only a few years older than I was this day, never saw the first wave of 180 attacking Japanese war planes, their fuselages displaying the same Rising Sun.

Hawaii was our first stop. Onshore, I found my way quickly to Waikiki Beach, the surf pounding rhythmically before me, iconic Diamond Head off to the left. Here it is, prominent, between the beach and bubblegum pink Royal Hawaiian Hotel: the giant banyan tree memorialized in a Robert Louis Stevenson poem.[27] Then it was on to military airfields, the naval base and armed services cemetery at Punchbowl Crater, hearing more at each stop about the Pearl Harbor attack and ensuing four years of warfare in the Pacific.

BUNKS, INFIRMARY TERRORS, RED LIGHTS—A YOUNG SEAMAN'S LIFE

On board the USS Mann, our 750-foot transport ship heading to Japan, we rotated duties in groups of five, chipping paint, washing dishes and working in the engine room and more. Bridge watch with young lieutenants supervising three of us at a time in fifteen minute rotations was the best duty: port lookout, navigation, helmsman, radar watch, starboard lookout, coffee break, even aft steering.

Keeping a seven hundred foot ship on course is an art form. The wind pushes in one direction, the ocean currents in another. Waves can push you off course by as much as two to five degrees before you can correct. After awhile, we mastered the ebb and flow, leaving a zig zag wake for miles, keeping our ship within one quarter of a degree of what our officers set as a desired course direction.

Our biggest test on the ship's bridge came later, on our return voyage heading east, when a massive typhoon forced us off course, northward toward the Aleutian Islands. Bracing for what seemed like hours against the impact of sixty foot waves crashing down was exhausting. The acceleration and compression was so powerful as the ship rose and fell, from trough to peak, it seemed you were only two feet tall, then stretched out to twelve feet! If this were a smaller ship we would all be done for, I thought. Yet the bridge officers were calm, reassuring. All of them had been through this before. I did not get seasick then, and only once early on the trip when coastal waves off California first rocked us. I never had a problem later on the ocean during my travels.

The thirty of us bunked deep in the hold with young crewmembers and dozens of Army G.I.s heading to assignments somewhere in Asia. The berths were stacked four high. We slept on a length of canvas that was stretched on each side over rectangular metal pipe. My berth was at hip height on a narrow passage. Each morning, my eyes opened to a long line of twenty or thirty naked butts queuing for a turn in the forward head. This, I thought on those many mornings, is different. Life on a navy ship? You get many lasting impressions like that one.

Infirmary duty was another kind of basic training on sexually transmitted diseases, lessons that aided my judgment later at the onset of the AIDS epidemic. Ninety percent of shipboard clinic operations was treating STDs. These crewmen and G.I.s were in serious pain. Here sits one with what the medics call blue balls, a jet black scrotum that was four times normal size. The treatment? A blue solution, copper sulfate, for fungal infections.

I winced again when medics informed a young seaman his pain came from boils emerging in his urethra. Treatment A: Breathe deeply. Place the penis on a thin stainless steel anvil. Tap a rubber mallet sharply to break the boil. Treatment B: Insert a catheter into the penis, push a button to release tiny sharp blades that pierce the boil. Either way, Ouch!

Infirmary terrors aside, sailors and marines had other things to talk about. Sexual fantasies, prior sexual encounters, sexual encounters anticipated. Talk of sex, morning and night. Inevitably, more consequences appear of prior sexual encounters. To wit, one morning about 10 o'clock I walk into the triangular forward head (translation for nonsailors: restroom near the front of a ship). Toilet stools with no privacy partitions line the steel bulkheads, ten to each side. Naked G.I.s occupy each one. Nobody is talking. A few heads turn toward me with blank stares. Or were they seething? Embarrassed? This was otherworldly, I thought. What was going on? A cloistered initiation rite? What?

The floor I waded through had become a small lake five inches deep, remnants from an overnight storm. Each of these crewmen is straining, oddly, awkwardly, to stay motionless on their perch. Heavy currents rock the ship from side to side. Water sloshes to one side, then the other. I had stumbled into another mandatory STD treatment, one requiring a bizarre choreographic sequence. (Milos Forman, Oscar winning director years later of *One Flew Over the Cuckoo's Nest,* could not have done better.) As a new wave ripples toward them, occupants on one side of the room raise their feet in unison, contorting to remain seated. Each, I realize, is immersing his penis in a paper cup. The cups are filled with a bright blue solution. Mystery solved!

Our first steps off the USS Mann footbridge onto the naval base take me and two buddies into what for us then was a truly foreign realm, raucous night life and the world's biggest red light district. Why is all of that there? Yokosuka Naval District is the biggest military population center in East Asia of American armed servicemen. Walking along loud bars, crowded tattoo parlors, and souvenir shops, dodging drunken sailors with arms wrapped around young Japanese women, we agree, wide eyed, this scene is straight from that movie, *The World of Suzie Wong,*[28] plus ten!

I am thinking, *I knew the world outside the United States was different. But, WOW! I never imagined it to be this different!* Peering down at my little red English-Japanese translation book, I hear approaching light footsteps. A young woman is next to me now, laughing. Perhaps I was a caricature to her, a pubescent kid standing pensively with my buzz cut, dark rimmed glasses and shorts. I glance up. "Hi, American," she coos with breezy sarcasm. "Are you looking for the word *f**king*?"

Next morning, up early, my two pals and I catch a train for a day in nearby Kamakura, birthplace of several Buddhist sects still a feature of modern Japan, including Zen. I had done my homework. The Great Buddha of Kamakura, or Kamakura Daibutsu in Japanese, is forty feet high, a 13th century bronze statue with an interior large enough for people to stand and trace by eye or hand the redoubtable bronze handiwork.

I wanted to see a different side of Japan, a classic cultural side. The Daibutsu was a good beginning. We also took motorized rickshaws to the bamboo groves at Hokokuji Temple and the Hachimangu Shinto Shrine, and a taxi for lunch on Enoshima Island, home to statues honoring a Buddhist goddess, Benzaiten. I wish I knew what we ordered. No one in the restaurant spoke English; we certainly did not speak Japanese. I do know I never again want to eat the meal we blindly pointed to on the menu that day, but never mind. I have loved Japanese food for many years.

WHAT THE LOSING SIDE LOOKS LIKE

The Navy granted me special permission to spend twenty four hours with family friends living in Tokyo. They took me to the top of Tokyo Tower. Erected after the war, it was fifteen meters taller than the Eiffel Tower and painted orange. From the top you could see little patches below where new buildings had cropped up. You could see the Imperial Palace, which American bombers had spared (and where I would dine three decades hence with fellow HIV/AIDS scientists and members of the Emperor's family).

Later that day we strolled along lovely moats and gardens on those grounds, and visited, at my request, the Imperial Hotel adjacent to the palace. The hotel was a mix of Aztec and Mexican architecture that Frank Lloyd Wright designed. My hosts that day were gentle, peaceful people. I became fast friends with Hajime, a son my age. We were together only that one time, but stayed in touch via letters over many years.

On other days during the two weeks' stay in Tokyo our Navy hosts bused us to sites in and around the city. Vermilion temples of Hakone at the foot of Mount Fuji. Serene Shinto shrines with white clad priests. Solemn ceremonies of a Sumo wrestling match. The delicacy of a dinner hosted by geishas. The quiet beauty of emerald green rice patties.

Yet Japan was only beginning to recover from a devastating war. Large sections of Tokyo were flattened. The stench of raw sewage was so rife you could smell the foul odor ten miles out at sea. "Night soil" was carried on foot from neighborhoods out to distant fields in "honey buckets," wooden pails suspended from each end of a shoulder pole. This, I thought, is what the losing side looks like after nations go to war.

Most vehicles were glorified motorcycles, little cars and trucks with one front and two rear wheels. Japan's export business was nascent—inexpensive transistor radios and cameras aimed at America's growing middle class, and cultured pearls for upscale foreign buyers.

The Japanese economic miracle of the '60s, '70s, and '80s—capped briefly by trophy purchases of Rockefeller Center and Pebble Beach golf club—has passed. Stagnate since the mid-'90s, Japan's economy has been sapped by a declining and rapidly aging population, deep cultural resistance to immigration, heavy corporate and national indebtedness and the rise of other Asian economies. Will this also be the fate of China in another generation?

Learning those weeks about how Japan tells its side of World War II in the Pacific planted ideas that tempered my youthful assumptions about nations and politics, gradually, in important ways.

I arrived in Japan harboring an unsurprising opinion formed on a U.S. military base. The U.S. was always virtuous, always on the side of right. Our enemies were always oppressive, evil. A stark us versus them. In this case, an increasingly militant Japan, already dominating China and Korea, was expanding into Southeast Asia. To prevent U.S. interference in those ambitions, Japan launched a sneak attack on Pearl Harbor to cripple our fleet. With great sacrifice, we fought back, ending the war with two atomic bombs dropped on Japan's homeland, an act that forestalled what would have been horrific final battles inevitably forcing Japan's surrender.[29]

The Japanese had a counter narrative. Japan was pushed against its will by U.S. naval forces' Admiral Perry in the mid-19th century to enter the modern world. Japan then learned as much as possible about the western world. It built western influenced institutions: economic, political, military, social and educational. Japan's leaders observed that countries with colonies gained tremendous economic advantage, and concluded that it was an internationally recognized right of strong countries to take advantage of the weak. France, Germany, Britain and the United States each carved out their own spheres of influence. Thus, Japan's aggression to colonize Korea and China was fully justified.

With Britain (Hong Kong, Singapore) and the U.S. (Philippines) active with footholds in Southeast Asia, Japanese leaders foresaw that at some point Britain and the U.S. would move militarily to thwart Japan's expansion. The Pearl Harbor attack was intended to reduce that threat, but the vehemence of America's response to Pearl Harbor was unexpected.

The narrative now enshrined in Tokyo's Yakasuni War Museum asserts that the U.S. was aware by July 1945 of Japan's intention to end the war; the atomic bombing of Nagasaki and Hiroshima was unnecessary. The U.S. ignored the overtures because the U.S. intended to showcase atomic weapons to restrain the Soviet Union from advancing further in Europe and Asia. Put bluntly, the U.S. was willing to demonstrate the power of the new super weapon on Asians, but not on Europeans.

I did not then and have never agreed with that Japanese interpretation of the war. However, as I said, discovering the counter narrative did begin a subtle change in my thinking. I became more open to criticism about our political, cultural and social history. As we will see, it would not be long until I personally became more than a critic—eventually, a determined activist— against America's role in another war in Asia.

UNITED NATIONS PILGRIMAGE

There is a wonderful yet, regrettably, little celebrated service society today in America called the Odd Fellows and Rebekahs. The organization, a 19th century offshoot of the Masons, dates to 18th century England. Many local lodges were founded to organize cemeteries in small towns.

Members mainly hail from small towns and rural areas, not big cities. Their fundraising events and donations bankrolled a trip to the United Nations each summer for rising high school juniors across the country, including twenty five from eastern California.

The summer after my Japan and naval sea voyage, I was tapped again for an adventure in the opposite direction, this time by bus, to New York City.

My theme for the speech part in the competition among eight of us at China Lake was motivated in part by those lessons from Japan. At mid-point in my remarks, I invoked John Donne's "No man is an island," and summed up this way: "The effect of each life is that of a pebble dropped into a pond. Ripples of each action go outward, affecting a wider and wider pool of our fellow men and women. Your actions reverberate throughout the world. Collectively, we are the world."[30]

The purpose of these trips was for young people to see more of our country, meet local people, and learn and appreciate more about this fledgling United Nations. The Odd Fellows and Rebekahs organized them soon after the U.N. was created in the wake of World War II. They wanted the U.N. to succeed.[31] Their ideals embodied a core idea in the Odd Fellows and Rebekahs' credo, "the universal brotherhood of Man."

Riding in the bus, I fancied at times that I must be traveling through a dense jungle. All green on every side! Accustomed to my life in the desert, I was fascinated by the seemingly endless green farmlands, by thousands of miles of hills and valleys. The expansive natural beauty of this great country was dazzling.

When we reached a destination for the night, we often gathered in church basements or modest homes for dinners prepared by our hosts. Local Odd Fellows and Rebekahs turned out in force. They welcomed us into their homes, sometimes parceling out spare bedrooms amongst them. They served delicious home cooked regional favorites. We reciprocated after the meal with short talks about our lives and what we were learning on the trip, and answered polite questions.[32] Groups like ours were en route from across the country, converging for two weeks together in New York City. Three hundred teenagers in all. Meeting these Americans from all over the country was for me the most profound revelation of the entire trip.

My first impressions of the big city were not good. Buildings coated with soot. Dirty streets. Overcrowded sidewalks. But those thoughts faded quickly once we entered the U.N. headquarters, gleaming beside the East River. We attended General Assembly sessions, met in small groups with ambassadors and embassy staff from countries allied with the U.S. and from Cold War adversaries.

The high point was a private meeting with Dag Hammarskjold, the U.N. Secretary General. A Swedish economist by profession, Hammarskjold was an influential world leader. He died tragically two months later in a Congo plane crash, an event that remains clouded by questions of sabotage. His daughter, a noted HIV/AIDS scientist, later became a friend and colleague.

We participated in mock debates on important issues of the day: Fidel Castro's Cuba, the Cold War, divided Berlin (just weeks before construction of the Berlin Wall began in August), power struggles in newly independent Congo (a former Belgian colony), and more. I was apolitical and somewhat conservative, yet found the give and take in these debates engrossing. And, at times, troubling. Some opinions supported European socialists. Others were proudly racist. Both came as a shock. Yet I liked these individuals as people, listening and arguing with them as they did with me.

Permanent representatives of Czechoslovakia and Yugoslavia, both firmly aligned with the Soviet Union, challenged our assumptions about American power and ideology, far beyond my discovery about Japan's narrative on the causes of World War II. Their questions echo louder for me today.

"If your system is so much better than ours, why are so many in the United States poor, unable even to feed themselves?"

"What do you think about racial discrimination, about Jim Crow laws in your South?"

"Is everyone in America really equal, including black people and American Indians?"

"Why are a decent education and healthcare truly available only to those who can afford it?"

Then, a carefully aimed attempt at a rhetorical coup de grace.

"We survived the terrible war in Europe, which devastated major cities and killed millions. You were protected by your oceans. Yes, we have inequities but we are trying to get rid of them. We are trying to treat everybody equal. Maybe we do not allow everybody the same freedoms you have, yet. Maybe someday we will. But you should look first at what you do to your own people before you criticize us."

I was not buying their argument about a socialist utopia in the making. But, once again, I found myself uneasy, quietly questioning staunchly pro-American views accepted as gospel at China Lake.

I am forever grateful to those kind people of the Odd Fellows and Rebekahs. Not rich or privileged, they were hard working men and women doing much of the work others shun. Our political views did not always align nor our outlooks on the world, especially as we traveled through the Deep South on the eastbound trip and the Pacific Northwest heading home.[33]

I mainly remember their warmth, sincerity and kindness. What I learned about the American people on that trip would inform my antiwar activity a few years later, just as it does my hopes for our country today.

TWO WHEELS, GOURMET BUDGET, WESTERN EUROPE

Sending children on a summer trip to Europe after high school and before college is a family tradition. My planning for that opportunity was very serious and deep. I knew exactly where I wanted to go, what roads I would take, how long I would stay and what I wanted to see. I mapped out each route carefully to see as many art museums, cathedrals, battlefields, monuments, forts, castles and Roman sites as possible during my two and a half months on the road.

I was part of a group organized by American Youth Hostels, four boys and eight girls. Our plan was to bicycle for six weeks as a group, travel four more weeks on our own and rejoin the group for the trip home. I took the train from California, stopping only in Chicago, and connected with my fellow travelers in New York City.

We set sail in mid June on the Aurelia, a small slow Italian liner. All passengers were students ages seventeen to twenty. With music bands and bars for and aft, beer a nickel, whiskey sours a quarter and plenty of nooks and crannies to canoodle, our Atlantic crossing was a ten day party! What a blast. I can still sing "Brigitte Bardot, Bardot" in Italian.

Our first overnight stop was in Bath, a ninth century mill with sagging roof and working waterwheel. We had journeyed from Southampton through Salisbury before our eyes fixed on Bath's monstrous Bathwick Hill, a steep incline we had to nearly scale, carrying our gear before staggering into the old mill.

Cycling to London took us across a hundred miles of windy rolling back roads. After crossing the channel by boat (no Eurostar train until 1994), we cycled from Rotterdam north to Amsterdam, then southward to Belgium and northern France. We wanted to explore the west and south of France,

Normandy to Brittany, then inhale more magic of deep France country through the Loire Valley on our approach to Paris.

I became close friends over those days with two buddies who were happy to match my pace. If you really want to see the countryside, ride a bicycle. You are completely free to see it at whatever speed you wish. This is where (and, importantly, how) my deep love for rural European getaways began. *La France Profonde*, the Italian Marche and Tuscan Hills, the vineyards of Bavaria and rolling hills of South England.

The countryside rolled by gently no matter how hard we pedaled. We passed fields laden with fruits we would be eating that evening. Cathedrals rose in the distance as we eclipsed a hilltop, and disappeared as our two-wheelers descended. First a tip of the spire, then their full form majestically unfurled as we drew nearer with each rise along the road.[34]

After Paris we were on our own. I headed south on my bicycle more than four hundred miles to Carcassonne near the Spanish border, eastward to Arles, Nimes and Aix then down to Marseille, all with centuries of fascinating history and great food. Trains next were my best option. They took me more than five hundred miles past Nice on the French Riviera, onto Genoa and Florence in northern Italy and southward as far as Rome.

At every overnight stop, whenever possible, from Marseille to Rome, I headed for one of what my Michelin guide said were the best restaurants. Still my mother's sous chef, I was conducting the research she outlined months before. "Order the best dishes at the best restaurants. Record your impressions. When you return home, I will make each dish, then you compare what I have made to what you ate on your trip."

What a job for a sous chef! I did my duty. And eat I did. By this point in my travels I was well practiced in my customized art, lone traveler fine dining. In London, the initiation was at the great Indian restaurant of the day, Veraswamy. In Amsterdam, the best place for Indonesian cuisine, Five Flies.

Before cycling to one of these two- or three-star restaurants, out from my tiny saddlebags came my drip dry Sears & Roebuck suit and a tie. Amazing my servers, I ordered two of every course—two appetizers, two first courses, two second courses and two or three deserts—and washed it all down with two bottles of wine, one red, one white. How does it feel to steer your bike after two bottles of wine? The bike comes alive! A mind of its own. You have the devil's own time to keep it straight. Oh, to be seventeen again and able to eat without restraint.

An overnight ride along the rails from Rome got me to Holland in time to board with my group the Dutch liner *Grote Beer*,[35] the start of another ten day Atlantic crossing party!

CRYSTALIZING PLEDGE, PURPOSE

Europe in the early nineteen sixties of course was not today's Europe. England, Holland, Belgium, France and Italy were only fifteen years removed from World War II. The northern cities, including Paris and London, were dark with soot. Bomb damage in East London and Rotterdam docks would not be cleared for years. Highways connecting most major cities were still only two lanes. Towns and villages typically were connected by pretty single lanes lined on each side with trees. Wider Autobahns (Germany), Autoroutes (France) and Autostrada (Italy) and super speed trains linking major cities were decades in the future.

Foreign travel, especially when you are young, opens your mind. I knew from those experiences that I never wanted to go back to China Lake, to live there permanently. What I learned laid a foundation for planning a far grander trip, one we'll retrace in a later chapter, that took me around the world into communities of desperately poor and dying people.

These three summer trips collectively and individually helped crystalize for me a pledge and a purpose that would propel me further across the next decade of my life. They accelerated my ambitions to have a global impact, to make a difference in improving human life. They helped me appreciate the equal value of human life everywhere.

This perspective soon became a very deep part of my philosophy, the motivation throughout my work in science and for what I still do today. We live on a globe. We are connected. We have to do our best to help everybody.

6

OPENING OF THE MIND

"WE ARE SORY..."

Within a few days in early April of my senior year in high school, I received in the mail one envelope and one post card. The envelope, a thin one, was from my first choice, Harvard. It was a rejection, with the typo above in the first sentence. The post card was from the University of California at Berkeley. On the back of the post card were two small boxes opposite the words: "Accepted" and "Not Accepted." The box next to "Accepted" was checked. I was on my way to university!

Looking back, that Harvard rejection letter was a lucky twist of fortune. Berkeley in 1962 was an ideal place for me. It was free of social hierarchy. Anybody with a B average in a California high school was accepted. The student body was socially, ethnically and culturally diverse. There was no adult supervision, no *in loco parentis*. It was a wonderful place to find yourself, to open and broaden your mind, to widen the range of your experiences and to meet and learn from people with different life experiences.

An excellent university demands that you have a broad education. Although I was enrolled as a premed major, with math, chemistry, physics and biology courses mandated the first two years, I also had requirements in political science, history, literature and a language—French, in my case. This broad exposure to ideas and people is one of the great advantages of the American system of higher education. I much prefer it to the European system, which funnels you quickly into specific job skills or career tracks at age seventeen or eighteen.

ORGANIZATION QUELLS ANXIETY

I did not go to Berkeley to party. I went for survival. My parents' commitment to support me was explicit, a clock ticking. I would be entirely on my own financially whenever I completed, or abandoned, my studies. Sitting in my freshman dorm room in the fall of 1962, I was scared. Could I make it? Could I achieve the high goals I set for myself?

Nobody looked after you at Berkeley. What you did and how hard you worked were decisions left entirely up to you. At our opening lecture for freshman chemistry, the professor declared from the stage of the crowded lecture hall, "Welcome to Berkeley. You are one of three thousand first-year chemistry students. Whether you can stay is totally dependent upon your grades. If you look to your right and to your left, only one of the three of you will be here at the end of the year."

My solution to anxiety was planning, organizing and preparing. Before arriving, I had already decided to use the same meticulous approach and execution of my European summer for acclimating to university life. The analogy seemed to fit: a sprawling campus, with multilayered overlapping cultures and subcultures of faculty, students, administration; the immediate Berkeley community, gritty working class Oakland to the south and alluring San Francisco across the Bay Bridge. Thus, make detailed plans: daily, weekly and monthly. Find a place to live, set a routine. I scheduled all my classes to start at 8 a.m. and finish by 1 p.m. The afternoon and early evening were for study, with break for dinner then back to the books. I would be in bed by 9:30, wake at 6:30, sometimes earlier. In class, I always sat in the front row to avoid being distracted by other students. My focus was the professor only!

After lunch, it was immediately back to my dorm room to analyze every line of my notes. This habit of immediate immersion gave me a deeper understanding of new material and created opportunities to ask professors or instructors questions about anything I did not understand. I rewrote all of my notes, incorporating details from references I had looked up. I then asked myself, what key issues would the professor likely require us to cover on quizzes or any kind of exams? Bearing down, I wrote out essay answers so specific they noted and summarized references, including some I discovered in my own reading. This rigorous approach, unusual as it was among my peers, always paid off.

"You drive me nuts!" a teaching assistant in a history class told me one day. He had just finished grading first-year student midterms. "I cannot imagine that you remembered all this detail. One of your references was so obscure I had to spend a whole day just trying to figure out whether you had cheated or not. I thought you made it up. I finally found it." He was complaining about my note on Eusebius, a Hellenic scholar in the fourth century AD known mainly as author of a seminal biography of Roman Emperor Constantine. I did not make it up.

Weeks later, I was extremely nervous heading into final exams. To settle down ahead of my first exam in math, I looked up past exams and studied them closely to make sure I understood all the concepts and calculations. To my relief the questions were similar. Walking out of the lecture hall after filling my blue book with precise answers, I was elated, confident. "Boy, this is great!" I thought. Later, when our final chemistry grades were posted, I collected another A. My first semester grades were all As. For this agitated teenager from China Lake, it was a *huge* relief. A thought crossed my mind, "OK, I can relax," but I quickly barricaded that notion. "Not too much! I am going to keep my focus."

Persistence and determination matter. Strength of will matters. Developing confidence matters. Knowing your purpose matters. Learn to tap into your strength of will so that whenever some obstacle is in your way, even if that obstacle is massive and poorly understood, you silence any doubts in your mind that you are going to work through the problem and get past it. You just keep going until you do.

NATIONAL PRIORITIES

We touched earlier on America's surging commitment to train a new generation in science and math after the Soviet Union launched Sputnik in 1957. Congress allocated more than one billion dollars annually in federal funds starting in 1959 to bolster science education in the rising generation, my generation.

President Eisenhower and President Kennedy used their White House platform to win public opinion for post-Sputnik science and keep the money flowing. Only a few years after President Truman signed the authorizing bill in 1950, the National Science Foundation had become a prestigious federal agency, a pillar of national security with a mission that remains the same today: "to promote the progress of science; to advance the national health, prosperity, and welfare; and to secure the national defense."

Much of that grant money flowed to the nation's leading universities. Berkeley's College of Chemistry made the list, expanding research opportunities for top faculty into applied chemistry and basic research into the building blocks of chemistry and physics.[36] Part of the grants funded programs to recruit, train and develop top students to assist in that research. Federal support for medicine came through the National Institutes of Health.

Before the end of my freshman year at Berkeley, a brilliant educator and scientist had picked me out, laying plans to divert my path from medicine toward science. Looking back, this was extremely fortunate. Yes, I was working hard at my studies. But in the big picture of national priorities, there is no doubt that I also was in the right place at the right time.

Chemistry lab was required for freshmen premed students after first semester chemistry. That was fine with me. I was enthusiastic about the experiments, curious at each turn. I guess it showed. One day that winter, a very senior professor came over and said to me, casually, "You know, Dr.

Pimentel would like you to stop by his office when you have a chance." I knew Dr. Pimentel was chair of the chemistry department but wondered why he wanted to see me.

WISE, VIGOROUS, PRINCIPLED

George C. Pimentel soon would become the paramount mentor of my life. He taught at Berkeley for four decades, a revered and beloved man until his death in 1989. He was a fabulous educator, a tireless and endlessly innovative scientist. His legacy is enshrined in Pimentel Hall, a dazzling theatre-style auditorium with seating for five hundred people. In the building's main entrance today, you can see a large black and white photograph of this wise, vigorous man surrounded by students. One of those students is me.

SCIENCE BEGINS WITH OBSERVATION

George Pimentel was one of the most influential forces in high school education for the sciences of the past two generations. Requiring teenagers to begin science courses with theory, he believed, was mind numbing, dispiriting. Determined to change that, he overhauled high school chemistry curricula, underscoring for thousands of teachers that discovery in science begins with *observation,* not theory.

See the three or four colors in that flame? The gap between the wax and the flame? Why is it dark in the middle? Then blue, then orange, then darker orange? What do these colors mean? What does the shape mean? The CHEM study materials he developed in the early 1960s, funded by Sputnik-inspired government funding, were calibrated to instill excitement in students about chemistry and science broadly.

Pimentel was a broad thinker beyond chemistry, envisioning where science might be headed, and implications for society. One day he asked us, "I want you guys to think about what is going to happen when work gets replaced by automation, when we have a society of leisure. How are people going to handle leisure?" His point was not for us to determine whether a society of leisure was or was not on the horizon, but to have us imagine conditions in which leisure might be the normal life.

Pimentel was "a master of empirical physical models... always looking for the biggest challenges and for truly new phenomena," C. Bradley Moore, Pimentel's successor as chemistry dean, wrote in a tribute published two decades after Pimentel's death.

Moore emphasized two points. First, that Pimentel's "transition from an impoverished working-class and service background to international fame makes the quintessential American dream a reality." And second, that my mentor's "intense loyalty to the University of California and to chemistry were grounded in the opportunities they afforded him to transform his life and his mind."[37]

That day I walked into his office, Pimentel had been at Berkeley for fifteen years, including his PhD studies. He had invented tools for analyzing molecules through spectroscopy, a huge advance in identifying, preventing and curing disease. He had coauthored what became the classic book on hydrogen bonding, a cornerstone of modern chemistry, and he had directed a national program to enliven teaching materials for high school chemistry, emphasizing experiments and observation over abstract theory. He taught freshman chemistry class with boundless enthusiasm to thousands of students, even during the painful last stages of colon cancer a quarter century on.

Raised in poverty by his mother during the Depression, George Pimentel had worked his way through UCLA to earn a diploma in physical chemistry. He moved to the Berkeley campus for his first job, a secret government project, where he examined chemical processes in the separation of plutonium. Once he learned the true purpose of the Manhattan Project, though, he quit and enlisted with the Navy, serving on a submarine in the Pacific for the final years of World War II.

Twenty years later, then in his first years as chairman of Berkeley's chemistry department, Pimentel placed first in a NASA competition to develop scientist-astronauts. But he was barred from the training after physicians detected a minor abnormality in one of his retinas. His passion for space exploration undimmed, Pimentel led design and production for NASA of an infrared spectrometer to study Mars's atmosphere, equipment that captured vital information during the 1969 Mars flybys of the Mariner 6 and 7 spacecraft.

Pimentel required eminent senior faculty members to spend time in the student labs, keeping an eye out for promising students—premed students mostly—that he hoped to attract toward the sciences. He then vetted these nominees, candidates for a summer retreat with elite scientists that he designed for prospective acolytes. Pimentel covered the program costs with National Science Foundation funds, the government's post-Sputnik money.

"WHAT ARE YOU INTERESTED IN?"

I was one of a dozen students in 1963 that he and his field marshals fished out of that freshman chemistry pool of three thousand students. This evangelist and mentor for careers in science was seated now across from me.

"What are you interested in?" he asked me.

"We just learned the molecular orbital theories of a scientist named Coulson," I replied. "It changed my conception about the structure of atoms and how they combine."

Molecular orbital theory, identified by British chemist Charles Colson and a colleague in 1949, describes how electrons are arranged in chemical structures, and illuminates how chemical bonds are made or broken. "You can figure these things out, and maybe predict what they are going to do. That really interests me."

"Colson is giving a lecture here in a couple of weeks. Would you like to meet him?

"Yes, yes!" I said. "It would be super to meet him!"

"I am looking for people who could work here in a summer program," he continued. "We pay enough for room and board. I cannot guarantee you will get a place, but I think you might like it."

I did not hesitate. "Sure!"

Pimentel's concept for that summer was simple: Nurture in these young people an excitement for science. Start them thinking about a life in science, and what that could look like. There were fifteen of us. We needed to find our own place to live. I chose a fraternity house near campus that let out rooms for the summer. Each week for six weeks we reviewed and studied the experiments and related papers of one elite scientist. This was the stellar lineup Pimentel assembled:

Melvin Calvin, the biochemist who elucidated the biochemistry of photosynthesis, the process by which carbon dioxide in the atmosphere is converted to the molecules of life. He was a pioneer in the use of radioactive carbon available in abundance for the first time from nuclear reactors. His work is enshrined in all textbooks on biochemistry as the "Calvin cycle." In 1961, just before we met him, he received the Nobel Prize.

Harold Urey, the physical chemist who applied the theory of isotopes to predict and discover "heavy hydrogen," deuterated water comprised of hydrogen enriched in deuterium. The theory of isotopes asserts that one element could have atoms with the same number of protons but different masses. He also discovered how lightning in a primitive atmosphere containing the elements of hydrogen, ammonia, methane and water contributed to the origins of life. He was awarded the Nobel Prize in Chemistry in 1934.

Owen Chamberlain, the physicist who discovered along with Emilio Segrè, his Berkeley professor, the subatomic particle known as the anti proton. It was a foundational discovery because further experiments with anti protons across the past sixty years have added clues for solving the mystery of the origins of the universe, the Big Bang. Anti protons have the same mass of a proton but a negative electrical charge. Chamberlain and Segrè were awarded the Nobel Prize in Physics in 1959.

Luis Alvarez, the experimental physicist who observed in the late 1950s how molecules fall apart when bombarded in a hydrogen bubble chamber. This was extremely important for understanding the fundamental structure of the universe. He was awarded the Nobel Prize in Physics later, in 1968.

Joel Hildebrand, the chemist hailed by the *New York Times* as "one of the most venerated faculty members ever to teach" at Berkeley.[38] More than forty thousand students took Hildebrand's freshman chemistry class before he was required at age seventy one to step down from that role. We met a half year after I had practically memorized for that course his classic textbook, *Principles of Chemistry*. He had a vibrant curiosity, and lived to age one hundred and one. Riding in a car with me one day, he remarked, "One side of my face is more wrinkled than the other. The left side. That's because the sun comes in from the left when I am driving the car." Those little details.

MASTER CLASSES

We spent a day talking with each of these brilliant scientists. It was tremendously exciting, thrilling to spend time with them. Urey, Chamberlain and Alvarez, for example, had been essential contributors to the Manhattan Project. These were master classes. It later occurred to me that Julliard students must feel the same way after rehearsing the works of some great musician for a week, then are tutored by this maestro for a day.

Listening to these people, understanding how they saw the world, and how they came to ask the questions they did and design experiments to answer them was a life changing experience. Profound, intimate. They talked about their lives, how they came to their major discoveries, and what they were doing now. One of them, Melvin Calvin, told me, casually, "Maybe you would want to work in my lab one day." It was the capstone to an exciting year of opening my mind to new possibilities about science.

Awestruck as I was, I came to realize that at some level these heroic figures were human, too, with distinct personalities and temperaments. Yes, they have super brains. Yes, they have made a huge impact. Yet, and yet, their Olympian achievements now seemed more vivid, more accessible. An unexpected spark flared in my teenage brain. If they once were just guys like me, maybe...

7

IS THERE LIFE ON MARS?

By THE NEXT SUMMER Pimentel was well into research to design an infrared spectrometer that could detect and analyze gases and other elements in Mars's atmosphere. NASA was building the first satellite for a Mars flyby, and these experiments were a key piece of the mission.

With his encyclopedic understanding of infrared spectrometer chemistry, Pimentel stood tall in the vanguard of scientists racing to answer the question: Is there life on Mars?

A scientist named Sinton had published data that suggested aldehydes were present in the Martian atmosphere. Finding aldehydes meant they were being constantly produced, and the only likely sources were living creatures. That was big news! Yet aldehyde has only a short time in nature before decomposing. George had good reasons to question Sinton's interpretation. Earth has abundant life forms, but why then, he asked me, is very little aldehyde in our atmosphere? And how could they exist in Mars's atmosphere?

BELIEVE YOUR MEASUREMENT, BEWARE YOUR INTERPRETATIONS

"Bill," he added, "you are going to help me find the answers." He paired me with a talented graduate student, Jim Shirk, to design and conduct the experiments. Jim and I hit the books immediately, analyzing spectra, wavelengths of electromagnetic radiation that an object emits or absorbs. A chemistry graduate student, he was both a collaborator and sub mentor with whom I could comfortably explore ideas and hunches.

If aldehydes did exist in Mars's atmosphere, we believed, the amount likely was very small because aldehyde molecules did not stay stable for long before decomposing. The spectrum of heavy water, Harold Urey's deuterated water—water with an extra hydrogen neutron—absorbed infrared similar to that of aldehydes but the light heavy water absorbed was in a narrow band, not the broad bands observed by Sinton and those of aldehydes. Had Sinton mistaken deuterated water for aldehydes?

I had read that an aldehyde spectrum would blur under pressure, so I set about creating a series of model atmospheres. Measuring the light that passed through each synthetic atmosphere, I eventually reproduced the pattern Sinton had observed. Our interpretation of the pattern data was that Sinton indeed had detected evidence for heavy water in Mars's atmosphere, not aldehydes. His conclusion—the leading scientific argument at the time supporting the idea that life might exist on Mars—was wrong. We speculated that Mars's surface gravity, which is about one third of earth's surface gravity, allowed normal water to be released into space in preference to heavy water.

"We need to publish these results as soon as possible," George Pimentel said. Jim and I had been meeting weekly with George, describing our progress, planning next steps with his insights. "Bill, you conducted the experiments. You take the lead in writing. We'll submit it first to *Science*."

The prospect set my pulse racing. *Science*, then as now, ranks with *Nature* as the most influential publications for scientists. Getting published in either one is extremely competitive, highly prized by even the most accomplished scientists. Only ten papers are published in each issue. My very first published scientific paper... in *Science*!

George wanted the article sent first to *Science* because the journal's editors had published Sinton's original observation. Our dissenting paper appeared (with very few modifications) in the January 1965 issue of *Science*.[39] A librarian in the Chemistry and Chemical Engineering Library, alerted to my request, handed me the copy as soon as she spotted it in the mail. "Here," I thought, savoring the moment, "is *my* contribution to human knowledge on a major question: Is there life on Mars?"

That was not the end of the Sinton band story, however. When I was a senior, a third paper on the topic appeared in *Science*. These authors agreed that we accurately described the spectrum for pressure broadened heavy water, but there was a problem. The heavy water was not in Mars's atmosphere, they wrote. It was in *earth's* atmosphere. Why? When Sinton measured earth's atmosphere by pointing his telescope at the moon, the humidity was very low. On the days he observed Mars (during its closest approach to earth) the humidity was high.

This story demonstrated a fundamental truth about the scientific method, one that I emphasized with students in every course I taught. "Science does not reveal truth. Science provides tools for testing ideas, hypotheses. Your measurements may be correct, but your interpretations may be wrong."

LIFE: A LIVING SYSTEM, CAPABLE OF REPRODUCING ITSELF, WITH ERRORS

That summer George Pimentel asked our group to ponder another question. What might life be like on another planet? In another galaxy? In another universe? In other words, what distinguishes life from other forms of matter and energy? This is a question that has fascinated philosophers for millennia. The answer had a practical aspect. If NASA were to design instruments to detect life in our universe, what were they looking for?

We met each week to discuss our thoughts with him. The discussions were lively, pushed along by Pimentel in classic Socratic dialogue. He never said, "This is what I think." He always asked, "What do you think?" We read everything we could find on the topic including Erwin Schrodinger's classic, *What is Life? The Physical Aspect of the Living Cell*.[40]

For our group, I came up with this simple formulation that I continue to hold today: A living system is one that is capable reproducing itself, with errors. The errors allow a self replicating system to acquire complexity and to adapt to its environment. This description of living systems is independent of substance. Life on earth is based on carbon. Other living systems may be based on other elements such as silicon or even on energy alone.

I have never stopped thinking about the nature and origin of life.

In time I added one additional condition to what is necessary for any form of life: sustained energy input. One of the fundamental observations of our physical world is that energy dissipates. Without sustained input of additional energy, order gives way to disorder. Life on earth exists in a thin energy rich shell. The crust of our planet is continually enriched by the flow of massive amounts of energy, the radiation energy of the sun from above and the intense heat from our molten core below. If we do discover other living systems on a distant planet we will only find them in energy rich environments.

That second year of summer duty in George Pimentel's lab was an extraordinary gift in many ways. I was at the front lines of science, probing a question millions of people shared. Is there life on Mars? It would have been fabulous to be known as the Berkeley undergrad who found evidence of life on Mars. Disproving Sinton's hypothesis was deeply satisfying in its own right, but more important was the rigorous grounding in the process of science. And that includes having your own interpretations overturned.

Moreover, talking with and studying the lives of great scientists at Berkeley crystalized for me an understanding of how scientific knowledge is passed from generation to generation. Somebody makes a discovery. People fight about it: Is it true? Is it not true? They come to a consensus: this most likely is true. That consensus enters the textbooks because it is a consensus, not necessarily because it is true. Textbooks are created by individuals. They are not authoritative compilations of truth. The contents are the result of the authors' understanding of some topic, some codified understanding of fundamental research. But people continue to create knowledge. Somebody may come along and say, "That old idea is not true. I have a new understanding."

When you do science well, the only thing you really believe is your measurement. A good measurement can be repeated. Then you are free, as Linus Pauling observed, to believe whatever the data says.

MOLECULAR BIOLOGY AT MIT, A FORESHADOWING

"Where would you like to spend this summer doing research at another university," George asked me. My junior year spring semester was winding down, the summer of '65 approaching,

"I'd like to go to Harvard," I replied.

"Make another choice," he said. "You are likely to do your graduate work with friends of mine at Harvard. Pick another school."

I wrote to Alexander Rich at the Massachusetts Institute of Technology. He was a leader in what was then the new field of molecular biology, understanding living systems by understanding how the information in DNA was used to direct the production of specific proteins. I had learned of his work from my undergraduate advisors.

Rich replied by return mail. "That is a great idea," he said. "You can work in my lab all summer. I already have something in mind for you."

Alex speculated that one enzyme might enable cells to replicate RNA independently of DNA. My task was to purify the enzyme and see if this theory was correct.

Working with Alex was an eye opener. Each graduate student and postdoctoral fellow, about twenty in all, was working on a different project. All were related to understanding the fundamental aspects of living systems, some using the techniques of chemistry or biochemistry, or to study biological structures with X-ray crystallography.

My first task was to purify the enzyme of interest. That project alone took two thirds of the summer. The second was to test Alex's hypothesis. No matter how I tried, the enzyme never performed as Alex thought it should.

My last week in the laboratory we met one final time. "I tried every possible approach but I cannot get the results you thought we would," I said.

"I guess that wasn't such a good idea," he replied. "Thanks for trying. You did a fine job."

Alex was not upset in the least, nor was I. I had worked side by side with wonderful scientists, learning many techniques that would serve me well, and made a friend for life in Alex.

DECIPHERING NUCLEOSIDES, SUPERCHARGING LASER LIGHTS

Before heading to Alex's MIT lab in Cambridge, I had my first experience with what would become my passion at Harvard, molecular biology. A Berkeley chemist, Ignacio Tinoco, was interested in the fundamental properties of DNA and RNA.

"I am working on a theory that would enable us to predict the shape form sequence," he explained to me. "You can help me with the experiments." To accomplish this goal, we needed to understand the fundamental properties of each of the units called nucleosides, the basic building blocks of DNA and RNA.

"Your job," he continued, "will be to determine the solubility of each of the units in a solution that mimics the interior of a cell."

This required me to seal small amounts of each compound in a mild salt solution, then rock them gently in a warm body temperature bath for several weeks. I then measured the amount of light absorbed by the liquid. That allowed me to determine the concentration and therefore the solubility of each unit. These numbers, the results of my third year Berkeley biochemistry project, are still cited in fundamental chemistry text books.

My senior thesis project was fun, a return to another space science project. "We need to learn more about transmitting messages from earth into space with lasers," George told me. "Brad Moore can help you get started." C. Bradley Moore, an assistant professor who had recently completed a chemistry PhD, was one of the first chemists to use lasers. Working with Pimentel, he made important discoveries on energy transfer in molecules, the kinetics of chemical reactions and photochemistry—all vital to our understanding of atmospheric and combustion chemistry.

"We want a clearer understanding of vibrations between linked atoms," Brad said, framing my role. This project was NASA funded research to improve clarity and reliability in voice communications between ground control and astronauts' command module. The clock was ticking on JFK's goal to get American astronauts safely to the moon and back. "We need to look at how light is emitted and absorbed by molecules."

The light emitted by lasers in use at the time could be absorbed by the earth's atmospheric carbon dioxide. Obviously, that was a problem for space communications. Messages communicated with these state of the art lasers could not be transmitted from ground control through our thick atmosphere to astronauts in command modules anywhere above the atmosphere. I thought about my earlier work with heavy water. Might light emitted by a carbon dioxide laser with a heavier isotope (O18) replacing normal oxygen (O16) solve the problem?

"Heavier oxygen slows the speed of vibration," I confirmed with Brad. "If we substitute heavier oxygen for normal oxygen, could that change the character of the emitted light so that it could pass through our atmosphere without losing intensity?"

"Good idea," he said, and we set about designing experiments to test my hypothesis.

Throughout that semester, I worked on building successively more powerful CO2–18 lasers. Eventually, it worked! My hypothesis was correct. To demonstrate this, I sent light beams from Latimer Hall on the Berkeley campus across the bay to San Francisco so powerful they could drill a hole through a brick wall. We proved that CO18 lasers were more than capable of carrying messages beyond our atmosphere. My paper on these findings, "Atmospheric Absorption of CO2 Laser Radiation," was published in November 1967 by the respected physics journal *Applied Physics Letters*.[41] Brad

Moore, a future dean of Berkeley's chemistry department, and J.C. Stephenson were my coauthors.

MOMENTUM

That disappointment from Harvard College's rejection was far behind me, long forgotten after my first two years at Berkeley. Confronting my doubts and fears—with rigorous organization and discipline, and hard work—had yielded straight As and drawn the attention of outstanding professors.

I discovered from long hours in laboratories, meeting remarkable scientists, and seeking to answer big questions that I loved science. Publishing the deuterated water findings in *Science* was a thrill. Yet I also was reminded through requirements of the broader curriculum that the humanities embraced human drama with questions and observations that science lacked.

Meanwhile, the federal government's enthusiasm and burgeoning funds were advancing the nation's capacities in science and technology. These national policies, designed to bolster America's standing opposite the Soviet Union in the Cold War, were opening doors. The inner confidence I needed, the knowledge that I could perform at a high level and pursue a life of purpose, for improving human health, was mounting.

‖ 8 ‖

MAKING MENTAL MAPS

I LOVED LIVING IN THE BAY AREA.

Sometimes I would hike alone into the golden rolling hills and forest just above my dormitory on Dwight Way. It was a short walk out the back door and into these Berkeley Hills that included trees planted by Jack London, the novelist, decades before. On weekends, I would set out on foot—twenty miles out and back—across the Bay Bridge to San Francisco, past Fishermen's Wharf or through Golden Gate Park, all the way over the Golden Gate Bridge to the picturesque enclave of Sausalito.

Strong winds coming in off the Pacific and warm afternoon sunshine were invigorating. I joined the sailing club. We might be out all day on a weekend, tacking westward across the bay to Sausalito for lunch, over to Fishermen's Wharf in San Francisco for dinner, then racing the evening fog back to Berkeley before dark. Once a month, thanks to my mother's generosity, I enjoyed a fabulous meal alone at one of San Francisco's great restaurants.

I began to loosen up a little, at least socially in these ways, at the start of my sophomore year. I was even elected social director of our combined dormitories. My responsibility was to plan social events—hayrides into the eucalyptus forests above the Oakland Hills, and big parties too.

One of those parties was a mock casino night. As people gambled their party chips for prizes, playing poker or roulette, some fellow conspirators and I charged into the room at the appointed moment, toy guns blazing. A casino bank heist. Bang! Bang! Bang! Sheriffs, in on the scheme, quickly got the upper hand. I was captured, doused with molasses, feathered, put on a rail, and ridden around the room. Then, hoisted to the rafter, I began jerking my body to and fro, blood seemingly oozing down my chin as I squeezed little red capsules hidden in my mouth. Some people started screaming. What a scene! It was great fun, but getting the molasses off my body later was not. It clung like tar.

I was genuinely fascinated by the diversity and character of the students. Race, skin color did not matter. My first year roommate was a black student from Los Angeles who went on to become an emergency room physician and, after retiring, served again during the COVID-19 crisis. My second year roommate was a Pakistani who became a great friend. Our dorms were segregated by gender—that is the way it was on most college campuses until the 1970s. Men and women did share common areas for meals.

By my junior year, with a transcript of straight A's and a Phi Beta Kappa key engraved with my name, I was increasingly confident. (The fellow sitting on my left that first day in freshman chemistry dropped out before the final exam; the fellow on my right made it through freshman year, then departed.) Fifteen of us, top students among six thousand in my entering class, were invited into luxurious accommodations—luxurious compared with dorm life—in a large house on Arch Street. Even better for me, the house was situated in the northwest corner of campus, the biochemistry corner.

Life was looking good. I was a Berkeley underclassman with free room and board as well as free tuition. I had my own room, with no roommates, and excellent meals prepared by a dedicated kitchen staff. All expenses were covered entirely by the Telluride Association, a non profit group championing intellectual achievement and social responsibility on campus.[42]

BEST PART OF HUMANITY

Although I loved science, I began to realize that the scientific method is not self directing.

Science is a tool that can be applied to answer many questions including weapons, commerce and health. Yet the priorities of scientific inquiry need to be aligned with human need. Science can take you very deeply, as deeply as you want to go, into any subject. Science can answer extremely important questions, *big* questions. But to determine those questions, you need a broad understanding of human history, the arts, physical and cultural anthropology, philosophy and literature. You need to know where society has been and insights into where it may be going.

Science is an intensely human endeavor, asking questions to satisfy our curiosity in ways that can improve our lives. The priorities of science are directed by human need. To know which questions to ask, we need a deep understanding of why different tribes, different cultures emerged, triumphed, wavered and collapsed. What technologies did they wield? What values? What rituals and traditions. What diseases did they contend with? What social hierarchies prevailed?

I have pursued this broader understanding of human need and human activity at least as vigorously as science since my Berkeley days.

What I started with my systematic review and rewriting of class lecture notes has always continued—in a disciplined way, in many forms. I have continued to learn.

My habit is to go to museums at home in New York City and wherever in the world I travel. Inside the exhibits, I photograph, now with my iPhone, as many of the displays and captions as time allows. Each photo then is saved to an album stored on my computer, where I will add my follow-up research on the same topic and then compile a photo essay that I share with a wide group of friends. This process enables me to preserve each exhibit as an element of my mental map of the world, my continuously expanding mental map. I have more than a thousand topics in this compendium.

To illustrate, I recently made more than five thousand photos from the entire Egyptian collection in the Metropolitan Museum of Art in New York City. For each of these five thousand photos, I made notes. For any unanswered question that arose in making the notes, I logged onto the Met's website or to Wikipedia to learn more. And then I added details and explanations to my notes.

I am interested in how ideas, history, culture and art are connected. Art is a window into what is happening at any given period of history. Look at Delacroix. Much of his work depicts life in North Africa. Why? Because he was painting in the 1830s when France had just colonized Algeria. Are you interested in what was happening in the world in 5000 BC? Which came first, the Harappa civilization of the Indus Valley in northwestern regions of South Asia or the Ur civilization of the Fertile Crescent in southern Iraq? Is it possible these civilizations influenced each other? Why did civilizations of the Fertile Crescent begin to interact with the early Egyptians?

My art collection is idiosyncratic. I prefer objects that reflect the interface between civilizations. The sculptures of Gandhara are a great example. These Buddhist images from the years 100–300 AD were made in what is now northern Pakistan. They were derived from Greek and Roman prototypes, a consequence of Alexander the Great's forays down the Indus Valley some four hundred years earlier.[43]

Life has tremendous conflict. It may be brutal, harsh. This is the nature of human existence, and probably the existence of all living things. When you look out at the world, you see how brutal people are to each other. A daily assault, collectively and individually, that has to be upsetting to anybody.

Yet, after all the conflict is burned away by time, what is left is beauty— great beauty, great achievements, great intellectual achievements. This is a completely different part of humanity, a part of humanity that we can celebrate. Our accumulated knowledge remains. Our mathematics. Our language. Our music. Our art. Our science. Our technologies. So we can enjoy this great beauty. It is part of what can keep you very happy, with the capacity to enjoy the moment, every moment. Whenever I am in these museums, I identify with what I regard as the best part of humanity.

ANTHROPOLOGISTS, HUMAN DRAMA

A great strength of U.S. higher education is the opportunity—at Berkeley, the obligation—for you to take courses outside of your area of concentration. Courses required in my physical chemistry major filled half of my curriculum. But the other half was up to me and I took as much advantage as possible. I picked cultural anthropology as a minor, and also studied political science, western intellectual history and several history courses—China, Japan and South America.

Anthropologists study the human drama, which is not what scientists do. Anthropologists ask very different questions than scientists. Our Meso-american civilization course surveyed Aztec, Mayan, Olmec, Teotihuacan and other ancient cultures spanning the region of what is now southwestern Mexico to Guatemala. In Guatemala, we examined ruins for a few weeks, searching for offshoots of the Mayans.

One archeological site under development at the famed Altar de Sacrificios intrigued me, so one day I climbed alone on one of the unexcavated pyramids. When I reappeared at our base camp and peppered my professor with the details, he was nonplussed. "You did *what?*" Tiny snakes with a lethal venom were active on that site, he explained. The locals avoided it. If you were bitten, there was no hope.

Our readings included a fascinating paring of books by two famous anthropologists who reached very different conclusions about disintegrating folk culture and social change in the same Mexican village, Tepoztlán. The first, Robert Redfield, of the University of Chicago, described a well ordered, hierarchical society in his 1930 book, *Tepoztlán, a Mexican Village.*[44]

The second, Oscar Lewis, of the University of Illinois and perhaps the world's most famous anthropologist during the 1950s and 1960s, saw unalloyed class warfare. He illuminated a microcosm of disorienting change in poor communities as their countries modernized, and how welfare programs for so called backward areas all over the world might be improved. Lewis's meticulous study over five years, *Life in a Mexican Village: Tepoztlán Restudied*,[45] was published in 1951. He dedicated his volume to Redfield.

A major takeaway for me was always to be alert to how academics' political views influence their collection and interpretation of data. Redfield later conceded many errors. "(Lewis) has once more shown the power of social science to revise its conclusions and to move toward the truth," Redfield wrote in his review.

An anthropology course on China looked at the culture of fishermen and their families living in a small village called Ping Shan. It was situated at Mile 21 along the circular road traversing what then was one of China's southernmost regions, the New Territories south of Shenzhen and across Hong Kong's northwest border.

Soon after taking that course, I was surprised to meet one of my professor's graduate students when I visited Ping Shan. (Ping Shan was one of many destinations on the around the world trip I made after graduating, a mélange of amazing experiences and our focus in a later chapter.) The PhD student was living with his young family on a tiny sampan tethered to the dock, studying the Hakka language of the boat people. Sounds idyllic, but this was hazardous duty, potentially. The boat people were regarded by villagers with suspicion and sometimes killed.

I have been back to Ping Shan many times. The area is unrecognizable now, surrounded by a forest of towering housing blocks. That floating sampan village near Tseun Wan is home to what may be the world's best seafood market. You pick out whatever live fish or shellfish you want for a meal, then, selection in hand, walk across the street to a restaurant waiting to prepare a plate to your liking. Delicious.

I learned years later that the Central Intelligence Agency provided funding to support our professors' research linked to these anthropology courses. The CIA wanted a clearer understanding of peasant life in the wake of Mao's revolution in Communist China. What are the roots of peasant rebellions? What counter-insurgency strategies would forestall or defeat peasant rebellions?

These studies were yet another way the federal government created life changing opportunities for me at Berkeley.

|| 9 ||

POLITICAL AWAKENINGS

ONE DAY WHEN I WAS EIGHT YEARS OLD, the married couple living on the other side of our China Lake duplex moved away. I was sad. They were friendly and their big St. Bernard dog let me ride him around in the yard. A month or two later, the same thing: a young guy down the street who drove a classic Jaguar sports car moved out.

What happened? Why did they leave? I asked my dad. What was that all about?

"Son," he began, somberly. "Never sign a piece of paper that can get you into trouble later in your life." What was the connection? "Well, they didn't declare everything when they came to the base—all of their past associations, especially when they were at university."

Still confused. What past associations?

Dad kept going, chary perhaps of careers in government, Hollywood and beyond already ruined by four years of red baiting McCarthyism, then at its peak.

"No matter what you do, avoid all political associations. Be extremely careful. Do not sign. As we have seen with these neighbors, you never know what can happen, what the political mood will be."

SOCIAL INJUSTICE FLARES ON CAMPUS

The Civil Rights movement across the Deep South was parent of the Free Speech Movement at Berkeley. African Americans teaming with volunteers to end decades of voter suppression in Alabama and Mississippi were attacked over the summer of 1964 by police dogs, blasted with water cannon and beaten by police with billy clubs. Three hundred were jailed.

Some were murdered. Public outrage at the violence was a major force pushing Congress to pass the Civil Rights Act of 1964.

Students and other activists returned to Berkeley with plans to recruit on campus for demonstrations to protest racial prejudice in nearby Oakland. For generations, campus groups of all stripes—theatre troupes, campus guides, religious centers, political organizations, choirs and many others set up their tables for recruiting and pamphleteering near the heart of campus, Bancroft Way and Telegraph Avenue. Campus political groups that year ranged on the right from Youth for Goldwater (Barry Goldwater, the Republican senator and presidential nominee I would meet twenty years later with Elizabeth Taylor in Senator John Warner's office) to the Socialist Alliance. The Freedom Riders expected to be out there as well.

But just before classes were to begin, those recruiting tables were gone. All of them. The most powerful member of the University of California Board of Regents, William Knowlton, had maneuvered to ban them. A former majority leader of U.S. Senate Republicans, the defeated Republican candidate for California governor in 1958, Knowlton was owner and editor-in-chief of the *Oakland Tribune*—and chairman of the Board of Regents. He had fumed for more than a year that the Berkeley campus was a haven for left wing radicals. Now he saw an opening to bar local Freedom Riders from organizing busloads of students and picketing his Bay Area newspaper.

When I first arrived on campus as a freshman, my politics were mainstream Republican—Cold War, Eisenhower Republican. It seemed that almost everyone I knew in China Lake carried the same mantle. But this edict banning all groups from recruiting and pamphleteering on campus was jolting. I did not like it. Neither did my new Telluride housemates or friends across campus. We seethed for weeks. It was not moral, not right, for somebody with intimidating economic and political power, Knowlton, to suppress legitimate protests against social injustice.

I had not thought much before about power structures in society—who owns what, but this situation began to open my eyes. "What kind of world is this?" I thought, naïvely perhaps. "What is going on?"

Small protests against the solicitation ban became larger, with chants and speeches rallying crowds against university administrators inside Sproul Hall, the seat of power. Students defied the ban, setting up tables to recruit and hand out pamphlets even closer to the heart of campus, the walkway beneath Sather Gate. Thousands of students, faculty and others passed daily through that iconic sea green wrought iron arch. This was my first political awakening: injustice.

"I am not only going to join the protests," I decided. "I am going to speak out, and help lead them, too."

FREE SPEECH MOVEMENT, DAY ONE

On the afternoon of October 1, 1964, I took my place on the left side of steps on the upper plaza leading to Sproul Hall's entrance.

"The university unfairly revoked privileges that students have had for decades!" I shouted to a small group listening on the main plaza below me. "The right to advocate for a cause. The right to campaign for their groups. The right to free speech."

On the other side of the steps, near a tall, spreading loquat tree, one of the Freedom Riders, a grad student and teaching assistant in the math department named Jack Weinberg, was arguing the same points to a larger group. "This is an injustice by the university... *against all students*!"

Suddenly, a campus police car pulls to a stop on the plaza. Jack had refused to show his ID earlier at a recruiting table for CORE (Congress on Racial Equality), and the officers were back now to arrest him on a charge of civil disobedience. Two officers jump from the car, run up the steps, grab Jack, pull him down the steps and force him into the back seat of the car.

"That car is not going anywhere," I thought impulsively, and rushed to plant myself on the ground within a few feet of the front bumper.

I heard somebody yell, "Sit down!" and immediately a large contingent of students is surrounding me. This police car is not going anywhere. Jack is in the back seat, an officer beside him. Hundreds more students and other onlookers soon crowd around us. The car is marooned in a sea of people that soon would exceed three thousand, twenty to thirty deep.

Now comes a parade of speakers—onto the roof of the police car. The first is Mario Savio, in stocking feet, a graduate mathematics student and another summer of '64 Freedom Rider. "The administration is taking away a fundamental right," he shouts, to cheers and applause. More on free speech, on social injustice, on the urgency to act. The next evening, thirty two hours later, the police drop the charges and Jack Weinberg is freed.

This one event, more than anything preceding it, marked the birth of the Free Speech Movement.[46]

Protests drawing larger crowds continued over the next two months until late one evening, on December 2, a few thousand students massed along the steps and plaza before Sproul Hall. I was among them. This was going to be a sit-in to protest the expulsion of four demonstration leaders. The goal? Shutting down the university if the right to assemble and solicit for political activity on the plaza were not restored. Would I go inside too?

A sit-in would be illegal. Arrests would be in the hundreds. If I joined the sit-in, jail time and a police record could be my fate as well. Most students outside Sproul Hall that night seemed delighted, excited by the prospect. I definitely was not, troubled instead by my father's admonition to "avoid all political associations," and this stern warning that he added that day years ago: "Do not get arrested. It can destroy your career. It can destroy your life. Just remember what happened to the people next door."

I had not worried at all about getting arrested when I dashed down to the police car with Jack Weinberg inside. But I did become uneasy the longer I sat that afternoon and the crowd swelled, so I left after a few hours. Standing now with hundreds before Sproul Hall, however, the prospect of my arrest was much higher. Mario Savio and other leaders were advocating civil disobedience, expecting that *all* of us might be arrested. In his remarkable speech moments before, Mario said as much:

There's a time when the operation of the machine becomes so odious, makes you so sick at heart, that you can't take part! You can't even passively take part! And you've got to put your bodies upon the gears and upon the wheels... upon the levers, upon all the apparatus, and you've got to make it stop! And you've got to indicate to the people who run it, to the people who own it, that unless you're free, the machine will be prevented from working at all![47]

I admired Mario. He was authentic and eloquent that day,[48] tapping into two themes of modern life, alienation and impersonalization, and political injustice. I personally did not feel alienated, but I understood what Mario was talking about. At the same time, the intensity of my father's warning was overwhelming—*Do not get arrested... It can destroy your life... Just remember.* What unknown forces might bedevil my career ambitions if I ignored Dad's warning? I did not join the sit-in.

The next night, more than eight hundred students were arrested, many dragged down several flights of stairwells and into waiting police vans. All were released after spending a few hours in jail. That confrontation brought forth even more rage and protests from faculty and students.

In another month, the faculty Senate forced the administration and Board of Regents to back down. The expulsion of four protest leaders was reversed along with a campus ban against six student groups. The faculty vote backing the student protests was overwhelming, seven to one. I made mental notes about confronting the misuse of power through nonviolent political activism, and would not forget them.

In 1997, a plaque was dedicated on the elevated plaza some twenty yards in front of four tall Greek columns marking the entrance to Sproul Hall. It reads: Mario Savio Steps. "The most beautiful thing in the world is freedom of speech." – Diogenes of Sinope (4th century BC)

"WHY ARE WE FIGHTING THIS WAR?"

My second political awakening that year was the antiwar movement. Lyndon Johnson had been elected to a full term in the fall of 1964, campaigning as a peace candidate opposite the hawkish Goldwater. Johnson's posture was far from the truth, as we learned later. While speaking passionately about peace, Johnson was secretly ramping up the war in Vietnam.

By the end of 1965, 189,000 American combat troops were stationed in Vietnam. In another two years, by the end of 1967, Johnson's buildup would push those numbers beyond half a million.

Like millions of college age men, I paid closer attention to the war my junior year, trying to grasp reasons for and against. Every male was required to register for the draft at age eighteen. Federal law mandated that we carry draft cards issued by the government's Selective Service. Classmates from high school and people I had met my first two years at Berkeley were being drafted. If I had not had a student deferment, the draft might take me as well.

My friends in the Free Speech Movement by the spring of 1965 had turned their sights to organizing antiwar protests and teach-ins. The first one scheduled several speakers I wanted to hear, such as philosopher Alan Watts, comedian Dick Gregory, California politicians Willie Brown and John Burton and folk singer Phil Ochs.

As I walked toward the rally at a campus athletic field, some half naked guys yelling crazily, wearing brightly colored vests and waving toy guns, stormed out of a parked bus painted with psychedelic colors. "This is Berkeley. I thought I'd seen everything," I thought. "But, what is *this*?!!" I had no idea until I read Tom Wolfe's *Electric Kool-Aid Acid Test* a few years later.

What I saw was Ken Kesey and his Merry Pranksters crashing Opening Day of the Berkeley antiwar movement.

Many speakers questioned why Americans should take up arms against the Vietnamese. I had no particular opinion about the war at the time. I knew that Kennedy came to China Lake in 1963, just a year earlier, for briefings about guerrilla wars and peasant uprisings. He wanted better ideas, better tools to win counter-insurgency wars. My dad became enthralled with how Gurkhas fought in southern Nepal and India, wielding their long, wide, sharply angled, vicious looking knives. Listening to speakers during the Berkeley rally, I thought: These people have a point. Why are we fighting this war? Why was the war escalating? There is no reason for this war. This is not like Korea.

By the time I arrived in Cambridge and Alex Rich's MIT lab for my internship in the summer of 1965, my politics had moved far beyond China Lake, from very conservative toward the left. The antiwar surge was spreading to campuses in Boston and Cambridge. Not only students but many outstanding professors at Harvard and MIT, including Alex, were involved.

I was inspired by them, eager to participate. People I knew would be going over to fight and some would be killed. What were we fighting? The domino theory? What kind of theory is that! Nonsense. This was not a matter of me abandoning the Republican party for Democrats. It was the Democrats who controlled the Senate, the House and the White House—the only period in my lifetime, so far—and Democrats were escalating the war.

One night some friends joined me to hear novelist Norman Mailer speak at Harvard's Lehman Hall. We arrived early to get seats; more than five hundred stood outside, listening over loud speakers as Mailer's angry, signature antiwar speech reached crescendo. "Hot *damn*! Got me a war in Viet-*nam*! Lyn-*don*. John-*son*. He wants his picture everywhere. So hang his picture everywhere but hang it upside down. He looks like a light bulb!"

WHERE ARE U.S. POLICIES TO PROMOTE SCIENCE?

We do not have national policies today promoting science and technology, international diplomacy and many other career professions that enable America to lead in the world.

It is extremely important that we have political leaders at the top who say these skills are important, and that science especially is important. The cascade of federal dollars into science—when well timed, well reasoned and competently executed by leaders in Washington, delivers immense benefits to our society and our world.

Federal budget priorities, advocated by presidents, enacted by Congress through legislation and funded through dedicated research organizations have unrivaled power to make an *enormous* difference in the first steps of young scientists, of young people, starting out.

I know because, as I have said, federal funding made a huge difference in enabling me to make contributions to society for improving human health. To wit, George Pimentel had grant money for his spectroscopy experiments and other projects from his College of Chemistry dean that opened tremendous opportunities for me; that dean received funding direct from the National Science Foundation; that government agency created in 1950 and its advisers were authorized to spur post-Sputnik funding for science and technology, and the White House and Congress set that policy.

Yet the message to young people today in the absence of inspirational national policy is quite different. The message for them in the 21st century is, "Make *money*. Become a financial *whiz*. Get into *hedge funds*. Drop out of *college*. Get into *dotcoms*."

This is a disaster for young people, and a disaster for our country.

‖10‖

AROUND THE WORLD IN NINETY DAYS

"Driver, can we stop at the famous Kali temple on the way into the city?" A woman's lilting voice, unmistakably from the American South, is floating over my shoulder here in northeast India. "We would like to look around."

The bus driver taking us from Dum Dum Airport into Calcutta glances back at two older ladies seated behind me, as if to ask, "You want to be dropped off at *that* temple?" His expression, incredulous and wan, makes me wonder, fleetingly. The Kali temple is the first thing on my sightseeing agenda for tomorrow morning.

Within minutes, tin shacks lining both sides of the road come into view, large throngs milling about.

"My goodness, look at that, and that!" one lady says, glancing to her left. "Why, look over there, too," her companion shudders, pointing to the right. "What are all these people doing out here in the middle of the day? Don't they have a job?" A pause, a recalibration, then in an urgent loud voice, she adds, "Driver, never you mind. Please take us directly to the hotel."

Before leaving Berkeley, I bargained with my father to use savings from funds unspent during my last two years on campus to journey into several countries from Japan to England, through the Indus Valley and Fertile Crescent. This trip now across northern India, by train, bus and an occasional rickshaw or hired car, after flying into Calcutta from Thailand, would be the defining experience of my three month circumnavigation, and one of the most significant of my life.

CALCUTTA

Stepping outside my hotel the next morning in the city center, I received a shock from which I still recoil. Dead and dying people filled the streets. Bodies were being loaded onto carts to be taken who knows where for disposal. Here was the depth of human experience. People with leprosy, people with no hands, no eye, no nose. People whose bodies were horribly twisted. I thought, "This is what Siddhartha must have seen on leaving his family palace grounds for the first time, staggering under the impact of human suffering."

The Kali temple along the Hooghly River is ringed by two thousand beggars desperate for water, many horribly crippled.[49] The scene as I approach seems to concentrate all the horror I had witnessed along the way. Human misery, chaos and ritual animal slaughter unfolded before my eyes. I see people with only one leg and twisted spines, their emaciated frames little more than bones. A pile of severed goat heads is dense with flies.

Three well fed priests, nibbling fruit and being fanned by turbaned acolytes, sit relaxed in a shaded pavilion in front of the temple. To the shamans, this chaos apparently was quite normal, nothing of concern. I had seen some of the poorest towns in the United States, ridden through the rubble of post-war Tokyo, and cycled passed European cities blackened by coal dust and still recovering from the devastation of World War II. But what I was looking at now was something completely different.

In 1960, eighty percent of the world's three billion people[50] lived in real poverty, starving.[51] In Calcutta I was witness to the depths of human experience, what life was like for most people for most of history. As jarring as these terrible scenes were, they reinforced the conviction that my purpose was to help others live better, healthier lives. This experience in Calcutta's misery, more than any other, bolstered my desire to do what I could to heal the sick of the world.

KHAJURAHO

The temples of Khajuraho, in central India near main rail lines and bus routes connecting Calcutta and New Delhi, were built originally for Hindu worship between 950 and 1200 AD and later converted to Jain worship.[52] Train or bus were the only options for me to reach the ruins' site, with train schedules promising faster conveyance at about two hours to the nearest railhead.

But the printed schedule did not allow for new precautions mandated in the wake of attacks by an indigenous Maoist movement, the Naxalites, who had been blowing up tracks along the route. My train proceeded only as fast as three men perched on the cowcatcher could run, each taking turns to inspect for bombs hidden beneath the rails.[53] That two-hour trip took at least ten hours. By nightfall, I had a bad case of heat prostration. It was the pre-monsoon wet heat, close to forty five degrees centigrade (one hundred thirteen degrees Fahrenheit). I spent the night under a wet sheet cooled by a fan in a government rest house, the only accommodation near the Satna rail station.

Moments after boarding a bus the next morning for the sixty mile trip to Khajuraho, I spilled some juice from a fresh mango. Flies gathered by my feet. I did not think much of it. At the next stop, though, the bus driver signaled to locals with a flick of the hand. Flick, flick, flick. Caste system dynamics were about to play out before me, *because* of me. The hand signal sped quickly from person to person—flick, flick, flick. Soon a lower caste sweep, dressed in red, steps onto the bus and walks back to clean up my mess.

The sun was boiling hot when we finally reached the temple grounds. I was too weak to walk the spacious expanse, across more than two square miles. There were twenty two structures. Mostly, I crawled on hands and knees from one temple to the next, flipping from my knees onto my back as I approached, catching my breath and staring up at the carvings. Some rose more than one hundred feet above the ground.

I must have looked pathetic. Local gardeners hosed me down from time to time. Sounds miserable but I don't remember it that way. The temple carvings were worth it. The most exquisite I have ever seen, before or since—and stunningly erotic, with depictions of assistants buoying men and women in every possible position—on mats, on swings, right side up, upside down. A celebration of the full range of human sexuality.

I hired a rickshaw in late afternoon to ferry me back to the guest house. The one-manpower vehicle had giant wheels, but the driver was not making much progress. Weak as I was, I scrambled out of my seat to lighten the load, then helped haul the rickshaw up a hill to the guesthouse. I rushed in, gathered all my gear quickly, then hustled out to hire a car for the two hour drive to the Satna rail station to catch my train to Delhi.

My only option, an open 1920 roadster, would have become a museum piece long before in the United States. Nonetheless, we departed. As the Satna station came into view in a deep valley, I also caught sight of smoke from the coal-fired engine of the train I needed to catch!... the only one to Delhi that day. Puff, puff, puff. We will just make it, I thought, but my driver had more immediate concerns. Stopping at the side of the road, he grabbed a coconut and a few flowers, walked over to a shrine, and prayed for a few moments. Then we were on our way again, speeding toward the station. I jumped onto that train to Delhi with only seconds to spare.

I have returned to Khajuraho many times since that first trip. No rickshaws, no 1920 roadsters now required. You can fly directly to a new airport and stay in modern hotels, a progress marker for that great nation.

ANGKOR WAT

"What is that guy drinking?" I ask the bartender.

I was killing some time before boarding an old DC3 heading from Phnom Penh, Cambodia's capital in the south, to my destination in the north, Siem Reap. The French guy next to me had downed a couple of stiff shots.

"He's drinking absinthe," the bartender replied.[54]

"Is that legal?" I knew that imbibing absinthe was not legal in the U.S.[55]

"Of course. We have been drinking absinthe for a hundred years."

I turned to the French guy, "You really like that?"

"*Bien sur!* I drink a lot of it. Try one on me."

The bartender mixes in water and the green absinthe turns cloudy. The taste is horrible, like a heavy Pernod Anis Liqueur gone bad. A terrible taste.

"You know, all that drink is bad for your brain," I said, a feeble attempt to recover.

"My brain seems fine."

The boarding call for my plane crackled from loudspeakers.

"Got to go. That's my flight," I said. "I don't want to be late."

"Don't worry," says my French friend, amused. "You won't be late. I am the pilot."

What??!! Not a reassuring thought.

For the next ninety minutes, with three live pigs trussed up in the back next to an open door, my pilot will demonstrate the fineness of his brain—or not. We head north at an altitude just two hundred feet above the fertile delta. This can't be normal, I am thinking. When the wheels of that DC3 touched down, I breathed a sigh of relief.

Siem Reap is the gateway to Angkor Wat, the world's largest religious monument, with more than fifty temples situated across four hundred acres.[56] The city was becoming an active site for engagement by all parties in the widening war in Vietnam.

Cambodia in 1966 was spiraling slowly into the war next door with its own military buildup, the seeds of a distant, looming tragedy for that country. Looking out from the veranda of the colonial French hotel, I spotted Cambodia's ruling monarch, Prince Norodom Sihanouk, resplendent in a white uniform, surrounded by high ranking American military men. They were all relaxed, chatting informally. Sihanouk at the time was juggling Cambodia's national interests among antagonistic American, Chinese and Russian leaders who were mounting regional propaganda campaigns over Vietnam.

For the next several days I journeyed into Angkor Wat, traveling in the back of a rickshaw powered by a motorbike. We regularly passed groups of five to ten men, clad in black pajamas and conical hats, heavily armed and stationed on long trails between clusters of temples, typically four or five, every fifty meters. I was getting anxious, thinking, I am an American. These guys must not like Americans. What if someone decides to take a pot shot? I felt like a duck in a shooting gallery.

A half dozen North Vietnamese regulars in neatly pressed khaki uniforms greeted me atop many of the temples. Most seemed bored, not suspicious. One senior officer was eager to talk. We were about the same age, both fluent enough in French. He was curious. Why are Americans fighting us? Why do Americans care about what is going on in our country? This is between us and our neighbors. We understand why the French fought us. They used to have the place. But we do not understand Americans. What do they want?

What irony. If I had not been protected by my student deferment my encounter with this fellow might have been violently different. We could have been eyeing each other through rifle scopes, forefingers poised by the trigger, somewhere across the Vietnam border to the east. "Well, this American does not think we should be here," I replied in broken French. "I have got nothing against you guys."

I have often thought about those days in Cambodia. How could those friendly, smiling people that seemed so peaceful have turned on one another which such ferocity? From 1975 to 1979, the Khmer Rouge regime killed one third of their fellow countrymen, by pickax, gunshot, overwork and disease. (The graphic Oscar winning film, *The Killing Fields* is a harrowing account of the Cambodian atrocities.) The experience taught me never to accept surface appearances as political reality.

KARACHI

When I arrived in Karachi, Pakistan's largest and most cosmopolitan city, the family of my college roommate and close friend, Bashir, was on a mission to find a suitable wife for him. They took me along on visits to the family homes of prospective brides. Muslim traditions were carefully observed on each occasion, men enjoying an elaborate meal and entertainment entirely separate from women.

In time, after I left, I received news that Bashir married one of the young women of these families, sight unseen. (They remain married, living in Karachi and Lahore where Bashir is a businessman.) During the week I lived in his family home and visited the family mango plantation, I never met a single female member of Bashir's family—not his sisters, mother or even grandmother.

One day Bashir and I toured the archeological site of an early civilization in the Indus Valley, Mohenjo-Daro, a trip that ignited a lifelong interest.

The Mohenjo-Daro civilization began to form as early as those of the Fertile Crescent and Egypt, possibly earlier. Mohenjo-Daro culture prospered here for about five hundred years; people had writing, weights and measures. Population centers were well organized, especially skilled at managing the water supply. Scholars put its rise to something approaching a city-state at around 2500 BC, but the origins go back another fifteen hundreds years to 4000 BC.

Innovations from this Harappa culture (renamed from Mohenjo-Daro by Indians after the 1947 partition) made their way into Mesopotamia, further west in the Fertile Crescent. Archeologists have discovered both Mesopotamian and Harappa artifacts in the same burial sites, near the Merv River in Turkmenistan. The site is along the major trading route from Northern Asia into Central Asia, across Afghanistan and through the Indus Valley into India.

Why did the Harappa disappear? All evidence points to an Aryan invasion, which forced dispersion of the people into the center and south of

India where they were lost to history, only faint genetic traces of the original population remaining. Food and clay bullets used in slingshots were still in the houses Bashir and I explored that day.

TEHERAN

Persia is deeply embedded in the narrative of western culture, if only for the famous encounters with Greece and conquests of Alexander the Great. Yet Persia plays a far greater role in the history and culture of South and Central Asia. I was eager to visit the capital of this dynamic country then governed by Shah Reza Pahlavi.

Teheran of the 1960s was a bustling cosmopolitan modern city, and, for me, a well timed refuge where I was able to relax over several lovely days. The fashions, cafes and shops reminded me of Paris, especially young women strolling in short skirts. The food was a blend of French and eastern flavors. One day I bought a kilo of the finest caviar for fifteen dollars, a freshly baked loaf of bread and a bottle of champagne that a friend and I consumed at one sitting. Oh, to be twenty one again!

Inside the Bank Melli vault, emeralds and rubies the size of robins' eggs were piled in heaps. Sparkling cut diamonds were arrayed, row upon row, in order of size from eighty to twenty carats. Everything it seemed that could be encrusted with jewels was on display: goblets, knives, shields and chairs. The *piece de resistance*? The famed Peacock Throne, looted from Delhi by an adventurous Persian ruler, King Nadir Shah, after his 18th century defeat of the Moghul Empire.

I could not have predicted the fate of Iran and its Islamic Revolution at that time. The country I experienced seemed so intent on becoming part of the modern world.

I returned to Teheran not long ago, finding the city a sad shadow of its past splendor. Shop fronts exhorting all Iranians to greater efforts against the great Satan had replaced fashionable stores. Towering apartment blocks, erected higgledy-piggledy, belied a deeply corrupt society where bribes make juicy land parcels available to developers and a tip into the right palm secures protection for ignoring building codes. No caviar except for foreign money and at outrageous prices! The jewels in the vault remained.

DAMASCUS

"Get out, right now! We mean *now,* not an hour from now. There is going to be a coup. Get. Out!"

The Indian embassy in Damascus had seemed a pleasant, secure retreat for a few days in Syria. But now, well before sunrise, the Indian ambassador himself was rousting me out of bed.

I was fresh from a two week stay with friends in Beirut to the north, then a wonderful oasis of beauty, education and delicious food. The journey to Damascus took me through eastern Lebanon's fertile Bekaa Valley, with stops in Baalbek and walks near two of the largest Roman temple ruins, the Temple of Bacchus and Temple of Jupiter.[57] Massive discs of some fallen columns had been arranged cleverly into a modern stage for classical opera and dance theatre. What a setting!

Damascus is one of the world's oldest continuously inhabited sites, settled at least four or five thousand years ago along a north-south Egyptian trade route to Asia Minor. As you approach by land from a distance, the outlines of Damascus first appear rather mysteriously, rising along a big mound.[58] The modern city today sits atop buildings from the past stacked at least thirty feet deep. Walking the streets, higher in places than roofs of occupied homes, I could peer into houses extending three floors below the surface. Literally, walking on history.

But now I was scrambling from the embassy, tossing belongings into a zip case, rushing to a waiting car. As I learned, the backlash to a successful military coup months earlier in Syria was unfolding. The vise of martial law would stifle civilian life. Roads would be closed, jails overwhelmed.

We barely made it through the mountains, heading south to Jerusalem. Had I been a little slower, I would have been stuck in Syria for a long, long time. The border was closed three hours after crossing into Jordan. No one was allowed in or out of Syria for several months.

JORDANIAN JERUSALEM

Many of the great holy sites of Jerusalem were in east Jerusalem, then part of Jordan.[59] I walked through Bethlehem, and along the Mount of Olives, Jericho and the massive limestone blocks rising more than sixty feet at the Western Wall,[60] all in Jordan.[61] I did not cross into western Jerusalem on this first journey, but since have traveled across much of contemporary Israel.

Those first experiences still fascinate me but the most searing image from that trip was not featured in any travel guide. It was a Palestinian refugee camp. People by then had been living in those camps for more than twenty years, hoping someday to return to legacy homelands within what became the borders of today's Israel. That sad history continues. The great grandchildren of some of those people I saw live today in refugee camps in nearby Lebanon.

Little did I know in 1965 that I was witness to the first trickle of what in the 21st century would become a flood of human suffering by refugees counted in the millions. This humanitarian crisis defines our times now, not only in the Middle East but in many parts of the world, a shameful reality brought about by cultural, economic and military conflict.

CAIRO

I had read in high school about Ramesses II, the most powerful and exalted Egyptian pharaoh. Ramesses II reigned for more than half of the thirteenth century BC, greatly expanding Egyptian rule militarily in northern Africa and into Syria.[62] Now, here I was, staring into his three thousand five hundred year old face, standing a few feet away in the great Cairo museum.

Ramesses's ancient forebears from perhaps three thousand years before his time may have historical links to the very early Harappa culture that my friend Bashir and I had contemplated only weeks before in Pakistan. Those ancient forebears might also have lived in early Samaria, an antecedent culture of Babylonia in an area now part of southern Iraq, between Baghdad and the Persian Gulf.

My appreciation of Egypt's history on this first visit was due largely to what I had read as a Burroughs High freshman in J.H. Breasted's classic, *Ancient Times: A History of the Early World*. It was Breasted, in that very book, who gave the Fertile Crescent its name.

Egyptian culture is one of the wonders of the world. I travel to Egypt as often as I can, mixing foundation projects, museum visits and sightseeing.

Many years after viewing Ramesses's mummy at the Egyptian Museum, I toured with Kent Weeks the subterranean tomb preserving the remains of Ramesses's ninety two sons. Kent is the American Egyptologist who led excavations in the 1990s of this massive complex, considered the largest tomb in the Valley of the Kings.

INCOMPREHENSIVELY BETTER

If you compare the state of the world in 1966 to today, there has been enormous progress, uneven but enormous. India then was in repeated cycles of starvation. You could not go into China, but almost every Chinese was desperately poor. Tens of millions of Chinese died of starvation during Mao's "Great Leap Forward," and millions more during the Cultural Revolution in the 1960s.

There certainly were pleasant parts of the world you could visit, but only five percent of humanity lived comfortably. More than eighty percent lived badly, very badly. Even in the late 1950s, when we rode by car on two lane roads to my father's home in Wisconsin, the United States that I saw gazing out from the back seat was not rich. Cheap hotels dotted the roadway.

Two billion people in my lifetime have risen into the middle class from poverty—abject, subsistence level, starvation poverty. Now the only famine you hear about is war induced famine. Fewer than ten percent of the world's population fall below the poverty line, down from eighty percent or more in the 1950s. People in India, China, Latin America and Africa may not be as privileged as some others but they live incomprehensibly better. My hope is that the COVID-19 pandemic will have marked only a brief stay on their upward trend.

When I arrived that September in Boston, I was extremely grateful, very grateful, for my one bedroom apartment. Here I had running water. I had a shower and a toilet that worked. The heating worked. The plumbing worked. People were not starving all around me.

I realized that we are extremely privileged. I have felt deeply grateful ever since for the circumstances that allowed me not only to live comfortably but also to do the work I love. It is a privilege beyond compare. Each morning, in a short meditation, I remember my good fortune and look forward to the day.

As I settled into my first courses as a Harvard graduate student, I was determined to make an impact in global health. The question was, what career trajectory would enable me to make the biggest impact? As a physician, or a medical scientist?

PART III

11

DESTINATION: HOT LAB

HARVARD WAS DOUBLY ACCOMMODATING THAT SPRING OF 1966, helping me confirm plans to take graduate courses in advanced sciences in the fall. I knew that I was not going to be a chemist or physicist as I prepared to leave Berkeley, but I was determined to study the sciences as broadly and deeply as possible before deciding on medicine or medical science.

"It is fine with us if you want this first year on campus to take the advanced science courses," Harvard said. "We will accept you into medical school the following year, or into the PhD chemistry program. You decide what you want to do."

Actually, as events unfolded, Harvard was triply accommodating.

After arriving in Cambridge, I was able to switch to physical chemistry studies from chemical physics. This change meant that I could master advanced theoretical physics, chemistry and applied mathematics. Completing these courses would give me tools I would need to explore a wide range of scientific questions related to health, whether I became a physician or medical scientist. I did not want to be limited by a lack of knowledge in any of these fields.

BRILLIANT INSIGHTS I: DEEPER INTO BASIC SCIENCES

Many of these advanced science classes this first year were taught by Nobel laureates or future Nobel laureates. Advanced biochemistry was about how the body transforms food into energy and the material necessary to sustain life. How do you make the cells that are not DNA? What happens to sugar? How does it make energy? What are the chemical conversions that go on?

Dual physics courses covered both field theory and statistical mechanics. In field theory, particle physicists examined two types of basic building blocks of matter, quarks and leptons. Statistical mechanics explored how to measure energy in matter as small as molecules, and how it changes as the composition of that matter changes.

Structural biology was my favorite course. This was an introduction to molecular biology following material developed by Cambridge University's John Kendrew, who received a Nobel Prize for determining the structure of hemoglobin.[63] (My professors, Carolyn Cohen and Donald Casper, had studied under Kendrew.) The course introduced me to the logic and beauty of biological structures. Ever since, whenever I look at the leaves of a tree or the shape of a sea shell, I marvel at the function and beauty of their form. Mother Nature invented form follows function; it was not invented by architects.

Our cells reproduce with an engineering tolerance so minute that it is equivalent to one-tenth of an angstrom. (An atom's diameter is approximately one angstrom.) Thus, every living thing at this most basic expression of a life form is a nanomachine. Cells are comprised of a number of discreet small objects called proteins.

I gained even greater insight into the intricacies of structural biology when another professor in the department, John Enders, tutored me privately. We spent hours together examining three dimensional models of proteins. I even helped him build some of these models. Many years later that experience helped me guide my daughter Mara as she designed and assembled sprawling sculptures, some dozens of feet long, of actual protein structures.

The collaboration with John was literally hands-on learning, creating models to replicate a precision that the human eye by itself cannot detect. Each protein is specified by a gene. A gene carries instructions for a miniscule three dimensional object that does the work to make chemicals for the cells in your body. As I say, our bodies are comprised of nanomachines. So is every tree in a redwood forest, some standing taller than three hundred feet.

Material science is approaching this same cellular precision, creating minute machines designed to integrate with our bodies. Effective medicines work at this level to accelerate the power of proteins or inhibit or alter their capacity to achieve a specific physiological change. Outstanding scientists in synthetic biology are crafting new materials at this same level of architecture. Create gasoline from sugar, not fossil fuels? Yes. Generate cannabinoids from sugar? Yes. If I were beginning my career now, scanning the horizon for approaching waves of science innovation, I would give synthetic biology careful consideration.

This was the most advanced coursework you could do in physical chemistry. I was increasingly confident as those weeks turned to months that I could do the physical chemistry professional work at a high level if I decided to be a scientist.

BRILLIANT INSIGHTS II: POLITICS, ECONOMICS AND POLITICAL HISTORY

Harvard graduate students have the privilege of auditing undergraduate courses. This is a cornucopia of intellect, offering brilliant scholars and experts speaking in every important field of study. I took advantage. Over both semesters, I gained knowledge in politics, economics and political history that has served me well ever since professionally and personally. Better yet, sitting in on one of these non-credit undergraduate courses is how I found my way into molecular biology, not readings or lectures for any of my advanced science graduate courses.

We will get to that improbable story shortly, but first, to underscore my convictions about pairing deep knowledge in the humanities with science, let me give you a quick summary of the fabulous humanities courses and their lecturers.

My first choice was a lecture course on international relations presented by an obscure (at least to me) assistant professor. I took my seat in the front row for the first lecture, and quickly found myself lost in time. The lecturer, in his thick German accent, was riveting. "International relations is merely domestic politics manifest on the international scene," he asserted. A simple insight, I thought then, one we know now has resounded through the first decades of the 21st century. "This course will illustrate the basic principles of international politics by study of 19th century *realpolitik* leading up to the Great War.

"Countries pursue their own interests either in concert, or in isolation," Henry Kissinger continued. "There is no such thing as international politics independent of a country's internal interests." In the coming weeks, he walked us through the clashing politics of Metternich (advocating balanced interests among European powers) and Bismarck (a Germany First nationalist) and how those played out through World War I, then onto events shaping the Cold War and nuclear standoff between the United States and the Soviet Union.

The course readings and lectures formed core elements of Kissinger's classic 900-page treatise, *Diplomacy,*[64] which was not published until nearly thirty years later. This was 1966, two years before Kissinger joined Richard Nixon's cabinet as National Security Advisor and, in time, Secretary of State. A master class in understanding contemporary international politics, with lessons highly relevant today.

As the year wore on I was welcomed to lunch discussions at Kissinger's Center for International Affairs[65], with Kissinger presiding. A rising West German political star and future chancellor, Helmut Schmidt, was one of many world leaders Kissinger attracted as guest speakers.[66]

John Kenneth Galbraith, the liberal economist, prolific writer and adviser to Democratic administrations of Roosevelt, Truman, Kennedy and

Johnson, had returned to teaching at Harvard after three years as JFK's U.S. Ambassador to India. His course, "The New Industrial State," asserted that big corporations and their large scale production processes had achieved primacy over free market competition. Much of the material was published in his best selling book with the same title a year later.[67] Galbraith brightened these lectures with anecdotes from his years as a diplomat and public servant, illuminating the human drama of policy and politics.

A course on Germany's doomed Weimar Republic and the rise of Nazism after World War I taught enduring lessons about human nature, politics and divided democracy, especially how societies reeling under great economic stress can embrace totalitarianism. The answer to the course's central question, "was German Nazism a real philosophy or a solely political opportunism?" was clear by the final lecture. Emphatically, political opportunism, not a philosophy. The professor, Richard Hunt, later served for twenty years as Harvard's head of protocol and coordinator of prominent visitors and events, a position known as University Marshal.

The deans of Asian studies at the time were John K. Fairbank and Edwin O. Reischauer. Both had advised American governments during and since World War II. They were widely known for public lectures, best selling books[68] and commentaries and interviews published in prominent journals and news media. I was eager to hear their lectures on the histories of China (Fairbank) and Japan (Reischauer) through the Korean War, and especially their views on the war in Vietnam. Neither opposed America's involvement, which I found disheartening.

One of Boston's nearby suburbs had a large sanatorium for mentally disturbed patients, one of several institutions supported through a public service organization affiliated with Harvard, the Phillips Brooks House Association. Still deeply troubled by my mother's mental illness, I volunteered for a year on Friday afternoons in what was known as the men's violent ward, hoping to learn more about mental disease and eager to assist the professional staff.

That experience deepened my sympathy for anyone suffering mental illness. The men's violent ward was an eerie place. Most of the time the patients sat quietly in drug induced stupor. Occasionally, however, the orderlies rushed toward the sound of a dull pounding; one patient viciously beating the head of another against a wall. We had to contend occasionally with sudden threats of personal danger as well. "Duck!" a voice from down the hall shouted at me one day. I did, flinching, as a meat cleaver flew passed, inches above my head.

COZY PHYSICS LECTURE HALL, NEXT MENTOR

With Boston's winter closing in, I preferred the warm, cozy physics lecture hall to pass the hour between my 8 a.m. class in field theory and 10 a.m. class in statistical mechanics. I decided to audit whatever course was scheduled.

That course turned out to be an introduction to molecular biology, the new science that excited Ignacio Tinoco when I assisted him in his lab at Berkeley.

A brilliant associate professor was teaching. Instead of lecturing, Walter Gilbert, a young University of Cambridge physics PhD, assigned students current papers from scientific journals, then led us through rigorous deconstructions, tearing apart the authors' methods and conclusions. I was dazzled. This struck me as basic training in critical thinking at the highest level.

Gilbert's process:

First, examine details from each step of the experiments.

"What methods did these researchers use to obtain their results?" he began, methodically. "Are you confident you could follow these same methods in the lab and obtain the same results? Are there too many gaps? Are the details precise, exhaustive?"

Next, pull apart the results.

"Were these answers genuinely meaningful? Were they statistically significant, or simply a minimal adjustment to what was already known?"

Finally, stress test conclusions from the data.

"Were the authors' interpretations logical, based on all we know? Were the speculations they drew from the data reasonable? What other interpretations might be equally valid, or more persuasive?"

Let me cite one example. In a brilliant series of experiments in his own lab, Wally had shown that ribosomes slide along the messenger RNA in the process of making new proteins. This soon became a central dogma of molecular biology: DNA → messenger RNA → proteins.

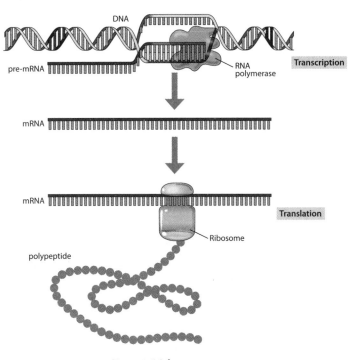

Figure 1. Making new proteins

RNA is a long polymer that is asymmetric from end to end.

The unanswered question was, in which direction did the ribosomes slide? Was it from what was called the 5 prime end or the 3 prime end of the RNA genome?

By chance, two published papers Gilbert had assigned examining and answering that question were written by scientists I knew personally. One paper was by authors led by Alex Rich in his MIT lab (my summer internship home two years before), and the other by authors led by Gunter Sent in his lab at UC Berkeley (a professor I knew and respected).

Both papers asserted that ribosomes began protein synthesis from the 3 prime end. None of us in Gilbert's class could spot any gaps in the authors' methods, but we all struggled to interpret their data. It was left to Gilbert to explain that these eminent scientists were wrong. They had presented the answer backward. Gilbert demonstrated that protein synthesis begins at the 5 *prime* end, not the 3 prime end.

Wally Gilbert's analytical approach ever since has been mine.

Analyze the tools used to produce the data.

Eye the data critically.

Be precise and cautious interpreting even the most reliable data.

Reality may lurk at unimagined depths.

These are essentials for conducting scientific investigation. You can believe *the data* when an experiment is done well, but you do not have to believe that *the interpretation* is beyond question. Data is data, conclusions are theories. Wally drove home the point that papers in scientific journals carry incorrect interpretations of data much more often than believed.

I was convinced from all I had learned in Gilbert's class that the field of molecular biology would progress rapidly. "Not only is his approach a brilliant way to critique science, this new field of molecular biology is going to transform medicine," I thought. The implications for the future of medicine and human health were staggering; to me, self-evident. *Our bodies are made of genes.*

What about other fields in science and math? Might they develop breakthroughs that could match molecular biology? I did not think so, given what else I had learned during those same months.

"Physics is going to be static," I believed. "Chemistry is not going to move very fast. Mathematics is a discipline I cannot practice at the highest level to make it a consideration."

"But molecular biology," I kept thinking, "this is something I can do that could be a very powerful tool for medicine."

Gilbert could be a fabulous mentor.

DECISION TIME

"We will take you, but because you turned us down once, we want you to talk to our top scientists who are also physicians. Then you can tell us what you want to do."

This guidance from a counselor in medical school admissions—*talk to our top scientists*—was unexpected, and welcome. The fall semester was coming to a close; so was my window for deciding whether or not to enter Harvard Medical School.

An elaborate experiment was unfolding when I walked into a semi-darkened laboratory for the first interview arranged by the admissions office. A monkey was fixed to a chair, his eyes propped open and staring at a black bar on a white screen. An electrode connected to a microphone emerged from the monkey's shaved skull. Two men in white lab coats a few feet away gazed intently.

The taller of the two men turned to me. "Watch this!" he said. The other turned a nob and the black bar began to rotate slowly. When the angle of the rotating black reached precisely seven and a half degrees, an amplifier emitted a rapid series of staccato clicks. As the angle shifted, the clicking volume rose or fell.

"Look!"

The taller scientist, visibly thrilled, explained to me what the experiment, an historic event in science as it turned out, was proving. "The brain is pre-wired to respond to specific forms." Fourteen years later in 1981, these two men, David Hubel and Torsten Wiesel, received the Nobel Prize in Physiology or Medicine for "their discoveries concerning information processing in the visual system."

Still energized from what we had witnessed, David Hubel sat me down in his cluttered office and read the summary provided by the admissions office. He listened carefully as I explained why I was there, paused for a moment, then in a quiet voice began to talk.

"I know something about your dilemma. I am a doctor who loves science. I thought I could do both. I am a doctor; I see patients. I am a scientist; Torsten and I are very excited about our work. We believe we are learning something profound about our brains.

"I am also a husband and a father," he continued. "For me, that is one too many responsibilities. I don't believe I can do justice to all three.

"If I had to do it again, I would devote all my time to science and family. I suggest you ask yourself a question I wish I had asked when I was your age: Are you compelled, really driven, to place your hands on a sick person to heal them? If so, then and only then, you should become a doctor."

He went on, "I see from your background you love science. Let me give you my opinion. You can do more for human health through science than you ever can as a doctor."

Thinking back on this now, I might have been a bit stunned by his candor. I nodded often as this future Nobel laureate confided all this, but kept silent. In any event I thanked him deeply for his time and advice, then departed. But there was no doubt: his words hit me like a thunderbolt.

Did I like being around sick people? No, frankly. I could get squeamish at that time in my life around sick people. Did I like the idea of putting my hands inside someone's body? No. I knew I never would be a good surgeon because my hands did not work necessarily at my command. Being ambidextrous probably contributes to having an agile mind, as I speculated in the Parallax Vision chapter, but it is not good for eye-hand coordination. You need fine motor skills to stitch someone up properly.

I saw clearly now my path should be a life devoted to healing *through science*, not medicine. Within a few days, I formally declined Harvard Medical School's offer to enroll and study to become a doctor.

THE "HOT" LAB

One day as other students filed out of the physics lecture hall that winter, I approached Wally Gilbert on the stage.

"Can I work in your laboratory as a graduate student?" I asked. "I want to do my PhD thesis in molecular biology."

He recognized me from my comments during class. His reply was encouraging.

"Well, my laboratory is full just now," he said, evenly. "Why don't you apply to work over the summer in the laboratory of my friend Jon Beckwith. If you do well there, I will consider you for work in my lab in the fall."

Beckwith was a young genetics professor at Harvard Medical School, highly respected. Within a few years he would lead a research team to a major discovery, isolating a gene for the first time from the chromosome of a living organism, a bacterium.

Jon did not accept me on the spot. He quizzed me, then posed several problems that required written answers. Evidently, he liked my answers. I spent a wonderful summer learning basic microbiology lab techniques and making many friends.

Beyond providing an audition for the Watson Gilbert lab, Jon helped me appreciate more clearly how and why discoveries about genes and the genome would transform medicine and medical research.[69] You approach genetics through observation, making mutations and watching behavior. Jon made deep inferences about behavior that were proven later through molecular biology.[70]

With his recommendation in hand by late summer, I still had another hurdle before I could join Wally's lab, an interview with James D. Watson, or "Jim," as he asked everyone to call him. I had no idea what to expect, and that might have been a good thing. Sitting in a hard wooden chair to the side of his desk, I labored to field Watson's staccato style interrogation, unable to finish even one sentence before his next scorching volley.

But, at last, I was where I wanted to be, admitted. A "hot" lab stocked with many of the world's finest scientists. I would be working with Watson, who two years before had won the Nobel Prize for his co-discovery with Francis Crick of the double helix structure of DNA, and the brilliant Gilbert, also destined for a Nobel Prize.

Meanwhile, I was unaware that Harvard was creating a new PhD program in biophysics. The idea was to encourage scientists trained in physics or chemistry to transition to life sciences. This was perfect for me, tailor made. Enrollment was limited to six to ten students per year. I was lucky to be one of them in the first year.

The Harvard Program on Higher Degrees in Biophysics, as it was called, had two great advantages: one, we could design our own curriculum, and two, we could choose any professors to study under in the vast network of affiliated Harvard institutions, including any hospital, any department of the medical school. This program, created by Arthur K. Solomon, became one of the university's most successful graduate programs. In my day, nearly eighty percent of the graduate biophysics students went on to become tenured Harvard faculty.

This extra year of studying science at the most advanced levels gave me tools that have enabled me to be an informed observer of spectacular advances in fields beyond medical science: cosmology, planetary science, physics, material science and information science.

Moreover, I have had no hesitations to pursue answers to scientific questions that fascinate me regardless of what tools were required, and especially to pursue questions related to medicine and health. The excitement never ends.

12

NO POINTS FOR
DISPROVING THEORIES

IN THE ENTIRE HISTORY OF SCIENCE, Jim Watson is one of the greatest contributors to human welfare and knowledge, one of the greatest scientists of all time. In coming centuries, he will be in the pantheon beside Archimedes, Al-Biruni, Galileo, Newton, Darwin and Einstein.

His discoveries with Francis Crick are that profound, with enormous consequences for our lives. Jim Watson answered an age old question, What is inheritance? The implications of that discovery for life and health will reverberate through the ages. More than any of his peers, he established the field of molecular biology as a discipline in the United States and around the world. What he opened up for medicine, for business and for our curiosity is amazing.

Working for Watson and Wally Gilbert in their Harvard molecular biology lab was like learning at the feet of Plato and Aristotle. They taught me the importance of how to choose and solve an important problem, then move on to the next. They showed me how to understand the deep implications of my work, and how to create that impact.

A decade before I joined the lab, Jim Watson and Francis Crick discovered the scientific answer to one of life's most fundamental questions, How does like beget like? Why, for example, do family members share certain physical traits? The answer lay in the structure of DNA. Watson and Crick found that DNA is comprised of two strands twisted about each other, the now iconic double helix. Each strand is a perfect mold for the other. As the two strands separate, one defines the precise structure of the other, yielding from the original form two identical copies.

Figure 2. Replication of DNA

Built into each strand of DNA are the instructions to make proteins— the micro machines that make life work. One length of DNA specifies information for one protein. Each length of DNA can be copied many times into messenger RNA. It is messenger RNA that directs the cell to make specific proteins. Copies of messenger RNA from one region of DNA produce one specific type of protein. This, as I touched on in the prior chapter, is the central dogma of molecular biology: DNA → messenger RNA → protein

The goal of the Watson-Gilbert laboratory at the time was to fill in the details of how this process for making proteins happened. I and my fellow students were the shock troops.

At the time I joined the lab, Jim was busy writing what became the classic text of this new field, *The Molecular Biology of the Gene*.[71] For his part, Wally also had solved a major problem, how proteins turn genes on and off. He also defined how ribosomes move along RNA, and, perhaps most impressive of all, how to sequence DNA.

As we know, I had an instinctive feel that molecular biology would eventually revolutionize medicine, providing new ways to understand human health and disease. But before I was given the opportunity to participate in this great adventure, I was required to demonstrate that I could make important contributions on my own. This is what defines graduate scientific training at the highest levels: identifying and solving major problems through disciplined, creative laboratory research.

WHAT MAKES ONE CELL DIFFERENT FROM ANOTHER?

In the Watson-Gilbert lab, each graduate student had responsibilities and freedoms similar to independent professors. We would choose our research topic. We would order what we needed to conduct experiments and decide the best approach. The onus was on us to design process and details for our experiments, which we did mostly by learning from one another.

The great news was that the lab was chockablock with extremely intelligent, highly motivated students, many of whom would become lifelong friends and colleagues.

Wally and Jim encouraged us to attack the two big problems of the day: How does DNA reproduce, or copy, itself? And what makes one cell different from another?

Arthur Kornberg at Washington University had discovered an enzyme, DNA polymerase, that could accurately copy DNA.[72] DNA has two strands. Nobody understood how one enzyme could read two strands at the same time. This was the first question that I tackled.

We had an idea of what must happen. All cells have one common set of proteins that make up the basic machinery of life. Each specialized cell also has a unique collection of proteins that account for specialized functions. Because we knew that messenger RNAs specify individual proteins, we knew the answer must be that different sets of messenger RNAs were present in each cell type, each representing copies of different parts of the common DNA.

Think of DNA as an instruction manual for a car. Each chapter in the manual describes how to make a separate component, an engine, an axle, a steering wheel. In this analogy, the set of messenger RNAs of a specialized cell, for example the cells of a hair follicle, have copied the chapter for that separate component: how to make a strand of hair.

Before the big questions could be answered, we needed to know some basics. We needed to know much more about the enzyme that Arthur Kornberg had discovered, the RNA polymerase, that could copy DNA into RNA to produce messenger RNA.

A fellow student in the lab, Dick Burgess, took up the challenge at his seat near my bench. He worked out how to isolate the enzyme and characterize its component parts, which led to a significant discovery: a loosely associated protein that is required for the polymerase to begin copying DNA at the right spot. Dick called the protein *sigma*. A related question arose: What was the signal to stop the DNA copying? My bench mate Jeffrey Roberts discovered that.

Dick and Jeff both devoted their careers to more deeply exploring these questions they first answered in the Watson-Gilbert Lab. Almost all of my fellow students followed the same path, building careers on the research they began as students. They pursued science for the sake of science. I had to perform in the same milieu, also answering big scientific questions, but I knew that my mission in life was different. I wanted to advance science in the service of human health.

HOW DOES DNA COPY ITSELF? WHICH WAY DOES THE CIRCLE ROLL?

All biology texts have a figure illustrating DNA replication. The knowledge underlying that seemingly simple diagram did not exist when I began my work at the bench. Wally Gilbert had just proposed a theory he called the "rolling circle model of DNA replication."

A small bacteria virus called PhiX 174 contains a circular piece of DNA. Wally proposed that if one strand remained as a circle, copying it could produce a very long opposite strand simply by rolling along the newly made DNA. Earlier, a Japanese molecular biologist and onetime Fulbright Fellowship student of Arthur Kornberg, Tsuneko Okazaki, had discovered with her husband Reiji that numerous small bits of DNA are made and later linked together during DNA replication.[73]

Wally added these small bits, or fragments, to his rolling circle, pointing out that the DNA opposite the strand that was forming a circle could be copied by making small bits of DNA and linking them together. Wally based his theory on the observation that what soon would be known as Okazaki fragments were made from only one of the two DNA PhiX strands during replication. (A graduate student in a neighboring Harvard lab had made that discovery.)

For my first set of experiments, I decided to see if Wally's theory applied to a larger bacterial virus called *phage lambda*. Many leading scientists had used *phage lambda* as a model organism. In fact Francois Jacob, Jacques Monod and Andrew Lwoff shared a Nobel Prize for their work using *phage lambda* and other small organisms.[74]

The excitement around their discoveries was that a detailed understanding of *phage lambda* would unlock secrets to much of biology writ large. Francois Jacob's memorable aphorism making the rounds then captured the vision: "What is true for *phage lambda* will be true for the elephant." Well, not quite, as we all learned later.

The question: Were the Okazaki fragments produced during *phage lambda* replication made from only one strand as Wally's theory predicted, or from both? Separating the two strands was a difficult process technically, a process I followed from published studies. I then tested the hypothesis, that one strand of DNA produced *phage lambda* replication. What did I discover? To my surprise, Okazaki fragments were made *from both strands*!

I reported these results at one of our lab's weekly seminars. Jim was uncharacteristically effusive.

"You have done a beautiful piece of work, Bill. Technically demanding and definitive."

Wally had been away after proposing his rolling circle model, on a sabbatical year at the Pasteur Institute in Paris. I reached him by phone in Paris and described my results. I did not know how he would respond, so I softened my closing comment as best I could.

"Wally, this is the evidence," I said. "What can we do?"

He was not pleased. From his perspective, the only one that mattered for me, my study and conclusions would not merit the follow-up for a PhD thesis. I could not proceed to the next stage, writing the paper for my thesis.

"Your study and conclusions, as accurate as they are, are unpublishable," he said. "No one is interested in the disproof of a popular theory. You have reached a dead end."

This was deflating, unexpected. I was stunned, momentarily, then decided to try another tack.

"Might there be something more subtle at play here?" I suggested. "Some other explanation of the Okazaki fragments coming from both DNA strands that I could try to find?"

Wally was not interested. He cut off the discussion. "You will have to find another problem to solve."

Six months later, at a conference on DNA replication, a Japanese scientist confirmed my experiment results, but had a different interpretation of them. During his presentation, he asked, "Why must a circle roll only one way? This result does not contradict the rolling circle model of DNA replication. The *phage lambda* circle rolls both ways!" That turned out to be the correct answer.

A leading journal published his *phage lambda* study, a paper that indeed disproved a popular theory, Wally's theory. With a little more patience on Wally's part and a little more self confidence on mine, that published journal article could have been my paper. Looking back, this entire episode is an example of how scientists too often seek to prove, not *test*, their pet theories—a fundamental error, obviously.

Imagine how many of the ancients proved to themselves that the heavens circle the earth. The brilliant Central Asian polymath, Al-Biruni, had the smarter, contrary analysis over a thousand years ago. If you will permit my paraphrasing, here is what Al-Biruni wrote: "My mathematical descriptions of the heavens are consistent with either the earth as the center of the heavens or the sun as the center and the earth circling the sun. The mathematics is simpler assuming a solar centric system. I do not now have the means to determine which is the case."

The mathematics is simpler is the operative phrase. Occam's Razor asserts the simplest explanation most often is the correct one; not always, but most often. Al-Biruni's simpler explanation was of course the correct one of his two hypoteses of which was at the center of the spinning solar system, the earth or the sun? The lesson for science, what Al-Biruni was getting at, is that the theory must fit the data, not the reverse.

As we will see, the setback from my first inquiry was not the only time I bumped up against the predilection of scientists to justify pet theories. Yet there was no mistaking the immediate lesson Wally had for me. With a year's worth of intensive and, in Jim Watson's estimation, "beautiful" experiments under my belt, I was no closer to completing my PhD program than the day I started. I urgently needed a new thesis project.

"YOU SCREWED UP"

Wally intended to remain in Paris through that summer, which was a relief. The extra time would give me several months to clear my mind and focus on some new project for my thesis. Ideas were already surfacing in my thoughts.

A few hundred miles away from Cambridge, along the northern shores of Long Island, Jim Watson was in the early stages of taking over as director of the once preeminent but then fading institution of life sciences research, Cold Spring Harbor Laboratory.

"I want you to spend the summer here at Cold Spring Harbor," he said over the phone one day. He had it all planned. The outgoing lab director, John Cairns, was in the final stages of a great experiment, one he had planned over several years, on DNA replication, a quite different approach than the one Wally had taken with Okazaki fragments. Jim, aware of my experiments and growing expertise in DNA replication, wanted me to assist John Cairns.

Cairns designed his experiments to isolate a strain of E. coli bacteria DNA that could replicate without DNA polymerase. If this were possible, it would contradict Arthur Kornberg's finding that polymerase enzyme is essential for DNA replication. How John had that insight about bacteria DNA I do not know.

Observing carefully as John worked to solve the problem, I thought, "This must be the way a master watch smith works." Here was the classic execution of science… at its best. John's notebooks were a model of precision and clarity. He meticulously prepared each phase of the experiment. For each colony of E. coli bacteria, he developed a simple, high volume test for the presence of the polymerase enzyme. For each experiment, he developed mathematical models.

In my very first days in his laboratory, John had his Eureka! moment. He isolated several variants of bacteria, not just one, that were devoid of Kornberg's famous DNA polymerase. Flush with this success in isolating the variants, John headed off for several weeks' holiday. Before leaving, he gave me an assignment.

"I want you to begin looking for another type of DNA polymerase," he said. "We know from the E. coli study that surely another one must exist. The question is, without Kornberg's polymerase enzyme, how do bacteria copy their DNA for reproduction?"

I decided that before looking for the new enzyme, I would do a bit more work on Kornberg's original polymerase. I reasoned that since we knew now that there was a variant, we should be able to quickly determine where the variant was located on the bacterial genome. "Maybe the second enzyme will be near Kornberg's polymerase," I speculated, and began mapping the gene.

I was making good progress when John returned. He. Was. Furious. "Why haven't you already begun the hunt for a new polymerase?" he thundered. "Other labs surely are working on this!" he shouted. The answer to a problem he had worked years to solve, and expected to continue research grounded in that answer, was now available to any lab focused on DNA replication. John suspected, rightly, that some of these labs might already have overtaken him.

John complained to Jim. I soon received an abrupt summons. "Bill," Jim said. "You screwed up. John is very angry. You must leave Cold Spring Harbor by tomorrow morning. Return to our Harvard lab." He paused briefly, then offered some reassurance. "Your scientific career is not over. Go back and work hard."

I had messed up, without question. We soon learned that others indeed were hot on John Cairns's trail. A few of these others would find not just one, but *two* new DNA polymerases; in time these researchers would build significant careers on these discoveries. Humbled, I took this as a lesson: "I am truly an apprentice, with no more rights than a medieval stone mason learning his craft." This refrain played in my head for many months: "I am just an egg, but an egg with a burning desire to fly."

PSI FACTOR: ON-OFF SWITCH FOR RNA?

Our gut bacteria undergo repeated cycles of feast or famine. After a meal they are flooded with nutrients. During feast time they reproduce wildly, doubling in number every forty minutes. During famine our bacteria are idle. They do not reproduce, but they survive by scavenging for whatever few nutrients in our gut may be about.

When they are growing, bacteria produce all the proteins necessary to make more bacteria. In idle mode they make an entirely different set of proteins which are suitable for the scavenging life cycle. All of this was on my mind as the outlines for a new thesis project took shape. My thought was, "Might understanding how a bacterium makes the switch from feast to famine, from growth to scavenging (self preservation), reveal a profound answer?"

Andrew Travers, a postdoctoral fellow from England working just down the hall from me in the Watson-Gilbert lab, thought the answer was yes. His experiments suggested that RNA polymerase, with or without Dick Burgess's *sigma* factor, could not copy those regions of E. coli DNA that were needed for growth. More specifically, RNA polymerase could not make the genes required to start the process, the cellular machinery for making proteins. The pieces of this cellular machinery were ribosomal RNA, transfer RNA (tRNA) and the genes for ribosomal proteins.

Andrew had found that an extract prepared from rapidly growing bacteria provided the substance necessary to copy ribosomal RNA. He called this the *psi* factor. Without *psi* factor, the ribosomal RNA piece of the machinery for replicating ribosomal proteins was incomplete. Based on this finding, he proposed a simple model for differential gene expression: First, each set of genes requires its own initiation factor. Next, the *sigma* protein is needed to copy genes that are required to maintain the cell's life but not to make new cells and the *psi* factor is needed to copy the ribosomal genes. Whichever initiation factor is most abundant will determine in what form genes are expressed, otherwise known as differential genes expression. The results were reported in *Science* magazine.

Travers's theory was elegant and easy to understand. It met with instant acclaim and enthusiasm. Might this be the answer to the fundamental question science had been asking: What makes one cell different from another? Perhaps higher order cells contain different types of *psi*-like factors, each enabling production of separate components required for each type of cell. *Science*, the authoritative journal, was impressed, and put their story about Travers's paper on the cover.

The upshot was this: If molecular biologists could identify the *psi* factor, they could understand how different cells read different RNAs. To read ribosomal RNA, they would have one *psi* factor. To read other genes, they would have others. Was this the paradigm for DNA differentiation? The science world believed so.

Yet, and yet, Travers had not actually identified the *psi* factor. He had only shown the effect from using an extract from growing cells that contained many differences substances. I saw an opportunity to take his finding a step further. "Why not identify the *psi* factor in pure form," I told myself. "I can then go on to unravel exactly how it works. What a great thesis topic." Wally and Jim agreed.

Over several weeks, I purified E. coli DNA, added the ingredients needed to make RNA, and measured whether or not I had made ribosomal RNA. The answer was entirely unexpected. The experiments showed that I was able to make ribosomal RNA *with no added factors*. I double and triple checked, and more. I even developed an entirely new way to detect ribosomal RNA. The same result every time: no extra factors were needed. How was I to purify *psi* factor if it was not needed to make ribosomal RNA?

I took the result to Wally, who had just returned from sabbatical.

"Andrew left only a few months ago," he said. "The DNA and RNA polymerase he used might still be in the fridge. Why don't you try that?"

I did, with the same disturbing result. *Psi factor was not needed to replicate ribosomal RNA.* Wally and I discussed the situation with Jim. If my observations were true, they would contradict what by now was widely accepted as a major scientific advance.

Jim immediately grasped the issue. "This is so important," he said, "that you should do the same experiments in Andrew's lab under his supervision."

Andrew Travers was in England now; he had been hired as a full professor at the University of Cambridge, ushered into the laboratory at Mill Hill, a mecca for molecular biology where Jim Watson and Francis Crick discovered the DNA double helix structure. Clearly, Andrew was a rising star in molecular biology.

Jim told me, "We can ask Andrew if he is willing to host you in his laboratory."

Andrew more than agreed. He was most gracious, inviting me to live with him and his wife while conducting the experiments. But the atmosphere was uncomfortable, charged even. If the experiment confirmed my results, not his, the impact on his reputation would be... well, we did not talk about that. We did not talk much at all outside the lab.

It was springtime. For two weeks we traveled back and forth to his lab through the blooming English countryside. The experiment Andrew designed for our collaboration was slightly different from the one I had done at Harvard. My task now was to measure production of transfer RNA from E. Coli DNA—with and without *sigma* factor, but with no *psi* factor extract. Andrew would collect samples from my experiment, then place them in a machine to read the results. He would know the answers. I would not.

NOT INTIMIDATED

Wally and Jim had agreed that I should go directly from England when my work with Andrew finished to present my results at a prestigious scientific conference. This was the annual Gordon Conference in New Hampshire, the venue for my first real scientific debut addressing world experts.

Just before I left England, Andrew handed me a sealed envelope with a letter he had written inside. "After your talk, have this letter read," he told me. "Do not open it." "OK," I replied.

Andrew's letter was burning a hole in my pocket, but I kept my word. When my turn came to speak, I handed the sealed letter to the moderator before I began and asked him to read it to the sixty scientists in the audience, all experts in the field, after I finished. It did not escape me that three of the most respected molecular biologists of the day were sitting together in the front row, Ekke Bautz from Germany, Charles Weissman from Zurich and Jerry Hurwitz from Albert Einstein College of Medicine in New York.

I needed only ten minutes to review my experiments, then concluded, "You have seen the data. I do not confirm the Travers result regarding *psi* factor. No additional factor is required to make ribosomal RNA."

The audience was silent for a moment. Then Ekke Bautz stood. "My lab repeated the experiments," he said, firmly. "You do need *psi* factor to make ribosome RNA."

Next, Charles Weissman. "We conducted similar experiments in Zurich. You need *psi* factor in ribosome RNA."

Now, Hurwitz. "I did these experiments with my own hands, and you need *psi* factor to make ribosomal RNA."

What was I going to say? I was a young graduate student presenting at my first major conference. Three legendary giants have directly contradicted me. For somebody who had not been trained to defend independent research findings—as PhD candidates were regularly during interrogations by Watson, Gilbert, Matthew Meselson, Mark Ptashne and others directing the Harvard lab—it could have been devastating. I did not back off or feel intimidated. I held my ground. "I did these experiments. I did not make up this data. These are the results. There has to be an explanation, and I am happy to explore it further with you."

The letter? What about the sealed Travers letter? The conference organizer stood, facing the audience.

"We have a letter here that Bill brought with him in a sealed envelope. The letter is from Andrew Travers. Bill repeated these experiments in England under Andrew's direct supervision. Even Bill does not know the results of their work."

The organizer opened the envelope and began reading: "To my dear colleagues. I oversaw the experiments Bill did in my own laboratory in Cambridge. I deeply regret to inform you that you are able to make transfer and ribosomal RNA without *psi* factor with RNA polymerase alone."

Again, silence, then a few barely audible gasps. The session ends. No one came forward to offer congratulations.

People in science dislike it intensely when a popular hypothesis is disproved. It is hard enough for anyone to learn something complex. People really hate it when they realize that something they learned is wrong. As I spoke in New Hampshire, dozens of new grant proposals based on the *psi* hypothesis were wending their way through the review process. Now, with Andrew's confirmation of my results, few if any of those proposals would be funded.

What about Andrew Travers? Andrew stood up, admitted he made a mistake, then carried on. If my memory is correct, he even published a note confirming my results. A man of high integrity, Travers continued his research for many years into how ribosomal RNA synthesis is initiated. To my mind Andrew is an excellent scientist and a fine human being. Yes, he made a mistake. That happens. In science, you will have disappointments.

I never received any explanation from Bautz, Weismann or Hurwitz about mistakes they must have made, but Andrew's *psi* factor hypothesis was dead.

So was my second thesis project! More than two years into the Biophysics PhD program and, yet again, I must go back to square one. Disproving theories does not earn you any points at Harvard. The standard at Harvard is: What big important problem have you solved?

13

MAKING MAGIC SPOT

Back in Cambridge after the Gordon Conference, I was determined to stay with the problem. How do different cells read different RNAs and replicate? What causes ribosomal RNA to be made, or not made?

"Travers had gotten it wrong, but I will get it right," I thought. "I will create a system in a test tube that mimics starvation. That will be my thesis."

My idea was to examine the synthesis of ribosomal RNA by breaking bacteria apart in whole concentrated extracts. One set of experiments would examine synthesis under conditions of excess nutrients. The other set would examine synthesis during starvation.

A problem with earlier experiments might have been that we all were using unrealistically *diluted* forms of high purified extracts of bacteria that do not mimic natural conditions. Highly *concentrated* whole extracts, I reasoned, should better replicate the behavior of the living organism.

A scientist at the National Institutes of Health had demonstrated recently that two small molecules accumulate in bacteria starved for amino acids. The scientist, Michael Cashel, called these molecules magic spots one and two. These findings were highly valuable for me, brought to my attention by a newly appointed tenured professor in the Watson-Gilbert lab, Klaus Weber.

Guanosine triphosphate (pppG) provides the power for protein synthesis, much as adenosine triphosphate (pppA) provides the power for most of life's processes, including muscle contraction.

"If I can create conditions in a test tube that really mimic conditions of a living cell," I reasoned, "the starved system should mirror Cashel's results and produce magic spot in a test tube."

Wally was enthusiastic. "Bill, fantastic idea, great idea," he said. "How are you going to do that?"

"I am going to add guanosine triphosphate labeled with radioactive phosphorous to a Zubay system that either has or lacks amino acids."

A Columbia University scientist, Gordon Zubay, had developed a system that was able to make both RNA and proteins simultaneously in a highly concentrated extract of E. coli. By luck, another biophysics graduate student working on the lab bench directly across from mine, Ricardo Block, was learning to use the Zubay system at the time.

"Ricardo," I said, "I'm trying to understand how ribosomal RNA is transcribed to proteins. Do you think the Zubay system would work for my experiments?"

"Sure, sure!" he said, and showed me how to work with the highly concentrated E. coli extract.

ALPHA POSITION, NOT GAMMA

Wally had listened carefully as I explained all this. Then, he stopped me and offered what would be a critical piece of advice. "Be sure to use guanosine triphosphate with the radioactive phosphate in the alpha position nearest the guanosine (ppp*G), not the gamma position (p*ppG)," he cautioned. "The gamma phosphates will exchange too easily with other molecules." Alpha and gamma positions refer to different locations in a chemical molecule.

I had been planning to use gamma labeled guanosine triphosphate, but I made this adjustment: use alpha labeled guanosine triphosphate. I started my experiments immediately, typically working from 10 a.m. to midnight to perfect the system. Most of the work required removing stray amino acids from the concentrate. I knew I was on the right track when amino acids I added to the extract restored protein synthesis after I had removed the free amino acids. Removing free amino acids stopped the synthesis; adding amino acids restarted it.

Late one afternoon, I added guanine triphosphate to the mix at the location Wally had coached me to use, *alpha labeled* guanine triphosphate—with and without amino acids. After letting it cook for half an hour, I placed a drop of the reaction on filter paper to separate the guanosine products, placed the filter paper over an X-ray film, and left for a quick dinner.

When I returned to the lab to develop the film, Eureka!!! Two spots on the film! These were the magic spots, one and two, right before my eyes. I had made magic spot in a test tube!

In a flash I saw the future. "I know I can take the system apart and discover exactly how magic spot is made. This would be a breakthrough, one that could lead to understanding what determines the difference between growth and scavenge modes in cells."

If I had not followed Wally's advice, I would have missed the big discovery! This story illustrates dramatically why working under a brilliant mentor can make a huge difference. The feeling I had in that moment was incredible. Finally, I was certain I had my thesis: making magic spot.

"Jim! Jim, I made magic spot in a test tube!" It was early the next morning and I had reached Jim Watson in Cold Spring Harbor. "Ahhh," he replied, with a touch of delight. He did not offer any explicit praise or ask questions. "Now," he added, "you are going to be a scientist."

Jim knew that I was a determined anti-Vietnam War activist and had published a series of critical magazine articles about how the U.S. government was conducting the war.[75] He and I never discussed the articles or anything related to them, but I was certain he and Wally had tracked them.

COMPETITION IN THE CAMP

I had no time to lose. The race was on to carefully document my magic spot experiments, then write papers and a dissertation. We knew other scientists were trying to figure out how magic spot was made.

"Klaus, you'll never believe it," I said, exuberantly, to the first colleague I met walking into the lab before sunrise that morning. It was Klaus Weber, the new tenured professor who had given me the tip about Michael Cashel's NIH studies. "I made magic spot in a test tube!"

I expected he would be delighted. How naïve. I will never forget the look on his face. Pure agony. Klaus immediately grasped the significance of my discovery. He seemed jealous. When you work with the best people in the world, you learn how best to approach and solve a problem. You also learn how competitive science is in that upper echelon. Think Olympic level competitive drive. A big discovery or breakthrough is rarely met with praise or cheers.

Ricardo Block joined me in the race. We worked as hard as we could for nine months, literally living in the lab twenty four hours a day, sleeping only during the brief periods we let the reactions cook—often only twenty or thirty minutes. We rushed home only on Sunday afternoons to do laundry and other basic errands, then returned by nightfall.

One day, we discovered that one of Klaus's graduate students was reading our notebooks in those rare moments when we were not there. He and Klaus were trying to beat us to the answer of how magic spot was made!

Yet, the timing of our discovery of their intrusion was lucky for us. Ricardo and I had not yet corrected a mistake we previously recorded in those notebooks Klaus's graduate student had copied.

Our error was that we had spun the centrifuge too long and too fast when separating the ribosomes from other proteins in the crude mix. Proteins that normally would be loosely associated with the ribosome, but were not actually part of the ribosome, spun to the bottom of the tube along with the stripped ribosome itself. We had caught the error after we had gone maybe two steps down a false trail. Klaus and his team probably went twenty steps down that false trail. They fell far behind.

One essential clue helped us pad our lead by isolating the enzyme responsible for magic spot production. We were looking for a so called relaxed variant of E. coli that continued to make ribosomes even when the variant was starved for nutrients. The variant was known as relaxed gene, abbreviated *rel*.

We knew we had isolated that enzyme after comparing a batch of purified samples from cells that made *rel* to a batch that did not allow us to purify the *rel* protein. The finding? Ribosomes with *rel* present could make magic spot. Those without could not. This was information we needed to publish our first journal article on the research. We had won the race.

I learned a lot about myself and about science during that period. It was a wonderful feeling being so focused on my work. A fantastic feeling. Through those many long weeks in the lab, every bit of my being—my emotions, my intellect, my physical activity—was focused on one and only one thing. This is what creativity demands: obsession and total focus to the exclusion of all else. I envisioned myself as a fighter pilot closing in on a target, my hand reaching out to switch off all external stimuli: social life, politics, friends, family... everything, to focus on one and only one goal.

The experience changed me forever. I never again fretted about working long hours. I did have to be admitted to a hospital, a patient for nearly a week after the first nine months—exhaustion, dehydration—but I recovered quickly. I had confidence I could face the rigors of the science life. I could focus totally, engage all my capabilities, and succeed. Many times later, whenever I faced a demanding stretch of activity, I knew that I would be below my capacity if I needed to go twenty four hours or less without sleep.

I HAD NO CHOICE

Ricardo and I were beyond dismayed that day when we discovered Klaus Weber was racing to beat us but we were even more upset when we learned that Wally Gilbert, my mentor, had been passing details from our research directly to our same rival down the hall.

One day I confronted Wally. "How can you do this when you know he is trying to beat us?!"

Wally was unfazed. "It does not matter who wins," he said, nonchalantly. "The answer will emerge faster this way. Science will be better off the sooner we know."

"Wow," I thought to myself. "Better for science but not better for me." I knew then it was a good thing that Ricardo and I had worked ourselves to exhaustion.

When Ricardo and I were putting the finishing touches on the manuscript for the first journal article on our findings, I received a call from Jim. He was abrupt, irritated. Klaus had been insisting to Wally that his name be included with mine and Ricardo as one of the paper's authors.

"Bill, I hear you are about to submit the paper on magic spot to *Nature*," he said. "I want you to add Klaus's name to the paper."

"But," I stammered, "Ricardo and I did all the work. We made the discovery. We worked night and day for months for that answer. You know that Klaus tried to beat us, don't you? He even secretly read our notebooks."

Jim did not dispute any of what I said. He just ignored it, and gave me this directive, "Bill, you have a choice. Put his name on the paper or leave the lab without a degree." And hung up. I was stunned. Five years of distinctive work on three projects, with no PhD? No future in science? I had no choice: add Klaus Weber. (I learned later that Klaus was threatening to leave Harvard and accept a job in Germany if his name were not included.)

Attempting to soften the blow, to add a plus from my own initiative to the minus Jim had forced on me, I went to Wally. "You should put your name on the paper, too," I said. He usually never added his name to his students' papers. "Sure, I will do that," he said. With that, the paper went to press.[76]

Eventually I came to terms with what had happened. Klaus was a constant source of support and encouragement in the months Wally was away. It was he who put me onto the trail of magic spot. I would never have done what he did, but I do understand.

EVERYTHING I NEEDED

The day I returned to the lab from the hospital, I knew I was on my own. Ricardo had had it. He was not willing to commit many more months with barely any sleep for the urgent push I planned next for magic spot research. Ricardo's choice was an early sign that a life in science would not be for him.

The question the results of that first experiment raised, and I now wanted to answer, was this: What was the specific trigger that caused ribosome to produce magic spot?

To make proteins, ribosomes assemble amino acid building blocks one by one. This takes place when transfer RNAs, each carrying a unique amino acid, attach to the surface of the ribosome, one waiting to be attached to the growing protein and the other in what is called the acceptor site ready to move into the attachment position. The sequence of the RNA messenger determines the order in which the RNAs line up.

Over the next six months, I purified every component needed for this intricate ballet. I added a specific component after each reaction. These precise steps, executed in sequence, gave me the answer: The signal to make magic spot is given when an empty transfer RNA without its amino acid arrives at the acceptor site of the ribosome to assume its place in line. The ribosome cannot continue to slide along the messenger RNA; it stalls in place. That is the signal!

I knew I now had everything I needed to publish a second paper.[77] The details at every step in this experiment could be followed by any scientist, in any lab, and, if executed properly, deliver the same result I had just produced. My data explaining the signal were clear. I was confident my interpretation of the data was correct.

I knew I had accomplished everything I needed to write my thesis, which I would entitle *Magic Spot and the Stringent Response*, and complete my PhD.

As I said, science is competitive. As I was waiting for my manuscript to be published a Danish group beat us to the punch. Our two studies came out weeks apart. We later became close friends and, for a while, colleagues. I was a visiting professor one summer in their lab in Copenhagen and one of them became one of my very first postdoctoral fellows when I was beginning my career as an independent scientist.

BELIEVE YOUR MOTHER

It is hard to be a scientist. You fail most of the time. You compete with your colleagues and friends. Sometimes you must work for years, not knowing if your well planned experiments will yield an important, or trivial, answer. You must constantly look for financial and institutional support. You depend on the work of your students for your success, some of whom may be spectacular, others disappointing.

Not long after receiving my PhD, I had a conversation with a famous biomedical scientist that summed up the mental toughness scientists require. Harry Eagle, a physician and medical scientist, was the driving force behind the creation of the Albert Einstein College of Medicine, a tireless advocate for biomedical research. He was chairing the Helen Hay Whitney Foundation when we met over breakfast at a retreat for postdoctoral fellows the foundation supported. I was one of the postdoctoral fellows.

"So you want to be a scientist," he began. I was slightly surprised. I had already earned my Harvard PhD and now, sometime in 1973 or 1974, was immersed in important research in David Baltimore's lab at MIT. The Whitney Foundation was funding my research. "Of course," I said. "That is why I am here."

But Harry Eagle had a point to make, so he continued, "You know, only young men and women who have been told by their parents that they are God's gift to the world—and who believe what they are told—can be scientists. We all face too many failures and too few successes to persevere without rock solid self confidence."

"No problem," I replied. "I believe what my mother told me."

My years in the Watson-Gilbert lab prepared me for the challenges and realities of a life in science. It was scientific boot camp. Tough, unforgiving, but excellent preparation for what was to come.

Performance at the top of any profession is demanding, competitive. Success demands many talents. Innate ability is one of them. Ambition, desire for achievement, and social and political awareness are also critical. Above all is perseverance: the ability to keep striving despite setbacks and hardship, always with your goal in mind.

But science was not my only passion as a graduate student. I also was pushing back against American militarism, caught up in the political and social turmoil of the 1970s.

‖14‖

WHAT HAVE
WE LEARNED?

A FEW YEARS AGO, I saw the Broadway revival of the 1967 musical *Hair*. When the curtain fell on the final act, my mood descended into deep sadness.

Fifty years earlier *Hair's* nudity and uninhibited celebration of hippie counter culture were shocking. Not this time. Time had burned away all but the essence of the story—a young generation, my generation, struggling against the war in Vietnam. We were fearful we too might be drafted to fight a war that we believed meaningless, then, like Claude in the last act of the play, some returned home in a coffin, mourned by friends and lovers.

Those of us on college campuses with student deferments in the late 1960s and into the early 1970s were off limits to U.S. military recruiters, for a time. Deferment notices would expire whenever studies ended. Yet as *Hair* became a sensation in 1968, *the* hot ticket on Broadway, the *Hamilton* of its day, the war news from the other side of the world deteriorated further, and no one could say with any confidence what was to come.

CRUCIBLE: WAR IN SOUTHEAST ASIA

By the final years of the 1960s, more than a half million U.S. troops were stationed in Vietnam.[78] Several of my high school friends had been drafted and were dead, either on the battlefield, killed while training or shot from the sky as reporters covering a battle.[79]

All of us young men faced the draft. Each had to question himself. "If drafted would I serve? Would I leave the country?" Almost everyone I knew opposed the war by the late 1960s. It was not a question of left or right, Republican or Democrat. Two Democratic presidents pushed us deeper into the war, Kennedy and Johnson. One Republican president, Eisenhower, vehemently opposed the war, while a second, Nixon, prolonged hostilities in the Indo-China peninsula by six painful and costly years, all the while saying he had been elected to stop it.

For me the situation was acute. My father and his friends developed the very weapons now being used in Vietnam. I knew exactly how Vietnamese civilians and soldiers were being killed. For example, cluster bombs. These horrors indiscriminately rained down machete-like slivers that tore the flesh of any soldier or civilian in their path. Cluster bombs were invented by my neighbors in China Lake. When John F. Kennedy came to China Lake in June 1963, he was planning counterinsurgency wars, looking for new weapons to overpower peasant armies.

In remarks to the graduating class at West Point a year earlier, Kennedy outlined his vision of these conflicts, and how the U.S. intended to fight them.

"This (revolutionary war) is another type of warfare, new in its intensity, ancient in its origin—war by guerrillas, subversives, insurgents, assassins; war by ambush instead of by combat; by infiltration, instead of aggression, seeking victory by eroding and exhausting the enemy instead of engaging him... It requires in those situations where we must counter it... a whole new kind of strategy, a wholly different kind of force, and therefore a new and wholly different kind of military training."[80]

ANTIWAR BRAIN TRUST

By the time I left Berkeley in 1966 I was firmly against the Vietnam War. Not virulently, but I considered it unquestionably immoral and probably illegal. I could visualize better than most the gruesome suffering American weapons inflicted. The Free Speech Movement helped me grasp for the first time that even democratic governments can do things that a majority of people do not support. At Harvard I went to more antiwar rallies, listened more. What were we as scientists being educated to do? How was science influencing this war? How were the generals and politicians directing science? What should *I* do?

Several mentors and colleagues were counseling me, a brain trust of revered scientists such as Paul Doty, Alex Rich, Matthew Meselson, Jonathan Beckwith and David Baltimore. Paul Doty, biochemist, was committed to banning nuclear and biological warfare. Alex Rich teamed with Doty at Pugwash conferences to halt the spread of nuclear weapons. Matt Meselson, molecular biologist, worked tirelessly to ban the use of chemical and biologic weapons by all nations. Jon Beckwith was an early member of Science for the People, and David Baltimore a member of the Union of Concerned Scientists.

Once more, George Pimentel was my signature inspiration. Recruited in the early 1940s from his Berkeley PhD studies to work on the Manhattan Project at Los Alamos, Pimentel quit when he learned his assignment was to help design an atomic bomb. He served then as a common seaman, enlisting as a volunteer submariner in the Pacific for the remainder of the war.

I regarded questioning the role of science and scientists in waging or preventing war as part of a scientist's duty to society. I saw many of those I respected not only advocate that science be used responsibly, but also protest vigorously and publicly that it be permitted to do so. As a result, I began to think much harder than I had at Berkeley about how wealth is created and distributed in American society, and America's unequal social conditions. I needed to understand the geopolitical implications of American military power in Vietnam, and to decide how I should respond as a scientist.

As we wrestled with these questions we looked to history. In his 1930s book, *The Social Function of Science*,[81] J.D. Bernal argued that science in the past had been a servant of commerce, a lever for accumulating and wielding money and power, not a dispassionate discipline for better understanding nature's laws.[82]

"The scientist is no longer, if he ever was, a free agent," Bernal wrote. "Almost universally he is now a salaried employee of the State, of an industrial firm, or of some semi-independent institution such as a university which itself depends directly or indirectly on the State or industry... Although many, if not most, scientists are opposed to the use of science for war, it is extremely rarely that a scientist refuses to do this kind of work. He knows too well if he does he stands to lose his position, and someone else will be only too willing to take it."

I came to believe, and still do, that every society supports science in the expectation that there will be a return for that support, a benefit. Most individual scientists pursue science for its own sake, but their work is supported by others expecting to benefit one way or another.

As we will see, my interest in science to improve human health, carried from my youth, was forged more decisively in this antiwar era. These experiences would, in the next decade, help fuel my desire to take up arms through the science I knew best, molecular biology, in the fight against HIV/AIDS.

TIME TO ACT

My opportunity for direct action came in 1969 when I heard that a new antiwar research group of the American Friends Service Committee had bought big books detailing every Congressional grant, including military contracts. Grants were catalogued by each of the four hundred thirty five Congressional districts, which meant that a little detective work could uncover the government's war footings anywhere in the country.

"This is a gold mine of data for educating the public about the war, a natural fit for me," I thought. "I was raised in a military community that relied on science to prepare for and win wars. I understand how weaponry is developed and what the effects of each weapon are. I can use this to describe for people how a weapon or some other military asset connected to their community is being used in Vietnam."

I volunteered to create a research center for the Quaker group—the National Action/Research on Military-Industrial Complex, or NARMIC as it was known.[83] Soon I was invited to speak with other NARMIC members all over the country, on college campuses, in small towns and big cities. On occasion I was accompanied at these forums by antiwar journalists such as Flora Lewis, a *New York Times* op-ed columnist, and Fred Branfman, who uncovered stories of secret U.S. bombing raids in Laos that our government never acknowledged.

My role was to make clear for each local audience the connections between local military activity and its impact in Vietnam and other countries.[84]

"Do you know that in your community, in this building at this address, casings are made for bombs that rain down cluster bombs in wide areas? Let me show you what cluster bombs do to human beings. Are you happy with the fact that your community is making cluster bombs? Do you know that in this very classroom tomorrow night our government is going to educate Brazilian police on torturing people? Are you happy with that?"

I was occasionally amazed and always buoyed by the enthusiasm of local antiwar activists who welcomed us into their homes. They reminded me of the friendly people who hosted us along the Odd Fellows and Rebekahs travels to the United Nations a decade before. One local coordinator invited me to his small town Kansas home for dinner. To my surprise, and delight, his wife prepared a fantastic meal of Chinese food. By my second and third years in the PhD program, in 1969 and 1970, NARMIC activities were consuming half of my waking hours even as those first theses projects in the Watson-Gilbert lab took wing, then crashed.

These were turbulent times. Everyone had to make their way through them, with no comprehension of when the nightmare would end. Comfortable assumptions we held about American life in the American Century were crumbling, certainly on college campuses. Some sought refuge from the draft by enlisting in the National Guard. Some renounced their U.S. citizenship and emigrated to Canada. Some enrolled in divinity schools.

To be sure, the majority did follow orders and reported for duty, but by March 1968 opposition to the war forced Lyndon Johnson to not stand for re-election. By the summer, two leading voices opposing the war were silenced: Martin Luther King Jr. and Robert F. Kennedy, shot by assassins. King opposed the war as another form of racial injustice. When Kennedy entered the Democratic presidential primary a few months before his death, ending the war was a pillar of his platform.

Protest marches that drew thousands to the Washington Mall starting in 1965 surged to a half million in November 1969. (I drove down from Boston to several of them.) That spring seventy Harvard students protesting Harvard's institutional role in framing military strategy and conducting weapons research took over the campus administration center. I did not participate, still owning my father's directive, *Do not get arrested.*

Some students threatened administrators and staff, including eight deans, forcing them from the building.[85] Others rifled through secret files, discovering documents confirming government funding for Kissinger and his Center for International Affairs that so captivated me. Not far away from University Hall, the administration building, I witnessed with alarm protestors storming into the Center's building on Divinity Avenue, forcibly ejecting its administrator. Kissinger had decamped by then to Washington. He was Nixon's head of national security.

More than two hundred protestors were arrested the next morning. Squads of helmeted state troopers and local police descended on the scene, collaring students from inside the building, clubbing and bloodying demonstrators outside. The police action stunned the campus, students and faculty, myself included, touching off an eight-day strike and stoking more intense antiwar activity.

A month later, students and faculty at more than thirty other campuses focused their ire on scientists' role in the war machine. Some led teach-ins, others protests. Some abandoned their labs for that day to show solidarity with what was known as the March 4th movement.[86]

The March 4th movement provided scientists across the country with their first opportunity to unite in protest against the war and confront fundamental questions publicly.

How is financial support for science generated in our country? What are the actual outcomes?

What are the consequences for us as scientists and for other people around the world?

Should we work on military problems?

Cambridge, the epicenter of the movement, overflowed with military scientists. One semi serious comment making the rounds was that the missile race was between two MIT labs, not the U.S. and Soviet Union. Scientists at MIT's Draper Labs dreamed up new guided missiles; scientists at MIT's nearby Lincoln Labs figured out how to shoot them down.

I was friendly with several MIT graduate students and faculty members who produced March 4th. In the aftermath, we seized the momentum to channel the protestors' negative energy into something positive and enduring: raising public awareness about science in politics and current events. Our vehicle for this was Science for the People.[87] Eminent MIT and Harvard faculty and others formed the Union of Concerned Scientists. Both groups believed science must benefit people beyond the narrow short term interests of whichever politicians and corporations happened at the moment to command the levers of government.

TIME TO TEACH

One day a friend and chemistry PhD candidate, Frank Mirer, said to me, "Bill, we ought to teach a course at Harvard about science and society." I instantly warmed to the idea. We were assembling all this knowledge for the public about science and current issues. Why not take the toolkit and tailor material for Harvard undergraduates specifically? We understood the

Harvard academic system. We were products of the system. Then it hit me. "We are only graduate students," I said with a sigh. "It is a good idea, but graduate students cannot teach a course."

Well, yes and no. We could not propose or offer a course ourselves, but a professor could and we then would commit to handle everything. Within a few weeks we had our sponsor, and the critical path defined for the task ahead. (The sponsor, Fotis Kafatos, was a molecular biology professor and neighbor in the Biology Building.[88]) Undergraduates in Harvard College were required to take a science elective in a general studies track known as Natural Sciences. Our course, Nat Sci 26, would be one of six or seven options for the 1969 fall semester.

Frank, a few others and I designed a series of lectures we would deliver, a general overview of issues in modern science. We added special sections requiring students to go off campus and investigate some high profile public policy issue that revolved around a scientific question.

Should nuclear power plants be built in your cities?

Why is the pharmaceutical industry marketing drugs that cause cancer or abnormalities in the womb?

Should you support biological and chemical warfare, or agitate to prevent it?

Today climate change surely would be a topic, as would pandemic control.

We recruited a marvelous set of experts in the community as teaching fellows. All were activists in their respective issues. I taught one section devoted to issues surrounding research on, and use of, chemical and biological weapons.

Biology and Social Issues was the course title. The purpose was to expose Harvard students to critical science policy issues of the day as well as prepare them as future leaders in society to grapple confidently with quandaries and conflicts rooted in science for the rest of their lives. We had forty students the first semester but within a few years four hundred undergrads were enrolling.

ANTIWAR JOURNALISM, FIRST STEPS

Alternative weekly newspapers were a phenomenon in the '60s. They broke the mold with florid unrestrained commentaries and vibrant graphics about movies, arts, music and politics. Alternative weeklies—alternatives, that is, to mainstream newspapers—were hip, experimental, popular.

My career as investigative war journalist debuted in the pages of *Boston After Dark*.[89] The editor, Derek Shearer, enlisted me from NARMIC. "Bill, you know a lot about weapons," he said one day. "You should write for us." "Okay," I said. "Let's do it."

Derek had information at the time from some high placed source in Vietnam about an aircraft manufacturer just west of Boston, in Lexington, Massachusetts. The company advertised very short takeoff and landing planes as perfect for the modern commuter. The owner happily agreed to my request for an interview.

The exposé we published hit hard. It reported all planes being painted black, rolled out of the Lexington plant and shipped to CIA operatives in Southeast Asia. There were no commercial sales. None. Our informants knew that the CIA deployed the planes on secret flying missions from one location in Vietnam to another in Laos.

Before the cover story ran, I called the manufacturer, read some passages from my draft and asked for comment. He was not happy.

"That is so unfair!" he protested.

"What do you mean *'unfair'*?" I retorted. "You are not selling your planes to commuters. You are selling them to the CIA. You are selling a lot of them, painting them all black. That is what you are doing."

We learned from an inside source that a company was testing nerve gas within a few blocks of a suburban Boston elementary school—Arlington, a fashionable bedroom community six miles northwest of Boston. A leak during testing could have sickened dozens of schoolchildren and their teachers and, if not quickly treated, been fatal from asphyxiation or heart attack.

In fact, we knew there were leaks, but lucky for everyone the leaks were from a test using material that was not actual nerve gas.

Nerve gas testing within a few hundred yards of an elementary school? Seriously? Nerve gas had been prohibited for use in warfare by the 1925 Geneva Protocols. Worse yet, the government was secretly carting nerve gas through Boston to and from the test site.

After we finished our reporting, Arlington school officials gave us permission to hold a press conference inside the elementary school. Some newspaper and TV reporters covered it. A few became frustrated, though, when police blocked them from checking out the test site. The government by then had halted the operation and sealed off the grounds. Our story had compelled the government to shut it down.

Who was Derek's high placed source? I did not know at the time but later learned it was Major General Edward G. Lansdale. Lansdale was a determined, nuanced CIA operative on counterinsurgency in the Philippines and Vietnam in the '50s and '60s, earning the trust of leaders there and advising U.S. military and political leaders at the highest level in Washington. But he chafed at U.S. policy in Vietnam after the Kennedy White House backed the military coup that ousted and killed South Vietnam's president, Ngo Dinh Diem. This happened a few weeks before Kennedy himself was assassinated.

Lansdale[90] opposed U.S. strategy throughout the Johnson years. The massing of foot soldiers and terrifying bombing campaigns alienated most Vietnamese, he argued. The strategy was too aggressive, badly misguided and doomed to fail. Lansdale encouraged leaking the Defense Department's secret history of the U.S. military in Vietnam through 1967, the Pentagon Papers.

The documents described how four administrations—Truman, Eisenhower, Kennedy and Johnson—misled the American people about U.S. military activity in Vietnam. Daniel Ellsberg, a top analyst at RAND Corporation advising Lansdale in the Pentagon, covertly provided printed copies of the Pentagon Papers to reporters at the *New York Times* and *Washington Post*. A series of Page One revelations followed during the summer of 1971.

WHAT HAVE WE LEARNED?

As I stood to leave the *Hair* performance that night, I asked myself, "What did we learn? Did we perfect the tools we need to resist senseless military adventures in the future?"

The answer clearly was, and remains, no. We then had been at war in the Middle East for fifteen years. I was as opposed to the second Gulf War as I was to the war in Southeast Asia; both pursued without thought for the consequence, both unnecessary for our security. The only difference, I feared, was the war in the Middle East would be endless and pose far greater danger to us and the world.

History has shown that none of the dire geopolitical consequences predicted by generals and political leaders of "losing South Vietnam to the North" came to pass. Vietnam is now an ally of the U.S. Dominoes did not fall. Our invasion of Cambodia did trigger the rise of Pol Pot and the subsequent genocide.

As concerned citizens, we may have learned little about how to prevent or stop a war. However, those in the government and military who plan and fight America's wars learned everything from their dissection of the antiwar movement's impact. Heirs to journalists who played such an important role filing dispatches from war zones in Vietnam have been neutered since the first Iraq War. We see on cable news few dead soldiers in Middle East war zones, few mangled civilians, few burned homes although surely they abound.

Reporters now, even the most intrepid, are "embedded" with the troops, meaning they are shepherded and censored. We fight with an all volunteer army recruited largely from the poor and voiceless. Middle class college kids and their parents need not worry about a military draft or dying in yet another war with which they may personally disagree. We fight this endless Middle East war with only two to three per cent of our GDP barely disturbing the good times at home.

My generation protested in the streets, the halls of government, town halls all across the country. We were driven to stop the deaths of tens of thousands of young America men as well as two or three million more people dying under the fire from our military in Southeast Asia.

With all these thoughts and memories racing, I walked from the theatre, downcast. Pondering Claude in his coffin, I again asked myself, what have we learned?

15

INVESTIGATING THE
WAR MACHINE

"HI, I'M ONE OF NADER'S RAIDERS."[91]

I looked up from my bench in the Watson-Gilbert lab. I was not expecting any visitors, but a young woman was walking slowly toward me.

"Hello," I said.

She introduced herself. "I just spent the summer in Washington. I would like to be a teaching assistant this fall in your course."

My visitor described her qualifications for one of the graduate student teaching assistant positions we offered in my Biology and Social Issues course. I recruited teaching assistants for NatSci 26 from the ranks of people who had been active in social issues that involved science whether or not they were part of the university. In fact, the majority of the teaching assistants were not. Impressed, I said I would get back to her.

Before leaving, she added, "Oh, and I need to give this to you."

She handed me a folder with a document inside.

"I was walking down a long hallway at the National Institutes of Health. Suddenly, a man opened a door just in front of me and handed me this envelope. He said, 'Take it to somebody who knows what to do with it. Believe me, it's important.'"

"I had no idea what he meant," she continued, "but I thought you might."

CIVILIANS BEAR THE MAJOR BURDEN

When I read what was in the folder later that day, I was stunned. This was an unpublished summary of National Cancer Institute studies, commissioned four years earlier, on possible carcinogenic, mutagenic or teratogenic properties in Agent Orange. The man who handed her the papers was an author of the studies, Marvin Legator.

"Agent Orange 2,4,5-T causes birth defects in animals! The army is spraying Agent Orange like crazy all across Vietnam," I said to myself. Military tanker planes by then had been spraying Vietnam forests and croplands with the chemicals for nearly eight years, since 1962. "This is big news!"

I immediately took the summary to Matt Meselson, a Harvard biology professor who worked just one floor up in the BioLabs. As I noted in the prior chapter, Matt was an international expert on the dangers of biological and chemical warfare. He worked to abolish those deadly weapons by international treaty. Matt understood immediately. He soon was able to get a copy of the full report through his contacts at the National Academy of Sciences. The implications, as we grasped the contents of the full report, were clear: Agent Orange is going to cripple a generation, and possibly more, of Vietnamese people and our own soldiers who handle it.

We needed to get this story out. Matt introduced me to a Yale plant biologist, Arthur Galston, and one of his Yale graduate students, Robert Cook, who could add their botanist insights. The three of us quickly drafted the article that *New Republic* editors rushed into the next available issue, January 10, 1970.

"What Have We Done to Vietnam? Deliberate Destruction of the Environment"[92] described the shocking extent of U.S. and South Vietnamese chemical warfare and the impacts. Villages destroyed by napalm-ignited flames; caves and bunkers saturated with tear gas; crops destroyed, and jungles stripped of leaves.

"It is the civilians who bear the major burden of this assault," we wrote.

This was the first of three articles I authored for the *New Republic* about multiple horrors the U.S. military was inflicting on the land and people of Vietnam. This first article described what we were convinced was an authoritative scientific argument that U.S. chemical warfare most likely was the reason behind rising birth defects in Vietnamese babies.

"Since 1962 huge C-123 cargo planes, equipped with tanks and high pressure nozzles, have released more than one hundred million pounds of chemical herbicides over more than four million acres, an area larger than the state of Massachusetts... To decrease the number of flights necessary over enemy fire, the chemicals are sprayed in concentrations up to ten times those recommended for use in the United States. This spreads nearly thirty pounds of herbicide over each acre of land."

We explained that the herbicide was simple to manufacture, with equal parts of two weed killers commonly used across the U.S., 2,4-D and 2,4,5-T. The mixture dropped from American warplanes was designed to lay bare trees in dense highland forests and jungles controlled by indigenous Vietcong and North Vietnamese soldiers. These were staging areas for attacks by those enemy forces across South Vietnam. Agent Orange also was weaponized to destroy the enemy's food supply, crops in the fields.

By 1967, more than a million acres a year were being polluted with Agent Orange. (The compound when manufactured generates a fraction of dioxin. Dioxin is nasty, regarded today as potentially lethal or causing birth defects in human fetuses.) In a few more years, a Vietnamese journalist wrote that two maternity hospitals in South Vietnam were ordered to send all files on miscarriages and malformed babies to the Ministry of Health, where these files then disappeared.

WITH LASTING CONSEQUENCES FOR ALL MANKIND

Meanwhile, in Washington, the Nixon White House announced a policy to ban the use of 2,4,5-T on crops in the United States, but downplayed the risks, implying approval for continued military use in Vietnam. "It seems improbable that any person could receive harmful amounts of this chemical from any of the existing uses" in U.S. agriculture, Nixon's senior science adviser said. We pointed out that this policy might have been influenced by the U.S. herbicide industry, which generated thirty five million dollars in annual sales from 2,4,5-T products.

The White House also ignored important findings of the National Cancer Institute's studies. Scientists there determined that 2,4,5-T, one of two Agent Orange weed killing agents, caused high rates of fetal deaths in rats and "serious developmental abnormalities" in survivors. We speculated in the article that Agent Orange was most likely the cause of rising human miscarriages and birth defects. The broader implications, we added, were profound.

"We have failed to consider the long-term hazards from the intrusion of chemicals into a system that has evolved its intricate arrangement for many millions of years... [I]n Vietnam, we can detect the beginnings of a new military tactic in limited warfare. No longer is scientific technology used only to kill the enemy; chemicals are also employed to destroy the economy that supports him.

"This environmental warfare has been conducted without any broad examination of the question whether any cause can legally or morally justify the deliberate destruction of the environment of one nation by another.

"The United States must begin to grasp the concept that belligerents in hostilities share a responsibility for preserving the potential productivity of the area of conflict. Otherwise, our technology may convert even the most fertile area to a desert, with lasting consequences for all mankind."

It was important to write that story, which was the first in any national publication to warn the public about the dangers of dioxin especially for pregnant women. Within two years, the military removed Agent Orange from its chemical arsenal. Dioxin in Agent Orange was teratogenic, meaning a cause of miscarriages and birth defects.

Chemical warfare by United States forces has been restrained in recent decades. Admirably so. It is gratifying to think that *New Republic* story made a dent, causing people to think more cautiously about using chemicals against our enemies in Vietnam. Agent Orange stories throughout the '70s and subsequent years made a lasting impact on the public consciousness. Even so, I have no illusions. I expect the Pentagon would rebuild our chemical warfare stockpiles quickly if any adversaries used chemical weapons or were intending to use them.

AUTOMATED DEATH

Richard Nixon campaigned in 1968 on a platform to bring the Vietnam War to a rapid close. He did pare back American troops on the ground, but not bombers in the sky. Nixon's Pentagon rained down nearly three million tons of bombs in Indochina in the first one thousand days of his presidency—more tonnage than the U.S. dropped on enemies in Asia and Europe combined during World War II and the Korean War.

The Pentagon for years experimented with airborne computerized weapons systems to reduce the need for combat troops. A secret project, code named Igloo White, first tested the approach in Laos in 1967, then expanded it over Cambodia in 1970. A year later Igloo White was pummeling the Ho Chi Minh Trail region with torrents of bombs. In my second *New Republic* article, "The Automated Air War: The Illusion of Withdrawal,"[93] I described for the first time in any publication the sophistication and futility of Igloo White.

Igloo White was the Pentagon's first generation of technology for the electronic battlefield. That vision to use technology whenever feasible to fight wars, to inflict heavy casualties on the enemy and limit American casualties, is far more potent today because the technology is vastly improved. This strategy was on display in Syria during both the Obama and Trump administrations.

In Vietnam, acoustic detectors dropped from aircraft and hanging in trees were designed to transmit noise to aircraft—either manned or automated drones. Seismic sensors that are partially buried detect ground vibrations. Two IBM 360–65 mainframe computers in Thailand, seventy five miles west of the Ho Chi Minh Trailhead in North Vietnam, analyzed the data. Printouts were relayed to a Battlefield Control Center. Then, in theory, "Bombs away!"

But there were problems. Sensors dropped from planes flying hundreds of miles an hour could be scattered across several miles of terrain. "If you don't know where the sensor is," I explained, "you don't know where to attack." Moreover, the sensors made no distinction "between friend or foe, civilian or soldier, adult or child, man or animal." The outcome invariably was "automated death on all who cross" the sensors' path.

My principal source for the Igloo White story was the transcript of Capitol Hill testimony. People I knew and trusted, and who trusted me, wanted the public to know. Parts of the testimony proffered ideas so ridiculous as to cast doubt on the logic of the entire operation. For example, surveillance aircraft were equipped with urine "sniffers," sensors to detect ammonia scents on the ground.

When the Vietcong and North Vietnamese figured this out, they had troops pee in the same pot, hang it on a tree, then dash off into the hills before the bombs dropped. By the way, most Americans believe guerrilla tactics caused the American defeat in Vietnam. Not at all. By the end of the war the North Vietnamese military was well equipped, highly sophisticated. They won primarily by deploying heavily armed divisions in direct combat against American divisions.

The Pentagon spent more than two billion dollars developing Igloo White and related systems during the mid-'60s and early '70s. Officials considered it a success. But effects on movement of enemy men and materiel along the Ho Chi Minh Trail to the south appeared negligible.

Shortly before my article was published in the fall of 1971, I inserted this fresh anecdote: "Communists launched a massive offensive in Cambodia in the midst of the rainy season and the heaviest floods in North Vietnam's recent history... It is not only cynics who suspect that supplies have been moving down the trail much as they always have."

DEEP CRATERS, AS FAR AS THE EYE COULD SEE

Horror and devastation by chemical weapons. Bombing raids more vast, more unrelenting, than the world had ever seen. Then there was more, what our generals termed "land clearing."

Massive American bulldozers brought to Vietnam leveled thousands of square miles of once arable, hospitable, beautiful land. A botany professor at a small college and I examined the staggering impacts in my last *New Republic* piece, "The Wasteland: Beating Plowshares into Swords."[94]

Defoliation campaigns were the rationale for Agent Orange and two related chemical compounds known as Agent Blue and Agent White. But by the early '70s nature had partially restored plant-based protection from U.S. aircraft surveillance for the enemy. Ground below trees killed from above by chemicals was overgrown by dense brush; and dead trunks wrapped by climbing vines.

"Land-clearing" was championed as the solution. "The U.S. Army Corps of Engineers is now using giant bulldozers to level hundreds of thousands of acres," we wrote. "The Engineers are cutting through trees, abandoned farms and scrub, leaving the soil grey, bare and lifeless."

The biggest threat to Army teams operating large bulldozers was not enemy snipers; snipers did take their toll, so much so that tanks and armored personnel carriers were assigned as bulldozer escorts. Yet the biggest threat was the deep craters, pockmarks over lands often as far as the eye could see, grotesque signatures left by exploding American bombs.

Concerns of local Vietnamese farming in most any area were not a factor when the Americans decided where to send in the bulldozers. The commanders' concerns simply were to aid American air power and reduce casualties to friendly ground troops.

"Shortly before an operation starts, the villagers are told via their village chief to leave the area, which then effectively becomes a free fire zone. Each morning before the bulldozers move out and each night after they return, the area to be cleared is saturated by artillery fire. During an operation, the armed escorts shoot anything they see that moves."

Our assessment in the article of tragedies ahead for the Vietnamese people was equal parts common sense and anger.

"Forests cut down will not return. Some one hundred twenty six thousand acres of prime tropical hardwood timber and over twenty five thousand acres of rubber trees have been destroyed. Wildlife habitat has been devastated. Erosion will be a serious long term danger on cutover hilly terrain. With the elimination of the enormous water holding capacity of the forests, heavy monsoon rains cause severely damaging floods."

THE INDOCHINA STORY

Experts on U.S. policy in Southeast Asia had known for years of covert military operations across that region. In the fall of 1969, an informal group of Asian scholars saw an opportunity to get the public more interested in their knowledge and policy ideas. They would attempt to explain America's activities in Vietnam, Cambodia and Laos in an anthology: *The Indochina Story, A fully documented account by the Committee of Concerned Asian Scholars.* Pantheon Books agreed to rush the three hundred fifty page book into print by January, 1970. More than thirty academics were recruited to contribute chapters collectively answering these questions:

- Who is the U.S. fighting in Indochina?

- Why is the U.S. fighting in Indochina?

- How is the U.S. fighting in Indochina?

- What can the future hold?

I was invited to draft the chapter examining American weaponry in Vietnam. Looking back now, I would not change or revise any of those four thousand words. The analysis was comprehensive. The examples rich and fact based. The logic sound. The conclusions compelling and, as events played out, I believe, accurate and enduring.

"The war in Vietnam is a war against an entire people and an entire country," I began, putting to words six years of my accumulating knowledge, and dismay. "Nowhere is this more apparent than in the tactics and weapons used by the United States."

"NO PLACE TO HIDE, NO WAY TO PLEAD"

Here are a few excerpts from my chapter:

"[Antipersonnel weapons] are primarily effective against decentralized agricultural populations; they devastate broad areas, killing people yet leaving property relatively unharmed; they are designed to be used against defenseless people; and they demand undisputed air superiority to be effective. Use of the weapons results in the indiscriminate slaughter of civilians and soldiers alike.

"Another weapons system designed specifically for counterguerrilla warfare is 'Puff the Magic Dragon.' Puff is a C-47 airplane mounted with three miniguns each capable of shooting eighteen thousand rounds a minute. It is used to saturate suspected enemy positions with bullets, and in three seconds can cover an area the size of a football field with one bullet to every square foot. A Quaker working in Quang Ngai, South Vietnam in 1969 describes Puff in action:

"'...As I watched it circle overhead last night, silhouetted against the low clouds in the light of the flares, flinging indiscriminate bolts of death earthward, I could vividly visualize the scene below. Men, women, children and animals, caught like rats in a flood. No place to hide, no way to plead their case of innocence to the machine in the sky, no time to prepare for death. The beating the civilians are taking in this war is beyond adequate description.'"

Medical teams described the primitive, gruesome care that was all they could offer victims who survive bombing attacks first and then a harrowing journey to hospitals. Rereading this account from Quaker Robert Crichton fills me with shame as an American citizen, just as it did when I inserted it in the chapter.

"'CBUs (Cluster Bomb Units) have created a need for drastic new surgical techniques. Because there is neither time nor facilities for X-rays, a CBU victim, if hit in the stomach, is simply slit from the top of the stomach to the bottom and the contents of the stomach emptied out on a table and fingered through for 'frags' as a dog is worked over for ticks. When the sorting is done the entrails are replaced and the stomach sewed back up like a football. This 'football scar' had become the true badge of misery in South Vietnam.'"

My opinion of American society and American democracy darkened during the long Vietnam War, a consequence of my political activism and my investigative journalism. Yet, disillusioned as I was by unconscionable failures of American government, I never was discouraged about my own situation. My scientific discoveries, my peers and mentors were too exciting for that. How could I be discouraged?

My PhD thesis and related journal articles describing experiments to make magic spot in a test tube would be finished in less than two years. Then, with Harvard biophysics doctorate in hand, I would move a few miles down the Charles River and be among the first to leap into the new DNA research at MIT that would ignite the biotechnology revolution.

ǀ ǀ16 ǀ ǀ

ON THE TRAIL OF VIRUS
AND CANCER

IN THE EARLY 1970S ANIMAL VIRUSES were the only way molecular biologists could study the complex biology of higher organisms. The ability to work with individual human or animal genes came later in the decade, but virologists already were making huge strides in understanding how viruses invade healthy cells and use the healthy cells to establish and accelerate infection.

David Baltimore was at the forefront of this group. His research into the late 1960s had focused on the polio virus, paralytic poliomyelitis, which caused a global epidemic after World War II into the 1950s. More than a half million people each year were paralyzed or killed.[95] By the late 1960s, David had moved on to study viruses known to cause cancer in animals, and, as he and others believed, viruses that might also cause various kinds of cancers in humans.

What David and two other biologists discovered fifty years ago—the process some of these viruses mastered to replicate within healthy cells—became a cornerstone of the biotechnology revolution to come.

I knew and respected David for his work on the polio virus and more directly for his concerns over the government's potential abuse of science in waging the Vietnam War. We had worked together a few years before in the March 4th Movement and in establishing the Union of Concerned Scientists.

HERESY: COPYING RNA INTO DNA

By now, in 1973, I was aware that David had made a major discovery, that some of these animal viruses contained an unusual enzyme, one that copies RNA into DNA. This finding reversed what was considered the central dogma of genetics, that DNA initiates cell growth through RNA to a specific protein. The discovery illuminated the little understood process of how viruses multiply: viral proteins, encoded by messenger RNA, can take over a healthy cell and make more of the same virus particles.[96]

This discovery propelled David's laboratory at MIT to the forefront of animal virus research, exactly where I wanted to be. He welcomed me into his lab and, with his support and commitment to serve as my mentor, I soon received that Helen Hay Whitney Foundation fellowship to fund my postdoctoral research.

As far back as 1911, the dawn of virus discoveries, a pathologist and virologist at Rockefeller Institute in New York, Peyton Rous, identified a virus that induced tumors in chickens. He described these as a "filterable virus." In the early 1950s, Ludwig Gross demonstrated that other members of this family of virus could induce leukemia in mice. Other members of the family were shown to induce cancers in other animals, including cats, cattle and even monkeys.

What about humans? Do viruses cause cancers in humans? By the late 1960s, viruses were known to cause lymphoma, liver cancer and cervical cancer. If viruses are a major cause of cancer might an anticancer vaccine be in the offing? Might an anticancer vaccine replicate the recent success of the polio vaccine in nearly eliminating that disease?

There was great enthusiasm for answering that question and understanding more broadly how the viruses worked. Mary Lasker, a powerful voice in shaping presidential perceptions about science and championing funding in the halls of Congress for cancer research, was among the most prominent advocates.

The National Cancer Act approved by Congress in 1971 had pumped new money into the search for viruses that might cause cancer. The section of the legislation known as the Special Virus Cancer Program covered an entire family of viruses that were now known, thanks to David Baltimore's discovery, as retroviruses. As I weighed my options in the spring of 1973 for a postdoctoral fellowship in university research labs, the field of retroviruses was red hot.

A DANISH DETOUR

In the months after finishing in the Watson-Gilbert Lab, I spent a delightful summer as a visiting professor in Copenhagen, welcomed by those two Danes who had outraced me into print with their journal article on magic spot. I was able to isolate and characterize a second protein made by bacteria that also made magic spot. This protein was produced by the so called relaxed 2 gene, or *rel* 2. What was its function? I speculated that the *rel* 2 protein acts as an emergency backup for bacteria that lose the primary ability to make pppGppp.

The Copenhagen lab was well known. Jim Watson had spent a short time there in the early 1950s before joining Francis Crick for their DNA double helix discoveries at the University of Cambridge. The setting was beautiful, a park in Copenhagen's city center. This was my first exposure to life in Scandinavia and a balm for me emotionally, the first time I felt that my values were well matched to a nation's culture. Most people opposed the Vietnam War. Most believed in the equality of men and women. Most displayed respect for all with no regard to appearances or personal wealth. A robust social safety net protected everyone, young and old, from the vicissitudes of life.

Children were prized, a sentiment obvious in even the smallest details. For example, every "polser" (read: hot dog) stand was fronted by tiny steps that enabled very young children to step up for a look inside. Danish men played a more central role in family life than in America. One day, when I saw an injured child run for comfort to her father, not her mother, I was

> pleased and surprised, another delightful vignette from a relaxed and happy summer... a year short of my thirtieth birthday... when I was so in tune with the prevailing ethos. Not in conflict with it.

David's work was based on the groundbreaking insights of a scientist in Wisconsin, Howard Temin, who across more than a decade had developed the idea, yet to be proved, that the RNA of some viruses is converted first to DNA which is then used to produce new viral RNA: RNA → DNA → protein.

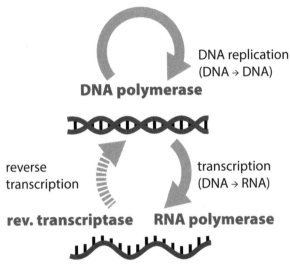

Figure 3. Process of Reverse Transcriptase

This was a heresy of sorts. The central dogma of molecular biology, articulated by Francis Crick in the 1950s, held that genetic information written in nucleic acids of DNA is transferred to nucleic acids of RNA which then becomes a template for making a specific protein: DNA → RNA → protein. The central dogma also held that genetic information cannot be transferred back from protein to nucleic acid.

Howard and David simultaneously published the discovery[97] that polio retroviruses contain an enzyme that does just that, copies RNA into DNA. David gave the enzyme the name *reverse transcriptase*. (The enzyme causes transcribing of genetic information in reverse; hence, reverse transcriptase.)

I was already in the lab when David took the call. He and Howard Temin would share the 1975 Nobel Prize in Physiology or Medicine with Renato Dulbecco for separate yet highly related discoveries of reverse transcriptase. Dulbecco had mentored Howard as a PhD candidate at the California Institute of Technology and David as a research associate at the Salk Institute.

The lab was jubilant. David arrived smiling ear to ear, as relaxed and happy as I have ever seen him. What a great day for all of us. His physical prize, a solid gold medal, has a raised profile of Alfred Nobel on one side and the specific award citation on the other. When I had the chance to hold the medal in my palm after David returned from the ceremony in Stockholm, my thoughts were a mix of awe, delight and admiration. Any scientist would feel that way, I think.

ORIGINS OF GENE-SPLICING

Simple retroviruses of the type studied by Temin and Baltimore make two types of RNA. One is a complete copy of the genome, and a second shorter version.

"How does that happen?" David asked me. This, we quickly agreed, would be my first problem to investigate: a puzzling aspect of retrovirus replication. I had already confirmed in an early experiment after joining his lab that a specific type of leukemia virus indeed made the two types of RNA, the long and the short.

"Is there a start in the middle of the RNA and the DNA that was converted by reverse transcriptase from RNA?" David added, a reasonable hypothesis, a good guess really, but it was only a guess.

I thought about the problem for a while. "If I can use reverse transcriptase to convert purified RNA of a virus (viral RNA) to DNA, that would mimic in a test tube what occurs in nature. Once I have the viral DNA copy, I can design experiments to determine how the RNA was made."

Conveniently for me, two of my colleagues in the Baltimore Lab had begun using reverse transcriptase in experiments to copy cellular RNA (such as the types of cellular RNA that specified human hemoglobin). I already knew from my experiments in the Watson-Gilbert lab how viral RNA was made.

The methodologies I had in mind were basic techniques of what we know today as gene-splicing and recombinant DNA. Daniel Nathans at Johns Hopkins and Paul Berg at Stanford were learning how to cut and splice DNA; that is, to isolate sections of a genome code, extract that section from the genome, then combine that piece with one or more other pieces of genomes.

Enzymes discovered earlier by Werner Arber, a Swiss microbiologist and geneticist, naturally cut DNA molecules at certain defined locations in the DNA. These enzymes, called restriction endonucleases, protect bacteria two ways: by chopping up the DNA of infecting viruses to restrict the virus growth, and by modifying the bacteria's own DNA in such a way as to protect it from being cut itself.

The enzymes discovered by Arber chop the DNA in very specific sequences.[98] Two pieces of DNA cut by the Arber enzymes could be rejoined to create a hybrid DNA—even if the two fragments had widely different origins. For example, a fragment of DNA from a bacteria could be cut and joined to a piece of human DNA.

Nathans and Berg demonstrated that a bacteria would copy the new hybrid DNA *as if it were a natural part of its own DNA.* If the new piece of DNA specified production of a protein, the bacterial would make that foreign protein as well!

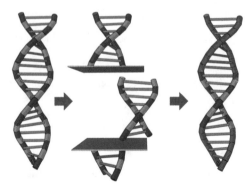

Figure 4. Genetic engineering: cutting, splicing DNA

My Lifelong Fight Against Disease

These discoveries had profound implications for modern science as well as modern medicine. Bacteria with human DNA spliced into its genome could produce functioning human proteins. This immediately raised the possibility that proteins vital for modern medicine, such as insulin and human growth hormone, could be sourced not only from the human pancreas or brain.[99]

What Nathans, Berg and Arber had discovered were the foundations of genetic engineering.[100] Proteins could be *engineered* to grow in bacteria. The biotechnology revolution was about to explode.

"THE EXPERIMENT IS OFF"

It took me several months to assemble all the components needed to make a faithful DNA copy of the virus RNA. I knew I could manipulate the viral DNA more easily in test tubes than viral RNA, something no one else had attempted. More specifically, I would be slicing and rearranging genetic sequences—the nucleotides of As, Cs, Ts and Gs—into shorter, hybrid pieces of DNA; or, as the lexicon soon developed, into recombinant DNA. It was an exciting several months, imagining potential contributions my discoveries might make to medical science, pharmacology and human health.

Most of that early work took place in MIT's old bio building, Building 56. David shared lab space with another young professor, Harvey Lodish, and the atmosphere was chaotic, more cramped than my chemistry lab back at Burroughs High! The lab was packed with David's rapidly growing roster of fellows and other researchers, most of whom were funded by new grants from the federal National Cancer Act.

I was allotted one square meter of lab bench, with one small drawer. At one point, I decided to clear space for mixing reagents on my small work space by rigging a tray and suspending it from my neck. This actually was more fun than it sounds. We all knew exactly what each of us was working on, precisely how we were doing it, and how to negotiate sharing essential equipment such as centrifuges. When at last we moved into our new building, a renovated candy factory on the edge of campus, the accommodations seemed palatial. David was allotted more than half of one floor. I had an entire lab bench and desk to myself!

One morning, finally, my gene splicing experiments were ready to begin. The goal was groundbreaking: to copy viral RNA into DNA, then insert that DNA into a bacterium to copy *that* DNA. An ice bucket with ten test tubes, each filled with a chemical reagent, was next to me at my bench. Just before I planned to start, Dave asked me to wait a few hours. I noticed Paul Berg and several other prominent scientists entering a conference room not twenty feet away.

Now I had to wait. I could hear animated discussion from time to time but could not make out the words. I had no sense of what was happening. After three hours, with water from melting ice slowly filling my bucket, Dave opened the door and walked straight to me.

"The experiment is off," he said. "Do not begin."

Just like that, no apology. Several months of work down the drain. My buoyant expectations for a great scientific coup, dashed.

"We need to invite many more scientists, ethicists and lawyers and figure out guidelines any scientist will have to follow for research in recombinant DNA," he continued. "We have decided to hold a more formal meeting."

It is very likely, as I anticipated, that my experiments would have led to exciting discoveries. Other biologists soon confirmed that the role of RNA splicing in gene replication is similar to a film editor's. It eliminates unnecessary elements of a DNA molecule and connects essential parts into a completed segment that matches the gene segments.

In fact, the RNA splicing process turns out to be a major distinction between simple organisms such as bacteria and more complex organisms such as plants and animals. Splicing is what allows the virus to make different proteins of its structure from a single genome transcript.

Within a few years, two friends of mine, Philip Sharp and Richard Roberts, working at Cold Spring Harbor Laboratory, discovered RNA splicing with a DNA virus that did not require recombinant DNA methods. They later shared a Nobel Prize for that excellent work. At the award ceremony in Stockholm in 1993, the prize committee praised their discovery of split genes as "revolutionary, triggering an explosion of new scientific contributions" in biology and medicine.[101]

As disappointed as I was that day in David's lab, I understood and agreed with the concerns. As it turned out, that meeting in our conference room was a prelude to what became the celebrated Asilomar Conference of 1975, to explore whether or not scientists should create a voluntary set of safety rules for recombinant DNA research. Those guidelines soon were codified into regulations for any work funded by the National Institutes of Health, then quickly adopted as global standards.

Any recombinant DNA experiments must be conducted in special containment laboratories

The experiments could be done only with organisms grown in a containment laboratory

The organisms grown in a containment laboratory could not be able to survive in nature

Different levels of physical and biological containment were assigned for experiments with different levels of risk

The experiments I had planned for Dave's lab did not meet these requirements. You might have seen photos of people in bubble like protective gear working with dangerous virus. That is what was required for the experiments I had planned. Only a few places had such facilities. MIT was not one of them.

COPYING VIRAL RNA TO DNA

For me it was back to the drawing board.

The first PhD thesis in the Watson-Gilbert lab ran aground because Wally Gilbert was unimpressed that my experiments disproved his theory about Okazaki fragments. The second was abandoned after I demonstrated Andrew Travers's *psi* factor was not required for making ribosomal RNA. Now, my initial postdoctoral research in the Baltimore Lab is halted abruptly, in the eleventh hour, because of legitimate ethical concerns that my genetic engineering could set loose a molecular Frankenstein monster into the world.

Even so I was confident, undeterred, ready to rebound. I knew the value of persistence. You assess and appreciate what you learn in any experience and move on. If one avenue of exploration closes there are always others.

I remained interested in how retroviruses replicate.

One puzzling result researchers had noted was that producing viral DNA from intact virus in a test tube yielded only DNA fragments, not one long strand DNA as expected.

"How can these short fragments then be joined to make an intact copy of the viral DNA?" I wondered. "That viral DNA copy has to exist to enable bacteria to manufacture the viral DNA."

There was a clue to the mystery. A collection of small transfer RNAs (tRNA) was packaged in the virus particle along with the virus RNA and reverse transcriptase. I remembered there was a bacterial virus with an RNA genome that had a structure, or coding, of nucleotides, similar to transfer RNA, at the 3 prime end of the genome. This structure allowed the viral polymerase to latch onto the end of the genome to begin the copying process.

"Might the reverse transcriptase in the collection of small transfer RNAs packaged in the virus have a method similar to the RNA genome in the bacterial virus? If so, the copying process might begin with the reverse transcriptase attaching to the transfer RNA."

To test this idea, all I needed to do was demonstrate that the purified protein could bind tightly to one of the many cellular transfer RNAs.

A lab mate in Cambridge, an Israeli scientist, showed me how to separate the biologic molecules. An expert on tRNA molecules at the University of Wisconsin, Jim Dahlberg,[102] helped me identify which transfer RNA bound tightly to the reverse transcriptase. I conducted each of the experiments in Cambridge, then shipped the new substances in packages of dry ice to Madison for Jim to analyze. We determined that reverse transcriptase bound only to one transfer RNA.

ICE CREAM

There was a light-hearted side benefit to my work with Jim Dahlberg. Wisconsin of course is famous for dairy. The University of Wisconsin has a renowned dairy science department, and Jim's lab was within a few steps of the department's creamery. Every time Jim shipped my package of test tubes in dry ice back to Cambridge, he added some experimental flavor of ice cream. Pumpkin pomegranate or durian pecan, anyone? I would not recommend either if those creations are still on the menu. Pumpkin fudge or blueberry kiwi? Much tastier.

My reciprocal offerings to Jim were whole frozen lobsters. When he decided to boil one of them, a whole lobster, Jim reported that the outcome produced enough foam to fill a kitchen. This is why, I explained to him, you can only buy frozen lobster tails.

Next question: Can I show that the polymerase employed the transfer RNA to begin copying viral RNA to DNA? The simplest way to do this was by using only highly purified components instead of molecules prepared from a whole virus. I still had the purified viral RNA from my earlier experiments. That became one component for this next experiment. The other two components were purified transfer RNA and purified reverse transcriptase.

The experiment worked!

THE ENDS... ARE IDENTICAL!

I now had definitive proof that new copies of viral RNA produced in bacteria began by elongating the transfer RNA, and that the process began at only one location, not the widely accepted view that the location was random.

But, where did the process begin? The answer turned out to be a big surprise.

DNA and RNA copying always flows in one direction along the genome, from what is called the 3 prime end to the 5 prime end. It never goes in the opposite direction. I thought it most likely that the transfer RNA attached to the 3 prime end of the viral RNA to copy the entire viral genome. But wait. The DNA fragment I made was only 150 units long (that is, only 150 characters of nucleotide coding), not the ten thousand units of the entire virus genome.

"How could that be?" I wondered. "Is it possible the transfer RNA actually is located near the opposite end, the 5 prime end? More specifically, is the transfer RNA actually located only 150 units from the 5 prime end?"

I left the Baltimore Lab with that question unanswered—my two year fellowship was ending—but soon resumed the chase when I was assigned my own lab in the Sidney Farber Cancer Institute at Harvard. With research colleague John Coffin of Tufts Medical Center, we proved the unexpected: that viral RNA is copied into DNA as one continuous chain, from one end of the genome to the other. It was not copied as small fragments of DNA being linked together.

The only way I could imagine virus replication beginning at the 5 prime end and continuing to the 3 prime end was that the 5 prime and 3 prime ends of the virus RNA must be identical, at least for a short stretch. This would allow the new DNA copy to attach to the 3 prime end, then replicate the entire viral RNA all the way to the 5 prime end.

John and I proved this indeed was the case: retrovirus genomes do contain the same sequence of nucleotides at both ends. We named this terminal redundancy. Then, to dispel the idea that replication occurred by linking small bits of DNA together, I applied another new technique in recombinant DNA to show that the viral RNA is copied into DNA as one continuous chain, from one end of the genome to the other.

TAKING STOCK

Young people making decisions about their careers are keenly tuned in to what opportunities they perceive to be available to them. After Sputnik, the government's enthusiasm for science education created for me and my peers an abundance of mentors, programs, projects—and funding through my Harvard graduate studies. Then, as the implications of David Baltimore's stunning discovery of reverse transcriptase and other research on animal viruses reverberated, a new wave for human cancer research was forming at a perfect time for me.

Those two years in Dave's lab were the capstone of my graduate and postdoctoral training, vaulting me to the forefront of experimental science in biology.

Over the thirteen years since the thrill of seeing my first byline in the pages of *Science*, I had made significant contributions to the scientific literature in biophysics and molecular biology. My graduate course studies had given me a deep understanding and facility for what was known in physics, chemistry and biology.

Moreover, I appreciated how essential collaboration and knowledge sharing are in advancing science. I had learned how to work with research colleagues within elbow's reach, in neighboring laboratories and in distant cities and countries.

As a skilled medical scientist on the cusp of my career, I could see far ahead... across landscapes of endless possibilities and real impact. It was time to apply all that I had learned to the great questions of human health and disease.

But, where should I go, and what exactly should I do?

PART IV

||17||

A HARVARD PROFESSOR

I HAD NOT SEEN BOB SCHLIEF for a few years since he worked down the hall from me in the Watson-Gilbert lab, but I recognized his voice immediately when I picked up the phone.

"Bill, there is a job opening at Brandeis for someone with just your background," he said. A serious, precise researcher, Bob now was a biology professor at nearby Brandeis University. "I am on the search committee. We would like you to give a seminar and meet the other department members."

Good timing, I thought. I was finishing my postdoc work at MIT and had just begun to look for my first real job. "Sure," I said. "Set the date and I'll be there."

LOOKING FOR A JOB

The appointed day began as scheduled with an early coffee with the chair of Brandeis's biology department. But he had bad news.

"I am sorry to tell you that last night I received word from our president that the job no longer exists," he said. I was stunned. My first job interview, no less. "He told me we just don't have the money for a new position. But please, since you are here, meet our faculty and give your lecture." The phrase I then silently repeated over and over again in my mind is not printable, but I am sure you get the idea. I gave the lecture, privately fuming.

A few days later the phone rang again. One of my contacts on Berkeley's biochemistry faculty, Peter Duesberg, a virologist, was on the line. It was midafternoon on a Friday and Peter's voice was animated.

"Come out to Berkeley on Monday," he insisted. "We are voting on a new faculty member for our department on Tuesday. I mentioned your name and everyone is excited. Can you make it?" At the time I considered Peter a friend (that changed years later when he bizarrely asserted in papers, speeches and testimonies that HIV did not cause AIDS). We had worked on similar problems.

"Peter, are you sure?" I said, guardedly. "It seems very short notice."

"Would I ask you if it wasn't for real?" he replied. "Please come. I assure you it will be worth it."

The idea of returning to my alma mater had some appeal. "Okay," I said. "I'll be there Monday morning."

I knew Berkeley's Stanley Hall well from my undergraduate days and expected several people to be around when I walked in at nine thirty that Monday. Instead, only eerie quiet. The halls were empty. A few doors opened and slammed shut. One faculty member, spotting me from a distance, quickly ducked away like a scared meerkat.

After an hour of this, I wondered what the hell was happening. A disheveled Peter showed up at eleven o'clock.

"So sorry Bill. Over the weekend, after a bitter fight, we hired someone else."

Now he tells me. My kindest thought was, *What a jerk!*

Things went better after that. I was offered two jobs in New York, one at Alfred Einstein College of Medicine in the Bronx and one at Sloan Kettering Memorial Cancer Hospital in Manhattan. I really enjoyed my visit to Einstein. I would have been very happy there. Many faculty I met on that visit became close friends and colleagues, including the chair of the department, Matty Scharff, and Bernie Fields and Barry Bloom.

Matty made a generous offer and we all enjoyed a fine meal that night at a Chinese restaurant. I might have accepted if a better offer had not come along soon.

Twenty five years later, Matty took me aside and pointed to a yellowing slip of paper tacked to a poster board outside his office. It read, *Wait, a better offer will come soon.*

"That is from your fortune cookie that night we took you to dinner after your job interview," Matty said. "Believe me, we *never* took another candidate to a Chinese restaurant again!"

THE AUDITION, THE OFFER

The job I accepted came along obliquely. Jack Strominger was a biochemistry professor at Harvard's BioLabs on the same floor as Watson-Gilbert. Jack was renowned for discovering in the '60s how penicillin kills bacteria. From time to time he had invited me down the hall from my PhD warren to speak with his students over lunch.

One afternoon when I was at my postdoc bench at MIT, he called. "Bill, I see you are doing great work on retroviruses. Do you have time to stop by for another brown bag lunch sometime soon?" Sure. When? "How about the day after tomorrow?" Okay, I said, but it will be informal. "No problem," he replied.

I showed up in Jack's conference room in jeans, unshaved. Crowded around the table was the entire biophysics faculty, all my most esteemed mentors and role models, Nobel Prize winners included. Not anything I had expected, disheveled as I was after working all night at MIT. "Gee, Jack," I said. "I always knew you had good people in your lab, but this is really a surprise!"

My presentation, it seemed obvious that morning, was an unannounced, unremarked upon audition for a faculty position in the BioLabs. Jack called me the next day. "That was a great seminar. You knocked it out of the park. Everyone was excited. Me too," he said. "I have an offer for you."

What came next was totally unexpected, and, to be honest, thrilling for me as Jack's words rolled out.

"You might know that I am the Chair of the Department of Biological Science across the river at the Sidney Farber Cancer Institute. (I did not.) The Farber has just been designated a comprehensive cancer center by the National Cancer Institute. That means we are first in line to receive infrastructure and cooperative development grants.

"I have the mandate to hire four junior faculty members," he went on. "My job is to recruit scientists like you that have an interest in medicine as well as science. I want you to join us. You will have your own lab right away and a much bigger one when we finish our new building. Tom Frei, Farber's president, and I are best friends. He is one of the country's leading cancer docs. I've known him since medical school. I told him about you, and he is excited. I know you will love him."

Then came the truly dazzling part, with outlines of a professional role I had visualized and worked toward since those initial studies on campus before my PhD research. I wanted to be at Harvard. I wanted to work closely with doctors in a teaching hospital. I wanted to learn about their problems, then research and apply what I learned to help them cure cancer and other disease.

"You will be able to work right next to leading cancer therapists and other researchers," Jack said. "Not only that, you can be a member of any Harvard Medical School department you want. You can teach if you want but need not if you don't."

Wrapping up, he added, "We can give you startup research money. Your salary will be almost twice what we could give you at the BioLabs."

"Wow, that seems too good to be true," I said. After a pause, I added, "I do have one request." To build a team of top researchers quickly for a lab, I knew I would need two fully funded postdoc assistants right away. With two positions funded, and significant lab discoveries likely to be accelerated, I could more easily attract grant money to add more positions.

"Ye-e-e-s?" Jack's reply was cautious.

I chuckled to myself, remembering that when a good fairy comes along you are granted at least one wish. My one wish then, to Jack: "I would like a guaranteed salary for two postdoctoral fellows for two years."

"Done!" he replied.

My job search had ended. For those looking for your first job (or any job), a bad start (like mine) doesn't necessarily lead to a bad ending. For me the result couldn't have been better.

HARMLESS VIRUS, LETHAL VIRUS

My early months as a young professor were exhilarating. I was free, free to choose my own problems to solve, to hire whomever I wanted and to work how and when I wanted. Harvard's expectations for new faculty are very clear: be the best in the world at what you do and raise on your own whatever funds you need to succeed.

I wanted to use my newfound skills in science and molecular biology to make a difference to medicine, but how?

What follows is a journey of discovery. Asking questions, seeing where they lead. Trying this, trying that, always with the ultimate goal in mind— how will my work help heal the sick, how will my work help people in need? I could not see the detailed path that lay ahead, but I knew my destination.

From my postdoctoral research in virus replication, I knew that one type of retrovirus grew in mice and caused leukemia and another closely related strain of that same retrovirus did not. This sparked a question I wanted to pursue: Might knowing why this difference was true lead to an understanding of the cause of human cancer?

I described the experiments I planned to my new postdoctoral fellows, Finn Skou Pedersen and Jack Lenz. (Finn was a Dane I met during my summer as a visiting professor in Denmark.) They both were brave enough to join the lab of a brand new professor, filling the postdoctoral fellow positions Jack Strominger promised me.

"Let's begin by verifying what others report," I said when the three of us huddled to plan the retrovirus research. "We will need to obtain two nearly identical strains. Jack, you inject them into mice and follow what happens. Finn, you will work in the biocontainment lab upstairs and make DNA copies of both viruses. We will use the DNA copies to make new copies of the virus. Jack will check that they both breed true."

Meanwhile I pursued a different line of research, studying fundamental aspects of virus replication, and sought more talent to expand our studies. The experiments went well, leading to more research manuscripts, review articles and several more grants. As soon as Finn and Jack received independent funding from outside sources, I invited two more postdoctoral fellows to join the lab.

ORIGINS OF REGENERATIVE MEDICINE

Richard Gardener, an English scientist, discovered that he could grow very early mouse embryo cells in the lab that, under the right conditions when planted in the womb of a female mouse, resulted in a pregnancy and birth of a fully functioning mouse. The newly born mouse was a *clone* of the parent.

Richard also described what happened to mouse embryo cells attached to the plastic surface of a petri dish: These cells transformed into many different kinds of tissues, nerve, kidney, heart muscle cells and more.

I was enthralled. Richard was demonstrating how animal embryo cells can be replicated in the lab. One of his students who had returned to the U.S. sent me some of the mouse embryo cells replicated in Richard's lab, at my request, and I began to tinker with them, noting various changes when different chemicals and hormones were added.

These early experiments were laying a foundation for what within a few decades would become known as the field of regenerative medicine, the science of restoring weakened or damaged cells to their normal function in the tissues or organs of humans or animal cells.

Gardener's experiments lead directly to the birth of "Dolly the Sheep" in 1996, the first cloned large animal.[103]

The remarkable story of regenerative medicine and its dramatic potential to bring us longer, healthier lives deserves its own chapter, which awaits in Part V.

A few months later Finn and Jack appeared in my office with big smiles. "The experiments worked," they said. "Strain A grows well in mice. None are sick. All the mice infected with strain B have leukemia, some are dying. What's next?"

"Let's begin to switch the parts," I said. "We will add the left half of strain A to the right half of strain B and the right half of strain B to the left half of strain A. If we are lucky, we will know which half makes the difference."

We were lucky. A few months later Jack announced that the leukemia inducing element was in the left half of strain B.

"Okay," I told them. "Now let's chop the left half into small bits and substitute the smaller bits of strain B for the analogous bits of strain A. Again, if we are lucky, we will find the bit that makes a difference."

We found what we were looking for. One small bit near the end of strain B made the difference.

At one of our next weekly lab lunches, I set the stakes for the crucial work still ahead.

"Now the fun really begins. We will determine the complete DNA sequence of both viruses, concentrating first on a comparison of the two bits of virus DNA that make the difference—for healthy mice or sick mice. If we do determine the complete DNA sequence of both, we will have two firsts: the first complete genome sequence of a retrovirus, and the first discovery explaining why strain B causes leukemia and strain A does not."

The answer was surprising. Except for the short region, the viruses were identical. The short region that was the exception was no longer than one hundred units of nucleotide base pairs near the beginning of the viral DNA. I called the group together.

"What could be going on?" I asked. "Notice that the difference lies just before the signal to start making new copies of the virus genome. Maybe it works better in some type of cells than others. We can test that easily. Who wants to try?"

Several hands went up.

Jack drew the honors... a seniority call. He had the longest tenure of anyone in the lab. His specific task was to determine what happens to the small element just before that start signal to make more virus RNA from the strain that causes leukemia. The answer: The small element works well in lymphocytes and not well in other types of cells. Just the opposite was true for the nonlethal strain.

BREAKTHROUGH: TISSUE SPECIFIC ENHANCERS

I opened our next meeting with a question. What is the role of that small element just before the start signal? Its location was interesting, just before RNA transcription begins. Maybe there is a new type of control element, one that determines what type RNA can be made and in which type of cell the virus can grow.

Here I was getting at what we all knew was one of the big unsolved problems in biology: What makes one cell different from another? All cells contain the same information. What makes them different is that the information they extract from the DNA, the process within each cell by which specific genes are expressed, is different. For that reason, in each cell, different parts of the DNA are read into different RNAs. How can the DNA that is the same in every cell give rise to so many different types of specialized cells?

Many elements like ones we found might be responsible. "Let's test that idea," I said. I had been down this road before with colleagues in Watson-Gilbert, searching without success for answers to what causes cells to express genes in different ways, but I thought Finn, Jack and I now were very close.

Bingo! BIG INDEPENDENT DISCOVERY. A short DNA sequence can determine in which type of cell RNA will be made! In other words, a short DNA sequence is what causes all cells which carry the same genetic information to reproduce in myriad different ways. We named these short DNA sequences *tissue specific enhancers*. Simultaneously, different laboratories working with other viruses and other genes found more short DNA sequences that determined the cell type in which nearby DNA was copied into RNA. An MIT laboratory found short DNA sequences as well for very similar retroviruses.

Today it is widely accepted that tissue specific enhancers explain a big part of what makes one cell different from another. Short sequences usually determine, in or near a gene, whether or not RNA polymerase can load onto DNA, which is how synthesis begins. This finding is similar to Andrew Travers's *psi* hypothesis but differs in one important aspect. The tissue specific enhancer is not the same as the signal to start RNA synthesis. That signal is the *promoter*.

Bacteria generally lack enhancers. The cells of plants and animals do have enhancers. In plants and animals the RNA polymerase must first load onto the DNA at a tissue specific enhancer to begin synthesis.

The question we asked—Why did one strain of virus cause cancer and not anther?—did not lead immediately to a new understanding of human leukemia. However our results did provide the first step for a sustained, multiyear effort by scientists around the world to understand how and when genes are regulated in health and disease. That knowledge is pivotal in our ability today to understand and treat cancer as well as other disease.

As we celebrated our discovery, I reminded my colleagues of important principles for conducting breakthrough experiments in science.

"Remember this story as you set out on your own. Ask important questions. Devise experiments to find an answer. Do not presume you know the answer. Keep an open mind. If your experiments are well crafted, you will find the answer. The answer may be trivial, but, if you are lucky like we were, it may be profound and answer one of nature's riddles."

|18|

FRONTLINES OF NEW CANCER TREATMENTS

By the end of the first year, my lab was brimming with energetic postdoctoral fellows and a few graduate students, all working on retroviruses. Our research was supported with grants from the National Cancer Institute, the American Cancer Society and the Leukemia Society of America.[104]

It was a good time for me to take the next step, and that required a chat with the president. Emil Frei (everyone called him Tom) had been the Cancer Institute's president since the death of founder Sidney Farber, and physician in chief since Farber recruited him for that role in 1972.

Calm, approachable, unimposing in owlish spectacles, Tom was one of the most distinguished cancer specialists in the country. He and a former colleague at the National Cancer Institute, Emil Freireich, years before pioneered the use of two or more drugs simultaneously to develop the first cures for childhood leukemia.[105] They called their novel approach combination chemotherapy.

WITNESS TO MORNING ROUNDS

Tom, I asked, how can I apply molecular biology to improve cancer medicine?

"Bill, the first thing you need to know is what we don't know. That will be your jumping off point," he said. "I can't tell you what you will find, but I can tell you where to look.

"The best way to learn about what we know and don't know is to attend morning rounds," he continued. "We are a teaching hospital. We analyze what is best for each patient one by one. That is how our doctors learn to treat patients. I will ask our attending physicians to introduce you as an observer."

If the snow wasn't too deep or the roads too icy, I would ride my bike the five miles from my Cambridge home to the hospital in Boston. (I can still feel the winter chills seeping into my bone marrow.) Usually, I joined pediatric rounds starting at six thirty. Senior physician Steven Sallin reviewed each child's chart, one by one, then opened discussion for best treatment options.

I attended the daily sessions of these disciplined, compassionate teams for two years whenever I could. These were some of the most inspiring, motivating experiences of my life, a tremendous privilege. I was witness to the very best of what one group of highly educated, dedicated people can do for a fellow human in serious trouble.

As the cancer medical teams puzzled out what to do next, patient by patient, I listened and observed as closely as I could to learn what they knew, what they didn't know and what they needed to know.

A key to discovery is to map the limits of the relevant unknown. That was my role during these hours as a medical scientist working on behalf of the pediatric cancer team. All too often we assume that we know more than we actually do, or, perhaps even more dangerous, we assume that what we know is true. In words often attributed to Will Rogers, "The trouble ain't so much about what we know. It's that so much of what we know ain't so!"

Science leaps into the darkness, the very edge of human knowledge. That is where we begin. Doing cutting edge research is like being in a deep cave facing a black wall of hard stone. You do not know what is behind the wall, but you know some truth is there. Your job is to chip away at that hard rock face, not knowing what you are going to find on the other side. It is extremely difficult to explain how unknown that unknown is. Some people chip away for a lifetime only to have a pile of flakes at their feet.

DNA DAMAGE AND CANCER

One day after my *Cancer and Society*[106] lecture on discoveries about the human genome and their potential to cure or prevent cancer, a sophomore from New Jersey, Alan D'Andrea, came up to me.

"That was really interesting," he said. "Are you working on solving some of the problems you mentioned? If you are, do you think I might spend some time in your lab?"

A week later Christina Lindan, another sophomore in the same class of two hundred and fifty Harvard undergraduates, made a virtually identical request. Alan and Christina were both premed students, taking the course not to satisfy their science requirement but from genuine interest. (Alan's mother, I learned later, was battling breast cancer at the time.)

Struck by this coincidence, I began to wonder, "What can I do?" Then it hit me. Young doctors on morning rounds had been asking me, "How do the drugs we use to treat these children really work? Can we combine them in new ways?" Mulling those questions took me directly to Alan and Christina's curiosity about molecular biology, DNA and treating cancer and then to a dramatic new discovery in DNA research that only a few scientists knew about.

I was one of those scientists. I knew that Wally Gilbert was about to publish a major paper with a colleague, Allan Maxam, describing how to determine the sequence of DNA nucleotides. This was going to be a profound revelation,[107] laying out for the first time every step for sequencing DNA.

Their method was to treat DNA with chemicals that attach to specific nucleotides. Wally had been tinkering with such chemicals during my last months as a graduate student a few years before. I remembered that many of those chemicals resembled drugs used to treat cancer. The framework for a molecular biochemistry experiment quickly took shape in my mind. The experiment could engage Alan and Christina immediately and, if successful, suggest valuable insights for the morning rounds physicians.

I envisioned two steps. First, isolate a target segment of DNA of known sequence. Then mix the anticancer drug in question with the DNA. Then compare the pattern of the DNA on what is called an analytical gel side by side with the actual sequence of DNA damaged by Wally Gilbert's DNA sequencing reagents. That way we would know exactly where the anticancer drug attacked the DNA. We would also know if its method of attack was similar or different from other anticancer drugs. In other words, we could answer the question the young doctors were asking.

"Come to my lab when you can in the afternoons and over the summer," I told Alan and Christina. "I have an idea that just might work."

The very first time Alan ran the sequencing gel in my lab, *the very first time*, the process worked. "This is unbelievable, Alan!" I exclaimed. "You have shown where the DNA is damaged" in cancer cells.[108] In a short time, we were able to identify the molecular impact of many classic drugs on cancer cells, and even for some newer cancer drugs. We brought out the champagne, then rushed to publish our results.

DRUGS TO KILL CANCERS

Treating defined sequences of DNA with several anticancer drugs did indeed allow us to understand exactly how they worked. We could identify exactly where damage was likely to occur.[109]

Alan came to me one day later and said, "Bill, I am puzzled. Some pairs of the drugs we sequenced, ones that doctors lumped together, damaged cancer cell DNA in very different ways." He did not realize it immediately, at the moment, but this observation was a valuable clue, a portent for new discovery.

As I explained to Alan, his observation suggested that the effect of using the cancer drugs together might be synergistic against cancer cells; not $1+1=2$, but $1+1=4$. In other words, as Tom Frei and Emil Freireich had shown years before, combinations of drugs might be more effective in treating cancers than a single drug.

I took the results to Tom Frei. "Bill, this is terrific," he said. He directed us to look further, to measure the ability of different combinations of drugs to kill isolated cancer cells. Smart call. We found that some combinations indeed were synergistic, as potent against some cancers as our DNA experiment had predicted.

Tom was elated. "You know what this means," he said when our results came in. Here was evidence that combining the right drugs will have a greater effect on treating the cancer, without damaging normal tissues. The effect on cancer is synergistic; the effect on normal cells is additive. "We will test these combinations in patients as soon as we can."

He decided to test the approach first in patients with head and neck cancer. Head and neck cancers are often hard to treat solid tumors. At the same time Tom convinced one cancer surgeon, Glenn Steele, to reverse the normal order of treatment. Instead of surgery first and chemotherapy later, chemotherapy would be completed before surgery. The idea was that the new combinations of drugs might radically reduce the size of the tumor, making surgery easier and less destructive.

Chemotherapy trials take time, typically several years. We needed ten years to complete these trials, treating head and neck cancer patients with combinations of cancer drugs, tracking outcomes.[110] But this change in treatment proved worth the wait. The new approach increased the five year survival rate for head and neck cancer patients from twenty percent to eighty percent! To me, that is science at its best... making a big difference to people's lives.

THE BIOCHEMISTRY OF ANTICANCER DRUGS

Tom quickly understood the power of applying the latest advances in biochemistry to understanding how cancer drugs work. For several years he had been trying to hire a top expert in the field, cancer pharmacology. None of the four or five world experts wanted to leave their jobs.

One day while pouring over data, Tom turned to me and said, "Bill, why don't you create a new division to grow our own cancer pharmacologists? We can solve our own recruiting problem and make a real difference to improving cancer care around the country."

Because I was only an assistant professor at that point, I was truly surprised. Yet here he was, the president of Dana-Farber Cancer Institute, suggesting that I become the equivalent of a department chairman.

"I'd very much like to do it," I said, after pausing a moment. "I have a few questions."

"Fire away," he said.

"I want to continue my work with viruses. Is that okay?"

"Sure," he said. "You can do any research you want. You will be your own boss."

"Great. But who will we train? How do you imagine that will work? Who will pay for the training?"

"Simple," he said. He then was so explicit about what he had in mind for creating a department specifically for research on anticancer drugs that it was apparent he had been thinking about this for some time. Not so simple, actually, but conceived with Tom's rare administrative talent of vision and precision.

"You will have the authority to hire about five or six junior professors. I will make sure they have salary and some research support. We may reassign one or two from existing divisions. That will be your faculty. Each year we accept new clinical fellows who join us for a period of five to seven years to become specialists in cancer treatment. Training grants will cover our costs.

"You and I will select one or two fellows each year," he continued. "Their first year will be devoted entirely to patient care. For the next two years they will learn how to do research with you or one of your faculty. We will promote the best as instructors and assistant professors. Hopefully one or two will stay with us. The others should be able to become department chairs at prestigious universities and cancer centers around the country."

I loved the idea. It fit my goal of applying science to the practical issues of treating patients.

I served as chair of what we called the Division of Biochemical Pharmacology for the next seven years. During that time, I continued my work on both viruses and DNA damage. The biochemical pharmacology division grew to include five faculty members. Many fellows became assistant professors. Several are now highly regarded physician scientists leading departments of cancer pharmacology. Just as Tom Frei foresaw.

Research findings from our DNA damage and repair laboratory and the Biochemical Pharmacology Division significantly advanced the understanding of a wide range of anticancer drugs. These included the nitrogen mustards and what at the time were newer drugs including cis-platinum, bleomycin, neocarzonostatin and adriamycin—drugs that remain the mainstay of most cancer treatment regimes today. We also made significant advances in understanding the effects of radiation therapy on DNA, as delivered via X-rays and by radioactive isotopes.

HOW DOES SUNLIGHT CAUSE CANCER?

"Don't most of the agents that cause cancer also damage DNA?" Alan asked one day. Yes, they do, I replied. "Then why don't we use the same techniques to discover how the agents work too?" Great idea, I said. We can study how both radiation and chemicals do their dirty work.

The approach turned out to be a gold mine. Over the next few years we gained new knowledge on many fronts regarding the effects of many cancer causing ingredients in food and the environment, such as aflatoxin, a toxin produced by mold that contaminates grains, and bento(a)pyrene, a chemical in charred meat that induces tumors in animals.

Here is a close look at one of many other important discoveries by our DNA damage and repair team in Dana-Farber's department of cancer biology.

Sunlight is a powerful force in human evolution. People who live in parts of the world where the sun is intense have dark skin to protect them from the deadly rays. Those who live in the far north have light skin needed for sun induced production of vitamin D. Sunlight is such a powerful selective pressure that the skin color of entire populations can change from dark to light in just a few thousand years. Analysis of ancient DNA reveals that the immigrants that settled Europe about seven thousand years ago at the end of the last ice age had dark skin.

"Huh," I wondered. I was staring at the pattern on a film where I had just exposed a short piece of DNA to ultraviolet light after separating the strands in a solution. "What are these breaks in DNA? They shouldn't be there."

It was well known that exposure to the ultraviolet rays of the sun caused the pyrimidine nucleotides (the Ts and Cs) in DNA sequence notation to fuse—to produce pyrimidine dimers. Normally bathing DNA strands in an alkaline solution as I did to separate the two DNA strands for analysis did not break DNA. I knew I was looking at something new and unexpected, a scientist's delight.

Years of research implicated the pyrimidine dimer as the reason sunlight caused cancer. That is what all the textbooks said. That is what nearly all specialists in sunlight induced cancers believed. I wanted to know exactly where in DNA the pyrimidine dimers formed. Using a defined sequence as the target seemed the ideal way to find the answer. What I found was entirely unexpected. It was ultraviolet light that sensitized DNA to breakage. The textbook explanations were incomplete.

I knew the sequence of the target DNA, which is why I quickly realized that the break occurred only at sites where the nucleotide T preceded the nucleotide C. (I called these the TC lesions.) That was an additional puzzle because it was well known that sunlight induces what are called cyclobutane dimers at sites adjacent T by preference. Not only that, the formation of a cyclobutane dimer does not cause the DNA to break in an alkaline solution.

"Wow. I think I've discovered a new type of sunlight damage! What could it be?" I hit the library looking for anything published about radiation induced changes to DNA. After several weeks of intense reading, I found an obscure reference in a Russian textbook that described an entirely different type of dimer, the so called 6–4 dimer formed between Ts and Cs.

Why a Russian textbook? In Stalin's time Russian scientists were required to adhere to Lysenko's views of evolution, that traits acquired by the parent, such as strong muscles that result from strenuous exercise, could be passed on to their offspring. That fit Soviet ideology, that society could be molded to create the perfect man. As a consequence, many Russian scientists, to their credit, became wary of dubious genetic experiments; instead they poured their efforts into understanding DNA chemistry. Hence the Russian trove of DNA chemistry data that I stumbled upon. Further experiments I conducted quickly revealed that DNA breaks were in fact caused by the 6–4 TC lesions.

Next question: Is it possible that 6–4 lesions, not cyclobutane dimers, are responsible for the cancer causing effect of sunlight? I knew exactly how to test this hypothesis: Expose bacteria to ultraviolet light and determine exactly where in the DNA the mutations occurred—at sites of adjacent Ts or at sites where Ts precede Cs? I was elated, practically jumping with excitement, when the results came in. Sure enough, almost all the mutations occurred at TC sites.

"We are going to have to re-write the textbooks on how sunlight causes cancer," I told my group.

"Will that upset many scientists?" one of the students asked.

"We'll see," I said. "I am giving the keynote lecture at the next annual meeting of scientists in the field. That is where I will unveil our new theory."

Organizers of this conference at a mountain ski resort in Colorado had invited me to give the opening keynote lecture about cancers caused by ultraviolet rays and how the damaged DNA can be repaired.

"Mutations do not occur where the pyrimidine dimers occur," I asserted in my presentation, the final outlines of my argument taking shape. "They occur at these TC lesion sites. The role of the more abundant cyclobutane dimer is to induce cellular DNA repair mechanisms. In induced repair, enzymes remove all of the cyclobutane dimers. They do not remove the 6-4 lesions.

Rather, a new error prone repair DNA polymerase reads over the 6-4 lesion, popping in an incorrect nucleotide opposite the C in the TC lesion. Those are precisely the mutations we find in sunlight treated cells."

Then, an emphatic concluding statement: "The TC theory of ultraviolet light induced mutagenesis and cancer fits more of the experimental observations than does the cyclobutane theory."

The reaction from this audience of four hundred scientists? Silence, nothing but silence. The first questioner was hostile. People clapped for that! I stood my ground, though, explaining the issue. I was describing in my presentation mutagenesis in double strand DNA; the questioner, single strand DNA.

Disproving a favorite theory is not popular, especially before a group of people who have worked for years on that favorite theory. A few years ago, I was pleased to learn that the TC theory of ultraviolet light damage, the theory I presented that snowy day, is now enshrined in biochemistry textbooks.

Looking back, teaching undergraduates was rewarding in many ways— some expected, some not. I believed I was carrying out the legacy of George Pimentel: to interest young people in a career in science. I believed I was performing a civic duty: to help future voters and decision makers reach more informed decisions on matters relating to science and technology.

Little did I anticipate that teaching my Cancer and Society course would provide the inspiration, sparked by a pair of inquisitive nineteen year old sophomores, Alan and Christina, for many years of exciting research in DNA damage and repair. But I am deeply grateful that it did.

‖19‖

HUMAN RETROVIRUSES

By 1980, OUR DNA RESEARCH ON ANTICANCER DRUGS was thriving but my initial Dana-Farber lab had encountered headwinds studying retroviruses and cancer.

The guardians of federal purse strings had lost interest in this research after funding a rash of failures around the world—and zero successes—from the mid-'60s through the early '70s.[111] The scientific quest for the discovery of human cancer causing retroviruses was mocked as "human rumor viruses."

We were among a small group of scientists anywhere in the world still keeping up the hunt to investigate the possibility that retroviruses can cause cancer in humans. A body of research, largely ignored, had shown that retroviruses could lie dormant for many years after primary infection, only later to appear as cancer causing agents in cattle and cats, and as immunological or brain and other diseases in other large animals. Those studies bolstered my convictions that we should continue this research.

"These viral cancer infections probably attack humans the same way they infect cattle," I thought. "None of those failed studies were conducted this way. I have to keep going." Most failed studies were conducted on small laboratory animals such as mice.

THE FIRST HUMAN RETROVIRUS, CONFIRMED

Then in the spring of 1981 came the unforgettable call from Bob Gallo. Bob was one of our small group of scientists working to isolate human retroviruses. He was exultant. "Bill, we did it! We discovered a human retrovirus that causes leukemia!"

"Fantastic! Congratulations!" I said. For all of us stubbornly carrying the conviction that virus causes cancer, Bob's message was a magical moment. We knew immediately that this discovery would open doors to new research in cancer viruses that might translate into millions of lives saved, healthier lives lived.

"What type of leukemia?" I asked.

"It is an amazing story," Bob replied. "Japanese doctors noticed an unusual T cell leukemia that seems to run in families. They suspect it may be transmitted from mother to child and maybe through sex. We were on the lookout for a similar case in the U.S. At last, we found one!"

"A Japanese living here?"

"No, not at all. An American, a Caucasian with a T cell leukemia."

The Japanese studies, it turned out, were based on clusters of leukemia cases identified in southwestern Japan in 1977. When virologists there discovered unusual cell forms in these cancers, they determined the disease was a distinct form of leukemia and named it adult T cell leukemia (ATL).

Meanwhile, Bob and his team had identified a new retrovirus like particle from the American patient. They then discovered that sera from the Japanese leukemia patients contained antibodies of that particle.[112]

But Bob could not grow the virus in his lab, an essential step to accelerate research. Why?

"I don't know," he said. "If it grows, it grows very slowly. Maybe infection is transmitted from person to person by infected cells. We are accumulating evidence that if we mix cells from the patient with fresh uninfected T cells, those cells start producing the virus too. It's just that we can't transmit the infection by cell free virus."

How do you know it is the same virus that affects the Japanese?

"That is a really exciting part of the story. Antibodies in the Japanese patient's blood react with our virus and not with any other. I am sure we have it this time."

What will you call it?

"The Human T cell Leukemia Virus, HTLV for short because it seems to affect only T cells."

Bob, what can I say? What a major discovery! I have some ideas we should explore.

"Great, I'd like that," Bob said.

A VIRUS THAT CHANGES THE HOST CELL

That call started me on one of them most exciting scientific adventures of my life.

The virus Bob described reminded me of a mouse virus I was studying in my lab at the time with a postdoctoral fellow, Joe Sodroski.

"Maybe your new virus has a T cell specific enhancer," I told Bob some time later. "That may be why it causes T cell leukemias. If you have a DNA copy of the virus, we can test that quickly."

Bob agreed. Meanwhile, his lab discovered a similar virus in west African patients with T cell leukemia. His lab sent us DNA copies of that virus first, then followed later with the DNA copy of HTLV-1.

With the material in hand, Joe and I were ready to begin in our lab. "If I am right, the HTLV enhancer should only work in T cells," I said to him. "Please test the enhancer for activity in as many cell lines as we have on hand, and in cell lines that produce HTLV-1 and 2 as well."

A few days later, Joe had the results. "The experiment worked!" he said. "The T cell enhancer works ten to twenty times better in infected cells."

"None of the other cells were as good?"

"None at all," he said. "Look at the data."

This finding puzzled me, but I thought there might be two explanations. One, that the virus picked a special sub-population of cells not represented among the type we tested. Or two, that the virus somehow changed the cell in ways that caused infected cells to make virus RNA abundantly.

The first explanation fit better with our earlier experiments. "Joe, I'll bet the virus picks out a cell type that we don't have in our collection," I said.

"I'll take that bet," he replied. "I think the virus changes the cell."

We needed to rule out one or the other. We were able to obtain in a couple of weeks a matched pair of cells that a scientist in England had made, one with the virus and one without. Joe and I were ready to try again.

"Look at this," he said a few days later, walking into my office. "I win! It is not the cell type that makes the difference. It is the virus that makes the difference!"

Another Eureka moment! HTLV was different from all other known retroviruses. *It activated itself.* We called this phenomenon *transactivation.* I immediately suspected that transactivation was also the answer to how virus caused leukemia. I thought, "If the virus could change the cell to favor itself, maybe it could also change the cell to favor the growth of those cells."

For the next two years, we designed and executed experiments to test the hypothesis. Progress was rapid. Another postdoctoral fellow, Craig Rosen, led our team to quickly isolate the element in the viral genome that responded to the transactivating signal. (Craig became an expert in the technology to do this by working on our studies of mouse virus enhancers.)

We named this element in the viral genome the *transactivating response* (tar) region.

But how did HTLV do this? A possible answer came from a Japanese lab. Mitsuaki Yoshida in Tokyo had determined the sequence of the virus, noting that HTLV had potential to make at least one extra protein from what he called the X region. He identified a novel long open reading frame, a DNA sequence that predicted a protein could be made, which he call *x-lor*.

X-lor was a long open reading from HTLV that certainly could make a sizable protein. The problem was that it lacked the start signal. That mystery was solved when we found that the start signal was supplied by splicing. We also discovered that the protein made from this region, later renamed *tax*, is capable activating the HTLV-1 enhancer in many different types of cells.

But, does the *tax* gene of HTLV cause leukemia? After several years of additional research, the answer was yes. Working with scientists in Germany, we found that *tax* causes normal lymphocytes cells to grow uncontrollably. Many laboratories have since confirmed the role of *tax* and discovered exactly how it causes cancer.

IN JAPAN, EXPLORING HOW HTLV BEHAVES

I needed to learn as much as I could about the natural history of HTLV, meaning how it was transmitted from person to person and how it spread in populations.

"The best way to understand this virus is to go where it causes the most trouble, Japan," I reasoned. "If I really understand how HTLV behaves, I will know where and how to look for the next human retroviruses." Taking the idea further, I wondered, "Maybe I can find a virus that causes breast cancer. We know that a retrovirus, the murine mammary tumor virus, causes breast cancer in mice. Why not in humans?"

In Japan, working with Japanese scientists as a visiting professor at the University of Kyoto, I learned that HTLV is transmitted from mother to child by exposure to vaginal fluids during delivery and through breast milk. Infection is also transmitted via blood transfusion and by sex from men to women, but rarely, if ever, from women to men. The infecting agent is not the virus alone but rather the infected cell. Cell-to-cell spread is a very unusual mode of virus transmission.

I also learned why it was so hard to find human retroviruses.

The disease occurs only after many years following infection, just like what we saw in cattle and other large animals. For HTLV, the period between infection and disease is quite long, typically twenty to forty years. Even then only about five percent of those infected fall ill. During the long quiet period very little virus appears in the blood, if any. With no virus in the blood, and absent disease, it is difficult if not impossible to find a new virus.

Our closeup studies of how HTLV was transmitted have not yet yielded clues to understanding breast cancer. But they did yield powerful insights that were soon critical for understanding another rare human retrovirus that was silently spreading, on its way to becoming a pandemic killer, lethal to anyone infected.

I am proud of our work on HTLV. We persisted, looking for human retroviruses in spite of scarce funding, skepticism and even ridicule, long after most gave up in despair.

But I am unhappy to this day about the public health response. Much more can be done to control HTLV infection, which remains endemic to many regions of the world.

I believe an effective vaccine to HTLV can be developed. Our immune response is more than ninety five percent effective in controlling the infection, one of the best indicators that a vaccine will protect. Such vaccines would save many lives if we develop them.

In fact, researching a vaccine for HTLV is what I planned to do next, but that was not to be. The threat of a deadly new disease, AIDS, sent me in a new direction.

||20||

HIV/AIDS: THE SCIENCE

It started with a question on a cold December day. A friend grabbed me by the arm halfway down the corridor between our two buildings at Dana-Farber.

"Bill, there is a new type of cancer that might be transmitted from person to person. That's just up your alley. It's Kaposi sarcoma in gay men, a type of skin cancer."

He had my attention right away. "Where can I learn more?" I replied.

"A doctor in L.A. just published a paper in *The New England Journal of Medicine*. That's where I saw it."

I rushed to find the paper. Michael Gottlieb, a young immunologist, and several other doctors at UCLA Medical School described a perplexing new illness they thought might be spreading. Over the past year Michael had seen a number of young men with the same set of problems. Common symptoms included *pneumocystis pneumonia*, a yeast infection known as oral *candidiasis*, infections and Kaposi's sarcoma and a rare cancer that appears in various organs as red, purple or brown blotches.

Michael had just learned in his previous job about the importance of white blood cells known as CD4 positive T cells for maintaining immunity, an insight that helped him recognize that this constellation of symptoms was common in people with badly damaged immune systems. These patients he was seeing all suffered from a profound depression in their number of CD4 positive T cells. CD4 positive T cell depression became a marker for the disease. Michael was the right man in the right place at the right time.

I couldn't get the story out of my mind. Over Christmas break, I read and re-read the paper. By early January I knew why.

"Maybe a retrovirus like HTLV causes this disease. It seems to be transmitted from one person to another, maybe by sex. That's similar to HTLV. The cells affected, CD4 positive T cells, are exactly the same as those HTLV infects."

I knew that retroviruses can attack the immune system. I had been working on cat retroviruses. Some caused leukemia and others caused an immuno-suppressive disease much like what was occurring in Gottlieb's patients. The fact that the UCLA scientists didn't find a new virus didn't mean much. As we saw in the previous chapter, viruses like HTLV go silent for a long time after the initial infection.

"I wonder what Max and Bob think," I mused. Calls to Max Essex and Bob Gallo in early January confirmed that we all were developing hypotheses along the same lines. Bob said, "It sure looks like a variant of HTLV to me. We already know two such viruses exist. Why not more?" Max agreed. "That is exactly what I have been thinking," he said. "The cat model of immune suppression by feline leukemia is the model."

At Bob's suggestion, we put together a small working group to collect as much information as we could about this new disease. The three of us met every four to six weeks along with a rotating cast of experts in diverse fields for the next eighteen months into the fall of 1983. Our research quickly narrowed exclusively on the hypothesis that the new disease was caused by a retrovirus and nothing else.

This was a risky bet. We knew our reasoning on what caused the disease, soon to be named Acquired Immune Deficiency Syndrome (AIDS), was good but not airtight. The original AIDS patients were infected with many different types of microorganisms, the consequence of their lifestyles. Infections including those with several types of herpes and hepatitis viruses, a variety of bacteria and even fungi were common. All were proposed as the cause of AIDS by one scientist or another.

Our core group investigating what we called "the retrovirus theory of AIDS" quickly expanded to include Jim Curran of the Centers for Disease Control and leading scientists from Germany, England and France. Data began to pour in from other sources. Donna Mildvan, an infectious disease specialist at Mt. Sinai Hospital in New York City, noticed that intravenous drug users were dying of a new degenerative brain disease. To test for the presence of a new virus Donna sent brain tissue from autopsies of these drug users to primate centers for testing in chimpanzees. Had the disease appeared quickly in chimps, Donna would have been first to find the virus. Instead, it took many years before her chimps became ill. Sometimes doing the right experiment doesn't lead to the right answer quickly.

Two New York City dermatologists, Bijan Safai and Alvin Friedman-Kien, began seeing an increasing number of young men with Kaposi's sarcoma like some of the initial patients in Los Angeles. The same was happening in cities throughout the U.S. and then in Europe. All of these patients suffered a profound deficit in immune function; specifically, very low numbers of CD4 positive T cells.

Then an entirely different population of patients appeared: infants born to mothers with the disease, blood transfusion recipients and a steadily rising number of hemophiliacs. This widening circle of infection reinforced our retrovirus theory; we knew that HTLV also transmitted from mother to child and by blood transfusion.

At one meeting Jim Curran of the CDC presented comprehensive, compelling studies of these AIDS patients—and a daunting, authoritative conclusion.

"I believe that no *known* infectious agent causes AIDS," he said. "We tested the outlier cases for everything we could think of. Many AIDS babies show no evidence of infection with any known disease causing microorganism. The same is true of most hemophiliacs and most blood transfusion recipients."

"If AIDS is caused by an infectious agent," he continued, "*it must be one that is new to medicine.*"

With all known virus and other microorganisms ruled out as the cause, the hunt for a new virus gained momentum.

ASSESSING THE KILLER

The first time I saw an image of the AIDS virus was a picture from a French lab. It looked like a retrovirus but at first glance not the one I knew. The center or core of the virus particle was conical, not spherical.

"Wait a minute," I suddenly realized. "I've seen pictures like these before. It looks just like the retrovirus that causes a brain disease in sheep. Maybe it's not an HTLV variant."

Within weeks the French lab and Bob Gallo's lab published back to back papers in *Science* announcing the detection of a new retrovirus from AIDS patients that grew in human T cells. Was this the cause of AIDS? How to tell?

The classic method for identifying an agent that causes disease was not in the cards for us. We could not rely on Koch's postulates, the time honored method that I had learned in high school (and used for a science fair project) to detect AIDS infection. Koch's postulates require isolation of the suspected agent, injection of the agent into a test animal, observing the appearance of the disease, and re-isolation. The major issue with applying Koch's postulates was that it might take years, maybe decades, before the disease appeared in test animals (in this case monkeys and chimps) and we could determine if the animals had been infected.

We did have one other option. Antibodies. Did people with AIDS have antibodies to the virus? New tests soon gave us the answer. Yes. *All people with AIDS had antibodies to the new virus.* We had discovered the cause of AIDS, a new type of retrovirus. A committee eventually gave the virus a consensus name, the *Human Immunodeficiency Virus* (HIV).

The ability to test people for HIV infection unleashed another bombshell. Many, many more people were infected with the virus both in the United States and worldwide than actually had AIDS. Not yet. Knowing these viruses as I did, I was afraid of what was coming. Many, if not most, of those infected might develop AIDS over time and die. The epidemic had already spread further than anybody had imagined. The disease we knew as AIDS was only the tip of a very large iceberg of infection.

I know this recounting of our actual laboratory work does not capture the excitement, the heat—you might even say acrimony—that exploded over who discovered the virus first and has been widely chronicled. Remembering back to my graduate student days at the time, I thought, "Maybe Wally Gilbert was right. Competition is good. The answer does emerge faster this way." For me, though, what mattered was not who was first but knowing that we now could begin the work necessary to stop an epidemic.

At this point in 1984, AIDS was always fatal, and spiraling out of control. I feared this disease would become a global pandemic with potential to kill hundreds of millions. AIDS had to be cured, and I was determined to play a role. The threat to global public health was so urgent, and my skills in medical science so well matched against the threat, I knew I had to shift gears at Dana-Farber and make combating AIDS my highest priority.

"Now is the time to apply everything you know," I told myself. "Use your knowledge of science and medicine to understand the virus and to discover drugs to stop the virus. Do what you can to gain more research dollars to recruit the talent we need. Use your knowledge of the biotechnology pharmaceutical industry to engage their capacity. Use your antiwar experience to raise awareness of the peril and to mobilize public opinion and research support."

One final thought threw down the gauntlet, a private exhortation that would keep me focused for the next several years. "Do this all at the same time. It will be a challenge of a lifetime."

HOW CLOSELY DOES HIV MIRROR HTLV-1?

The first challenge was fear, fear among many of my fellow scientists and physicians at Dana-Farber that my lab's working with the virus would endanger them and their patients. "Why bring a new and deadly virus, one that causes a disease with no cure, into our hospital?" several protested, some vehemently.

Baruj Benacerraf, the Nobel Prize winning immunologist who had recently succeeded Tom Frei as the institute's president, had an answer, courageous and firm.

"As medical scientists dedicated to using our knowledge to fight disease we have an obligation to do what we can," he announced. "We are fortunate that two of our scientists, William Haseltine, a virologist, and Stuart Schlossman, an immunologist, are world experts with just the skills needed; Bill with his knowledge of viruses and Stuart with his expertise in CD4 T cells.

"I will personally take the responsibility," he asserted, "to assure our work on this disease will not endanger either our patients or our staff."

Baruj gave me the green light to accelerate HIV related research and create a formal new research unit, the Division of Human Retrovirology. An entire department dedicated to retrovirology was the first of its kind in the world, as far as I know. Over the next few years, I recruited an excellent faculty; many were my former graduate students and postdoctoral fellows. By the end of the decade, we would number more than one hundred.

By great good fortune, we had just the laboratory facilities we needed for HIV studies. Several years earlier the National Institutes of Health authorized funds to build containment facilities suitable for working with dangerous gene splicing experiments. Dana-Farber received the funding to build one. I was on the design committee and made sure our faculty was equipped to work with potentially lethal viruses. The containment lab was just one floor above my office.

Our very first question: How closely did HIV resemble HTLV? By then we knew that both HTLV and bovine leukemia virus were capable of activating their own expression, transactivation. Was this true for HIV as well? To find the answer, all we needed was to look for the presence of transactivation in an HIV sample.

After running this test, Joe Sodroski and Craig Rosen were wide eyed. "Boy, does HIV ever transactivate," they told me. Transactivation, you remember, is what triggers rapid growth of a virus in infected cells. "The signal is ten to twenty times stronger than that of HTLV!"

Conclusion from this first impression: Yes. HIV is like HTLV.

Craig led the team to locate the transactivating response (*tar*) like element. I looked over his shoulder at the results. "How odd," I mused. "The responsive region is positioned after, not before, the site where RNA transcription begins. That's something new and unexpected." We chewed over what that might mean.

"Maybe the target for the HIV transactivator is in the newly made RNA itself," I suggested. If the transactivator was in the newly made RNA, I knew this would be a rare example of how gene regression is controlled in RNA, what is called post-transcriptional regulation. Post-transcriptional regulation was thought to occur in some cells but the details remained obscure.

I immediately brightened at the prospect that we could bring more clarity. "Great," I told our team. "We have an opportunity to describe a gene control pathway new to biology."

It did not take long to show that the target of the HIV transactivator was indeed RNA, a very short loop at the beginning of the molecule. Copying the virus DNA begins but then stops short unless the transactivator is present. This was the first of many occasions when a laboratory study of HIV revealed biological phenomena new to science.

HIV SEQUENCE, REVEALED

The race was on to determine the entire sequence of the virus. Gallo's lab made a DNA copy of one strain that grew especially well. He sent one half of the strain to my lab and the other half to another group at Washington University in St. Louis. When we combined our results with those from Washington U., at last we had it, the full sequence of the HIV genome.

In those days we printed the DNA sequence on a continuous piece of paper about fourteen inches wide and sixty feet long. The RNA sequence ran down the center of the page. The predicted protein sequence was printed above the RNA sequence. I tacked the entire printout at eye level around the four walls of our conference room. (It fit, with several feet to spare.) We then began to mark the printout at points precisely where we thought each protein was made. That long piece of paper became my constant companion over the next several years. On long flights, I would pull it out of my briefcase to see what more I could learn. At every opportunity, I studied it carefully.

Once we had the sequence of the virus we immediately understood many of its working parts.

"Look," I said to Roberto Patarca, a graduate student who loved working with DNA and protein sequences. I wanted to make sure he was aware of our latest insights and how they fit into what we already knew. "Some parts of the genome look just like those of other retroviruses we have sequenced. These genes must form the internal core of the virus. The predicted long precursor protein is just where it is in all the other retroviruses. Here too are genes for the enzymes the virus needs to copy itself, just where they should be. This must be where the gene is that makes the outer surface, the envelope protein."

Roberto interrupted. "But look here. The envelope gene is not where it is in other viruses. There are open spaces, one in the middle and a longer one at the end." We then began to examine those regions much more closely. Our first pass identified the possibility that three new proteins could be made in the central region and one larger protein could be made from the region at the far end of the genome.

This is the type of discovery that sends a scientist's pulse racing: four proteins unknown to science that make up what are likely to be important parts of a virus causing a new and deadly disease. Learning more about these proteins might help us fight the virus.

As we were about to publish our study of the virus genome we learned that a French group had done the same thing and would publish their results at the same time. When we compared the two published results, we were pleased to see that we had reached the same conclusions, right down to the fact that HIV had the potential to make an entirely new set of proteins.

Over the next two years, in a series of firsts, my laboratory was able to confirm each of the four proteins was in fact made. We described what some of them do to help the virus reproduce while evading the body's immune response. My own Dana-Farber lab, subsequently, and many around the world have spent years figuring out what they do. Some results are still coming in.

DISCOVERING THE TRANSACTIVATOR: TAT

I knew that we needed to find new drugs that stopped the virus from growing if we were to treat and hopefully someday cure people infected by HIV. To do that we needed to discover which proteins the virus needed to reproduce itself.

"Here is what we are going to do next," I said to my team. "We are going to introduce changes (mutations) all along the virus genome and see what happens to the virus. We are looking for changes that kill the virus. If any knock out the ability of the virus to make a protein then we know that protein will be a good target for an antiviral drug. Let's get to work!"

When the answers started to roll in, we learned that *all* the proteins HIV shared with other retroviruses, the major core proteins—the envelope protein, the viral protease, reverse transcriptase, ribonuclease H and integrase—were essential. However, the story with the new proteins was different. None was required for virus growth. We called these the non-essential genes. None was likely to be good targets for antiviral drugs. We now know that each plays a role in some aspects of HIV infection. Nonetheless, the virus can and does do well without them.

These experiments raised another question. The analogy with HTLV led us to believe that the *nef* protein would be the transactivator. After all the *nef* protein was in the same relative position. But no. Transactivation was normal in viruses lacking *nef* function. Even more puzzling, none of the new proteins *vif, vpu* or *vpr*, was the transactivator. "Where could it be?" I asked our team.

We did find that two of these regions we selectively damaged failed to transactivate. Careful inspection of the genome revealed that these mutants disrupted the ability of HIV to make another small protein. Follow up experiments proved that this small protein was the transactivator. We named the protein the transactivator and named the gene *tat*. Although very different from the HTLV counterpart in structure and mechanism, the transactivator in HIV did share one unusual feature with HTLV. The start site for the *tat* protein was contributed from a spliced messenger RNA. We went on to show that a small protein was indeed made in infected cells from the *tat* gene.

Our discovery of the *tat* gene and protein was doubly pleasing. We found a new protein that worked differently from anything we knew about in biology and, very importantly, we discovered a new chink in the virus armor. Bottom line: If we could find a way to inactivate *tat*, we could find a way to kill the virus. We had another new drug target!

DISCOVERING A REGULATOR OF RNA EXPORT: REV

A few weeks later Joe came to my office with a question. "Bill, look at the effect of these two induced mutations. They kill the virus yet all the proteins we know are intact including *tat*. What do you think is going on? Is it possible that there is another small protein in this region with the mutations that we overlooked?" "Maybe," I replied. "Let's look again."

Sure enough, we found a second small protein when we re-examined the HIV sequence and soon proved that this second protein was indeed made in infected cells. We named it *art*. *Art* was later renamed *rev* by an international nomenclature team so I will call it *rev* hereafter. Just as we had shown that all the other usual HIV genes—*vif, vpr, vpu, nef* and *tat*—made new proteins, we were able to prove that *rev* also made a small protein. That was the sixth novel protein in HIV, the final surprise among all the novel parts of HIV as compared to other retroviruses that were known at the time.

But what could *rev* be doing? What was its function? We were surprised to discover the entire virus genome was made normally by the *rev* defective mutants. There was no sign of any of the major virus proteins, not the capsid, envelope or any other. However, both the *tat* and *rev* proteins were made and were active.

We thought, "That is odd. All the RNAs are made but only some are used. There has to be a block somewhere for the RNAs to not function after they are made. RNA is made in the nucleus but must exit to the cytoplasm via a nuclear pore to serve as a template for protein production. If it cannot get out, that would explain why the proteins are not made. All the machinery to make protein lies outside the nucleus in the cytoplasm."

But how were the *tat* and *rev* proteins made? There was a clue. Both *tat* and *rev* are made from spliced messenger RNAs. These RNAs lack long stretches of the viral genome needed to make major structural and replicative enzymes. Perhaps there are "hold me in the nucleus" signals embedded in those regions of the virus genome that are not present in smaller spliced messages. Their "hold me in the nucleus" signals would be spliced away, allowing smaller RNAs encoding *tat* and *rev* to exit the nucleus.

How then could full-length RNA containing the "hold me in the nucleus" signals exit? Hah! I thought. That's where *rev* comes in. The *rev* protein must recognize "get me out of the nucleus" signals embedded in the full length genome and override the "hold me in the nucleus" signals.

That was our hypothesis, entirely new to biology. We postulated that both "hold me in" and "get me out" of the nucleus signals existed and that the *rev* protein binding to specific sequences overrides the "hold me in the nucleus" signals. It took several months of very intense work to find both signals. *Rev* worked as we had hypothesized!

Validating the *rev* hypothesis remains one of the most satisfying discoveries I have ever made. It was wholly and entirely unexpected for two reasons—first, that HIV specified yet another protein (discovered only by our random mutations), and, second, that we discovered cells can regulate RNA transit from the nucleus to the cytoplasm.

This discovery created a fundamental new insight into how normal cells function, with impact far beyond uncovering a quirk in HIV biology. The added discovery of yet another new target for anti-HIV drug, *rev*, was icing on the cake.

21

ANTI-HIV DRUG TARGETS

I CALLED MY TEAM TOGETHER TO FOCUS ON THE NEXT STEP in fighting the new disease: transforming discovery to treatment and cures.

"Our new mission is to use our knowledge to stop the pandemic. We can do it. A vaccine stopped polio. Drugs can cure herpes.

"We need to develop drugs to stop HIV/AIDS. We know better than anyone how to do so. We know the virus weak spots. We have discovered what HIV needs to infect and to reproduce. We can reduce each step to a simple yes/no test. Does a drug candidate stop that function or not? If 'yes' it is a drug candidate. If 'no' go on to the next.

"Our first task is to reduce each of the virus's necessary functions to such a simple yes and no test. We have the genes, we have the proteins and we have the knowledge of what they do.

"We have several great candidates, the viral polymerase, the viral protease, the viral ribonuclease H and the viral integrase. We can add to that the *tat* and *rev* proteins that we discovered and showed that the virus cannot live without. We will develop high throughput assays for each function. That will allow us and our partners to scan hundreds of thousands of new chemicals for anti-virus activity.

"We will be working to find any anti-HIV drug in partnership with bio-tech and Big Pharma companies. They have resources we can't match. But we can point the way and deliver the materials they need. Our job is to make their job easier."

KNOCKING ON DOORS

For the next three years, well into 1987, our lab set out to do exactly that. We developed rapid screening tests for the viral protease, ribonuclease H and integrase and for *tat* and *rev* functions. Others had already developed rapid assays for the viral polymerase. We filed patents on behalf of Harvard and Dana-Farber, then coordinated with our licensing office to make these new tests available to drug companies.

Meanwhile, the death toll from AIDS was climbing terribly (approaching fifty thousand in the U.S.[113]) as I predicted. I went on another crusade, this time aiming to forge partnerships with major pharmaceutical companies and universities to deliver new drugs into hospitals and clinics desperate to treat dying AIDS patients.

I began knocking on the doors of CEOs and research directors at major pharmaceutical companies and deans and presidents of elite research institutes. Many I knew personally either as research peers in life sciences or as contacts through my first company, Cambridge BioScience Corporation. Founded five years earlier, Cambridge BioScience developed an effective vaccine to protect domestic cats from a viral infection, often fatal, known as feline leukemia, that caused cancer.[114] The vaccine was the first to protect mammals from a retrovirus infection.

I was granted the meetings, but not any deals for funds. SmithKline Beecham, Bristol-Myers, Pfizer, Roche, Sandoz, Ciba-Geigy and Johnson & Johnson. Everywhere, the same story. "Sorry Bill. Funds for research are already fully budgeted for this year. No way we could start a new program now." Some added, dismissively, "Besides, there are many diseases much more important than AIDS."

Nonetheless I kept pushing these pharmaceutical companies, arguing that they should develop new drugs against diverse targets. My experience with Dana-Farber cancer treatments and the vision I shared with Tom Frei bolstered my convictions about the importance of combination drug therapy. Cancer cells are master escape artists. Give them one drug and they will find a way to survive. Give them two you might have a chance. Hit them with three and you had a good chance of winning.

The response in universities and research institutes was practically the same as Big Pharma's. And even more frustrating because I expected more. Renowned scientists leading infectious disease and microbiology departments voiced appreciation for our detective work to locate molecular vulnerabilities in HIV. But, in effect, they said their hands were tied.

"Wow, you really have made impressive progress," one said. "It is scientifically interesting. However, how can I hire new people or even convince my faculty to work on a problem for which there is little or no money?"

There was one exception, Joshua Lederberg, president of Rockefeller University. He was one of the most famous scientists of that era, prominent in leading the U.S. space program's search for life on Mars and for his Nobel Prize winning discoveries in bacteria genetics.

"Bill, you are right," he said. "AIDS is a serious threat to world health and to us right here in New York. I am sorry we can't do more. Money for AIDS research is just not available. History will judge us harshly for not doing more with what we know."

AN HIV VACCINE?

At a brief press conference announcing the discovery of the AIDS virus in the spring of 1984, the Reagan administration's head of Health and Human Services had painted a hopeful picture. The discovery opened the door to controlling the disease, Margaret Heckler said. She added that new diagnostic tests soon would be available to identify those infected and to protect the nation's blood supply from HIV contamination.

"We also believe," she concluded, that scientists will "develop a vaccine to prevent AIDS in the future. We hope to have such a vaccine ready for testing in approximately two years."

She was correct about the diagnostic tests, but not the vaccine. Twenty years later, she said in a public television interview that the question about vaccine timing was discussed among the briefing participants before the press briefing. "I listened to the leaders of the department, who said they did not know," she said. "I asked Bob Gallo... He said, 'two years.' In the press conference, I did say two years."

Meanwhile, as Cambridge BioScience ramped up production of our feline leukemia vaccine, I thought, "Why not a vaccine for HIV?" A protein I designed for the vaccine was a modified part of the outer protein (the envelope glycoprotein) of the feline leukemia virus. There were several indications that a similar new agent might work against HIV, offset by several red flags.

One encouraging sign was that antibodies for HIV soared after infection. A high concentration of antibodies that prevents viral replication is a good predictor for effective vaccines. For HIV patients, antibody counts were sky high. We had never seen such a vigorous prolonged antibody response. Some patients had lymph nodes swollen from working overtime to produce antibodies (a symptom called lymphadenopathy).

Yet, the antibodies did not stop the virus from growing. Somehow, the virus escaped. Moreover, once infected, AIDS patients were infected with HIV for life. That ruled out the simplest predictor for an effective vaccine, when infected people clear the virus once and for all. We also tested whether T cells from HIV infected people were active against the virus, a suggestion from the chair of infectious diseases at Massachusetts General Hospital, Marty Hirsch. A good friend, Marty lent me two of his very talented researchers, Bruce Walker and David Ho. The level of anti-HIV T cells they measured, working temporarily in my lab, was the highest ever recorded for a disease. Nonetheless, infection progressed.

All of this was bad news. There would be no easy win with an HIV vaccine. We lacked the basic research that had to come first. I concluded that it might take twenty five or thirty years, maybe more, before we had a vaccine. This was the message I had to get out, even though it would be dismaying for AIDS sufferers, their families and friends and the general public at a time of mounting hysteria surrounding AIDS.

The best opportunity would be the second annual HIV/AIDS global conference, set for Paris in the spring of 1986.

"A vaccine is not an impenetrable shield that prevents a virus from entering our bodies," I said in my keynote. "Rather, it is like a rapid reaction force that eliminates a virus once it starts growing. If the most active immune responses ever recorded can't stop the virus once it has gained a toehold, then it is unlikely a vaccine will either.

"A vaccine to prevent the spread of the AIDS virus *is not* on the near horizon," I asserted. "Given what we know, I cannot predict when or even if it will be possible to make one. What I do know is that we need to learn much more about our own immune system and the virus." Then I added, "But we should never say never."

The audience reacted angrily, prompting organizers to pull me from the stage. Yet today, as I write thirty five years later, there is still no HIV vaccine. But we should never say never.

STEPS FORWARD, BACKWARD

I was increasingly worried, very worried. With no vaccine, there would be a tidal wave of death for years unless we could develop drugs to treat infected patients and block HIV growth. HIV had remained my highest priority in Dana-Farber research, but it was not all consuming. My cancer pharmacology lab continued to make big strides in identifying combinations of drugs to treat cancer—just as Tom Frei and I had envisioned.

"Maybe a combination of antiviral drugs will work against HIV," I kept thinking. "We learned from cancer that one drug is not enough, but cancer cells have a much harder time escaping when two or more drugs are combined to attack different targets in the cancer." I briefed our team on the reasoning, and added a further thought. "If the drugs work to stop the virus in an infected person, maybe they can also prevent a person from being infected in the first place."

One of many missing elements in basic HIV research was a tool that could test the effectiveness against HIV of any proposed vaccine's biochemistry. When scientists frame an experiment, the first tool they have is analogy, or similarity. We ask, is what we are looking for analogous or similar to anything we have ever seen before?

I knew about a virus similar to HIV that affects some African monkeys. It was called the Simian Immune Deficiency Virus, or SIV. Our idea was to replace the outer envelope protein of the monkey virus cell with one from an HIV cell. If we could create a hybrid, an SIV-HIV hybrid virus (abbreviated SHIV), we then could conduct the search for a human vaccine against HIV much faster in monkeys. We succeeded.

Joe Sodroski was my lab expert on the cell envelopes of viruses, the outer shells of virus. We were both optimistic this hybrid concept would work. It did! These SHIV viruses we created—I called them sharp little knives that would cut through the thicket of vaccine development—became the backbone for many HIV vaccine research programs ongoing now in the U.S. and around the world.

The FDA announced the most promising news yet for an HIV treatment in 1986 when it approved the first anti-HIV drug, known as AZT. Recalling that a failed cancer drug blocked retroviruses in mice, Burroughs Wellcome had pulled samples from storage and repeated those experiments. The National Cancer Institute, intrigued by the Burroughs Wellcome results and better equipped with containment facilities, ran those tests successfully on HIV. They confirmed that AZT effectively blocked HIV growth. Toxicity studies in animals then showed AZT to be safe. Moving quickly, the National

Institutes of Health and FDA demonstrated AZT was safe for humans and in record time, five days, approved the drug for treating patients.

AZT worked as predicted. The concentration of virus in the blood of infected people dropped precipitously. People near death's door recovered. The CD4 population of T cells rebounded. Everyone worried about AIDS breathed a sigh of relief. But the optimism began fading as patients who initially responded to AZT began to fail. Their CD4 T cells blood count dropped. Virus isolated from these patients was no longer killed by the drug. These were signals to us that HIV mutated to become resistant to AZT and continued to grow. That indeed was the case. We learned that most AIDS patients developed resistance to AZT within six months to a year.

For me, this development was not unexpected. HIV is a master at escape. We urgently needed to find a new anti-HIV drug to pair with AZT and thwart this elusive HIV response. I was seeing too many dear friends descend to death after what seemed a miraculous recovery.

We needed combination chemotherapy to stop HIV, just as we had accelerated its impact against cancer in our Dana-Farber Division of Biochemical Pharmacology. In time, I became known among AIDS activists, HIV researchers and the press as "Dr. Combination."

The first real success came from combining two or more anti-reverse transcriptase drugs with protease inhibitors. Some people who received those initial combinations in the early 1990s are alive today. Now, the great majority of HIV positive people receiving combination drug therapy can expect to live a near normal life.

PREVENTING MOTHER TO CHILD TRANSMISSION

We knew this same year that about thirty percent of children born to HIV infected mothers also became infected. I wondered, "If AZT reduces the amount of virus in the blood, might treating mothers with AZT for a short time before childbirth protect their babies?"

As we had learned, HIV needed several months before it became resistant to AZT. AZT was already approved to prevent HIV infection in healthcare workers inadvertently exposed to HIV, the so called "needle stick cases." Why not for expectant mothers as well?

Officials I contacted at all the big healthcare bureaucracies and some philanthropies rejected the idea. The National Institute of Allergy and Infectious Diseases, World Health Organization, Doctors Without Borders and others. The same answer. "Not interested. Too dangerous. Probably won't work anyway."

I knew there had to be a way around this roadblock. The virus in monkeys that Joe and I had learned about, the Simian Immune Deficiency Virus, came to mind. I thought, "If we can show in tests with newborn monkeys that AZT prevents SIV infection, maybe people will listen." I found and hired a scientist, Ruth Ruprecht, to join my department to test the idea. She soon had the results. AZT prevented transmission of SIV to newborns. Human trials quickly were underway, and within months we had the answer: AZT reduced mother to child transmission. The new Burroughs Wellcome drug was approved for use with expectant mothers infected with HIV.

I was delighted to learn that this treatment based on our initial work dramatically reduced mother to child transmission of HIV, from thirty percent to five percent. Today, combinations of drugs given to the mothers before and a short while after childbirth virtually eliminate HIV infections in all newborns.

HOW DOES HIV ENTER THE BODY?

When I heard about a group of seven to ten women in Australia who had been infected with HIV from semen through artificial insemination, from the same donor, I was surprised. The common wisdom was that HIV entered the body through tiny blood vessels when mucous membranes received small breaks and tears during vaginal or anal sex.

"That can't be correct then," I thought. "Artificial insemination doesn't break or disrupt mucous membranes." How, then does HIV enter the body if not through the blood?

None of any of the immunologists I knew, when I asked them, had ever heard of any type of cells that crossed back and forth across mucosa including that of the cervix. Except one, Ralph Steinman of Rockefeller University. Ralph for many years had argued to little effect that a type of cell, dendritic macrophage, was the first to recognize foreign substances.

He called these dendritic cells sentinels, master educators of immune response. They are called dendritic cells because their branching structure serves as a wide net to capture invading organisms.

Most immunologists regarded the dendritic cell-master educator theory as nonsense. Ralph was the subject of scorn and skepticism, his papers rejected, his grant proposals repeatedly denied by skeptical review committees. The accepted theory of how our immune systems determine whether or not a substance is foreign put the spotlight on a more common cell in the immune system, the macrophage. I was aware of the macrophage theory because my mentor and boss at Dana-Farber, Baruj Benacerraf, won a share of the 1980 Nobel Prize for proposing it. It turned out that Baruj was right, but not fully right. That is very much how science goes.

Ralph explained to me in his office that humans have dendritic cells in all of our tissues, but especially in mucous membranes. Mucous membrane lining the cervix helps prevent infections. Dendritic macrophages migrate across mucosa of the cervix into the vagina then return to the surrounding lymph nodes.

"That's it!" I thought.

I was aware that uncircumcised men also have a bit of mucous membrane under the foreskin, and that dendritic cells travel back and forth across that membrane too. Ah, I thought. Dendritic cells could be the Trojan horse that carries the virus into the body. That hypothesis later gained support from studies showing the rate of HIV infection in circumcised men was far lower than their uncircumcised brethren.

I knew immediately that we needed to learn as much as we could, as fast as we could, in our lab about dendritic cells and their roles in the immune system. Yet very few people in the world had done any serious work with dendritic cells. "Is there anyone in your lab I can recruit to join mine?" I asked him.

"You're in luck," Ralph replied.

Erik Langhoff, a Danish physician, was finishing his postdoctoral fellowship at Rockefeller. He had been studying how the immune system responds to and often rejects transplanted tissues when the surging AIDS epidemic caught his interest. He studied what cells might be susceptible to growing the AIDS virus, centering his research on Ralph Steinman's singular expertise: dendritic cells. Ralph himself was not interested in HIV-related research and was happy to help Erik find another home.

"You'll like him," Ralph said. "He knows how to purify these cells. He's intelligent, hard working and easy to get along with."

Purifying dendritic cells in those days was more art than science, and Erik had learned from a Picasso. Yet scientists governing federal funding for AIDS were not interested in Erik's experiments. At least three or four of his grant applications were rejected during his first years in my lab. "Don't worry," I told him. "I have the money to support you. You will get that grant."

One day, he burst into my office. "Look at this!! HIV loves to grow on dendritic cells," he said. "I have never seen such wild growth." This was good work, but not the full story. We consulted with Ralph Steinman, and Ralph was happy to set us straight. He pointed out that what Erik had seen likely was a mixture of T cells *and* dendritic cells that turbocharged the growth of HIV. Many experiments later, my lab determined that all of us were right. Yes. HIV infects dendritic cells, but poorly. More significant was how the virus stuck like glue *to the surface* of dendritic cells.

This, we realized, was a deadly pairing. The virus rides into the body *on* dendritic cells as well as *in* dendritic cells. Dendritic cells become both infected with HIV and a messenger carrying HIV. They appeared to be sentinels for first responses in the immune system, carrying virus particles through the cells then providing support for the virus to replicate before the virus is released when infected T cells replicate.

In other words, when those dendritic cells bearing HIV on their surface or infected by HIV contact T cells, membrane to membrane, perfect conditions for rapid transmission and growth of HIV are created.

MASTER EDUCATORS: DENDRITIC MACROPHAGES

I began attending conferences on the biology of dendritic macrophages. I learned that they were not only sentinels, they were the master educators of what is called the adaptive immune response, so good at what they do that they could induce an immune response to a foreign substance even when presented with that substance outside the body. Once reintroduced, they taught the body's immune system to reject that substance. I was amazed when I learned that some researchers believed the body might even reject some of its own substances if the reintroduced dendritic cells had been presented with that substance outside the body.

"Wow," I thought. That means you can break tolerance, the body's process to protect against damage by our own immune systems. Maybe we can use the power of the dendritic cells to kill cancer cells. Cancer cells escape immune destruction in part because they are our own cells and the body tolerates them. I thought, "We will introduce the cancer tissue to a patient's own dendritic cells outside the body, then reintroduce the dendritic cells back into the body to teach the immune system to kill the cancer."

As I describe below, I created a new biotechnology company to test this idea, Activated Cell Therapy Inc., financed with start-up funds from my friends at HealthCare Ventures. The company, eventually renamed

Dendreon, developed what I believe is the first FDA approved cell-based immunotherapy, a drug (actually a cell-based procedure) to treat prostate cancer called Provenge.

EDUCATING THE IMMUNE SYSTEM TO TREAT CANCER

There were many times during these years when my knowledge of designing and treating patients with anticancer drugs helped me think through various HIV mysteries and find solutions.

We knew by now that we could stimulate the entire immune system of an animal with dendritic cells. When we exposed dendritic cells in a test tube to a foreign substance, then injected those cells back into the source animal, the animal's immune system snapped to attention. The foreign substance was subdued quickly, with no sign of illness impact.

"Suppose we purify dendritic cells from the blood of a cancer patient, then expose those cells to cells from the patient's own tumor?" I wondered. "Will that teach the immune system to treat the cancer as a foreign invader? Put another way, can we use dendritic cells to educate a patient's immune system to fight their own cancer?"

A good reason to start another company and find out. I learned that two Stanford professors, Ed Engelman and Sam Strober, had discovered efficient ways to purify dendritic cells from blood. Our company, initially called Activated Cell Therapy and later Dendreon, produced the first live cell cancer therapy approved by the Food and Drug Administration—a prostate cancer treatment that was derived from my HIV research, not my cancer research. That approval in 2010 validated long held expectations among cancer researchers and physicians that a patient's immune system could be mobilized to fight cancer.[115] Immunotherapies today are the great new hope for treating and curing cancer.

A SECOND WINDOW INTO INFECTION: THE M CELL

About two thirds of our immune system lies just outside of our intestinal tract. Its job is to recognize and protect us from all that is in our gut, which includes most of our internal microbial universe.[116]

HIV infections were known to be commonly transmitted through anal sex. I wondered, "Does HIV find another way into rectal mucosa other than through dendritic cells?" If there is another way and we are able to identify it, maybe that discovery would lead us to a drug or set of drugs that could block that path to HIV infection, or somehow stimulate immunity to HIV within the rectal mucosa against the alternative path.

I learned that a cell with unusual properties, the M cell, creates exactly such an alternative path in the lower gut. When M cells encounter a particle of a certain size and surface content—a virus being the right size—they engulf that particle, providing a window for the immune system to see what is going on with it. M cells then transport the particle, intact, across the mucosal membrane directly to a lymph node loaded with T cells on the other side of the membrane.

Could the M cell be another route by which HIV entered the body?

To test this hypothesis, we placed live virus into a short section of live intestine, sealed both ends, then sliced it into separate sections. This last step enabled us to produce fabulous electron microscope images that resembled still shots from a motion picture. We could see the virus traveling from outside the gut section to the inside, where infectable T cells waited to receive it.

Our hunch was correct. Some virus was stuck to the surface of M cells. Others were surrounded by the M cell membrane. Still others inside the cells were surrounded by a protective bubble. "We have our culprit," I told our team. "The M cells are a window for virus infection." What a tricky customer is HIV. Now we had identified two windows for how HIV is transmitted: by dendritic cells and M cells.

HIV RESEARCH BOLSTERS GENE THERAPY

Most retroviruses infect only growing cells. The vast majority of cells in our body are resting, not growing. Yet here was another characteristic that made HIV a unique retrovirus: HIV infects both growing and resting cells. I wondered if there might be some way we could exploit HIV's dual capacity for infection.

Gene therapy was one field that had this potential, because one of the main problems with gene therapy is introducing genes into resting cells. Perhaps a modified, harmless version of HIV could do just that. If so, counter intuitively, we could exploit the virus of the deadly AIDS scourge as a useful tool for a new medicine.

A new postdoctoral student just arrived in my lab from England, Mark Poznansky, was eager to try. After Mark created a strain of HIV that could enter but not leave infected cells, he replaced part of the virus genome with a gene that specified a protein that turned cells green. A population of resting cells exposed to this hybrid virus turned green as well. Mark succeeded in what we set out to do: Create a vector to bring new genes into either growing or resting human cells.

It was an important discovery. Modified HIV used to carry genes into cells for gene therapy is now the favored tool for gene therapy. The name has been changed to protect the innocent. They are now called lentivirus vectors, a name derived from the class of retroviruses to which HIV belongs.

A BITTERSWEET DAY

It would be accurate to describe Ralph Steinman as grumpy during those years he counseled me. As I said, hardly anyone in his profession respected his work or theories on dendritic cells going back to when he co-discovered them in 1973. Ralph was very proud of his discoveries. I am certain he found the criticism and opposition corrosive emotionally.

It was gratifying for me to see Ralph receive the recognition he deserved by the turn of the century, winning several awards. A great deal of the advancing knowledge and treatment of major medical conditions, infections, autoimmune diseases, cancer and more was based in part on his research.

The day he received the Nobel Prize for Physiology or Medicine, October 3, 2011, was bittersweet for all of us who knew him. Three days before, Ralph had died of pancreatic cancer at age sixty eight.

Ralph Steinman is the only winner of a Nobel Prize ever honored posthumously.[117] He believed in his work. He persisted.

22

AIDS: MOBILIZING
THE RESPONSE

How great a danger does HIV pose to the world?

I had my fears. But were they justified? I set loose a flurry of inquiries seeking more perspective, asking the best epidemiologists, doctors and medical scientists I could reach for their opinions and insights.

One physician and virologist specializing in infectious disease at the Walter Reed Army Medical Center had what appeared to be some of the best early data and answers. Robert Redfield[118] had recently completed a comprehensive study, testing for HIV infection in eight hundred thousand men and women on active duty in the U.S. Armed Forces. He was overseeing counseling for all those infected.

"I am very disturbed by what we found," Bob, a deeply religious man with a finely tuned social conscience, told me. "First the good news. Infection rates in our service members so far are low, less the two percent. I hope we can keep it that way."

"But here is why I worry," he said. "We developed a program for married couples. When one of the two was HIV positive, we brought the uninfected spouse into a private room for counseling. We were tough, saying, 'Your husband (or wife) is infected with a deadly virus that is almost always fatal.

There is no cure. If you have unprotected sex with your partner, the chances are very high that you too will become infected and probably die.'"

"Bill, what is your guess as to how many of them followed our warning to use condoms?"

"Most," I replied. "People don't want to die."

Bob looked at me for a moment. "That's what I thought too," he said. "Our data tells a different story. The answer is less than one third."

I was stunned. "If that is true there is little hope for controlling the epidemic through public messaging alone," I said. The three points identified for a public health campaign underway aimed at slowing the AIDS epidemic were: abstinence, be faithful and use condoms (designed for easy recall as A-B-C). "If people don't respond to the lethal danger of unprotected sex with their husband or wife we are in real trouble," I said. "Changing sexual behavior is going to be a lot tougher than giving up smoking, and that has been hard enough."

SCIENCE IS PART OF LIFE

Looking back now, public health campaigns did make a positive impact in subsequent years, helping reduce adult and teenage smoking by more than fifty percent. But human sexuality, the sex drive, is deeply imbedded in our nature. A movie from the early '70s, *The Emigrants*, about a Swedish couple struggling for a better life with their children in Minnesota, captures this dramatically. The character played by Liv Ullmann is warned that if she becomes pregnant again, "you will die." But, to no avail. She and her husband in the story, played by Max von Sidow, continue having sex, she becomes pregnant, and she does die.

In one sense, what Bob and I examined was a stark question of health and science, analyzing data and predicting human behavior. But it was more than that. Science is not removed from life. Science is part of life.

I trained my eye beyond science to understand the entire human experience as broadly as I could, all the complexities of history, art, culture and politics. To know the human spirit. Human culture is extremely deep. Our behavior, how we are built, the way we think goes back at least a billion years or more. A huge amount of information goes into making a living organism, especially a living thinking organism.

A DEEPER REALITY

Whatever you discover through science, you are only discovering one part of a deeper reality. All life in any environment is connected in many ways.

Across an environment as large as Planet Earth the possibilities for connections are limitless, unfathomable. You can never discover the full picture. For an environment as large as the universe... well, where to begin?

"It is very unrealistic to believe people will change their sexual behavior in a major way," I remarked during a 1986 public lecture in Cambridge.[119] "Let me give you an example. Everybody knew in the nineteenth century how syphilis was contracted. They also knew it was a very serious disease. Yet if you look at the statistics at the turn of the century, at least ten to fifteen percent of American citizens had syphilis. It isn't that people didn't know how they got it, it's that they didn't change their lifestyle accordingly."

The vivid memory of Liv Ullmann in *The Emigrants* contributed to my dark thoughts about how terrible this new epidemic could be.

Nearly all the early AIDS patients were thought to be in Europe, the United States or the Caribbean. I had a chilling premonition of why AIDS would become a global pandemic at a Paris meeting in 1983 of doctors from all over the world including Asia, Africa and South America. We heard first that Brazil, Mexico and Southeast Asia had a few diagnosed cases, but then Belgian doctors based Zaire, now the Democratic Republic of Congo, said, "No AIDS here. We report no cases."

Their counterparts, physicians working in Belgium, scoffed. "Then they must catch AIDS on the plane flying to Brussels," they said. "Our wards are full of patients with full blown AIDS from the Congo." Within a few months, a team organized by the U.S. Centers for Disease Control was reporting five new cases a week in just one hospital in the Congo's capital, Kinshasa. An unrecognized galloping AIDS epidemic had already hit Central Africa.

There was more. I relaxed slightly as the dean of Kyoto's Medical School was about to give his comment, expecting a candid scientific assessment. He was the administrator who hosted me in Kyoto the summer before for my HTLV research. I knew him well, or so I thought. But I winced when I heard him say, "No AIDS in Japan. We are not worried because there are no homosexuals in Japan." Neither statement was true. He knew this, and I knew that he knew.

"Denial of reality in the face of disease is worse than the enemy," I muttered to myself.

In the years to come fear, ignorance and prejudice were on full display around the world. There were a few exceptions. Two countries that had the most rapid and positive responses were Thailand and Brazil. Their governments and people confronted AIDS for what it was—a new and deadly disease, transmitted sexually from men to women, women to men and men to men. They all took whatever measures available to reduce infections and protect their people by promoting HIV tests, condoms and, eventually, free anti-HIV treatments. Every military in the world reacted the same way. Their view, "Let's not blind ourselves and pretend soldiers are saints. They are not. They behave as humans."

Bob Redfield's surveys in time would become influential in demonstrating heterosexual transmission of AIDS. Five years later, the Army reported that either the husband or wife in more than three quarters of uninfected couples in the study that did not use condoms became infected with HIV.

We learned more about the epidemic in Africa as the year progressed. It was not confined to the Congo. Many sub-Saharan countries were impacted, in some cases with infection rates as high as five percent of the population—and rising. Most infections in Africa were almost exclusively the result of sex between men and women, not men and men or intravenous drug use. In sex workers the numbers were much higher, twenty to thirty percent.

"If what is happening in Africa happens here in the U.S. we are looking at twelve million Americans dying of AIDS," I estimated. "Even half that number is horrible to contemplate."

I asked myself, "What is my responsibility in the face of a pending disaster of such magnitude?" The range of potential activities could have been dizzying at first. This is how I broke it down, a focused four pronged agenda for action:

Mobilize medical and science community.

Engage civil society.

Speak out.

De-stigmatize the disease.

We needed to mobilize the medical and scientific community to use our most powerful tools to find ways to treat and possibly cure the disease, but, as we saw in the opening chapter, we needed much more money for HIV research. Without the money we would not be able to recruit the scientists we needed.

We had to engage civil society, create nonprofit organizations like the American Cancer Society to raise money and convince government to do more.

I had to speak out in public forums, media interviews, private receptions, meetings with AIDS activist groups and more, applying all I learned as an antiwar activist to alert the public to the danger ahead and what they could do to protect themselves and their families. With cancer fighting strategies of the Lasker Foundation as a model, I was certain that an informed public would put pressure on Congress and the administration to do more.

To de-stigmatize the disease, I needed to dispel the image of AIDS as a disease of fringe populations... homosexual men, drug users and Caribbean immigrants. "Spread the message that you cannot contract HIV from causal contact, sneezing or otherwise," I told myself. "Let people know that sexually active people are at risk, including teenagers and even the elderly. Condoms will save lives."

SCIENTISTS, CELEBRITIES AND AMFAR

The first nonprofit group organized to confront the epidemic, the AIDS Medical Foundation, was organized in 1983 in New York City. Its leaders were Joseph Sonnebend, an infectious disease specialist who treated many of the early AIDS cases in New York City and an early advocate promoting safe sex in the gay community, and Mathilde Krim. Mathilde was a geneticist and immunologist with a long history of supporting cancer research and myriad social causes together with her husband Arthur Krim, head of United Artists and former Democratic Party finance chairman and adviser to Lyndon Johnson.

When we met, Mathilde was in the early stages of joining forces with the California based National AIDS Research Foundation, established by Elizabeth Taylor and Michael Gottlieb, the first doctor to describe AIDS in 1981. Their merged organizations officially became the American Foundation for AIDS Research, amfAR, later in 1985.

Mathilde and I hit it off immediately. She said, "You know as much about the virus as anyone. I agree with your priorities: fund research, raise awareness and de-stigmatize AIDS. Please join our board. We will need a scientific advisory committee. Are you willing to be the chair and recruit like-minded scientists and doctors?"

I was delighted to find in Mathilde someone with social and political connections who saw the disease threat as I did. For the next five years I worked closely with amfAR shuttling back and forth between our meetings in Los Angeles and New York as we established ourselves as the leading nonprofit anti-AIDS foundation. amfAR's close connection with Hollywood was a great help.

Elizabeth Taylor became the most famous advocate for research and for treating AIDS victims with compassion. She was one of the most passionate, articulate and effective public figures to warn of the dangers. Close friends of hers and even a family member (from a blood transfusion) were already infected. And of course, she was aware that Rock Hudson, a dear friend, was seriously ill.

It was through amfAR that I recruited Elizabeth to go to Congress later that year. Some people in the general public had the impression she was a diva but that was not true at all. She was warm, unpretentious, well educated and fun to be around.

At first the nonprofit's governing board was deeply divided when we met in the Westwood conference room of octogenarian oilman and cancer research philanthropist Armand Hammer. Mathilde, Michael Gottlieb and I wanted to use whatever money we raised to fund research. I proposed funding young scientists to begin HIV research in the labs.

"We can issue a call for rapid turnaround grants," I said, referring to a process we pioneered at the Leukemia Society of America when I was on the board to quickly channel funds into fields of priority research. "We will promise to review funding applications and distribute money within six weeks. To recruit as many researchers as possible, we should limit the amount per grant to cover the work of only one postdoctoral fellow per application, not multiple researchers in any given lab. We will give the grants to any postdoc who applies from a good lab."

A few singer-songwriters in the group, such as Barry Manilow and Carol Bayer Sanger, were not so sure. "Our friends need help," they pleaded. "We should give them money to live, or at least to make their last days more pleasant." Whatever money we raised should go for food, transportation, nursing care and other social support for people dying from AIDS, they said. Like other celebrities on the board, David Geffen counted many personal friends suffering from AIDS. He had deep ties in the entertainment industry as founder and head of Geffen Records and a former top talent manager at the William Morris Agency. Yet David also was passionate about stopping the epidemic.

"I understand the need to help those with AIDS," he said. "However, if we don't find a way to stop the disease, we will only end up having more and more people to support. We need science to stop the epidemic. I vote for Bill's proposal."

David was persuasive. His argument clinched the issue, setting the policy for what is now thirty five years of amfAR research grants. I could not have done it without him. Many of our country's leading HIV/AIDS scientists today got their start from those early amfAR grants. In all, through 2019, amfAR had raised more than five hundred fifty million dollars and funded thirty three hundred scientists in HIV research.

MEDIA BLITZ, ROUGH AND TUMBLE

The next two years were busy. Almost every day we were learning more at Dana-Farber about how HIV caused the disease, where we might attack the virus with drugs and other strategies to stop it. We weren't alone. With new money pouring in from Congress and private donors, scientists all over the United States were eager to join the fray. I crisscrossed the country speaking at universities and research institutes, responding to requests to explain what we knew about HIV and help jump start new research projects.

For a time I was one of the few scientists willing to talk about HIV and AIDS to the reporters. News of Rock Hudson's illness and rapid decline before his death in early October 1985 shook the nation, jolting people everywhere to ask themselves, Am I at risk? Are my children at risk? Will the disease be confined to a few risk groups: homosexuals, drug users, blood transfusion recipients? Is AIDS transmitted by casual contact, touching, sneezing, kissing?

The AIDS story, long shunned by editors and news directors of mainstream media, now was featured on the covers of *Time* and *Newsweek* and the front page of *USA Today*. AIDS segments increasingly were "next up," a topic for morning programs with millions of viewers, ABC's *Good Morning America* and NBC's *Today*, as well as network evening news programs anchored by Peter Jennings and Tom Brokaw. I was interviewed by them all.

One morning I was in the green room at NBC Studios in Rockefeller Center, waiting for my segment, a live interview by co-anchor Jane Pauley. A minute before air time, an assistant poked in her head. "Oh, by the way, we're going to have somebody on five minutes before you," she said. "It's a concerned mother who just took her kid out of school because of AIDS."

Shortly our segment is underway and I am sitting on the same small couch under klieg lights next to this distressed mother. Jane turns to the mother. "So you have pulled your two young children out of school to prevent them from contracting AIDS."

"Yes. I am terrified that some kids may bite or scratch or even sneeze."

Jane looks to me. "Doctor, how do you respond to her concern?"

"May ask a question?" I replied, then asked the mother, "Do you have teenage children?"

"Yes, two," she said.

"It is teenage children who are at risk, not your young children," I counseled. "The virus is not transmitted by causal contact but it is transmitted sexually. My advice is to focus your concern on your teenagers, the need for caution and the details of safer sex."

The public forum is rough and tumble. Medical and scientific fact clash continuously with political realities and religious beliefs. Facts do not change beliefs easily. Denial, deflection and blame are the coin of the realm.

For example, in a story at the end of 1985, "The Latest Scientific Facts" about AIDS, *Discover* magazine proclaimed: "Heterosexuals are virtually risk free," and blamed gay men for much of the epidemic. "Anal sex is the essential element in the AIDS story," the article asserted. The virus "may have come (to the United States) by way of Haiti, a popular vacation spot for homosexuals."

In 2005, *Discover* published a mea culpa of sorts with the headline, "20 Years Ago in *Discover*: Misunderstanding AIDS." The article suggested that interviews with more than a dozen "leading epidemiologists" in the United States, Britain and France, and authoritative reports in publications such as the *Journal of the American Medical Association* and the *Lancet* had led it astray.

The original article, the retrospective continued, did quote "one scientist whose decidedly minority views turned out to be correct. William Haseltine, then a pathologist at Harvard University, argued that the virus was fast becoming a heterosexual disease. 'To think that we're so different from people in the Congo is a nice, comfortable position, but it probably isn't so,' Haseltine told *Discover*. 'It's heterosexual promiscuity. The more lovers, the better the chance of being infected.'"

Bob Redfield and I were accused of being self aggrandizing alarmists by people with different political or social agendas and, sadly, even some of our colleagues and peers in science and medicine. We were attacked for speaking out, often viciously. I've learned over the years that what remains in many people's memories is that we were controversial, not that our opinions were correct. We both paid a price for that irony, Bob with his job at Walter Reed and I in a protracted tenure battle at Harvard.

THE PRINCESS AND THE AIDS BABIES

"You must meet her. You will love her," Deeda Blair is urging me.

A medical philanthropist *non pareil*, Deeda learned the art of convening people of wealth with scientists—who depended on that wealth to pursue vital cancer discoveries—at the side of Mary Lasker. She is guiding me in 1987 toward the good graces of Marguerite Lippman and, we hope, the inner circle of the United Kingdom's most influential AIDS fundraising organization, the AIDS Crisis Trust. Deeda added, "Marguerite has rounded up the 'great and the good' of London for AIDS Crisis Trust."

Deeda was right, and effective, as usual. Marguerite quickly recruited me as her scientific advisor. Her signature fundraising event for the Trust was a Hollywood movie premier hosted on Saturdays by Princess Diana and often attended by stars of the new film. In one of the Trust's bi-monthly strategy sessions, set in the living room of Marguerite's elegant West End townhouse, I made yet another appeal. I had been pushing for months for members of the Trust to use their social connections to persuade a member of the royal family to speak out about AIDS.

"It will make a difference not just in England but around the world," I argued. "People everywhere look up to British royalty." Marguerite, staunchly in my camp on this, added, "The Princess's best friend from the ballet world, Adrian Ward Jackson, has convinced her that she can make a real difference."

"The Princess" was Princess Diana, the Trust's headliner. Her mother, Lady Spencer, was a member. After a few weeks, Marguerite Lippman announced the welcome news—"Princess Diana is ready to visit an AIDS ward"—in her slow drawl. The same languid tones of Monroe, Louisiana, she used to coach Elizabeth Taylor how to "talk southern" in *Raintree County* and *Cat on a Hot Tin Roof*. Marguerite was a close friend of Tennessee Williams.

The pictures were stunning. Princess Diana shaking hands with men, weakened and obviously ill, some in wheelchairs. Princess Diana holding and hugging AIDS babies, their tiny fingers wrapped around one of hers. The images drew extraordinary coverage on front pages and newscasts around the world.

For the next eight years, until her tragic death, Princess Diana did more than anyone else—visiting AIDS clinics in many countries with photographers present, shaking hands with adult patients, holding babies and young children—to soften the public's perception of people with AIDS.

Moreover, I am convinced that those images from the very outset did more to de-stigmatize AIDS than all government campaigns and pronouncements combined. Never again did reporters ask me, "Can I catch AIDS by being around sick people?"

DESPERATION AND COMPOUND Q

From the early '80s as AIDS infections began to soar, gay community activists became furious, staging angry protests against the FDA, NIH and scientific institutes. They demanded access to any experimental drug with a glimmer of potential to slow or cure the disease. But the FDA stonewalled, insisting on testing protocols that could span several years.

That pressure in fact did influence fast tracking of AZT for legal use after an initial clinical trial with thirty six people infected with HIV. Half were given AZT, half were not—this is how clinical trials are conducted. Within three months conditions of patients given the drug improved dramatically, patients not given the drug deteriorated further. Some AIDS activists were outraged that eighteen men in the trial were untreated, a searing expression of the emotional intensity of the times, despite the fact that the trial yielded the first real promise for an AIDS cure.

In private meetings at the NIH and amfAR, I saw this intensity surge over the next two years, pushing activists to new extremes in their desperation for any cure. Anthony Fauci, head of the National Institute of Allergy and Infectious Diseases and one our strongest allies in government for accelerating AIDS research, had recruited me earlier to his grant approving council, an official group that also sought or provided advice to people in government, civil and scientific communities.

Tony had included several leaders of the gay community and African American groups at these meetings. They were deeply suspicious—that the government was willfully too slow (gays) or their needs were being ignored (African Americans).

I got to know and like Martin Delaney, an intelligent, courageous leader of the gay community, through these meetings. Martin never tested HIV positive, but had dozens of friends who had died from AIDS and more among what by the late '80s were hundreds of thousands of people living with AIDS and no known cure.

Martin had organized what he described as "medically supervised guerrilla trials" in previous years that did not have federal approval. He now was championing a Chinese abortion and anticancer drug, derived from a cucumber plant grown in southeast Asia, because it had been shown to kill HIV-infected cells in a test tube. The drug, trichosanthin, widely known as Compound Q, was quite toxic. Martin, a lay person with deep knowledge of AIDS research and clinical trials, as many AIDS activists had, organized and promoted a trial of the drug for AIDS patients. With news photographers capturing the scene, he openly handed out envelopes containing trichosanthin.[120]

"Look, what you guys are doing is dangerous," I told him later, trying to convince him not to proceed. "You need to do controlled trials, with careful dose escalation. We have decades of experience trying to solve really difficult problems like cancer with powerful toxic drugs. If you are not careful, people will die."

Remembering Tom Frei's counsel years before at Dana-Farber, I added, "The real heroes of cancer, and all this kind of experimental drug work, are the patients that are willing to trust you with their lives. That is really what they are doing. If you do not proceed very carefully, you can accelerate the demise of the people who are putting their trust in you."

"We understand that but this is an emergency," Martin said. "I don't believe you scientists and doctors are doing what you can. The way you do clinical trials is way too slow. Not only that, you insist on randomized trials where some people get the new drug and others don't. Don't you realize people are dying because they don't get the drug? We have to do something and you guys are taking too much time."

His Compound Q trial unfolded. It was a failure, not slowing the disease and, although I have not seen any published data, likely killing several of his and other gay leaders' friends. Martin, chastened, soon became a strong partner with us in pushing through reforms at the FDA. These reforms accelerated approval protocols for new and emerging drugs, reforms that have saved thousands of lives. After some early fireworks, African American leaders became vital partners, explaining the rationale for clinical trials and rallying their communities in other ways.

Martin was responsible for the NIH decision to require groups with strong interest in a new drug to participate in the review process. That policy is now a matter of law. Martin's legacy is enshrined in a special grants program the NIH named in his honor.

TEAMING ACADEMIC AND PHARMA LABS

After my HIV research funding appeal was rebuffed by the pharmaceutical companies, I suggested taking a different approach with Big Pharma to Tony Fauci and others on our council.

"Suppose we give them money in a new grants program to start AIDS research," I said. "I propose we make relatively large grants to academic labs interested in drug development."

"But they don't know how to do drug development," someone objected, immediately. I barely got the first sentence out.

"That's right," I went on. "But they do understand the virus and they have rapid screening tests that the companies can use. In any event, my lab has already done most of the basic work. These grants I have in mind would be conditional; applying labs would have to have a pharma partner. Once the companies hire a few people to start the research, they will have it embedded in their budget cycles. The proposals must be joint, one academic lab and one or more pharma partners. Our grants must be large enough to interest both parties."

The council embraced the concept. Soon agreements were struck with several top U.S. academic labs and companies such as Bristol-Myers, Pfizer and Johnson & Johnson. Grants initially were large, between six hundred thousand and eight hundred thousand dollars, with a quarter of that going to academic labs and the rest to the companies. That is how almost all of the major pharmaceutical companies got involved in HIV research. Many drugs

My Lifelong Fight Against Disease

approved today by the FDA owe their origin to this innovation, known as the Cooperative Drug Development Program.

In the grant program's first years, my Dana-Farber lab supplied the assays for *tat*, *rev* as well as integrase and protease proteins. We had discovered the HIV protease was a primary target for drugs, and in time these protease inhibitors became an essential biochemical ingredient in many AIDS drugs. Our lab licensed protease inhibitor technology to five companies. These inhibitors provided, when given with AZT or other reverse transcriptase inhibitors, the first durable remissions to AIDS and by the early '90s through combinations of drugs prevented those with HIV infection from ever contracting the disease.

The commercial development of this protease inhibitor was a direct result of the Cooperative Drug Development Program. My lab supplied the protease gene, and Cambridge BioScience, a company I started years before (the main story in another chapter), produced the protein in large quantities. Scientists at Agouron, a West Coast biotech company that developed drugs, determined the detailed protein structure and designed an effective inhibitor. It helped that one of Agouron's founders, John Abelson, had been a friend for years since we became drinking buddies at Gordon Conferences. The drug they created, nelfinavir (Viracept), was one of the first protease inhibitors to reach the market.

EUROPE CAMPAIGNS

The fashion world was devastated, with hundreds of high profile designers, models and executives succumbing to AIDS. Several leading designers reached out to me through their contacts with Hollywood and amfAR with urgent requests. Could I advise them, for example, on how to help de-stigmatize HIV/AIDS in their own country? Yes, of course.

I worked with Valentino and his partner Giancarlo Giammetti on gala events in Italy. The centerpiece, a major news story in Italy, was an award presented to Elizabeth Taylor one night at the international conference on HIV/AIDS in Florence, where I had the delightful honor of introducing her. "People living with AIDS need our love and support," she said in her acceptance remarks. "Please, please help them." Karl Lagerfeld and Chanel followed the same script in Paris; this time with awards to Catherine Deneuve and other celebrated French actors.

Easily the best experience for me among many AIDS-related events and campaigns in Europe was collaborating with Niki de Saint Phalle. A fabulous French-American sculptor, painter and filmmaker living in Paris, Niki put all her talent and energy into a book to help teenagers and children understand AIDS. Translated into German, Italian and Japanese, the book highlighted what was and was not risky behavior. *AIDS: You Can't Catch It Holding Hands*, an illustrated letter to her son Philip, was an arresting, creative way to educate and inform thousands of young people about the dangers of unprotected sex and needle sharing by intravenous drug use. In all, seventy thousand books were distributed free in schools. A 1988 *People* magazine article quoted me, quite accurately: "This book is crucial."

I met Niki through Etienne Baulieu, a great scientist and friend perhaps best known for his discovery of the "morning after pill" and even more for his advocacy for the pill in the face of fierce opposition in France and the rest of the world. "Niki is writing a book to help children and teenagers understand AIDS," Etienne explained to me over one of those delicious French lunches. "Please help her. Make sure all the facts are correct."

Niki became one of my closest friends. She died much too young from exposure to toxic chemicals she had used for her sculptures.

FAR SIGHTED RESEARCH

I got a lot of different people thinking about and working on AIDS. I was not alone. Other people helped, but I played an essential role in the early response, speeding up the whole process. It shows how one person can make a difference.

If you are really determined, energetic and have the right vision, you can make a big difference. That difference, if you are lucky, can save hundreds of thousands, even millions of lives. It is a wonderful feeling to know that I was able to do that.

That fact that AIDS appeared when it did, in the late 1970s and early 1980s, was fortuitous. Had the disease entered the international population earlier, say during World War II when men and women were moving en masse all over the globe, we would have been at a loss as scientists in knowing what to do.

But with two decades of intense research on retroviruses, and funding support through the government's Special Virus Cancer Program, some of us by the early '80s were prepared to meet the challenge. My lab and Bob Gallo's labs were already investigating another human virus, HTLV, that would closely resemble the microbiology and mode of transmission of the HIV retrovirus.

By 2020, thirty two million people had died from AIDS, almost forty million were living with HIV infection and, of those, twenty five million were receiving antiretroviral treatments, according to UNAIDS. Without timely warning and massive intervention by scientific and medical communities supported by private and government funding, the toll would have been much greater.

Those few of us who committed to the search for a human retrovirus had made a lucky bet with our careers. The three hundred twenty million dollars in supplemental appropriations Congress approved for HIV/AIDS research in the fiscal 1986 federal budget grew quickly, and for many years has remained steady at about two billion five hundred million dollars.

Far sighted research paid off in the early '80s, and, as millions of people with AIDS living nearly normal lives likely would agree, far sighted research has continued to pay off. It will continue to pay off if we as a country recommit to supporting our best and brightest scientists.

23

"AREN'T YOU BILLY HASELTINE?"

As the Reagan administration continued to ignore the gay community, scattered appeals from Congress and advancing science, it was clear by early 1985 that we had to rely on wealthy private donors in the near term to help fund more HIV research.

But, where to go?

Boston was a non-starter; there were some generous contributors, but not many. New York was locked up; yes, many wealthy contributors to big science, but the honey pots were surrounded by thousands of bees with stingers aimed outward to keep you away. London? Not much tradition there for supporting science research.

But what about Los Angeles? I thought Los Angeles could be interesting. The wealthy L.A. community was not accustomed to giving large donations to science, but they might consider doing so for a disease so devastating to one of their marquee businesses, Hollywood.

I thought, "If I go out there, and say to them, 'I can help you solve your problem,' I think I can raise a lot of money." A Harvard scientist working the L.A. entertainment world for money to fund AIDS research might pay off.

The strategy was solid. I would elicit hundreds of contributions and letters of gratitude for our work from many people, including donors themselves suffering from AIDS or with friends or family with HIV. But I would have raised millions more if Harvard's development office had been more competent.

The first disaster ruined a great relationship I was building with David Geffen through amfAR on my trips out to L.A.

One day David said, "I would like to give you twenty five million dollars to build an AIDS institute to treat patients and do research at Harvard."

Being well acquainted with Harvard's development office formulas, I immediately replied, as I saw David forming a cube with his hands, "We can leverage that to build a one hundred twenty million dollar building." David glanced at his hands, and added firmly, "... with my parents' name on the top."

I said, "Okay, I think we can do that."

I explained all this to Baruj Benacerraf as soon as I returned to Boston. "We have this twenty five million dollar gift that we have to leverage five or six to one. You have this space. You want to build this building. It has got to be a cube building, with the name on top."

It was not long before David called me. The deans of Harvard's medical school and school of public health had just left his office. "They want me to give my twenty five million dollars and let them decide how to spend it for AIDS research," he said. "I told them, and you can tell them again, that they are not going to get my money unless they come up with the plan I want."

As perturbed as David, probably more, I called Baruj. Baruj was a true hero of mine, a great scientist, mentor and wonderful human being. "What the hell is this?" I said. "We may lose this building now." Baruj was embarrassed. "I had to tell the deans, but maybe I shouldn't have," he said. "I will talk to them."

Whatever they discussed, the development executives must have deflected Baruj's appeal because they soon were bearing down even more. Not once, but twice in the next few months they descended on David at Geffen Records.

David now was dumbfounded, angry. "Bill, I have had it. They showed me a cockamamie building on top of another one, tall and twisted. Tell them to never darken my door again. I told you what kind of building I wanted, exactly what I wanted. Do not call me again. I am giving the money to UCLA. They agreed to build the building exactly as I wanted."

Years later, riding big screen blockbusters such as *Saving Private Ryan* through his partnership with Stephen Spielberg and Jeffrey Katzenberg in their movie studio DreamWorks SKG, David Geffen made the largest private donation ever given to a medical school in the United States: *two hundred million dollars.*

"Los Angeles is my home and I want to do my part in contributing to its future," he said in a news release announcing the gift. "I have great respect and affection for UCLA and my hope is that with this gift, UCLA's doctors and researchers will be better equipped to unravel medicine's mysteries—and deliver the cures for tomorrow."

Baruj told me later that relaying my report of Geffen's pledge for a Harvard building to those deans was the biggest mistake of his career.

PICASSOS, BRAQUES, DISMAY

An interior decorator from Miami, Billy McCarty Cooper, and I met through the AIDS Crisis Trust. Billy was elegant, fashionable, very funny and a wonderful person. He wanted to help.

"Bill, you are raising money for AIDS. Come out to Los Angeles. I will give you a million dollars. My friend Rose Tarlow and I will raise tons of money," he said.

Billy's home, the setting for this big party, was beautiful. World class collection of African art. World class orchid collection. A pool in which you could swim from dining room into living room. At every turn, Picassos and early Braques commanding your gaze. Adopted shortly before the death of his very close friend, Douglas Cooper, Billy McCarty inherited these priceless paintings.

As you might imagine, high society *cum* big science events are not put together easily. You need the right combination of people, timing, glamour… a whole lot of things. The guest list Billy and Rose assembled featured Hollywood crème de la crème capped by Marvin Davis, billionaire owner of 20th Century Fox studios, and several of his very wealthy Hollywood and business friends. Actor Sidney Poitier was coming too.

Our plan was for Billy to announce his gift of one million dollars at the appointed hour. I would describe Dana-Farber's mission to conquer HIV and AIDS, gently challenge people in the audience to match Billy's donation, then slowly ratchet down requests toward smaller pledges. We anticipated a big night.

All of a sudden, with hors d'oeuvres circulating and before I could speak, these big donors with their millions of dollars started leaving. Why? Had they already made pledges? No. That afternoon someone from Dana-Farber's development office had caught wind of our event. As I learned later, Davis had about fifty thousand dollars remaining on a comparatively small prior Dana-Farber gift pledge. The development guy left this message with Davis's office on the Avenue of the Stars in Century City. "You don't have to give anything to this Dana-Farber scientist who is coming to L.A. tonight until your other pledge is finished," he said. "Tell your friends they do not have to give either."

Can you imagine how angry I was? I might have collected five million dollars or more that night for my research! Well, I eventually did raise the money, but not the money I thought I was going to raise.

"A COUPLE OF QUESTIONS FOR YOU"

"Aren't you Billy Haseltine?"

Well, I used to be, I said, smiling.

I was in the home of Paramount Pictures' chief executive on another money raising trip to L.A. when this tall attractive woman approached me. She introduced herself as an executive vice president.

"We were together on that bicycle trip in high school, remember?" she said.

Of course. What a great time.

"I remember you very well. I have a couple of questions for you."

Okay, sure.

"First of all, you would get up in the morning and zip off, and we would not see you until the night. What were you doing?"

Well, I had everything mapped out. I wanted to see the museums, historical landmarks, architecture.

"The rest of us were enjoying our slow bicycle ride through the countryside."

I enjoyed riding in the countryside too, but I did it a little faster. I really wanted to see all these things.

"Oh, okay. That makes sense. I have another question. Every so often you would put on a suit, disappear and come back late. What were you doing?"

Well, I would go to these three star restaurants. I was seventeen. I had a huge appetite and a big budget. I ordered two of everything: two appetizers, two first courses, two second courses, two desserts and two bottles of wine. I was doing research for my mom.

"Okay," she said, apparently quite satisfied. "That settles some questions I have had for a long time."

I was very pleased to have answered them, too. In a short time, Paramount made a donation to our Harvard AIDS research.

HE'S BROKE

"The president of Harvard requests your presence at dinner tonight with Robert Maxwell. We will send the directions later."

In late 1990, Robert Maxwell was a powerful press baron and one of the most controversial men in London. Born in Czechoslovakia to Yiddish speaking parents who later perished in the Holocaust with several of his siblings, an American army hero in World War II, Maxwell controlled six newspapers through his Mirror Group along with printing and book publishing firms. On this chilly day he was in New York City negotiating to acquire the financially strapped *New York Daily News*.

Maxwell had advised Harvard President Derek Bok that he was considering a donation of one hundred million dollars (the equivalent of nearly two hundred million dollars today) to the university for an AIDS research institute. He wanted to learn more about our work from President Bok and a few deans and professors over dinner. I was at my desk that morning when I received the call.

We soon were instructed to meet at what turned out to be a Harvard owned home somewhere in the Berkshires. The site was a ninety minute drive from Boston. Maxwell and a few of his aides would meet us—President Bok, deans of the medical school and school of public health, Max Essex and me.

Maxwell arrived by helicopter moments after we did. The house was cold, the décor dated... last refurbished in 1909. Think of the Addams Family house. Before dinner, Maxwell arranged us in a semicircle with himself seated at the center then, addressing us not by name but by title, fired off a series of staccato questions, each segment beginning: "President... Dean One (Medical School)... Dean Two (School of Public Health)... Professor One (me)... Professor Two (Max)."

Over dinner, I was sitting immediately to his right. About half way through dinner, an aide whispered something into his right ear and Maxwell, a burly dark featured man with a booming voice, was beaming. "Now I own the *Daily News!*" he announced. Wow, congratulations. Immediately after dinner, he and his aides are off again—womp, womp, womp—in the helicopter.

"Okay, what are our chances?" President Bok asked. "I can't really tell, but I think it's pretty good. You know he's going to other universities, but we have a great team. We are well recognized and have been there (HIV research) from the beginning. I think we have a good chance." The three others said pretty much the same thing.

It was my turn. "Gentleman, I am sorry to tell you but we don't have a snowball's chance in hell," I said. "When he is doing a business deal, Maxwell's pattern is to divert attention or give himself leverage by claiming he's going to give a lot of money for academic research.

"This now is the fourth time he's done it, and there has never been any money given," I went on. "This is a scheme to enhance his prestige. Simply put, it is a negotiating tactic that has nothing to do with us."

"How do you know that?"

"Deep research. This is all documented, on the record," I explained. "I've been reading very descriptive, unvarnished biographies."

Maxwell had let it be known some time before that he was planning to fund an AIDS research institute in Europe or America, I continued. The University of Maryland, Duke University and maybe the University of North Carolina at Chapel Hill were on a list with Harvard. I wanted to learn all I could about him.

"Oh, I will tell you something worse," I added. "He's broke. Some of my good friends in the banking community in London tell me he doesn't have a dime. He has misused funds very badly and is about to go jail. The further we stay away from this situation, the better we are going to be."

In late March, Maxwell officially took control, fleetingly, of the *Daily News*. That fall he was dead, age sixty eight, his body found floating near his yacht in the Atlantic off the Canary Islands. British investigators soon declared that Maxwell had embezzled four hundred and sixty million British pounds from his companies' pension funds, the equivalent then of one billion dollars.

ENTIRELY CONFIDENTIAL, IN FRANCE

Around this time, anticipated advances in HIV research and AIDS treatments in France had fallen short of expectations. With HIV infections, AIDS deaths and public pressures soaring, government officials needed solutions.

"We are in a quandary," Jacques Attali, special adviser to President Francois Mitterand, told me. We were meeting privately in his elegant Élysée Palace office a few steps across from the president's. I had met Jacques through friends on many trips to visit scientific colleagues in Paris and enjoy France's great restaurants and museums. "I am receiving conflicting reports," Jacques went on. "Some say we are on the right track. Others that our top scientists are leading us astray."

The French government had been reeling from a scandal of its own making. High level officials had delayed by several months approval of a clotting factors screening test for HIV from the U.S., trying but failing to provide enough time for a French rival to rush its test into the market first. "Our health authorities were advised that 'HIV antibody positive' meant 'protected.' But it wasn't true," Jacques said.

I remembered it well. An estimated twelve hundred hemophiliacs were infected by HIV, mostly through transfusions, before testing began in August 1985. Some four hundred of those infected died. Those who gave the flawed advice were never held to account, but two officials who warned of the danger were accused of overseeing supplies of the infected blood and jailed.[121]

Jacques was a leading French intellectual, a brilliant scholar and political strategist who wrote and published a new book each year even while serving as Mitterand's chief of staff.

"Bill, would you be willing to advise me and the President on our HIV/AIDS research policy and programs?" he asked. The offer was unexpected, but I told Jacques I would do whatever I could to help. "You must keep this entirely confidential," he cautioned. "I would like you to be an informal advisor."

For nearly five years, I flew to Paris every six weeks to meet privately and discuss AIDS research and policy with Jacques. One of the first questions was who should coordinate France's HIV/AIDS research policy. Mitterand had lost confidence in the original leader, Luc Montagnier.

Montagnier had advised that HIV antibodies in the blood meant protection from infection. This was a disastrous extrapolation from his previous research on polio. He also advised the government that a person had to be infected by a bacterium, *Haemophilus influenza*, in addition to HIV to contract AIDS. This, again, was entirely incorrect, a misleading theory to which Montagnier clung despite overwhelming proof to the contrary.

I suggested several candidates to Jacques, one of whom was selected.

UNDER NO CIRCUMSTANCE

All my fundraising, media interviews, consulting, teaching and public speaking elevated my reputation into the late '80s as one of the world's leading and most accessible experts on HIV and AIDS.

I often heard from people urgently seeking medical advice either for themselves, family members or friends. I was happy to refer them to the best AIDS physicians I knew, summarize current research or quickly sketch salient aspects of the epidemic, as frightening as the details were.

These contacts occasionally led to bizarre experiences. One time, friends at AIDS Crisis Trust in London asked me to meet a wealthy British aristocrat who was coming to Boston. An invitation for dinner at the Four Seasons soon followed.

The man was accompanied by two others, a young man—his son, seriously weakened by what quickly was disclosed as HIV/AIDS, and a young woman who appeared to be not quite developed mentally... not able to follow the discussion.

My host wanted to know, is there any way his son's infected sperm could be cleansed of HIV so that he could impregnate this young woman? The aristocrat explained that he had lost another son to a terrible accident and now feared (and expected) that this young man would not live long. His solution was for this young woman to bear a child that might fill the looming vacancy for an heir to his title.

The idea of sperm cleansing at the time was impossible and I said so. Gathering he might proceed anyway, I was aghast. To make sure the young woman understood, as best I could, I told her: "Look, under no circumstance... do not let them do this. There is no way we know now how to make sperm infected with HIV safe. If you contract HIV, you are very likely to die from AIDS even if we treat you with a full set of therapies. AZT probably would put you in remission for no more than a year. In no circumstances do this."

I could not discern with any confidence whether she or the young man understood this. But the aristocrat certainly did. He became very angry. When the bill arrived, it just laid there for awhile as if he expected me to pay.

So I said, "Listen, you invited me for dinner. You made this outrageous proposal where you wanted my help with this young woman. What you are trying to do is immoral. If you want a child, why don't *you* impregnate her? Why bother with your son? That is how you could do it if you are not HIV positive."

Departing moments later, shuddering as I walked, I said to myself, "What a weird encounter. You are experiencing in this epidemic the full extremes of human behavior. This was one of them."

The young man died from his AIDS complications within a year or two. That aristocrat lived another twenty years. The young woman? I have no idea.

ENEMIES, FRIENDS, TENURE

The simplest way to describe the disputes over and preceding my Harvard tenure appointment is that I got famous before I got tenure.

Achieving tenure at Harvard is always, inevitably, a problem. It might be best understood as a hiring process. Harvard deans and department chairs are expected to find the best person in the world for any given field.

When you are up for tenure, a pan-university committee is convened. Is this person the best in the world at the specialized teaching and research he or she conducts? Do they attract abundant funding to support that research? What other candidates should be considered from outside Harvard? A letter is sent to every leading person in that field, asking for names. A list is assembled, including the institute or department's top candidate (whether or not a Harvard professor), then ranked by the tenure committee. A simmering stew of rivalries, friendships or alliances can tilt the process when the decision is made to award or reject tenure.

I knew from the start it would not be an easy ride; it rarely is, even for the most talented. My HIV/AIDS research was controversial. Many faculty felt strongly it endangered patients and staff and never should have been permitted within any Dana-Farber building. Many scientists considered my global public persona inappropriate, distasteful. I had started several companies. I was outspoken about my convictions, at times combative. I was sought after and befriended by the rich and famous. I wore suits instead of jeans.

I knew I had enemies.

John Cairns, now a professor in the school of public health, did everything he could to block me. His disdain swelled beyond the rage he voiced to Jim Watson over my lab diversions that got me banished from Cold Spring Harbor that summer fifteen years earlier. Cairns gathered every possible ally to oppose me. I will tell you what it felt like as the process dragged through the summer of 1987: I was a piñata. Anyone could take a swing. The difference: I was blindfolded and they were not. They knew exactly where to strike. I never saw the blows coming.

One afternoon that fall around six o'clock, Baruj called me in my office. "We won, Bill," he said. "You're going to receive your tenure. However, it cost me one of the most valuable things in life, which is a lifelong friend. It was a costly battle for me. I had to lose that friendship, but we won."

That is what you find in life. If you are successful, you can't expect everyone to be happy about your success. Not everyone, regardless of their own fame or status, will value your achievements. As Baruj put it, "People throw rocks uphill." As the Arabs say, "The dogs bark and the caravan passes by." This is why in any organization the mediocre are the enemy of the excellent.

This rule applies to organization leaders as well. A dean and professor I had considered a friend were weak when push came to shove. It was Baruj who prevailed for me.

In general, I have determined over the years that a weak friend is worse than an enemy when you are in a battle. Look at the ancient world. Most military battles were not won by overwhelming force. They were won because some key enemy generals defected at a critical moment. How do you conquer a fortress? Persuade a traitor on the inside to open the gate. The victors, believing that a person who turned against your enemies would turn against you, executed most of these traitors.

An enemy? You know where they stand. A weak friend? You cannot depend upon them.

I was awarded tenure because enough people thought I was making valuable and unique contributions. Nobody enjoys being judged, especially in a secret process. Do I think Harvard did a good job? Certainly. Am I happy with the outcome? *Very* happy, and proud. Being a tenured professor at Harvard means that I was judged the best person in the world at that time to do what Harvard wanted me to do. I had looked forward to this day for many years.

WORK OF THE WORLD

I would not be alive today if it were not for modern pharmaceuticals, beginning with the penicillin my mother procured for me in Jefferson Barracks when I was an infant. I may well have died on nine or ten different occasions.

Despite those many ailments that unsettled me in my youth, I was pretty healthy at Berkeley. My mother's frightful struggles gave me my purpose when I was young, to cure disease and improve human health, but disease in my own body also was a motivating factor then and, as it turned out, more so ever since.

I became allergic to aspirin when I was twenty one, a symptom that signaled the onset of what is called atopya, a triad of aspirin sensitivity, nasal polyps and asthma. Once every four or five months, my asthma became so bad I could not walk across a room. I had to be rushed to the hospital for adrenaline shots.

For the next two decades, as I was building my career, I needed a nasal polypectomy every six to eight weeks. The physician would fix a wire loop over a polyp—and yank. For each polyp. It was like having your eyeballs ripped out through your nose. I had several major operations. Brutal surgery that eroded bones in my nasal passage. Sometimes an eyeball would pop out.

It took me years to learn that all that disturbance from nasal polyp surgery exacerbated my asthma. A physician specialist in Philadelphia discovered that each time a polyp was removed, new wounds were created, setting conditions for a new polyp to develop. The cycle repeated.

Applying a cortisone cleansing rinse, budesonide, the specialist, Dr. David Kennedy, healed my polyp wounds every week or two for a year. He also used a minimally invasive technique in the nasal cavity, stereotactic surgery, to remove polyps. I was one of his first patients for these new treatments. He had my atopya under control by my mid-forties.

But then, a decade of migraine headaches. Cluster migraine attacks occurred frequently into my mid-fifties. The first time I was treated with sumatriptan pills was for a migraine that had lasted three days. What a relief! I still get migraines, but now thankfully we have sumatriptan pills.

Most people who know me do not think of me as a cancer survivor, but I am. I contracted head and neck cancer five years ago—those same tough cancers Tom Frei and I treated successfully at Dana-Farber with our targeted chemotherapies. A fractionated dose of radiation during my treatments at NYU Langone Health has left me quite functional, even sparing the salivary glands.

I had to have enormous drive to push through all this. I was never coasting. I was fighting to go to work despite my medical issues, just fighting every day.

My mother had a poignant way of expressing this attitude for outlasting personal health challenges, a mantra inspired I am sure by her own immense physical and mental struggles. She said, often, "The work of the world is done by people who do not feel well the day they do it."

24

THE LARGEST COMMITMENT OF ANY NATION

BEFORE TAKING OFFICE, George W. Bush was quietly determined to help Africa cope with the HIV/AIDS epidemic. That effort would be high on his first term agenda, a way to put into action the "compassionate conservatism" on which he campaigned.

A few months after Bush unveiled his program early in 2003, I was on a flight with two longtime friends and partners in mounting America's defense and the world's defense against AIDS, Dr. Anthony Fauci and Ambassador Richard Holbrooke.

We had just spent ten days in East Africa with dozens of evangelical Christian members of Congress and many of the world's prominent public health officials.

Our chartered plane with sixty passengers was about to land in Larnaca, Cyprus after a two thousand four hundred mile flight from Uganda. We had overflown the entire Nile from its source in Lake Victoria, the sprawling lights of Cairo and darkened waters of the Mediterranean.

It was a brilliant moonlit night. We needed to refuel in Larnaca before heading on to Munich. But there was a problem.

"Are we landing?" a heavyset city mayor of mayors asked me. He and I were wedged uncomfortably into jump seats immediately behind the pilot and co-pilot.

"Not on this glide path," I replied.

I could see airport landing lights rapidly coming into view, but we were way too high, about three thousand feet. A co-pilot pulled out a massive three ringed binder and I watched over his shoulder as he began leafing through pages. He paused, flipped a switch and pronounced, "Okay?" The pilot, focused and stone faced, replied, "Negative."

This terse exchange repeated for several minutes. We were circling, the remaining manual pages dwindling. The pilots showed no outward signs of emotion.

"Tower, this is flight 403 out of Entebbe," the pilot announces. "The flaps will not descend. Your runway is too short for a flaps up landing. Can we divert?"

"Sorry. No such airport is available within your flight parameters."

My eyes fixed on the co-pilot quickly turning more pages, I thought, "This has the makings of a calamity. Virtually the entire health leadership of the world is on this flight."

My fellow passengers—in addition to Tony Fauci, Dick Holbrooke and George W.'s members of Congress—included directors of the National Institutes of Health and the National Cancer Institute; Tommy Thompson, Secretary of the Department of Health and Human Services; and the president of the World Health Organization, CEOs of several American pharmaceutical companies and a former Navy SEAL tapped by Bush to lead his program.

My pulse was pounding. Down to the binder's final few pages, the co-pilot stopped, reached up and flipped another switch. I strained hard, trying to see how close the fuel gauge was to "E," but my line of sight was off. "Okay?" Immediately, the plane shuddered and a grinding sound filled the cabin. The flaps descended.

"I WANT TO LIVE LONG ENOUGH…"

On the day Bush outlined his plan in the State of the Union speech, the White House said the pandemic had killed more than twenty million of more than sixty million people infected, leaving fourteen million orphans. "Today, on the continent of Africa, nearly thirty million people have the AIDS virus—including three million people under the age of fifteen," the statement continued. "There are whole countries in Africa where more than one-third of the adult population carries the infection."[122]

Fourteen countries had the highest rates of HIV infection, accounting for nearly twenty million HIV-infected men, women and children—nearly seventy percent of the total in all of Africa and the Caribbean. Four of those countries—Zambia, Kenya, Uganda and Rwanda—dominated our itinerary.

Billed as a fact finding trip organized by the White House, this partially was a gambit by Bush to gain Republican Party backing for his ideas, to cover his flanks on the right. Congress had to approve his request for fifteen billion dollars over five years to fight AIDS in Africa, starting in the fiscal 2004 budget. He was counting on conservative support for what was called the President's Emergency Plan for Fighting AIDS Relief, PEPFAR. They had applauded when the president outlined his plans in the 2003 State of the Union address. They saw an opportunity to relieve the suffering of millions and perhaps save millions of souls with their religious fervor.

In Uganda, the young health minister took us to a tiny remote village, *his* village… an eight hour bus trip from Kampala followed by another hour for each of us on the back of a motorcycle. In this tiny village deep into the Ugandan countryside, we came upon a kind of haven, if you can conceive of a desolate haven. When a man died of AIDS, villagers blamed the wife, now viewed as a witch, and, along with all her children, forcibly evicted the family. Stigmatized, where could they go? One answer was small corners of remote churchyards.

An uncle, an aunt, a young child and a woman with three children were living in a mud hut on a small parcel of church land with a small vegetable patch. They were distantly related. AIDS had vanquished other members of the family, except two or three being treated by the health ministry.

Once a month, these survivors received a big bag of grain and had to make due with this diet and whatever their garden yielded. Every week, the health ministry dispatched someone by motorcycle to deliver HIV medication carefully sorted by week in a plastic box for each infected person. The infected woman told us, "You know, I do this because I want to live long enough so my oldest daughter can take care of the rest of my children."

This and similar visits by all on our fact finding mission proved to be a defining experience for everyone in our group. Expecting misery and despair, we instead found hope... evidence that a program of AIDS treatment could offer hope to desperate people. Bush had visited Africa twice in the first years of his presidency. I imagined at that moment that he might have seen something like this as well, and wanted my Congressional companions to be moved in the same way.

HAWKS, NOT PIGEONS

On our next flight, northward to Rwanda, I was struck by the expanse of Uganda's dense jungles, two thousand miles with no sign of a village or town. Then we crossed the border into Rwanda. Every piece of land as far as I could see was cultivated to the hilltops. The malaria belt went only as high as three thousand feet. Malaria keeps populations low but mosquitoes can not survive at higher elevation, enabling civilizations to avoid the plague and thrive in mountainous regions.

The purpose of our stop in Rwanda of course was to assess that country's AIDS casualties and the government's predicament. For me, though, two echoes of the genocide nine years earlier overwhelmed anything I heard those two days about AIDS. One came during a memorial event organized by the government, the other from my Rwandan seatmate's eyewitness account during a long bus ride.

Our accommodations were in the Hotel Rwanda. In the early morning, I looked out a window and saw what I thought was a flock of pigeons on the ground. Only these were hawks, not pigeons. The hawk population soared during the massacre, feeding off human flesh, and had not returned to normal.

Richard Holbrooke and I had been friends since the early '90s when he heard me speak at the Aspen Institute about the AIDS threat and the advancing treatments to contain it and my recent work on genomics and aging. "I need to learn more about this," he told me.

In his brief time as Bill Clinton's ambassador to the United Nations in 2000, Richard prevailed over scoffs and skepticism in elevating AIDS to a Security Council priority. "Look at the facts; it's not simply a humanitarian issue," he argued. "If a country loses so many of its resources in fighting a disease which takes down a third of its population, it's going to be destabilized, so it is a security issue."[123]

In 1994, when the massacres raged through Rwandan villages, Richard was Bill Clinton's ambassador to Germany. Meanwhile, after our first meeting, Richard did learn more about AIDS, much more.

As the White House finalized its manifest for this mission to Africa, Richard was on the list because he had built a nonprofit organization of businesses, the Global Business Council on HIV/AIDS, into a vital funding source. He called me. "I want you on that trip, too," he said. "You are the one who helped me understand AIDS."

We met for breakfast on the morning of the scheduled memorial for the massacred Rwandans. It wasn't long before he stopped chatting and dining. "I need to concentrate," he said, and began jotting notes for his speech. What a speech, one of my most indelible memories of the entire trip.

Standing quite literally on a field bearing skeletons of a hundred thousand butchered Rwandans, some bones even poking above ground, Richard touched on many themes, including the inaction of the U.N. and world powers independently that could have stopped the massacres. Once a young American diplomat in Vietnam who turned against that war, he admonished all of us, "Never say 'never again,'" because history warns that massacres will remain a deplorable element of human existence, even in the 21st century.

GENOCIDES CAN HAPPEN ANY TIME

The second episode took place that night after I flew into Nairobi. A woman sitting next to me on a ninety minute bus ride to the American embassy described her life during the Rwanda nightmare, chapter and verse. The story was straight out of "The Rime of the Ancient Mariner": *By thy long grey beard and glittering eye / Now wherefore stopp'st thou me?*

"You know that hotel you were in? I was there when the pool was chock a block full with bodies," she said. "The same pool you were swimming in was filled, from bottom to the top, overflowing with bodies... limbs, arms and heads everywhere. Storerooms were filled with as many bodies as they could fit. When I took a shower, tiny pieces of flesh came out of the water onto me."

Unbelievable stories, a chilling new perspective on where I had just been, one that matched my fresh memories of the hawks and of Richard standing over the remains of all the bodies.

Weeks later, reflecting on those Rwanda days and after reading more, I decided the 1994 genocide had less to do with tribal resentments than overpopulation. Rwanda inheritance tradition held that every son in a family received an equal plot of land. As the population grew on the mountainside, plots got smaller and smaller. Too many sons, too little land, and sons cannot support a family anymore. Neighbors turned to warring against neighbors, fighting over land.

Demagogues typically pick up on these issues and exploit them for their own power. In this case, it resulted in a million people dying in ten days of a civil war. With that kind of social pressure, people find religious or other reasons to kill and take what the neighbor had. In Rwanda before the war, the Hutu and Tutsi tribes were entirely intermixed across the country. Then they became neighbors who turned against each other.

The Rwanda experience was life changing for me. I saw firsthand how delicate the fabric of society is, what horrific conflicts can happen when things go wrong. People will, and did, kill a million others in a matter of weeks, not with guns but machetes. This was Richard's point. Never say never again. Genocides can happen any time. You have to be vigilant... all the time.

You do not need modern technologies to conduct genocides. The Aryan invasions of northern India killed everybody four thousand years ago, destroyed civilizations. The Mongols destroyed civilizations a thousand years ago that never returned; the skulls are still there. Thousands of people killed with bows and arrows, knives and swords. In Rwanda, a million people were hacked to death with machetes.

A MUCH BIGGER PLAN

Soon after George and Laura Bush returned from their Africa journeys early in his first term, the President called Tony Fauci over to the Oval Office.

"I want a plan for the United States to help Africa with AIDS," Bush said.

Tony was eager and prepared. He had sounded alarms, directed the flow of government money to research labs and advised physicians in the U.S. and around the world on AIDS patient care by then for two decades. African governments for years had turned to him and his teams for help.

At age forty three, when Tony took on the mandate as director of the National Institute of Allergy and Infectious Diseases in 1984, he was a prominent immunologist. He also was a physician struggling to treat early AIDS patients, as he has said, "with no effective tools; it was like putting Band-Aids on hemorrhages."[124]

A few weeks later, Tony returned to the White House and presented his plan. "I don't like it," Bush said. Tony braced momentarily, then brightened as the President continued. "It is not nearly enough," Bush said. "I want a much bigger plan, an entirely different initiative."

The President explained he wanted more funding. He also wanted an administrative design to avoid as much as possible bureaucratic delays in the U.S., high administrative expenses and the expected corruption that attends many aid programs in Africa. "I want to create a new way to get money directly to people treating AIDS in Africa," he said. "I don't trust our own bureaucracy; they tie things up. I don't trust the governments; they steal all the money."

Another few weeks, and Tony returns to the Oval Office. As Tony explained to me, Bush took those ideas and "crafted his own plan, the President's Emergency Plan for Fighting AIDS Relief. He created that. The plan I gave him was not as big or as bold as he wanted."

"I KNOW WHAT I DID"

Every American should be proud. President Bush carried out this mission from his understanding of the nature of the problem. From my point of view, this is exactly what American Presidents should do. He saw a problem, used the power of the American government and in doing so probably saved at least ten million lives. What is more, in my view, Tony Fauci continually exhibited qualities of the highest character that represent the best in medicine—a great scientist, dedicated physician and magnificent public servant. If there is one person in the world who has made the greatest contribution to prevention and treatment of HIV/AIDS, that person is Tony followed closely by President George W. Bush.

We have spent close to one hundred billion dollars to thwart the HIV/AIDS epidemic in Africa and the Caribbean, the largest commitment by the people of any nation to fight a single global disease. These funds have supported scientists conducting major research at American universities and institutes and people in cities and villages all across these countries. I have visited many of these sites. Millions of people avoided infection and millions more live relatively normal lives thanks to the regimen of affordable antiretroviral drugs and accessible test kits.

HIV/AIDS is the worst scourge of infectious disease ever encountered by any civilization. By the end of 2019, the global death toll from HIV/AIDS was thirty two million people. In all, seventy seven million had been infected, with estimates of another 1.8 million people being infected each year. Those are grim statistics.

But look what has been accomplished. Of thirty six million people living with the disease, more than twenty million are receiving full antiretroviral treatments and living nearly normal lives. More than a million of these patients live in the U.S. Of those twenty million, more than fifteen million receive these treatments through PEPFAR. Moreover, the American people are helping six million orphans and vulnerable children. I expect many of these children are like those kids we met in that tiny mud hut in Uganda nearly twenty years ago, when PEPFAR was only a plan.

We now have the scientific tools—through testing, treatment and education—to prevent HIV infection or make it nearly impossible for an infected person to transmit the virus to someone else. PEPFAR has been an essential part of this story.

Tony Fauci, I and others who have been fighting HIV/AIDS from the start, for nearly forty years, explain and emphasize this fact at every opportunity: We can eliminate the scourge of HIV/AIDS. These resources from the American people bring treatments and methods for prevention to millions more. The problem is reaching vulnerable people in areas of the world where they do not have easy access to these life-saving therapies.[125]

In 2018, President Trump embraced and Congress approved an extension of the program through 2023. On World AIDS Day that year, a former first term Congressman from Indiana who voted in favor of the first President's Emergency Plan bill in 2003, Vice President Mike Pence, proclaimed in remarks at the White House that PEPFAR "has been inarguably one of the most successful investments in healthcare and humanitarian aid in American history."[126]

Near the end of his second term, I praised George W. Bush for this achievement in a speech to an international conference of AIDS researchers.

"We as Americans should be proud of what our country has done, and is doing, to stem the tide of death due to HIV/AIDS," I said. "Unbeknownst to most Americans, and certainly in other countries, we are saving millions of lives in Africa each year. Many of you don't support this President for a variety of reasons, but we should all be grateful for what he has done."

After I finished my talk, a man I did not recognize approached me with a pleased look on his face. "That was a nice speech," he said. "Would you mind saying that directly to the President?" He was quite serious. It was Josh Bolten, White House chief of staff.

"It would be my pleasure and honor," I said. "I should tell you that I do not support all of his policies but, as I said, I do respect and applaud him for this amazing piece of work."

"We know," he said. "It doesn't matter."

"I would be happy to speak with him."

A few days later, Bolten called me back. "I spoke to the President about your speech," he said. "He said to say thanks but there is no need to speak with him. He added, 'I know what I did.'"

PART V

‖25‖

BIOTECH ENTREPRENEUR

CREATING A COMPANY WAS NEVER PART OF MY PLAN when I became a Harvard professor.

I had only a dim understanding of how corporations were organized and no understanding of finance. Growing up on a naval base, how could I? The government managed nearly everything, from officer, scientist and staff salaries and housing assignments to discounted pricing at the PBX. Moreover, my intense opposition to the Vietnam War in the '60s and '70s alerted me to the dark side of business... profiting from weapons made to kill and destroy.

Yet an awareness of how business could be a positive force for health was slowly dawning on me. Tom Frei and many of our young Dana-Farber doctors worked closely with pharmaceutical companies to test new anticancer drugs. This opened my eyes to how any drug targets my new lab discovered ultimately would be translated into drugs for treating cancer. I met with company scientists who developed adriamycin, cisplatin and bleomycin. "Do you have any more of these?" I asked. "Come and visit," they replied, and in these sessions I learned how clinical trials were done and who paid for them.

Then, too, the new age of biotechnology was gathering speed at very close range. I kept tabs as close friends left universities to join these nascent companies. Cetus was the first, founded in 1970. Then came Genentech in 1976 and Biogen two years later. Dennis Kleid, the postdoc lab mate at MIT who helped me solve the mystery of how retroviral genomes were made, now was a top Genentech researcher. Wally Gilbert not only was one of Biogen's founders, he resigned from Harvard's faculty after nearly two decades to become Biogen's first CEO.[127]

All were racing to apply the new techniques of recombinant DNA, gene splicing, to make new drugs and vaccines. Research scientists at universities might create a conceptual breakthrough, but I realized that bringing new drugs to patients was the work of business. My attitude changed. "Companies," I now thought, "are the practical part of connecting science to medicine." For Cetus, after it was acquired by Chiron,[128] the blockbuster was interleukin-2; Genentech, human growth hormone; Biogen, a vaccine to prevent hepatitis B. For a fourth startup, Amgen, a protein known as erythropoietin that stimulates production of red blood cells.

A West Coast trip I planned for collecting mouse leukemia viruses—for my investigations of retrovirus as a cause of cancer in animals—marked the tipping point for me. In Seattle, what excited cancer immunologist Bob Nowinski was the new company he had just organized with five million dollars in venture funding from a small firm in New York City formed by two brothers, David and Isaac Blech. The company was Genetic Systems.[129]

"They read about my work in *Scientific American* and now we are in business," he said. The Blech brothers. I made a mental note.

At Genentech, situated less than a mile north of the San Francisco International Airport, Dennis Kleid walked with me through his spacious new labs and introduced me to his first postdoctoral fellow, David Goeddel. "We are hot on the trail of insulin," Dennis said. "If we get it, the company will go public."[130] Wow, I thought. Things happen fast in their world. Dennis's "if" soon became reality. Two years later Genentech became one of the first publicly traded biotech companies, valued at eighty five million dollars.

On to San Diego where Richard Lerner, a research chemist at the Scripps Research Institute, had more samples of mouse leukemia waiting. Richard had been studying protein structures, specifically how to accelerate response

My Lifelong Fight Against Disease

of antibodies to bolster the immune system against infections. "Look at these results," he told me. "Antibodies to these peptide fragments recognize the whole protein." Peptide fragments are short chains of amino acids that help identify an entire protein. He added, "We don't need to purify proteins anymore!"[131] I understood immediately: using peptide fragments should be a faster, cheaper way to make vaccines!

IDEA FOR A COMPANY

On the flight back to the Bay Area and an evening with friends at Berkeley, I processed everything. The excitement Bob, Dennis and Richard projected, the science of their projects, their startup strategies and my own retrovirus research. *How can I apply this new knowledge? What should I be doing?* My neck began to tingle. I wondered, "Might it be possible to create new vaccines using small peptides rather than entire viruses or virus proteins?" Why wouldn't it be possible, given the results Richard had just shown me? "If so, how would I do it? With what viruses?"

I knew how long and expensive it was to develop new drugs, ten years and many tens of millions of dollars. Wouldn't these techniques shorten the time and the expense? I knew pets and livestock suffered serious viral infections. These often were lethal if the animals lived long enough. "Why not test the idea in animals? We won't need to go through the FDA," I thought. It would be a shortcut to demonstrate that a vaccine can prevent retrovirus infections that cause cancer. "I can create a company to do this."

"Eddie, this is Bill Haseltine. I am calling you from the San Francisco airport. Do you mind if I ask you a few questions?"

Ed Goodman was the only Wall Street banker I knew, a casual acquaintance through friends in Cambridge.

"Hi, Bill. No. Fire away."

"What kind of banker are you?"

"I am an investment banker."

"Is that related to venture capital?"

"Yes. That is the kind of investment banker I am."

"Are you free tonight for dinner? I have an idea for a new biotech company. Can we talk?"

"How about in the morning? I'm hosting Aaron Copland's eightieth birthday party tonight. I can invite you to the concert and a dinner later at Carnegie Hall. Will that work?"

"Sure—and thanks. I'll rush to get an earlier flight to New York."

Ed Goodman listened carefully the next morning as I outlined my idea. "The work will complement, not compete with, my Harvard research," I said, aiming to deflect any concern about how I would manage my time. Besides, I added, Harvard professors were barred from active management roles in companies and consulting was restricted to one day a week.

"I can't help you," he said, evenly. "You have an idea but I can't tell whether it is a good idea or not. My business is mostly leverage buyouts of mid-sized companies." In other words, he worked with companies that already had products or services generating one hundred million dollars or more in revenue, not startups like I had in mind. "But I know just the person who can," he added, now upbeat. "Deborah Ferris. She was instrumental in getting Biogen off the ground two years ago."

Ed gave me her phone number, and I thanked him before leaving his elegant Manhattan town house office on East 71st Street. That afternoon I dialed the number and gave Deborah my pitch.

"Ed mentioned you helped Wally Gilbert form Biogen," I said. "I hope you can help me, too."

"I love the idea and would love to help," she said, eagerly. "You probably don't know this but my father is a specialist in animal diseases. He works on Plum Island in a lab just offshore to prevent any escaping organism from devastating our livestock industry. The search for new vaccines is in my blood. My dad will be excited." That island setting was the only place in the country where research on dangerous livestock diseases—and vaccines to stop them—was permitted.

Deborah and I spent the next few days at my dining room table, outlining the technology to develop animal vaccines and a business plan to develop and sell it. We sketched out the market, the timeline, staff roles and projected costs. I penciled myself in as chair of the board of directors and scientific advisory committee, with Deborah as interim chief financial officer. Her compensation? Two percent of the founding shares. We named the company Cambridge Bioscience.

"THE WHOLE THING; NO PROBLEM"

Before heading to blue chip venture capital firms, such as Greylock in Boston and Venrock and Citicorp in New York, among many others, I needed a rapid education about venture capital and starting a new business as well as a sartorial upgrade. At the Harvard Coop, a landmark bookstore in Harvard Square, I exited with a bundle of five or six of the best books on those topics, then headed straight to Lord & Taylor's upscale emporium in Boston for a few new suits, shirts and ties... and a new briefcase.

Then, we prepared. At each meeting, though, the same cautious story. Everywhere. "We like the idea. We like you. We like the plan. You look credible enough. We will put money in *but first* you need a CEO and a lead investor, a fully committed venture capital group that will conduct due diligence." Due diligence is legal-financial jargon that essentially means kicking the tires of any individual or organization in question before putting money at risk.

We soon hired a CEO, but could not secure a lead investor. Round and round we went. Then one day, as we departed yet another firm's office, I picked up another startup business plan by mistake. A familiar name immediately caught my eye. The Blech brothers. They were shopping another company. "If they are still creating new companies, maybe they will be interested in mine," I thought.

They were. My conversation with David Blech took less than an hour. "We like the idea," he told me leaning over his desk in a small office in midtown

Manhattan. "I see you are asking for five million dollars to get the company off the ground. We will do it."

Do what?

"The whole thing," he said. "No problem."

I was taken aback. From what every other firm said, there would need to be at least a handful of investors putting up money to spread their risk of loss. It seemed to be the standard practice. There must be some hitch, I thought, some deal breaking condition or other hurdle David had not identified.

"The company will have to be near Boston, and I have to continue as a Harvard professor," I said.

"That's no problem," he replied. "But we don't like your CEO." I thought our CEO was a good man. He helped us work out some kinks in the business plan. Before I could say anything, though, David added, "Get started without one. We can help you find the right one."

And, that was that! Three months after Eddie Goodman graciously accepted my cold call, I was in business. We had the detailed business plan, we had the five million dollar commitment. But I had other reasons to worry: university politics.

There was no precedent for a Harvard assistant professor starting a company. Even for full professors, the idea of starting companies was highly controversial. Derek Bok, Harvard's president, had voiced skepticism. Other faculty across the university grumbled, some with outrage, at the notion that biologists or biochemists might turn discoveries developed at Harvard into a personal fortune.

Untoward outcomes from starting this company were conceivable, and vexing. I wondered, "If Nobel Prize winners and other famous professors are getting in trouble and fighting with the university about starting companies, what is going to happen to me? This is big-time politics and I am small fry here. Will starting a business endanger my career? Maybe I'll be accused of having a lack of focus."

B-SCHOOL DEAN: "I'D LIKE TO HELP YOU"

The lanky gentleman seated next to me on a flight back to Boston wanted to talk. I was returning from yet another business trip to New York because, to borrow from Willie Sutton, "That's where the money is."

"So you are a Harvard professor," the man said. "What is your interest?" I briefly described my research and mentioned that I was starting a company. His eyes lighted up. "I'm Larry Fouraker, dean of the Harvard Business School," he said. "This is a great idea. This is how good things start. I'd like to help you. What can I do?"

What great luck, I thought. Maybe he *can* help me. "Well, the president seems a bit leery about professors creating companies," I said. "I have some concern about any impact on my academic career."

"Don't worry," he said. "Derek Bok doesn't have it right. None of these guys have it right. An English professor writes a book and gets his royalties from the publisher, right? What the heck is the difference? Converting new ideas into new companies is exactly what our professors should do. In fact, universities now are required by law to create a technology transfer office for exactly that purpose."

He was referring to the Bayh-Dole Act passed by a lame-duck session of Congress just months before at the end of 1980. The law's intent was to promote commercialization of research funded by the federal government. Birch Bayh, Democrat of Indiana, and Bob Dole, Republican of Kansas, were the legislation's sponsors in the Senate. Jimmy Carter signed the bill into law.

"The law states that all universities and research institutes that receive federal funding must file patent applications on all discoveries with practical application," Fouraker continued, then added another detail that quieted my concerns. "They must make best efforts to transfer the technology to businesses for commercial development."

I thought, "What a mandate. This law is a green light for exactly what I am doing: transferring my knowledge of viruses to a business for commercial development." I learned later that it was Benjamin Franklin who put the concept of patenting intellectual property into the Constitution, believing that, as he put it, "a patent couples the fuel of self interest to the fire of invention." And so it does. The Bayh-Dole Act is recognized today as a stemwinder of the 1980's economic boom.

Larry Fouraker added that the chair of the university's governing body, the Harvard Corporation, was a good friend of his. "I will speak with him about this, and President Bok," he said. "But I have a request. Let Harvard share in your success. Pledge some shares of your company to the university's endowment fund."

"Thank you," I replied. "I cannot write that down but I promise you that if this turns into money I will give them five percent of whatever the value is. I will do it."

"That is fine with me," he said.

Larry Fouraker never accepted my offer to compensate him for his time and advice and never served on Cambridge Bioscience's board of directors, but he became a close friend and mentor for many years. His only request was that I speak to students at the B-School from time to time about entrepreneurship.

As it happened, the university rejected my offer to donate five percent of our founding shares outright. They hadn't worked out what they thought the ethics might be of such a transaction. I can assure you that by now they have. After Cambridge Bioscience went public a year and a half later, I sold the five percent and donated the cash. They were happy to accept it.

Adding outstanding faculty scientists to my venture would further bolster my ability to deflect political heat within the university, should any develop, and of course deepen my brain trust. I quickly recruited two colleagues, giving each five percent of the founding shares.

The chair of the microbiology department at Harvard's School of Public Health, Max Essex, a veterinarian and microbiologist, was an expert on animal viruses. The chair of the department of microbiology and molecular genetics at Harvard Medical School, Bernie Fields,[132] was an expert on viral infections. Max brought in Arthur Hurwitz, president of the New York Animal Center, the premier pet hospital in Manhattan. Bernie recruited another faculty member, Mark Green, a talented immunologist. Our scientific advisory committee, doubling as my political firewall, was complete.

ENTREPRENEURIAL WHIRLWIND

At Harvard, everybody is everybody else's enemy, more or less. Friendly rivals probably is a better way to put it. But for Max, Bernie and me, working together in the company bolstered collaboration in our labs, accelerating discoveries. We gained a level of trust that translated very easily. When you start a company, you are able to form remarkably tight associations. You all are working toward the same goal, trying to make a product and make money.

For example, I was working on HTLV when we organized the company. Max was also interested in HTLV. In another year he and I were sharing ideas with others on Bob Gallo's small team that determined the infectious cause of AIDS had to be a retrovirus. As we saw earlier, a retrovirus never had been detected before that caused cancer in humans.

Meanwhile, Cambridge Bioscience was developing its first product, a synthetic vaccine to protect cats from viral leukemia disease. Our team's blend of relevant, varied expertise gave us a quick start. I determined the entire genetic sequence of the virus's outer protein shell, essential for identifying targets for a vaccine biochemical structure. Art Hurwitz confirmed access to however many cats we would need to test the vaccine as safe and effective in killing leukemia cells.

Our chief scientist, Dante Marciani, worked on an adjuvant, a chemical agent that spurs the body's immune response to fight a specific disease with high volumes of antibodies. Adjuvants make vaccines more potent. We knew an adjuvant had to be part of the vaccine formula because we planned to use peptides, not proteins, for the vaccine. Peptides are small chains of nucleic acids, smaller than proteins and less well defined. They can regulate activities of other molecules, but they do not stimulate the immune system as well as intact proteins.

A Peruvian, Dante started his career at the National Institutes of Health. We hired him from a contract company where he led vaccine research.

"I have an idea," he said one day. "The extract of a soap bark tree is used in traditional medicines in Peru because it stimulates the immune system. If you approve, I have a good source who can provide the extract, then I can purify the active ingredient." We were enthusiastic. "Go ahead!"

In a few months, Dante succeeded. We coupled the purified protein with the adjuvant and *voila!* we had our vaccine. Today that adjuvant, which we named Quil-A, is at the forefront of research to create a vaccine to prevent COVID-19 and save both lives and economies. In less than a year, our tests with Art Hurwitz's cats proved the vaccine to be safe and effective. Our efforts were important for science as well as for saving cats. This was the first effective vaccine to prevent retrovirus infection in any mammal, one that is still used today.

Several vaccine companies that Art knew from his broad contacts in the animal vaccine industry bid for the manufacturing rights. A French company, Virbac, was the winner and became a great partner. Within another year, Virbac obtained regulatory approval and began selling on the market. We were making money and ready to go public, little more than two years after opening our doors.

Shopping for an investment banker to manage the Cambridge Bioscience initial public offering was fun. Competition for our mandate was fierce. The lead bank for an IPO typically raked in six percent of total funds raised, a handsome profit. We chose Fred Frank of Lehman Brothers as lead banker.

Fred was already a legend. His keen interest in our company brought us immediate credibility with potential investors. Fred was the first on Wall Street to discern the pharmaceutical sector as a distinct niche of the chemical industry, a niche that needed investment bankers with specific knowledge of pharmaceuticals. By the late '70s, with Cetus, Genetic Systems, Genentech and Biogen off and running, he leapt forward again, perceiving biotechnology as a subset of pharmaceuticals with phenomenal potential for growth and economic impact.

For our first road show, I prepared what I thought was a convincing slide show. "Bill, that is a great explanation of your company," Fred said, slightly amused. "But you have to tell me why I have to buy *now!* That is what your audience wants to know." I tore up the script and created a new one.

Road shows are intense. We flew all over the country to meet potential investors. Twenty minute presentations with ten or more questions over breakfast, lunch and dinner meetings and many others during the day. I learned to inhale my food; it was either that or starve.

On the day designated for our IPO, we waited anxiously at the closing bell at Lehman Brothers' midtown office tower. Would big investors buy? At the high end of the fixed price range? Fred and his team of bankers assembled the book of purchase orders as they were phoned in, each specifying an amount of shares at a specific price within the offering range Fred set. Our offer was oversubscribed... order volume topped the number of available shares. The next day, the first for public trading, was perfect. Investors bid Cambridge Bioscience shares higher than our offering price. We were elated. "Our science works and we have money in the bank," I reassured myself. "Cambridge Bioscience will have a clear run into the future."

NOT SO FAST

An appealing new opportunity soon arrived, developing kits to test blood for HIV infections. The U.S. government announced plans to award semi-exclusive contracts to five companies. This should be a quick win for us, I thought. It was hard to imagine another firm with as much expertise on the molecular biology of HIV, how to test for antibodies, and so on.

But our CEO, the one David Blech helped us recruit, badly botched our application. We fired him, then scrambled after the government window closed to get back into the fray. Our best option was acquiring one of the companies that had won a license, BioTech Inc. We quickly developed a five minute test for HIV that I hoped could be sold over the counter to thousands of people, and in time probably hundreds of thousands, who did not know but feared they had HIV infection.

But the government said no. The Food and Drug Administration refused to allow any HIV home testing. Reagan's Department of Health and Human Services maintained that such a test would allow people to hide the fact they were infected, if an infection was confirmed by the tests.

This tragic failing in a public health policy would stand with varying constraints for the next quarter century. In the mid-'90s, the FDA approved two over the counter kits for in-home blood sample collection that required testing in remote laboratories. Finally, in 2012, the FDA approved by a vote of 17–0 an oral test kit that would provide results in twenty minutes, similar to a home pregnancy test. One of its reviewers estimated that nearly three million people would use the test annually, leading to forty five thousand new positive test results—that is, forty five thousand people who would discover they were infected with HIV. The reviewer indicated that people infected with HIV could avoid more than four thousand new HIV transmissions a year if they knew the facts. Recent data show that home tests do increase the likelihood that people will seek treatment.

Stock manipulators play a spurious game of "pump and dump"—drive the price of a thinly traded stock sharply higher by aggressively persuading naïve investors to buy, then sell aggressively when the price spikes and leave late buyers with big losses as the artificial demand the manipulators created evaporates. Sometimes the cops at the Securities and Exchange Commission are close behind. Sometimes not. Think of the Leonardo DiCaprio movie, *The Wolf of Wall Street*.

I learned more than I ever wanted about "pump and dump" shops not long after our IPO. Some of these outfits in Florida began manipulating our stock, possibly with some help from inside our company. (We changed the name to Cambridge Biotech after the BioTech acquisition.) This forced us to make more changes to our board and management. I thought David Blech was in cahoots with the stock manipulators. I was right and we parted ways. He later was jailed after pleading guilty to repeated lapses into securities fraud. For a while, I was chagrined. "There is more to business than having good ideas and making money," I told myself. "You have to guard against crooks, too."[133]

By now our Dana-Farber HIV/AIDS research was becoming more urgent by the day. Health professions were desperate for an effective drug treatment. It was the right time for me to leave Cambridge Biotech's board, which I did, and concentrate on fast moving developments and discoveries in both of my labs, retrovirus and pharmacology.

The company's distress resumed, though. The interim CEO who had been chief financial officer was convicted of embezzlement and jailed, and Cambridge Biotech was sold to a Boston company. The good news is that the technology we created for vaccine development and other applications continues to thrive.

ALL THE SKILLS YOU NEED

Far from harming my career, creating Cambridge Bioscience turned out to be a huge plus. I developed trusting relations with two powerful department chairs. Max invited me to become a member of his department at the School of Public Health. And I became a role model and adviser to other faculty members in starting their companies.

For example, I helped Fred Goldberg create ProScript, the company that developed Velcade to treat multiple myeloma and other cancers. Tim Springer and I founded LeukoSite, a company focused on drugs to block disease-promoting actions of white blood cells, especially in cancers and inflammation.[134]

Eventually, Harvard's governing board and administration embraced the benefits of professors starting companies. While still teaching at the medical school, I was asked to chair a university wide committee that clarified rules governing relationships between professors and the companies they seek to start. The University now *requires* faculty to pledge a percentage of the founding shares as well as royalties received for startups based on a professor's patents.

People often asked me after I started Cambridge Bioscience, how can a scientist be a businessman? My answer was that as a Harvard science professor you have all the skills you need to be a successful entrepreneur.

You have to do your science and manage your lab as well or better than anybody else in the world. You have to raise all your money yourself, including your salary. Harvard helps you very little with that. And you have to communicate what you do so people—grant funding institutes, typically—will know what you have done and be willing to bet on what you will do in the future.

Your scientific reputation is your capital.

"The frog is very different from us on the outside but inside it looks like us." After dissecting frogs and explaining anatomy to other kids and parents at the junior high science fair in 1958, I went to bed happy that night.

As a four-year-old, enjoying the dazzling natural environment of California's Indian Wells Valley.

Cub Scouts, 1954, then Boy Scouts, were welcomed rites of passage while growing up on an isolated naval weapons research base.

Steaming into Pearl Harbor, 1960; first port of call on a
journey across the Pacific. A transport ship ferried me and
other winners of a U.S. Navy League competition to Japan,
along with hundreds of sailors, soldiers and officers.

At sophomore year science fair, 1960. My friend Jeffrey Besser
(pictured) and I created experiments demonstrating how bacteria
from my throat created boils in rats, and how antibiotics cured them.

A sophomore year pig roast at UC Berkeley, 1963. I had been an attentive sous chef for years at the side of my mother, a gifted culinary devotee.

Trying on a treasured heirloom at my ancestral family home; knight's armor, 1961.

A pool party, 1963; Pimentel hosting students plucked from his freshman chemistry course for all-expenses-paid studies that summer with elite scientists.

George Pimentel, at UC Berkeley. My paramount mentor, he taught freshman chemistry to thousands of students from the '50s through the '80s.

Mario Savio speaking atop a police car before a huge crowd at UC Berkeley, with me in a dark sport coat seated in front of the left headlights. Beginning of the Free Speech Movement, October 1, 1964.

My junior year at UC Berkeley, when *Science* published my first journal article, coauthored with Pimentel and a grad student, analyzing Mars's atmosphere.

Graduation Day, 1966.

Marching with other Vietnam War protestors
in New York City, 1967.

Attending one of many antiwar lectures and rallies during
March 4th Movement at MIT, 1969.

The co-discoverers of the double helix structure of DNA, James Watson, left,
and Francis Crick. With their model of part of a DNA molecule in Cavendish
Laboratory, University of Cambridge, 1953.

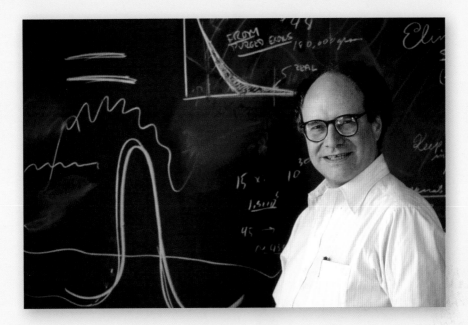

Walter Gilbert, my PhD advisor along with Watson at Harvard. Wally's lectures on molecular biology convinced me to pursue medical sciences, not medicine.

In my Dana-Farber office, for a *Life* magazine feature in 1985. Our urgent campaign in late summer persuaded Congress to sharply increase federal funding for AIDS research.

David Baltimore's discoveries in how animal viruses replicate became a cornerstone for the biotechnology revolution. My postdoctoral research in his MIT laboratory contributed new knowledge on viral RNA replication.

Tom Frei, president of Dana-Farber Cancer Institute, in 1978. He committed to creating a biochemical pharmacology department to design cancer drugs, then put me in charge.

Baruj Benacerraf, Tom Frei's successor at Dana-Farber and another prized mentor of mine.

With the board of directors of amfAR, the Foundation for AIDS Research, including Elizabeth Taylor. I headed the team of science advisors, beginning in 1985. By 2020, amfAR had invested more than $500 million to fund 3,300 scientists in HIV research.

Ronald Reagan, Nancy Reagan, and Elizabeth Taylor, with White House aide, moments before President Reagan made his first major speech on AIDS, 1987.

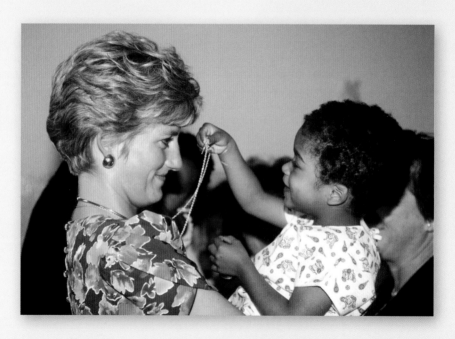

Diana, Princess of Wales, holding an HIV-infected child in Sao Paolo, Brazil, in April 1991. A striking event with global news coverage that I had encouraged for destigmatizing AIDS.

Dr. Anthony Fauci in 2004, his twentieth year directing the National Institute of Allergy and Infectious Diseases. Great scientist, dedicated physician and magnificent public servant.

President Bill Clinton with an AIDS patient at Georgetown Medical Center, December 1993.

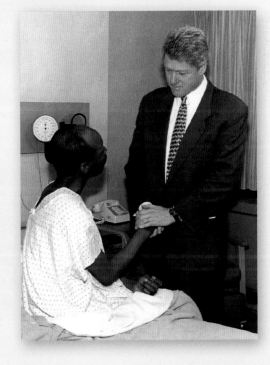

At Dana-Farber with the genomic sequence of HIV, a discovery that led to targets for life saving pharmaceuticals to treat people with AIDS.

In *TIME* magazine's feature, "The 25 Most Influential Business People of 2001."

A panel at the annual Aspen Ideas Festival, 2015. At the first Ideas Festival in 2005, I organized sessions on science and health. A mountain hike later that day inspired me toward a new focus: global health.

This bronze sculpture by my daughter, Mara, in the center of the science city Biopolis in Singapore, depicts the three-dimensional polypeptide backbone of the SARS protease.

A session during the U.S.-China Health Summit in 2018.

One of many live appearances with CNN's Anderson Cooper and Dr. Sanjay Gupta analyzing developments in the COVID pandemic, summer 2020.

26

A PERISHABLE DIAMOND

"A LOT OF US LAWYERS WISH WE COULD BE HARVARD PROFESSORS. You have a great role," Marty Lipton, one of the most renowned corporate lawyers of his era, was saying. "Why would you leave now?"

I had just begun over lunch to outline privately to him my plans to leave Harvard—my two Dana-Farber labs, my teaching positions at Harvard Medical School and Harvard School of Public Health. Why? To accept a fulltime position as chairman and chief executive of a biotech startup.

In many ways, I had to acknowledge, Marty was right. Why leave now? Funding was pouring into my HIV/AIDS lab. We were a world leader, unraveling more about the virus in the early '90s and identifying targets for drugs to contain its many mutations. Outstanding graduate students and visiting professors knocked on our doors. Invitations for keynote lectures arrived from around the world, far more than I could accept. I was juggling time with several companies, owning five to ten percent of each in equity and receiving supplemental income as leader of their scientific advisory boards.

"But," I explained to Marty, "I think I can change the future of medicine. I have been asked to take what we've learned about genomics in HIV research, apply advances in computing and robotics and establish a business to sequence genomes for every possible disease. But I cannot do it within the university. This is going to take all of my time and energy. It's an opportunity of a lifetime, just too big to pass up."

This chapter tells the story that I told him that day.

WHY ME?

Wallace Steinberg once had been Johnson & Johnson's director of research, but left in frustration after one too many of his proposals to push the pharmaceutical giant faster into biotechnology was rejected.[135] His belief in the future of biotechnology took him to Wall Street and the investment firm he organized in the 1980s, HealthCare Ventures.

We had worked extremely well together, respecting and trusting each other's expertise. Wally understood the pharmaceutical business and venture capital; I understood the science of biotechnology. For five years, meeting every month or so in Manhattan, I would hand him a one or two paragraph description for a new company. If he liked the idea, I would have immediate call on five million dollars to begin organizing the company.

Wally and Alan Walton, a like minded biotech investor at another venture capital firm, raised the money from investors. LeukoSite, ProScript, the Virus Research Institute and Dendreon were launched this way.

"Bill, I have an idea that will get you out of Harvard," he said.

"Wally, you're nuts. Why should I leave?" I said, a bit astonished at his suggestion. "I have a lifetime position at one of the greatest universities in the world. My work is going well. I love what I am doing there and what we are doing together."

We were sitting at the back table of a stylish Italian restaurant on Manhattan's Upper East Side. Wally had an extra gleam in his eye.

"Just a minute," he continued. "I want you to go to the National Institutes of Health and meet Craig Venter. He wants to leave NIH but only to work within a nonprofit institute that will commercialize his research."

Wally explained that he and a colleague were creating the institute—soon named the Institute for Genomic Research—and planning a private company to develop and market the technology.

"That sounds complicated. Why use any funds to create a research institute? Just create a company directly. You are asking for trouble if you depend on a nonprofit to do a key part of research. Plus, I've read that he is difficult. The guys running the Human Genome Project don't have good things to say about him. As I hear it, they will be happy to see him gone.

"Finally," I added. "Why me?"

I was not fishing for compliments. Wally knew me better than that. He had determined, he said, that across his extensive network of scientists, research directors and pharmaceutical executives, I was easily the best fit for this role. Credentials: elite research discoveries in DNA molecular biology and the biochemistry of drug development. Proven leadership in fundraising and building teams and organizations in science and business.

"I know you well enough to believe that you can take full advantage of this opportunity," he said. "You will jump at the chance when you see what is possible."

WALLY MAY BE RIGHT

I had to admit his pitch was tempting. I was getting restless at Harvard. Two years earlier, in 1990, NIH funding for HIV/AIDS was nearing two billion dollars and rising (to $2.5 billion today), a remarkable and gratifying increase from Reagan's meager allocation of one million dollars in fiscal 1985. Excellent scientists from all over the world were fully engaged in AIDS research. I had trained many. Moreover, pharmaceutical and biotechnology companies were introducing new drugs almost monthly and my lab was filled with bright young scientists exploring many aspects of the virus and AIDS.

I realized the pioneering phase of HIV/AIDS research was over, with one exception. The path ahead for HIV treatment was clear: continually developing drugs to keep pace with the virus mutations and combining them. Many able hands were at work. The one exception was the search for a vaccine to prevent HIV infection. At best, I reasoned then, that discovery would take another ten or twenty years. (Nearly thirty years later, there still is no HIV/AIDS vaccine.) "You could beat your head against that wall and crack only your skull, not the problem," I told myself.

If there is an opportunity to open a new frontier, why not take it? Genomics may be it, I thought. It was basic genomics, deciphering the sequence of the unique chemical bases, or letters—A, C, G, T—in HIV's genetic code that enabled our lab's key breakthroughs. We identified more targets for preventing growth than the biotech and pharma industries could handle. What is more, we developed these targets within weeks of defining the sequence, not years as had been the case in the past. If we could do this for HIV, why not for any disease?

"Wally may be right," I thought as the days passed. "If there really is a way to isolate human genes quickly, I can certainly figure out how to turn some of them into drugs."

We knew that each human chromosome contained some three billion pairs of the four chemical bases, yet fewer than two percent of the DNA specified the proteins. I thought regions of the genome that specified individual proteins would by far be the most useful as drug targets. The remaining ninety eight percent might hold some interest for science and, perhaps in the future, for medicine, but they were not of immediate interest. I thought, "Wow, having a full collection of human genes might do for all of medicine what having the sequence of the HIV genome did for AIDS."

I took Wally's advice and booked a trip to Washington, D.C.

BROWN BAG EPIPHANY

Craig and I met over a brown bag lunch on an outdoor terrace in Bethesda, Maryland, not far from the sprawling campus of the National Institutes of Health a half hour's drive north from Capitol Hill. He was in a good mood... relaxed, easy to speak with, eager to begin. I would never again see him that way.

When he showed me computer printouts summarizing some first results of the rapid gene identification technique the NIH lab had adapted to rapidly isolate and characterize human genes, I was stunned. There before me were descriptions of dozens of human genes. Some were similar to genes with well known functions. Others were entirely new, unlike any seen before.

In that instant, an epiphany. I visualized a sequence of three precipitous consequences that would revolutionize medicine and medical science.

Genomics would usher in a new era, opening new ways in medical science to find cures for most if not all disease.

I would build a pharmaceutical company applying genomics to bring new drugs to market, demonstrating the potential of gene sequencing to identify molecular targets of vulnerability.

Our success would inspire others to emulate our process, creating a formidable infrastructure in genomics to fight disease and improve human health.

To do all this I would build a company around a strategy with five core elements:

Quickly isolate a complete set of human genes that produce proteins, working as partners with the nonprofit institute (which we would support financially).

Create a copy of all human genes capable of producing active proteins within two to three years.

Create a new atlas of human anatomy to describe genes needed to make each type of cell, tissue or organ. (This would be the Human Gene Anatomy Project.)

Determine which genes were altered or damaged in disease tissue in contrast to normal tissue. (The Human Gene Pathology Project.)

Finance the company's early stages by licensing our collection of genes to pharmaceutical companies. This handoff of our intellectual property would speed the search for target enzymes and receptors for two reasons: One, Big

Pharma had immense research and manufacturing prowess. And two, they could select whatever targets from our collection of genes that matched the type of drugs they focused on in their business strategies.

SEEING FIFTEEN STEPS AHEAD

People who take what many others see as risk after risk, I have observed, have vastly different profiles of risk aversion than most people. The perception of the risk versus the reward is not daunting; the reward looks so attractive, the path so clear.

I have always had a particular skill for seeing an entire picture, to reconstruct an entire globe from a tiny grain of sand. Most people cannot do that. Some others have the ability to *imagine* the grain of sand and then construct a world. I do not have that ability. I need to see the grain of sand.

When I do see a path that is open, I see it so clearly that I think other people must not have seen it yet or are not seeing it the same way I do. I am aware of downsides, that things can fail. But I can see ten, fifteen steps ahead; what is likely to happen, what the end results will be. And then drive toward that end, anticipating what the barriers will be and how to overcome them.

Have I maximized impact and returns that might have been possible? That is impossible to know. But I have done fine.

In 1992, many if not most genomic scientists believed the primary goal of sequencing the genome was to understand the genetic basis of inherited differences, especially inherited differences that impact health and disease.[136]

In the early days of the Human Genome Project, officially launched by the U.S. government in 1990, many of its leaders were geneticists.[137] Jim Watson was the first director. They believed that understanding the genetic basis of disease would reveal clues to new cures. Once an inherited disease was described, knowledge of the complete genome would vastly accelerate the discovery of the responsible gene or genes. Knowing the gene and its function would open the path to new cures. "All disease is genetic," was their catchphrase.

I mention this because my approach was nearly polar opposite. If I had a single gene, I could tell what that gene does in the human body. If I can do this for one gene, why not for all genes? No reason whatsoever. And if I can do it for all genes, I can do it for all diseases that are inherited, and all disease linked microbes that are not inherited. "Genomics is not necessarily genetics," was my catchphrase.

I was convinced now that starting a new company was the right idea, and again met with Wally.

"You are right," I acknowledged. But, still cautious about this dubious organization pairing, I added that we would need to build our own independent capabilities for gene discovery as soon as possible.

"I am going to request a two year leave of absence from Harvard to serve as chief executive," I said, without hesitation. "They do not guarantee positions for longer than that for professors who leave for government service. I think they might be willing to make the same exception for me. (They were.) Let's meet next week and work out the details."

Today my vision of a genomics field within the rapidly expanding repertoire of biotechnology nearly thirty years ago does not seem revolutionary.

CATECHISM FOR PARRYING SKEPTICS

Let me take you back to the prevailing view of genome research at that time and, in this dialogue format, open a window into the skepticism I encountered—and how I responded. Did I convince everyone? No. But I did convince myself.

Bill, why in the world did you leave Harvard to start Human Genome Sciences? All you will have at the end of the day is a bucketful of genes that have no known function. As a geneticist, when I track down the cause of an inherited disease, I know what it does.

Well, as a geneticist you are the last specialist I would go to with a medical problem. You might be able to tell me why I have the problem, but unless I have one of the handful of inherited diseases for which there is a cure you will shake your head sorrowfully and say, "Someday we may have a cure." How many inherited diseases exist for which we already know the genetic causes? Many. For how many do we have a cure? Only a handful. That will not change in our lifetimes.

What a pessimist. Don't you want to know what causes all these diseases?

Let's get real. You and I know that at most only ten percent of diseases have a strong inherited component. For example, only ten percent of breast cancers are inherited. Same or even less for Alzheimer's disease. Your rallying cry, "All disease is genetic," is deceptive. Yes, all diseases involve genes. They also involve cells, tissues and organs. Saying all disease is genetic is the same as saying, "All human disease is human."

You say you can isolate all human genes. But you won't know what they do? That's of no use at all. At least when we find a gene using genetics we know what it does.

Let me play Socrates for a minute. Say I have one functional gene. (A functional gene produces an active protein.) We know it can make a protein but we have no idea at all what that protein does. Okay?

Sure. That is just what I was saying.

Yet once I have the gene in pure form in a test tube I can then discover easily in what cell, tissue and organ the gene is made. You will agree, right?

Yes. I can see how you can do that.

Then, if I make an antibody to that protein, I can easily know where in body the protein is made, in what organ tissue and cell it is made, and even where within the cell the protein acts even if I don't know what the protein does. Then I can discover whether or not the protein is more or less abundant in a diseased organ or tissue. Correct?

I suppose so.

Then I can find out what happens if I inactivate the gene or overproduce the protein in a cell or even in an experimental animal. I can do that too, can't I?

It may take a fair bit of work, but yes you can.

Then you agree that I can discover the function of any gene I isolate, as well as its role in health and disease. Am I right?

Yes, but there are a lot of genes. Are you actually telling me that you will not be looking at inherited differences?

Yes there are a lot of genes. But new methods are constantly being developed to allow us to do this work faster and faster. We have robots to do what you and I used to do standing for hours at the bench, transferring small drops of liquid from one tube to another. Robots do this type of work several hundred times faster. Besides we will only focus on a subset of genes that we think may be medically important. What we can do for one gene, we can do for many.

As for your second question, as latter day anatomists and pathologists, we ask what parts of the body are common to all people and diseases. My intent is to develop one drug for one disease for all people with that disease, not one drug for one person. I do understand that some diseases are very rare, affecting as few of five to ten people only. Yes, there is value in finding a cure for those diseases. But that is not my goal. I want to find solutions for diseases that affect many thousands if not millions.

My rallying cry is: Genomics is not necessarily genetics. It is also anatomy, pathology and drug discovery.

A JARRING NEW DETAIL

Early the next week when Wally and I met as planned, he opened the conversation with a stunner.

"Bill, you know Alan and I promised the Institute fifty million dollars over five years to support the nonprofit research institute. As CEO of the parent company, you have the responsibility to raise the money."

"What did you just say?!!" I exclaimed, startling diners nearby.

"I said, you are responsible for making good our promise," Wally repeated, firmly.

"You made the promise," I shot back. "You pay!"

"We can't," he said. "Alan and I at most can come up with twenty million for both your ventures. Our limited partners put a cap of fifteen million on any single one of my ventures and five million on Alan's."

"Do they know your limits?"

"We never told them."

"That's just great," I said, sarcastically. "I have to reconsider."

Wally must have anticipated my response, as well he should have. He didn't miss a beat. "But here is my idea," he said. "You remember I was research director at Johnson & Johnson. I know how they think. Once they realize we will come up with new and useful drug targets, they will be dying to get their hands on them. They will fight for rights to use our data."

He then laid out a plan to generate the funds for the Institute and our own requirements by licensing our data on specific genes to five or six different companies. "One will be able to use the data to find drugs to treat heart and vascular disease. Another will use it to discover new ways to treat neuro-psychiatric problems. A third can use it to discover new anti-pain or anti-inflammatory drugs. Each will pay us twenty five million dollars for access. We may even negotiate a separate fee for each gene, and a royalty, if they bring a drug to market.

"There will be a big premium on being first to develop the genome data," he went on. "That is why the deal with the Institute is so important. We can get started right away. All the NIH scientists have to do is change where they park their car in Bethesda. The Institute will be as close to the NIH campus as we can find. You should locate right next door since your company will have commercial rights."

NONNEGOTIABLE CONDITIONS

This scenario seemed feasible but only to a point. "I understand what you are proposing, but it is very risky," I said.

I realized I needed to create options to protect myself and my career. The first condition was to adjust my exit plan at Harvard to keep the door open at the medical school and Dana-Farber if I decided to return to my labs and teaching. "This is what I am willing to do," I said. "Instead of taking a leave of absence, I will take a sabbatical. That way all of my grant funding and lab work will stay intact, and I can return to Harvard anytime."

I told Wally after a quick mental calculation that we likely would need to raise at least fifty million for the Institute and another fifty million for our company. "If and when I see that we have the money we need, I then will convert the sabbatical to a leave of absence," I said. "But I cannot assume the title of CEO during a sabbatical." This restriction on sabbaticals led me to the second condition to protect my interests with Wally before moving ahead. "My caveat is that you must do everything I ask as if I were CEO," I said, flatly, firmly. "The moment you don't, it is back to Harvard for me with no hard feelings. Do you agree?"

Wally was unfazed, thankfully. "You got it, Bill. Let's shake."

If I did not have such faith in Wally's integrity, I would have dropped the entire proposal right there. Just the same, I did not waste any time before putting Wally's pledge to the test.

"Okay. Here is my first CEO decision. The goal of the company will be to discover, develop and market new drugs. Licensing our technology to other companies is not our purpose; it is only a financing strategy. This is nonnegotiable. Do you agree?"

"Yes. What you describe is a long and hard road, but I agree."

"My second decision is we will make a licensing deal with one, and only one, company. We are not going to parcel out discoveries one company at a time."

"I'm listening. What's your rationale?"

I had had so much direct experience by then with Big Pharma research directors and chief executives that I was certain they would pay a lot more for exclusive rights than the partial access Wally had outlined. Nothing in that part of his licensing scheme appealed to me.

"You know how insecure they are," I said. "If there are many hands in the pot, they effectively will be competing. Each company will be convinced one of the others will find the best candidates for drug development before they do."

Then I raised the matter of the unknown in drug discovery and development, and potential serendipity. "When you start a drug discovery program based on one gene, which will be the case, you cannot predict all the uses the drug may have," I said. "For example, a drug developed for anxiety might also stop a virus. I know of one that works against HIV."

Finally, the urgency for speed, of moving quickly to set the early pace in genomics research and development. "Negotiating with several companies to parcel out licensing access will take much more time than negotiating with one," I said. "We are selling a perishable diamond. Given time, and not much time at that, others will copy us. The value of our company will plummet. Agreed?"

"Yes. I agree."

This final point was prophetic, and no surprise. Several companies, such as Incyte and Millennium, were founded with a year. Both billed themselves as a new kind of enterprise, a bio-dot.com, with an initial business model to create and sell DNA sequence information, not develop or market their own drugs. They raised about ten million dollars or less from each licensing partner, but little or no royalty payments if their data were used in the discovery of successful drugs. As you will see, our financing strategy proved many times more valuable.

The tone of this conversation with Wally was essential for its salutary outcome. I knew that I must raise all concerns with him then, putting my cards on the table transparently and bluntly. He needed to know my hesitations, and my conditions to remove them. I needed to know what he would commit to, and any issues that might give him pause. Once our positions were clear, and we had agreed, there was just one more question to settle.

"What name should we give the company?" he asked.

"I like Human Genome Sciences," I replied. "The name signals what we do, and why we are different."

"I like it, too," he said.

ADVICE TO YOUNG SCIENTISTS: ON BUSINESS, TIMING

It is tempting for young scientists to think business is easier than science. It is not. Business is more challenging in many ways.

You are not going to be prepared for business as a scientist until you understand human motivation. As an academic scientist you are in a particular bubble, relatively isolated or protected. Human society is infinitely complex. It has many varied pieces. You need to develop your understanding of different kinds of institutions and people.

There is no barrier in business for an expert to appear who is better than you. Often there will be. In business, there are geniuses who think exclusively about making money. The purpose of capital is to make more capital. These geniuses are dedicated to making more capital.

One day when you are in business, inevitably, you will find yourself across the table from one of these geniuses, maybe two or three, and you will be outclassed. If you are a scientist you have a calling to do something different, some purpose that is not necessarily determined by money.

Young scientists should stay in their academic positions until they are well established, an expert in their field. Your knowledge and reputation take years to build as an academic scientist. Once your knowledge and reputation are established, they are unassailable.

If you believe a really big idea has come out of your research, ask yourself: What is the best tool to implement this idea? A university? A government lab? A startup company? A small company already established in the same field? A big company with massive research budgets conducting studies in the same field?

These are all wonderful tools. Analyze them for the best fit regarding your goal, your technology and which institutions would best enable your ideas to have the greatest impact in society.

MARTY'S VERDICT

Marty Lipton had listened keenly, patiently, occasionally lobbing in a question, as I walked him through all the twists and turns of this saga only a few days after sealing my commitment with Wally.

I wanted to hire him as my legal counsel in creating Human Genome Sciences. But I could tell he had concerns... as if I were about to leap from a schooner with five towering masts into an empty rowboat. He had seen that drama play out for clients many times.

After I finished, though, underscoring my conditions and Wally's buy-in to those conditions, I detected a hint of a smile. Maybe a touch of admiration and respect as well.

Then Marty Lipton gave me his verdict, agreeably and resolutely, "If this is what you want to do, I will help you do it."

And so we began.

27

HITTING THE MARK

My first idea for a potential licensing partner was Bristol-Myers, where I enjoyed a good relationship for at least two reasons.

The company had been a generous contributor just a year before to our HIV/AIDS research, awarding my Dana-Farber lab five hundred thousand dollars over five years.[138] Moreover, the company's recently appointed research director was a former Yale professor I knew well.

He invited me for a meeting, and immediately recognized the significance of my proposal to provide Bristol-Myers exclusive access to our data.

"Bill, you have a great idea," he told me as he walked me out the door of his office. "If I thought I could convince my management, I would sign an eighty million dollar agreement tomorrow. But I know them well enough to know they will never go for it. I wish you the best of luck."

Far from discouraged, I was energized by fortuitous insight: a price floor for future negotiations to license our data! Eighty million dollars.

THE REMARKABLE GEORGE POSTE

One piece of advice I gave my Harvard classes—undergraduates, graduate students and postdocs alike—was to treat everyone in those classes as if you are on a lifelong journey together because... *you are*. Make maximum efforts to stay on good terms with everyone you come across when you are young because they are going to be with you when you are old.

It is not enough to focus only on what *you* do and what you do well. Help everybody around you do as best as they can. People have broad networks and over time people in those networks will ask them about you. What do you think of him or her? Should we do this with them? Or do that with them?

During the 1970s, I met a British virologist named George Poste whose cancer research at the University of Buffalo also examined DNA damage and repair. A Formula 500 race driver in his young 20s, George was intense, brilliant and, literally and figuratively, hard driving and highly caffeinated (consuming thirty cups of coffee daily).[139]

By the late '80s, now heading all research of newly merged SmithKline Beecham, he was keenly interested in our lab studies on potential HIV drug targets. I considered him a promising prospect for licensing access to our genome data library. When I contacted George, he immediately agreed to meet me in Washington.

Walking toward me under the vaulted marble arches in Union Station, George extended his hand vigorously and, before I said anything, exclaimed, "Hi, Bill! Let's make a deal!" "Okay," I replied. "Let's do!"

Within two months of that handshake, we signed the largest single transaction of biotech's first two decades: one hundred twenty five million dollars from SmithKline Beecham for exclusive rights to data we were rapidly assembling on human genes for drug development plus a seven percent stake in Human Genome Sciences equity. We first agreed on one hundred million dollars, then George asked to include Takeda Pharmaceutical in the deal, which I agreed to for another twenty five million.

Human Genome Sciences retained rights to use our data for our own drug discovery programs, but gave SmithKline the option to develop a drug first, if it wished to, from a specific gene. If they did not exercise that right within sixty days, we were free to go ahead.

Whoever forged ahead first was required to offer evidence to the other partner of its continuing best efforts to develop the drug—or forfeit that exclusive right. Revenues would be split 80:20, with the developer-marketer receiving the eighty percent share. Each company would cover its own costs to develop drugs from our data library and related marketing programs.

When I met with Wally and other principals at HealthCare Ventures a few weeks after the deal was signed, I had already notified Harvard of my plan for a two year leave of absence. The HealthCare team was eager for details. "How did you do it, Bill?"

"George knew what he wanted before I said a word," I said, still mildly incredulous myself in the afterglow, and added that I speculated he had at least two motivations. First, I knew from past dealings that George as a scientist had bold vision and favored big ideas; our idea was about as big as they come. He also was new in his job and wanted to make a strong impression; this deal checked that box as well.

"That said," I continued, "we were just plain lucky to have him as a counter party. I don't know of any executive in the industry who would have done the same, especially so quickly." In a cover story eighteen months later on the biotech boom on Wall Street, "Genetics – The Money Rush is On," *Fortune* magazine seemed to agree with me, concluding, "Seldom has a major corporation put up so much money at such an early stage for a technology being developed by someone else."[140]

A TAXI WITH THE LIGHT ON

I believe you can never convince anyone to do a deal. They must convince themselves. All you can do is offer an opportunity for them to have what they already know they want.

You cannot change someone's perception of the world, their perception of you or their will to do something. You cannot sell something to someone unless they believe they need it. George Poste understood what genomics would mean for drug development before our tête-à-tête in Union Station. He had belief and will. He wanted access to our data library for diagnostics and chemical discovery.

You have to find people who already have decided to do what you can help them do. Then you will have a chance.

As we will see in the chapters on the global health think tank I created, ACCESS Health International, this conviction about motivation guides our work in many countries. We look for people who understand they need tools for improving public health and want to make that change. We share knowledge about how people do it better in other places and then we advise them. We help them make that change.

Either people are ready for a relationship with you or they are not. That goes for every aspect of life. As my brother Eric puts it, occasionally a taxi comes by and the light is on. You raise your arm, the taxi stops, you take a seat and move ahead toward your destination.

A PUBLIC COMPANY

Venture capitalists are by nature impatient. Custodians of funds contributed by investors, their limited partners, they are always under pressure to return capital to these investors as soon as possible. Limited partners all hope for quick outsized returns on their investment to compensate for putting their money at risk in early stage companies.

Investors in Human Genome Sciences were no different.

One way to return capital is to take a company public because once a company's shares are publicly traded, those shares can be cashed in. Our financial progress was so rapid, and publicity around our unprecedented research concepts so intense, that pressure for a public offering began to mount as soon as the ink on our contract with SmithKline dried. Then, too, market conditions that summer and early fall of 1993 were favorable; investors were eager to invest in biotech companies. I had witnessed dramatic ups and downs in public market appetite for early stage biotech companies during more than ten years of my active involvement in the industry. I knew: Now was a good time. The market was up.

"I think we are ready," I told our board of directors at the September meeting. "We have a great story and the market is hot. We don't need the money now, but we will. You have approved our plans for drug discovery and development. That is expensive."

One director quickly objected. "We are less than a year old," he said and noted, correctly, that for many startups initial public offerings did not happen until at least three of four years after the businesses were organized. (Apple Inc. went public in 1980, four years after its founding.) "True, we were incorporated in the summer of 1992, but we really didn't open shop until January when you came on board."

"You are right. We are new," I replied. "But Fred Frank at Lehman Brothers thinks we can do it and sell shares at a good price. Fred is the dean of biotech bankers. We've worked together on several deals. Let me add my two bits of hard won wisdom. In biotech, you take the money when the window is open. The financing window is open now. Who knows when it will close? When it closes, it closes fast and for a long time."

The board agreed in a unanimous vote, setting in motion plans for Human Genome Sciences to become a publicly traded company in less than four months, raising one hundred eighty million dollars on the last day of 1993, equal roughly to three hundred twenty million dollars now.

MORE LICENSING PARTNERS, MORE REVENUE

Around the time *Fortune* published that cover story, SmithKline's chief operating officer (and future chief executive) J.P. Garnier proposed expanding the licensing structure more broadly, jointly, to other pharmaceutical companies. Our partnership was working smoothly and SmithKline was well into developing its first drugs from our data.

"Suppose together we offer our collection of human genes and all we learn about them to other companies in return for upfront payments and co-rights to sell any drugs they discover from our collection," J.P. told me in his spacious office overlooking downtown Philadelphia. "SmithKline and Human Genome Sciences will split whatever we make fifty-fifty."

I immediately liked his concept, and especially welcomed his initiative. But I had to raise two concerns. Wouldn't prospective partners shy away, anticipating we had picked over the best gene prospects before making others available for them? Also, how extensive would the co-rights be?

"Yes, they will worry that we have first choice but once we show them the data, which we will have to do, some will be convinced," he replied. "The human genome offers more opportunities for drug development than all the biotech and Big Pharma companies combined can use."

"I want the maximum co-rights we can negotiate," he went on. "Some may be foreign companies. Ideally, I would like to share markets with them. Then we may be able to market the drug in the U.S. Others may not care about Asian, African and South American markets, which we could pursue on our own. At minimum I will ask for the same 80:20 arrangement we have. As for us, Human Genome Sciences and SmithKline will split all revenues equally, 50:50."

That approach, formula and rationale all made sense, and we agreed to get moving. Over the next year, we negotiated separate deals with Merck KGaA, a German company; Sythelabo in France; and Schering-Plough in the U.S. Human Genome Sciences and SmithKline collected three hundred and twenty million dollars upfront, then split those revenues equally.

These transactions pushed total revenues *booked and received* in our company's first eighteen months to two hundred and eighty five million dollars. And that did not include our rights to revenue from products other companies would develop and market from our data.

BOARD MISCREANTS, BIOTECH PORTFOLIO NEOPHYTES

The job of a public company CEO is demanding, a leadership role that spans strategy, operations, financing as well as communications with all employees and directors and all external constituent groups such as investors, regulators and journalists.

We were in uncharted waters with our strategy at Human Genome Sciences, inventing a new way to discover drugs and then proposing to use our discoveries to bring new drugs to market.

The first generation of biotechnology companies had a much simpler task. They typically applied a new manufacturing method, recombinant DNA technology, to producing drugs that already had established markets. Some of the newer companies, such as those I created with Wally, had narrowly defined objectives. ProScript's was to produce a drug to block protein degradation; at the Virus Research Institute, to create a new vaccine adjuvant.

Managing our early investors, the venture capitalists, required varying levels of collaboration and hand holding, and, occasionally, confrontation.

After several years a serious issue arose. We had been able to attract brilliant scientists in part because we offered a bountiful stock option package. Our key employees received additional stock options at the end of each year. To retain this talented team and hire additional staff the board needed regularly to increase the option pool. But now, with the pool close to empty, some venture capitalists on the board balked. They didn't want their shares diluted, which increasing the option pool would certainly do.

I enlisted the help of outside securities lawyers and two friends, both globally prominent investors who had each accumulated a fifteen percent stake in our company. Gaining the support of these two investors, though, required delicate diplomacy. There was bad blood between them unrelated to Human Genome Sciences, the fallout from earlier high stakes financial clashes.

I was fortunate to have a savvy diplomat at hand. I had recruited Richard Holbrooke, the former Assistant Secretary of State and future U.S. ambassador to the United Nations, to our board of directors shortly after we organized the company. We met when Richard approached me after my Aspen Institute presentation in the early '90s on genomic science and HIV/

AIDS. "This is really interesting," he said that day. "I need to learn more." We became close friends.

Richard now was a partner at investment firm Credit Suisse First Boston, stepping away from his diplomatic career for a few years. We agreed that I should explain the options problem to the two big investors in separate conversations and ask them to lean on the miscreant directors causing us problems.

"Once we are out of options we can't retain our best people," I told them, quite separately. "I won't be able to hire the new people I need to move into manufacturing and clinical trials. I have already lost two scientists I really wanted to keep. You own a significant share of the company and you understand this. Please tell these other board members they are failing their fiduciary duty; their obligations are to the company, not their limited partners or themselves. They have a short term perspective. You are interested in long term value. Let them know that you are willing to take the dilution because you believe it will create even greater value."

Happily, both investors relayed the message. The balking venture capitalists resigned, I appointed new directors and, with more options to give, proceeded to award valuable grants to our scientists and executives.

Communications with our public shareholders consumed a vast amount of my working hours, far more than anticipated. Institutional investors, big insurance companies, pension funds and investment management firms, mostly, owned the majority of our shares. These funds often managed several billion dollars, allocating only a small part to biotech.

Some managers of the biotech investment portfolios were true professionals with long experience in the pharmaceutical and biotech arena. Most were not. I often found myself meeting with a twenty seven year old Harvard or Yale graduate who might have been reassigned two weeks before we met from investing in the telecom sector to overseeing several hundred million dollars in a biotech fund. These were not fun conversations.

"Tell me about biotech," they would begin. "What is your competitive advantage over company X, Y or Z?"... in effect asking me to fill in cavernous blanks in their competitive intelligence. "So and so says you are not on the right track. What do you say?" After the hundredth iteration, and I am not exaggerating, these neophyte analyst conversations became tiresome.

My business friends and especially my chief financial officer counseled patience.

"Stick to your story line, Bill," they said. "Repeat the story no matter what the question. Never criticize another company; your comments will bounce back at you immediately. You may find these naïve questions irritating, but we assure you that your attitude will change the moment you want to raise more money."

All I can say is that I took their advice and did my best to remain patient during the hundreds of meetings that followed over the next ten years. As we will see shortly, I would indeed want to raise more money.

Finally, there was communicating with the investment community as a whole, the news media and the general public.

There was intense interest in what knowledge of the genome might bring. I was lucky to have gained confidence in speaking with the news media during my antiwar work in the '70s and the early days of the HIV epidemic in the '80s. Human Genome Sciences was featured in dozens of articles in business magazines and newspapers as well as the mainstream press. Most were positive, including cover stories in *Business Week*[141] and *Forbes* as well as *Fortune*.

THE WONDER YEAR: 1999

Despite rapid progress on many fronts, our stock price had been stagnant, rising and falling in a narrow range slightly above the offering price through the late '90s. No matter what the news, good or bad, there was little change. In 1999 things began to change—and change fast. It was the year of dot. com mania. Prices in tech stocks and telecom began to soar... beyond thirty, forty, fifty times annual earnings per share, as companies spent aggressively on information technology to forestall possible disaster from the forecasted Y2K debacle. A historic stock bubble was forming.

Soon biotech stocks, including ours, were lassoed into the center ring. The word on the street was genomics was hot, time to invest. And invest they did. The price of Human Genome Sciences shares was rising almost daily. I had never witnessed such a bubble before (and nothing to compare since). I was certain this was a unique circumstance. My role as CEO was to take advantage in the smartest possible way to bolster Human Genome Science's financial strength.

I persuaded our board to try a new financing strategy, issuing convertible notes. You had to be an optimist to issue these, believing your stock price was heading higher. And I was. Convertible notes are a form of corporate debt that carries a pledge for the note holder to convert the note to common shares. When the price of Human Genome Sciences common shares rose to a certain price, for example, a twenty percent increase over the purchase price of the note, we could demand conversion and, in the process, reduce our total debt burden.

There was a second advantage. The notes could be sold overnight with no road show. Every time we offered new stock for sale, we were required to conduct a costly, time consuming road show. (A higher expense item.) Moreover, existing investors fearing dilution would sell, dropping the final offering price for the new shares. (Probability of a lower stock price, actually or comparatively.) That could not happen with overnight converts.

The bank underwriting these note sales would carry much of the risk. The bank would buy the notes at the market price and sell them as they could. If our underlying stock price rose, so would the notes' market price. The bank would rake in the upside profit. However, if our stock price declined, the bank would face losses, forced to unload the notes at prices below what they paid us.

To give you a sense of how unpredictable these deals can be, Fred Frank's Lehman Brothers turned me down despite our previous history together. I went next to Merrill Lynch chief executive David Komansky. Years before he had invited me to serve as a juror on a tech prize that Merrill awarded each year. David himself was tempted to underwrite our note sales, but in the end, he told me, his bankers were too wary they might be left holding notes they could not sell.

Now what? Richard Holbrooke again delivered the solution, introducing me to Allen Wheat, chief executive of CS First Boston. After conferring with his group in the London office that handled convertible note sales, Allen said yes.

The transaction soon turned into a cliff hanger, especially for Allen and his bank. They were obligated to pay us full face value of this transaction, the first of four planned note sales, thirty days after the sale began. The full value was approximately two hundred and fifty million dollars. If the note price fell, they could take a big loss. After a stable first day, the stock price began a steady downward drift each day, first a decline of 0.1%, then 0.2%.

On day twenty five, the note price still substantially under water, I was cruising along the picturesque drive between San Francisco and Stanford University in Palo Alto when my mobile phone rang. It was Komansky.

"Bill, your friends at Credit Suisse First Boston are going to take a bath," he said. "Thank God we didn't take the deal." His tone was friendly, expressing privately his personal relief at avoiding a big loss for Merrill much more than needling me, although there was a touch of that too. I responded in the same spirit: "David, great of you to call. I appreciate the thought. It's not over yet."

Then, a sudden change of fortune. The next day our stock price began to rise, first to the original conversion price for the notes, and then well beyond. At the thirty day mark, Credit Suisse was able not only to sell all the notes but also what is called the green shoe, an allotment beyond the scheduled offering of two hundred and fifty million dollars. We received all of our planned proceeds, and Credit Suisse made many millions on the transaction. Courage rewarded!

I am a bit ashamed to say I did call David back. "Too bad, David," I said. "You missed out. You will miss out on the next one too. I'm sticking with Credit Suisse." He was gracious, as I expected. "Bill, what can I say? I am sorry for making that call to decline your deal. It wasn't right. I wish you all the luck you deserve."

ANOTHER CLIFF HANGER

Our stock price continued its meteoric ascent and we quickly met the conversion price; we now had all the proceeds from the note sale, and none of the debt burden. We followed that first convertible offering by three others in quick succession and by the end of summer had raised almost one billion dollars. The first three note offerings all quickly hit their conversion price.

With the scorching market for biotech equities still prominent in the dot-com bubble, we decided to schedule a traditional stock offering complete with road show, this time for six hundred million dollars.

Credit Suisse again took the lead, with a stellar group of supporting banks all eager to participate in and profit from our rising good fortune. After we filed required paperwork with the Securities and Exchange Commission in mid-September, we learned they decided on a full review that could take up to two months. By the third week in October, I was becoming more anxious by the day. The market remained smoking hot, but I felt the heat could dissipate rapidly.

One reason was Y2K. No one knew whether computer systems worldwide would collapse in the opening days of January, or the potential impact on millions of daily market transactions. Some predicted chaos. Then, too, looking ahead to the 2000 presidential election, I knew stock market history signaled trepidation. Market prices typically languish, moderately, amid uncertainty about presidential election outcomes. I figured George W. Bush versus Al Gore would be too close to call. If Gore pulled ahead in polls, the market might cool quickly.

Waiting for the SEC's clearance, I prepared, organizing three teams to conduct what would amount to an instant road show. We worked out a minute-by-minute schedule of presentations, with more than sixty planned for four days beginning on a Monday and finishing by Thursday. I would lead the East Coast and Midwest team. A second executive would take care of the West Coast and South. A third would cover European investors. Each of us had our own plane reserved to zip us from one city to the next.

The SEC's green light arrived late on a Friday, on Monday morning we were on our way and by Thursday midday we had our coveted outcome: a full book of orders at a price slightly above our target. "Over and done," I thought, eager and ready to relax and celebrate. But just as I stepped onto the tarmac ladder for the private jet primed to fly our group to New York, I received an urgent call from a major money manager in the Midwest.

He said, "If you drop the offering price by five percent and increase the size to accommodate us, I will buy an additional three hundred million dollars' worth of shares."

An unexpected windfall!... potentially. It now was almost the end of the business day on the East Coast, deadline for closing our stock offering, so I had to hustle. With only minutes to spare, I called our lead bank then quickly assembled a quorum of our directors by phone.

"I recommend this deal," I said, with as much conviction as I could muster. "You all know my thinking when it comes to raising money. This is a unique chance to add another year or more of operating cash to our bank account. There may be tough days ahead. When crossing a desert you need all the supplies you can carry. Please let me do this." They agreed and the bankers quickly accommodated our Midwest buyer.

We closed the plane doors and flew off to our celebration in New York City. A whirlwind four days on the road. Another nine hundred million dollars in our coffers, added to the one billion already tallied from our four note offerings.

What a year.

WHAT WE PROVED

My concerns about a reversal in the market proved prescient. Human Genome Sciences needed every penny of the $1.9 billion we raised that year to outlast what came next.

The dot-com crash began in the spring of 2000, touching off sharp declines in market values for another two years. The hung election of Bush v. Gore added to the initial turmoil, freezing markets in the final months of 2000.

Yet our company's finances remained strong. We retained nearly $1.7 billion in cash reserves at the end of 2001. With multiple licensing agreements still in place, and operations drawing down roughly eighty five million dollars a year in cash, Human Genomes Sciences' balance sheet was geared as I planned for the long haul. In 2001, *TIME* magazine named me one of the twenty five most important business executives in the world. (I stepped down as Human Genome Sciences' chairman and chief executive in 2004. The decision, as I turned sixty, soon led me to global health philanthropy and consulting, my principal activity now for fifteen years.)

Stock market enthusiasm for genome companies never revived. From the late 1999 high of $110, Human Genome Sciences shares began a long slide to near oblivion before ultimately bottoming at thirty five *cents* a share. The shares remained virtually moribund until the company's first drug was approved by the FDA in 2011.

Isolating the chemistry for this drug was an important discovery, extremely important for lupus patients. Using genome data we created the design for this drug in the lab in the mid-'90s. Years of trials began in 2001 before the FDA could begin its review process and, eventually, approve the drug for treating lupus patients. My experience with the FDA has always been positive. They do their best to help you get your drug to market as fast as possible. They are not a roadblock. They are an enabler. Unfortunately, political considerations seemed to interfere with FDA functioning at the time of COVID-19.

It took Human Genome Sciences sixteen years to develop and begin in 2011 to market the drug, Benlysta. News of the FDA ruling sent Human Genome Sciences shares soaring in value almost a hundred fold overnight, to $35. Later that year, Amgen took a serious look at acquiring Human Genome Sciences and bid $7 billion, roughly the same $35 a share. Human Genomes Sciences' board rejected the offer.

GlaxoSmithKline did buy the company a year later at half the Amgen offer, $3.6 billion, amidst another nadir of market interest in biotech companies. Glaxo's bid amounted to $14.25 a share.

Benlysta's odyssey since Glaxo's acquisition has become a classic example in demonstrating genome screening's power: identifying targets for and developing a new drug that has advanced over a quarter century towards near blockbuster status.

We proved in Human Genome Sciences that our brand of genomics could dramatically accelerate the search for genes and proteins as targets for new drugs to fight disease. When I began, the entire field could identify no more than two hundred valid target genes and proteins in all of medicine. Two years later, that number had soared to several thousand.

Yes, we could identify new targets. What we could not do is accelerate the process of drug discovery. Companies still must identify new compounds, then conduct human trials to ensure their safety. As we will see in the next chapter, especially through the Benlysta story, that process remains long, complex and costly.

‖28‖

GENES TO DRUGS

HUMAN GENOME SCIENCES HAD NO TROUBLE recruiting talented scientists once we explained our plans to rapidly sequence thousands of protein generating genes.

The first one I tried to reach by phone after my lunch with Wally Steinberg had been one of my top PhD students, a collaborator on several HIV/AIDS studies and published papers. Craig Rosen now was directing his own laboratory at the Roche Institute of Molecular Biology, in New Jersey, an elite organization of pure scientific research.[142]

"Cindy, is Craig home? I'm calling from D.C."

"No, but he will be back later tonight. He is already on the train."

"Okay, thanks. By the way, are you prepared to move to D.C. next month?"

"What??!! What are you talking about??!! We just bought a new house here in New Jersey. Craig didn't say anything about this!"

"Don't blame him. He doesn't know yet. He will explain what is happening after I speak with him this evening."

SCIENCE ALL STARS

Craig had the brains, the drive, the organizational ability and the instincts necessary for a superb research director. After our brief conversation that night, he was all in. He accepted my offer to become Human Genome Sciences' scientific director and move his family to D.C.

Within three months, we had a team as good or better than most universities. Craig, a marvelous recruiter, joined me in signing up several of my postdoctoral fellows and former students as well as skilled molecular biologists, biochemists and other scientists in his own networks.

One group focused on identifying new drug targets, a second on developing techniques to isolate and characterize new genes. The latter was essential for us to avoid depending on the Institute for Genomic Research. To do that, we needed our own library of sequenced genes for gene-based medicine. Within six months, we were isolating and characterizing human genes at an ever accelerating clip.

By mid-1994, our library had more than twenty thousand full length copies of expressed human genes—and a sophisticated system for retrieving details on each of those twenty thousand genes. Think of a Google search engine built solely for users of this rapidly growing information library. I named it *The Oracle*.

"You can ask our computer any question about a human gene and receive a meaningful answer in seconds," I explained in an orientation session for our young scientists, most in their late 20s.

"We know in what cell and tissue the gene is expressed. We know its abundance in that cell relative to other expressed genes. We know if the gene is active in normal cells, and how it changes in health and disease. The information we have is many times that available in the scientific and medical literature."

I asked them to consider which disease they most wanted to prevent or cure, then pursue that goal. And then I reiterated a fact I knew had attracted many to Human Genome Sciences.

"What would have taken you months or years you now can do in a few days," I said. "Do the research to know what cells and tissues are likely involved. Ask *The Oracle* what genes and proteins are likely responsible for the imbalance causing the clinical disease. If you find that it is a protein, let us know. We will evaluate it as a potential target for new drugs. Bring us new genes that we can use for medicine."

"CLONE BY PHONE"

Around that time, I heard from an eminent cancer researcher, a pioneer at Baltimore's Johns Hopkins University in the rapidly growing discipline of understanding genes that held cancer in check. "Professor Bert Vogelstein is on the line," my executive assistant said, poking her head inside my office door. "He says it is urgent."

I had known and highly respected Bert since the '70s. His most recent research illuminated ways that cells prevent themselves from growing out of control. He worked on proteins (called p53) that inhibit the formation and growth of cancer cells and other proteins (APC: adenomatous polyposis coli) that stimulate the immune system's production of infection fighting white blood cells. Mutations in either p53 or APC contribute to colon cancer.[143]

"Beautiful work, Bert," I said.

"In fact, that's why I'm calling," he said. "We may know the type of genes that are damaged in one type of inherited colon cancer. Geneticists call it heritable nonpolypoid colon carcinoma."

"Sure, I know about that disease. If I remember there is about a fifty percent chance that carriers develop an aggressive form of colon cancer," I replied, adding that I recalled there also was a chance for developing ovarian, endometrial (uterine lining) and stomach cancer.

"You're right. It is not only the risk of colon cancer," Bert said. "We've mapped where the genes are in the genome, but have not yet identified them. They might protect cells from making mistakes"—or, mutations—"during DNA replication. They might be mismatch repair enzymes—enzymes that clean up mistakes cells make when copying their DNA.

"I am sure we can find them using standard techniques but it might take a few years," he went on. "There may be a shortcut. Do you have any human genes in your collection that resemble the bacterial mismatch enzymes? If you do, I can quickly compare the sequence of those genes in people with the disease to the normal sequences."

"That's exciting," I said. By then our gene identification software, *The Oracle*, was running smoothly, tapping our data library for the twenty thousand full length DNA copies in our freezers. I reminded Bert that each was capable of making a unique human protein. "I'll get back to you right away."

My informatics team had the answer the next morning after an overnight *Oracle* inquiry. "Great news, Bert," I said. "We have copies of two different genes, each very similar to the bacterial mismatch repair genes of E. coli. Come down this afternoon. We will give you samples and you can get started right away."

Two weeks later, after examining the samples, Bert confirmed his hunch to me about the enzyme mismatch. "This is yet another example of how cancer cells escape control," he said.

"People with heritable nonpolypoid carcinoma inherit one of two defects. One set have damage to one of the mismatch genes you sent. The rest have damage to the other. Missing these enzymes in your body is like being exposed to the most dangerous carcinogens every day. No wonder people who can't repair these enzyme mismatches get colon cancer."[144]

This discovery was a landmark for colon cancer treatment and prevention. The news, coupled with Bert's impeccable reputation, immediately elevated Human Genome Sciences' standing, validating publicly the high quality of our science. Many of our critics faded away.

I found it mildly amusing that this seminal event for us centered on a discovery about inherited disease. "Genomics is not inheritance," I reminded myself, laughing. What irony. Well, in this situation, we had something close. Our genomics *illuminated* inheritance.

In his paper a few months later summarizing the research and discovery, Bert wrote, graciously: "Having a near complete, ordered set of human genes accelerated the pace of our work enormously. I want to thank Bill Haseltine and those at Human Genome Sciences who made this possible. This is truly a new way to speed the discovery of disease causing genes. I call this, 'clone by phone!'"[145]

WEAPONIZING A PROTEIN

One day the director of our immunology group, David Hilbert, asked, "What is the signal to activate a type of white blood cell, called a B lymphocyte, to produce antibodies?" David had a sweeping idea that, if proven, could open a path to a major medical breakthrough: protection from infections. Within a week, he designed and executed a test, directing our robots to sort through our collection of "signaling" genes to find one capable of making a protein that activated B cells to produce antibodies.

He came up with three prospects but one was much more potent than the others. We named it B-Lymphocyte Stimulator (or BLyS for short, pronounced "bliss"). What medical applications might this more potent protein have? Our first thought was treating people whose immune system could not make antibodies; some carried mutant BLyS genes.

But doctors who specialized in treating these patients were not enthusiastic. "We don't need a new drug," they told us. "Every two months we infuse our patients with gamma globulin. It's inexpensive and it works." They used purified human plasma to treat aplastic anemia, a kind of autoimmune disease that attacks stem cells in bone marrow. "We are sure your drug will be expensive and unnecessary." Strike one!

Our cancer team had another idea during one of our regular drug discovery discussions. "*The Oracle* indicates that the receptor for BLyS is found only on B-Cells, activated B-Cells and B-Cell tumors," they said. "We think if we attach a chemical poison to the BLyS protein, it will kill B-Cell tumors."

Our clinical team responsible for testing new drugs in patients loved the idea. So did the few research oncologists we consulted, including friends at Dana-Farber. In short order we made large quantities of the BLyS protein.

For a "poison" additive, I knew from my prior work that radioactive iodine was a good option. As it decays, radioactive iodine will kill a cell, blasting a hole in the side membrane. We soon signed up a Canadian firm with a cutting edge process to couple radioactive iodine (the poison) to the BLyS protein.

In a matter of months, the FDA allowed us to test the drug in a few patients who had shown no improvement from other treatments. The test results came in far better than hoped. "Look at these photos," said David Stump, head of our clinical trials group. "Radioactive BLyS is a great imaging agent." A trace amount administered intravenously to the patient had lighted up all the tumors.

"Look how much disease this patient has," David continued, pointing to multiple black spots. "You can see tumors all over his body and even in his bones." He then showed me images made before the patient received a high dose of radioactive BLyS and others made two weeks after treatment. Radioactive BLyS had nearly wiped out the multiple myeloma cells. "The tumors are almost all gone," David exclaimed. "This will be a home run!"

Not so, unfortunately. We could not persuade any oncologists around the country to enter some of their B-cell tumor patients in our planned trials. No one would agree. We were stymied, frustrated. We believed we had every piece of biochemical proof to give them optimism that radioactive BLyS would be effective against multiple myeloma, a cancer of plasma cells.

I finally asked one of my former Dana-Farber colleagues what the problem was. He said the roadblock had nothing to do with the drug, and agreed its biochemistry design was rock solid. "We like the data. We think the drug will work," he said.

The problem was organizational silos within hospitals' cancer treatment departments. "Your drug is part chemotherapy, part radiotherapy," my friend explained. "Radiation oncologists are uncomfortable using it" because of the chemotherapy element, "and so are chemotherapists" because of the radiation element. "Believe it or not, they refuse to work together. My colleagues in other hospitals have the same problem."

Without the willing participation of paired oncology specialists to test the drug on their patients, we could not proceed. We did not have the resources to conduct four or five trials simultaneously on our own. Strike two!

FIRST NEW LUPUS DRUG IN FIFTY SIX YEARS

Autoimmune disease happens when the immune systems cells malfunction and mistakenly attacks healthy cells, tissues and organs. Scientists have identified more than eighty varieties. Among the most common are type 1 diabetes, multiple sclerosis, rheumatoid arthritis and lupus.

One afternoon, discussing with our drug development team those first two candidates' setbacks, I mused, "Aren't some autoimmune diseases caused by overactive B cells?

"Why don't we screen arthritis patients, people with multiple sclerosis and others we expect will have high levels of circulating BLyS protein in the blood stream," I added, warming to the idea. "If BLyS is the cause, maybe we can develop an antibody to block it."

"Don't forget lupus patients," the two Davids, Hilbert and Stump, said at almost the same time. "They have such high levels of circulating antibodies that kidneys sometimes become plugged up."

I concurred. Lupus is an autoimmune disease that results when your body's system for fighting infections or healing an injury instead attacks healthy tissue. Inflammation occurs, often causing swelling and pain. Nine out of ten people with lupus are women, often between the ages of fifteen and forty four. "Let's make a test to detect circulating BLyS proteins," I said. "We can use it to test all different types of people with autoimmune disease, including lupus patients."

The test results a few months later ruled out arthritis patients (BLyS levels only slightly elevated) and multiple sclerosis patients. "But look at this!" David Stump said, pointing to a projected slide. "The levels of BLyS in the blood of one third of all lupus patients are off the chart, in some patients more than one hundred times normal. We are definitely on to something. I have never seen hormone levels so far out of whack!"

"Why only a third of lupus patients?" I asked. But then I remembered. Lupus is an episodic disease. Attacks come and go. "Let's follow a group of lupus patients over time," I suggested. "Maybe the levels of BLyS rise only during the flare-ups." That indeed was the case. Results of that test showed levels of BLyS spiking *before* a lupus flare.

We were sure we had our culprit. When we found that mice and rats mimicked lupus symptoms after being injected with BLyS, our confidence rose further. We soon contracted with an innovative young company in England, Cambridge Antibody Technology, to produce a human monoclonal antibody to BLyS.[146] Monoclonal antibodies can be constructed to bind specifically to almost any substance. All are clones of a unique parent cell, the basis for "monoclonal" in the name.

We designed our drug candidate to bind to and inactivate the BLyS protein. The point was for the drug to disarm the protein's damaging effects, which the drug did well in initial tests by preventing arthritis in animals exposed to BLyS.

CLINICAL TRIALS' LONG ROAD

The next step, limited trials with lupus patients, was far more difficult to execute. There was no agreed criteria among regulators for judging success in a drug to treat lupus. No one in recent memory had developed a lupus drug.

Yet FDA officials were accommodating, open minded and willing to work with us. As I've said, my experience with the FDA has always been positive. They have seen many drug failures, many adverse reactions. They know a lot more than you about potential dangers ahead because they have seen people who tried to develop drugs along the same pathway, or with the same class of compounds. There are good reasons when they raise warning flags if you are heading into dangerous territory.

Working with the FDA may be time consuming, but without the FDA no company could sell drugs. Their goal is to find the clearest, shortest pathway for patients to begin treatments with your drug.

They asked us to design a trial with our proposed measures of success, which we did... talking with twenty or so lupus doctors, hiring a whole clinical team and a team of FDA regulation experts. A year later, after canvassing lupus experts across the country for their reactions, the FDA established our trial guidelines. They accepted most of the pathway we designed, about ninety percent, and added a few more criteria themselves.

MANAGEMENT BY SERIAL DESTRUCTIVE TRANSFORMATION

We had to construct and redesign the Human Genome Sciences organization sequentially, abruptly, as work requirements evolved from one stage to the next. Each step required different people with different skill sets. We were not a giant pharmaceutical company that could afford to do everything at once.

We had to let go the very people who in each stage made us successful and ready to move to the next stage, which demanded a different set of skills. This was difficult. I called it serial destructive transformation. Building, destroying; building, destroying. At one point we expanded to two thousand employees, then a few years later were down to one thousand.

There were four or five stages. In the beginning, we made gene sequencing discoveries—raw discovery. Then, on to focused discovery and optimizing preclinical drug targets. Next, we shut down research to design preclinical studies and then conduct early clinical studies for our own drugs. Finally, there was manufacturing genes and administering them widely in late clinical studies.

Professional lupus societies were essential collaborators through these trials. They and their members, primarily people ailing from lupus and their families and friends, helped us with patient recruitment and ongoing discussions with the FDA.

We started controlled safety studies in 2001 with about twenty or thirty people, slowly ramping up treatment doses for half the patients, but not for the other half. Once positive results were confirmed, we moved to larger controlled trials. Lupus is a disease that flares in patients episodically over two or three years, so Human Genome Sciences' clinical teams had to monitor each test patient in both trials during that entire period.[147]

As we saw in the last chapter, the FDA approved Benlysta for patient use in 2011. GlaxoSmithKline, charting Benlysta's course since the pharma giant's 2012 acquisition of Human Genome Sciences, said in late 2019 that it hoped to broaden the drug's use for patients with all forms of lupus. It began controlled Phase III tests in patients with a lupus variation that attacks kidneys and intended to submit findings to the FDA in 2020.

We were overjoyed by the FDA's approval. It authorized for the first time in fifty six years a new drug for lupus patients.

Benlysta was not, however, the first drug from Human Genome Sciences to reach the market. The first, the story of the next chapter, was an antibody to treat and prevent lethal anthrax infections, rushed into place within two years of the anthrax terror attacks following 9/11.

FOUNDATION OF PRECISION MEDICINE

The biology of any animal is extremely complicated, the outcome of millions of years of evolution. Even today, we know just a tiny, tiny fraction of how the human body actually works. My analogy for medical scientists is we are trying to throw a monkey wrench into a very complicated engine, hoping it will work better.

When we were doing AIDS virus research, I described the challenge as the equivalent of asking a scientist or engineer around the year 1800 to figure out how a basic 20th century television set worked. They would take out one piece and put it back, trying to figure out what went wrong when the piece was removed. That is what we were doing with the AIDS virus. We broke one piece at a time to see what happened.

I often used these analogies in social settings, responding to people who asked why drug development took so long. "Where are all the drugs? Genomics looks like a failure." This happened often by the late '90s, a period when Human Genome Sciences had six drugs of its own in development and our licensing partners had many of their own.

"What are you talking about?" I would respond. "Genomics is a huge success. It was not meant to solve the problem of getting new drugs quickly. It was meant to solve this problem: *how you start* to find drugs. That is what we did."

By then more than thirteen thousand research and development scientists, backed by nearly three billion dollars in combined research budgets, had access to our library of gene sequenced proteins. SmithKline alone was allocating more than three fourths of its research spending for new drug development on genes selected from our library. I predicted that the majority of new drugs within twenty to twenty five years would be based on the kind of genomics we did—into anatomy, cell physiology pathology and pathology *to improve human health.*

Today, almost all drugs in the development pipelines of major pharmaceutical and biotechnology firms have their origin in the kind of genomics we practiced. Most cancer molecules are found this way, the targets for activating and directing the immune system to defeat specific cancer cells. Molecular biologists examine genes of immune cells that fight these cancers. If successful, the scientists determine the role of each cancer fighting antibody, manufacture them in high quantity and inject them in patients to attack cancer cells.

Our goal at Human Genome Sciences was to identify the subset of human genes, the functional genes, that secrete proteins likely to leave one cell and work on another. And that is what we did. About two thousand genes met that criteria, producing protein that triggers response in other cells.

These responses include triggering an auto-destruct program, triggering growth, inhibiting growth and signaling the cell to move. Other responses include initiating a process for changing the state of cells from quiet to active. This causes a cell to transform to a different state altogether, one capable of performing specialized functions—in other words, controlling almost all activities of the cells of our body.

This is the essence of genomics and now the foundation of precision medicine: the use of our genes to prevent disease and provide for particular groups of patients the most efficient and enduring therapies.

THE CASE FOR GENE PATENTS

From our first years at Human Genome Sciences, critics in government and academia sought to discredit our actions to patent genes we isolated in the genome for medical purposes.

Genes *as they exist in nature*, in our body or the body of any living organism, are not patentable. There was no controversy about that. Courts in the U.S. and other countries have affirmed the unpatentability of naturally occurring genes many times over.

However, once a gene has been removed from a natural organism and made useful by human intervention (the hand of man) it can be patented. It is then considered a human artifact. In genomics, we defined "genes" as isolated DNA sequences and proteins expressed by those DNA sequences. Recombinant proteins and the DNA that encodes them by then had been patented frequently by biotechnology companies for twenty years.

Bill Clinton and Tony Blair, Great Britain's prime minister, might have stirred some public confusion and anxiety about gene patents in their joint statement early in 2000. As I wrote a few months later in a commentary for *MIT Technology Review*,[148] Clinton and Blair called for free sharing of information on the human genome, but they also specifically emphasized the need to protect the intellectual rights to genomics-derived products and treatments.

"Nowhere are patents more central to the creative process than in genetic drug development, where human genes and their expressed proteins themselves are developed as therapies," I argued. "The biotechnology industry in the United States has brought a handful of these crucial new products (recombinant human insulin, to name one of the most familiar) to market and is on the threshold of a bonanza of genetic drugs and vastly greater relief for ill and aging populations around the world."

"Patent protection is the *sine qua non* of that bonanza," I continued. "Discovering and developing a new gene-based pharmaceutical product in the United States requires years of commitment and immense capital resources—as much as five hundred million dollars. Without the possibility of recouping investment that is bestowed by patents, no biotechnology company would be able to raise the financing necessary to develop these products."

Put simply, no gene patents, no gene-based products.

Rules governing gene patents then and now remain quite clear. The utility of the discovery must be supported by detailed, clearly documented experiments and details of how the discovery might be put to practical use. That is a tall order, requiring rigorous experimental proof in any gene patent application.

It would not have been sufficient for Human Genome Sciences to simply identify the sequence of a new gene, the natural function of the gene in the human body or even to prove that the protein product of that gene could be made.

What is a patent? A patent is a legal document enforceable by the court that prevents someone other than the patent holder from selling a product. Our founding fathers believed that encouraging inventions would be so important that they enshrined the right to patent inventions in the Constitution. To again quote Benjamin Franklin, "A patent adds the fuel of self-interest to the fire of invention."

To be valid a patent must disclose all information necessary to allow "someone skilled in the art" to replicate the invention. In return for disclosing these details, the inventor is granted a twenty year exclusive right to sell the product of the invention. Failure to disclose all relevant information invalidates their patent.

PATENTS AS TEACHING DOCUMENTS

I like to describe patents as teaching documents. They truly are. Patents are not secret. Most technical details that underpin our modern world are transmitted through patent literature, not textbooks. Then, too, patents encourage people "skilled in the art" to invent new and better ways to do related work.

The National Institutes of Health was then and remains *the largest single owner* of human gene patents. In fact, NIH and all university researchers supported by Federal grants are required by law—the Bayh-Dole Act approved by Congress in 1980—to patent all useful inventions, including inventions with a human gene as the subject matter.

In any event, the controversy quickly faded once the Human Genome Project was completed in 2003. The heat went out of the argument. University scientists, companies and federal laboratories continue to discover and patent new human genes without controversy.

|29|

DEFEATING ANTHRAX

THE 9/11 TERRORIST ATTACKS IN 2001 were the most lethal assault ever mounted by foreign aggressors on U.S. soil. Nearly three thousand Americans died, exceeding the number of sailors, soldiers and citizens killed by Japanese warplanes sixty years earlier at Pearl Harbor.

Driving home from downtown D.C. that September morning, I witnessed men and women who believed they were under attack, running for safety across the White House lawn. A few hours later, I closed our Human Genome Sciences offices after watching in horror with colleagues the collapse of the World Trade Center towers.

The nation reeled in the weeks immediately following 9/11, confused, stunned, fearful. What might be next? Bombings of public transportation and iconic government buildings. Poisoning of water supplies. Disruption of the electrical power grid. Each was seriously examined by public officials and journalists. None happened.

Yet something unexpected, bewildering—and frightening—did happen.

Deadly anthrax attacks, anthrax powder deployed as a bioweapon.

FEAR, NATIONWIDE

Five people died, including two postal workers at the P Street post office close to my Georgetown home. Operations in the building were shut down.

More than a dozen others in various locations along the East Coast were sickened, many permanently, painfully disabled. Each had inhaled anthrax from powder mailed in envelopes from Trenton, N.J., to several media organizations and two Democratic Senators on Capitol Hill, my friend and Majority Leader Tom Daschle and Patrick Leahy, head of the Senate Judiciary Committee.

Was this a second wave of al Qaeda terror attacks in America? Many thought so. News videos and photographs captured members of Congress and the Supreme Court evacuating their Capitol Hill buildings. As the *New York Times* recalled years later, "The letters prompted fear nationwide."[149]

"What can we do to help?" I asked myself. As chief executive, I was certain Human Genome Sciences had the nation's most gifted scientific talent and most advanced processes necessary to detect vulnerabilities in anthrax bacteria toxins and create antibodies to attack those vulnerabilities.

The spore forming bacterium, *Bacillus anthracis*, is most serious for humans when inhaled. Less than one in five people survive if they do not receive immediate medical care.

The Defense Department for decades had classified anthrax as a potential weapon of bioterrorism. A weaponized anthrax attack from the air could cause widespread panic and a breakdown of social order far beyond the site of attack.

I was determined to find a better way to cure people infected, protect others already exposed and design a vaccine to prevent these gruesome deaths or suffering from any new attacks many feared might be coming.

As the Centers for Disease Control and Prevention notes,[150] "If a bioterrorist attack were to happen, *Bacillus anthracis*, the bacteria that causes anthrax, would be one of the biological agents most likely to be used." Microscopic anthrax spores could be put into powders, sprays, food and water. The spores could be produced in a lab and remain potent for a long time in the environment. A single aircraft could spray spores over wide areas, sickening hundreds of thousands of people.

My Lifelong Fight Against Disease

I knew anthrax for the deadly killer it is. In my Biology and Social Issues course at Harvard, I lectured on how the Soviet Union and United States developed anthrax as their favored organism for biological warfare, and Japanese aircraft showered several Chinese cities with anthrax in the 1930s. Richard Nixon terminated America's bioweapons program in 1969 and was among more than a hundred world leaders to ratify the treaty in 1972 that banned biological and toxic weapons.

To prepare those lectures, I interviewed several scientists and technicians. Among them was Ken Alibek, the military physician and biological expert who, as a Soviet Army colonel, designed what the *Los Angeles Times* called "the most virulent and vicious strain of anthrax known to man,"[151] and later blew the whistle on Gorbachev's ongoing biological warfare agency in his book, *Biohazard: The Chilling True Story of the Largest Covert Biological Weapons Program in the World.*[152]

Weeks after the post 9/11 attacks, I told a solemn team of scientists gathered in our offices, "No one is better than you at using genomic data to find a drug target. No one is faster at converting that target to a drug candidate. Our doctors know how to test it. We have the manufacturing capacity we need.

"You find the drug and I will work with Congress and the Administration to speed approval and purchase," I continued, framing our respective mandates. "This is our duty to our fellow citizens and to all others who might be attacked."

FIND A CURE

John Mekalanos at Harvard Medical School was an expert on bacterial infections, consulting with health professionals around the world. I had been thinking John could be a key collaborator in sorting out how best to contain and kill anthrax cells. We were close friends. He had joined Bob Langer and me in creating the Virus Research Institute in the late '80s. Moreover, John had years of experience in research on infectious disease, applying those tools to understanding and treating cholera, another bacterial disease.

"John, let's team up again," I said when we connected via phone. "I'm committing Human Genome Sciences to find a treatment and cure of anthrax."

"Terrific, I'll be down right away," he replied. "We are on the same wavelength. Wes Clark and I are thinking of creating a company to do just that."

As we caught up, I was relieved to learn that John had largely recovered from a noxious parasite infection he had contracted a decade earlier in Bangladesh. He spent years in the fields there in combat with cholera. And I was pleased that he already was working with General Wesley Clark.

For the prior ten years, I had made it a priority to become acquainted with leading members of our armed forces. Senator Ted Stevens—the same Senator Stevens with whom I worked closely on HIV/AIDS funding—and I hosted monthly dinners in my Georgetown home with several members of the Joint Chiefs and other top brass. Wes Clark often was among them. I got to know Wes when he returned to D.C. from Europe after serving there as NATO Commander. He was a colleague of Richard Holbrooke in negotiating the Dayton Accords that ended the Bosnian War.

John Mekalanos was in my office two weeks later. We had two goals: pick a drug target and decide how we would work together.

"We think an antibody to the anthrax toxin is the best approach for a drug target," I said. "If we can block the toxin, we may be able to stop the infection even if the actual bioweapon has been made resistant to all known antibiotics." I knew from my Ken Alibek interviews and his book, published two years before, that his Russian anthrax strain (as well as others known to bioweapons experts) was resistant to antibiotics.

"We agree," John replied immediately. "Which part of the toxin, the landing pad or the toxin itself?"

Inhaled anthrax secretes a toxin, or poison, that kills cells. The toxin has two parts. One known as the landing pad attaches to the cell surface. It creates a passage for the second, active part of the toxin to enter. Once inside, the active part kills the cell. The bacteria grows extremely fast and can kill you in a couple ways: by killing cells or stealing oxygen from your blood system.

"I favor the landing pad," John continued. "That way the toxin never reaches the cell."

"Our team favors an antibody for the active toxin," I countered, amiably. "If we block the active toxin it does not matter if the full toxin attaches to the surface of the cell."

Ultimately, despite our strong friendship, John and I could not agree on business terms. He and Wes Clark formed their own company and ended up competing with us. Happily, nonetheless, we all remained friends.

My scientists began working on an antibody to block the active toxin, a process that began with making the active toxin. We shipped samples to Greg Winter's Cambridge Antibody Technology in the U.K., the same company that years earlier helped us create Benlysta for stimulating B cell antibodies to attack lupus antigens.

My assignment this time for the Cambridge lab was to create potent monoclonal antibodies for the active anthrax toxin. Within weeks, we had them: antibodies designed for humans that bound to and inactivated the active anthrax toxin. This was our drug candidate.

I knew that three federal agencies would be interested—the newly created Department of Homeland Security, the Defense Department and the Department of Health and Human Services. The main challenges were how to pick my way through the bureaucratic maze discretely and diplomatically, make sure we covered everything required by officials behind each marked door and—no small matter—how and when we would get paid. We intended to fund the entire project ourselves on the expectation that the government ultimately would buy the drug for a strategic stockpile... if we met whatever specifications were required.

DEPARTMENT OF DEFENSE

Vivid memories of my urgent, eleventh hour HIV/AIDS funding campaign sixteen years earlier returned. That experience and longstanding friendships bolstered my confidence. A first meeting was quickly scheduled with

William Cohen, former Republican Senator from Maine with whom I had worked on the AIDS funding and Bill Clinton's second Secretary of Defense. Bill and his wife, Janet Langhart Cohen, were frequent guests at our policy salon dinners in Georgetown. I first met Janet when she was a Boston TV news anchor during the early days of the HIV/AIDS epidemic.

Bill and his team of six experts at his Pentagon focused consulting group developed a procurement flow chart for our meeting. This was a customized road map of rules, agencies and decision makers I would have to navigate within the Defense Department, Homeland Security, Centers for Disease Control and the Food and Drug Administration. To say the flow chart was dizzyingly complex would be an understatement; it was as if someone had spilled a plate of spaghetti on the diagram. One thing was clear: the Defense Department was the final arbiter in the federal government for which drugs would and would not be stockpiled for bioweapons defense.

The high ranking Pentagon official urgently directing the nation's response to the anthrax attack was Paul Wolfowitz, Deputy Defense Secretary. Paul and I had met long ago as college undergraduates during annual gatherings of the two Telluride Association campus residences. He from Cornell University; I, Berkeley.

"It's great to see you after so many years," he said. "I hope you can help. We have a lot on our plate."

"I think we can protect and cure people exposed to anthrax," I said.

"That is just what we need," he replied.

A bioweapons countermeasures team he assembled was assessing "all potential threats," he explained, evaluating medical resources stockpiled to counter them and whatever gaps they discovered between threats and medical resources. Existing medical resources for infected citizens were shockingly limited. Something had to be done.

"I'll arrange for you to meet with the team tomorrow," he said. "Let's walk over to the Secretary's office."

On the short stroll over to Defense Secretary Donald Rumsfeld's office, Paul reminded me Rumsfeld had been a board member of Gilead Sciences Inc., the fastest growing biopharmaceutical company, for a dozen years. Rumsfeld was Gilead's board chairman the four years immediately before taking the helm at the Pentagon. "He got Gilead to focus on HIV treatments," Paul added. Gilead by then was on its way to becoming a powerhouse in antiviral pharmaceuticals.

Our conversation with Rumsfeld was brief but to the point. I was committing Human Genome Sciences to pursue quickly a cure for this virulent anthrax strain, and I would coordinate appropriately with Paul and his team. We would take the financial risk to develop the drug if they would promise to buy it if we met their specifications.

"I like the idea," Rumsfeld remarked as Paul and I prepared to leave. "Good luck. We'll see what we can do."

The next day, Paul's bioweapons team presented a complex chart with some boxes full, some partially full and some empty. One on axis, potential threats were listed. On the other, effective countermeasures. One anthrax box was half full, indicating a partially effective vaccine existed. The empty box signaled the nation had no effective way to protect an unvaccinated population from exposure to a strain of anthrax that was resistant to antibiotics for bacterial infection. The entire U.S. population, of course, was unvaccinated for the inhaled anthrax powder that had just killed five people and sickened another seventeen.

Pointing to the empty box, I said, "I am sure we can plug that gap. Please write detailed specifications for what you would consider the ideal product. We will design our drug to meet your specifications." Ten days later, we had those specifications.

REPRISE, TONY FAUCI

What about limited and expanded human trials required by the FDA for any new drug to be approved? How could you do that for any anthrax antibody when naturally occurring human infections were so rare? The answer: a normal limited antibody test was impossible.

The only other way to test humans was to infect volunteers with this virulent, lethal new anthrax strain, treat them with our new antibody drug and hope the infected volunteers recovered. But that was impossible, never a serious option. You cannot infect volunteers with a potentially lethal agent and then treat them with a drug not yet tested in humans. Too dangerous and highly unethical. Again, impossible.

I soon learned that Tony Fauci, then approaching his twentieth year as director of the National Institute of Allergy and Infectious Diseases at NIH, was actively developing alternate routes to dodge these roadblocks for clinical trials.

"Tony, we already have what I believe is a great candidate to protect and treat people exposed to anthrax," I said. "We expect it will meet Defense Department requirements. But you and I know traditional clinical trials are out of the question."

Tony agreed those trials had to be ruled out. In its place, he said, he and colleagues at the FDA would suggest an unconventional approach, testing drugs in two animal species, each exposed by inhalation (aerosol spray, in practice) to this new weapons grade anthrax.

"If a drug or vaccine against bacterium or virus protects animals, it should protect us," he explained. "We are targeting a foreign organism, not some part of the human body. Of course, we have to conduct safety trials on humans."

"That's great," I said. "We can develop that drug; it shouldn't take long."

But there was the other issue: money. We knew from our drug manufacturing operations at Human Genome Sciences that hundreds of millions of dollars would be needed to finance production in the vast quantities required for a national stockpile. The government would be the only source of demand. I assured my board of directors at Human Genomes Sciences that we could not proceed without federal commitment to pay us.

Tony had already begun working with the NIH, White House and Congress to establish a general mandate for the government to make such commitments.

"Tony, you remember my speech to the Senate calling for increased federal spending for HIV/AIDS research. I mentioned that HIV would not be the last time a new deadly virus would emerge from Africa or elsewhere," I said. He remembered.

"What do you think about including language in this bioterrorism countermeasures legislation that would provide the same flexibility to develop drugs and vaccines for new natural as well as manmade bio-threats?"

"This is exactly my thought," he replied, eagerly. "You work from your end and I will from mine to include language in the law that applies to *new and emerging threats, whether natural or manmade in origin.*"

The legislation called for rapid approval and purchase of countermeasures against bioterrorism, and for the Defense Department to stockpile the drugs and vaccines. It included language exactly as Tony had articulated that day. Both houses of Congress responded quickly, drafting bills then agreeing with solid White House support.

"It is a very good bill," Tony asserted in public comments hours before Senate approval in May 2004.[153] "It provides incentives for industry; it facilitates the research process; and it facilitates the emergency use of these countermeasures where necessary in time of emergency."

George W. Bush would sign the Project Bioshield Act of 2004 into law two months later, authorizing $5.6 billion over ten years to purchase new drugs and vaccines as countermeasures for bioweapons attacks.

"Bioshield should give you confidence there will be a market for our drug," I told our board. "Developing this drug is risky. That is true for any drug. But I believe a guaranteed market provides a better chance for a return on our investment than is the case for most drugs. It is also the right thing to do." The board quickly gave us the go-ahead to begin tests.

My team of clinical scientists estimated a sufficient supply of antibodies to test the drugs in animals could be made within six weeks. The FDA cautioned that safety tests could not start until we had favorable results from the animal tests. How many patients were needed for the human tests? "They tell us twenty to thirty people," my team said.

AS GOOD AS IT GETS

I looked to the Battelle Institute, an independent research laboratory in Ohio, to conduct the animals tests that Tony and I had discussed. Even with our containment labs, Human Genome Sciences could not work with weapons grade anthrax in any of our facilities. Battelle could. It often was hired by the government for special projects. The animal tests had to follow Tony's explicit conditions: two species of animals exposed by inhalation to the new weapons grade anthrax, then treated with our antibodies.

Battelle had stocks of the virulent lethal anthrax. They also demonstrated to the satisfaction of our inspection teams that they could carefully execute the experiment protocols and do so safely for all their staff. "The last thing I want is to endanger workers there or anyone else," I said.

These lab tests required several months, but the results could not have been better. Our antibodies *fully protected* rabbits and monkeys exposed to the inhaled anthrax, a one hundred percent clearance even for ten times the lethal dose. Moreover, the animals showed no signs of ever having been infected. Our drug, raxibacumab (which we branded as Abthrax), provided complete protection. We were not able to grow any anthrax from any of the exposed but protected animals.

This is as good as it gets, initially. We still did not know how long this protection would last.

Two months later, we had the answer. Protection remained complete. Moreover, seriously ill monkeys that received the medication were quickly and completely cured, even when close to death. What is more, these treated animals showed no sign of ever having been infected. Once treated, they became immune to any further exposure to the anthrax. We could not recover any anthrax from their blood.

Our initial safety studies on humans were conducted with twenty healthy volunteers. Different groups of volunteers were given a low dose first, then a moderate dose and finally the maximum dose. There were no serious adverse effects, even at the highest dose. A subsequent test with more than two hundred healthy volunteers had the same welcome result. Again, no serious adverse effects.

The FDA approved Abthrax before the end of 2003 after an advisory committee investigating our work overwhelming endorsed our presentation by a vote of sixteen to one. This was the first monoclonal antibody approved under the new rule Tony and I had discussed, the concept of permitting efficacy findings from what the FDA terms "adequate and well-controlled animal studies when it is not feasible or ethical to conduct trials in humans."

Abthrax was Human Genome Sciences' first drug to earn FDA approval. Time to break out the champagne.

"It has been just two years and two months since the anthrax letters were mailed," I told our board. "We must have set a record for new drug approval; two years from conception to FDA approval."

Of course, as we saw earlier, the usual timeline for approving a new drug for both efficacy and safety takes at least ten years or more. It takes that much time to complete animal tests and three phases of tests on people with a particular disease.

"We must all recognize that years of investment in Human Genome Sciences' fundamental research gave us the tools we needed to do this job," I went on. "A well developed industrial base allowed us to deploy those tools to maximum advantage.

"You authorized payment covering all expenses required to discover and develop Abthrax. You should be proud of our team and what we have done to protect our country."

ANTICIPATING NEW BIOLOGICAL THREATS

Our government can be efficient when faced with a crisis. That was an important takeaway from the anthrax bioterrorism story. There was no partisan disagreement and few, if any, turf wars among agencies that had to interlace their processes to create Bioshield.

We learned how to encourage companies to develop drugs that have no immediate market, drugs that protect us from new and emerging biological threats as well as bioterrorist threats.

In time, seven years, the FBI identified a microbiologist who had worked at an Army laboratory on anthrax vaccines as the likely assailant. The suspect, who had maintained his innocence, committed suicide as the FBI moved to indict him in 2008. The government said the suspect was the lone custodian of the particular strain of anthrax used in the 2001 attacks.[154]

In 2006, Congress created the Biomedical Advanced Research Development Authority (BARDA) to enable the discovery, development and stockpiling of drugs to counter the terrible effect of bioweapons on people. BARDA also had authority to protect our population from chemical and nuclear events, influenza epidemics and the emergence of naturally occurring new diseases.

We know which threats of naturally occurring disease are on the horizon. Highly lethal strains of influenza, coronaviruses, Ebola like viruses and hidden pathogens yet to emerge. My hope is that BARDA and other agencies will continue to seek ways to protect us.

A final thought for this chapter.

As I underscored in my opening Note to the Reader, I am doing all I can to encourage our government to develop new drugs and vaccines to combat the third and vastly more lethal coronavirus pandemic, COVID-19. I also am advising governments and public health leaders around the world on how best to contain and defeat this pandemic.

A crisis during the early months of 2020 has turned into an avoidable tragedy, a failure of leadership. The toll of lives lost globally by mid-October exceeded one million; in the United States, two hundred twenty thousand. A forecasted second wave is upon us as winter looms, with infections escalating in Europe and North America. In the United States, our public health system, starved for resources for decades in states, cities and local communities, will struggle to distribute effective treatments, and, possibly vaccines, once medical science has created them.

A global health tragedy seems certain to deepen global economic pain. Two prominent American economists, Harvard's David Cutler and Larry Summers, former head of Barack Obama's National Economic Council, estimate the long term reduction of this country's economic output from COVID-19 at $16 trillion, equal to *total* United States federal debt as recently as 2012.

Some of you might have thought at various places in the chapters thus far, reading during the pandemic, that "This is relevant to COVID." Or, more broadly, "This is relevant for fighting pandemics." The fundamental understanding of viruses. Of medicine and how it is delivered. Of how drug targets are identified. Of building and leading companies to make drugs. As we've just seen, all these elements were critical for rapidly confronting the anthrax threat. So were understanding the levers of government policymaking and, drawing from my anti-war and HIV work, how to be a persuasive public advocate.

It is as if the first seven decades of my life provided the range of tools and insights necessary to continue even now to pursue my purpose, to advance human health. I find myself with a distinctive platform from which I am able to visualize and campaign as actively as I am able for what is needed to combat and subdue COVID-19.

The COVID Commentaries, the focus of this book's final chapter, is a comprehensive collection of my writings, social media posts, media interviews and other observations on the pandemic. Published in tandem with this autobiography, *Commentaries* also includes a robust assemblage of links to important research and other resources.

‖30‖

BIRTH OF AN IDEA: REGENERATIVE MEDICINE

THE EUROPEAN MONETARY UNION'S DEBUT WAS APPROACHING, only a few months away on January 1, 1999. In another three years, marks, lira, francs and nine other national currencies would become relics, swept into the past as part of history's largest changeover of cash currency.

What would the future hold? Former prime ministers and presidents, finance ministers, economists, philosophers, historians, novelists and journalists from across the continent and the United States were here in northern Italy over a long weekend to examine the implications.[155] A handful of business executives and scientists were on hand as well at the conference venue, the elegant Villa d'Este hotel on the shores of Lake Como.

After lunch on Saturday, our host, the former (and future) Finance Minister of Italy, Guilio Tremonti, asked me to address the group before dinner that evening. "No one has even mentioned science yet," he said. "Several people asked if you could speak. You can discuss any topic you want."

After a few moments, I replied, "How about the future of medicine? Everyone needs a doctor even if they are not interested in science. Exciting things are happening. What do you think?"

"Perfect," he said. "We'll let everyone know you will lead an extra session and begin at 7 p.m."

By now it was late afternoon, a beautiful early fall day with a chill in the air as I paced the hotel gardens. "What is the best way to approach this? What can I tell them? How can I explain?" I repeated to myself, struggling to find a theme that would unify, simply, clearly, many ideas bouncing around in my head.

You, by now, are more familiar than most in the group with two ideas I was about to address, biotechnology and genomics. Other topics—stem cell research, tissue engineering and mind-machine interface—were on some but not many policy agendas: I knew all of these topics were laden with cultural baggage or would strain audience patience in other ways.

I paused for a minute, distracted by the lush green hills darkening now beyond the lake. Further away, I could see the fading rays of sun illuminating mountain peaks. "Soon, the leaves will drop," I thought, a bit wistfully. "This green will give way to the hard rock of winter. How fragile is life, how durable the stone."

Yet, in that instant, I was jolted by a concept so contradictory it registered almost like a physical blow.

"Wait! You have it backwards! It is life that endures and mountains that perish," I told myself. "A million years ago, an ocean where I stand was teeming with life. These majestic mountains will wear away and rise, once again to be covered by a soft living blanket."

"How many times in the last three and a half billion years has this cycle repeated?" I asked. Then, more profoundly, "How can life endure as mountains perish?"

I felt a tingle from the words, the logic, the insight.

"DNA, the immortal molecule," I thought. "All life is united by a single molecule, DNA, that has existed for billions of years, and may endure yet for billions of years to come. Yes, it takes different forms but all are variants of the original. One parent molecule divides and gives rise to two almost identical daughters. Both are originals. The immortal molecule continues its journey from the unimaginably distant past. We—all forms of life—are but its carriers, pausing briefly along the way."

"If the essence of life is immortality, why then do we as individuals perish? Might there be a way to link our individual existence to the fundamental immortality of life, the immortal DNA?

"Ah ha! I have my unifying concept," I realized. "Modern medicine seeks to restore our bodies to normal, whether injured by trauma, damaged by disease or worn by time. Isn't that what we really ask of medicine? To restore us to normal health, to be able to live and love in a healthy body and mind? Might the new medicine restore our mind and body *and* join our transient existence to our own unique immortal molecule?"

What name should I give this broad idea that would resonate? The first one to come to mind was Rejuvenative Medicine, but that sounded like hype. "What about *Regenerative Medicine*—that's it!" I decided. "Regenerative Medicine captures the goal, not the means, and the goal is what is important. I can explain all the different tools we use to achieve these goals under one name."

And, that is what I did that evening. Let me take you through my remarks, unencumbered with quotation marks and lightly edited for clarity, and a few highlights of the discussion that followed.

THE FUTURE OF MEDICINE

Looking out over the lake and hills, many of you may have shared a fleeting melancholy thought I had today. That this beauty endures, and we vanish. The language of poetry proclaims the permanence of earth while lamenting the transience of life. But, as a biologist steeped in the new knowledge of DNA, I recognize that this perception is, and always has been, false.

It is the mountains that erode, and life that endures. These hills will rise and fall, and rise again. But, on this exact spot, be it an ocean, plain or mountain, life will abound.

There is a grand mystery to life, one you and I know, but until now had no way to understand. All living forms, including we *Homo sapiens sapiens* (that's us), create youth from age. To illustrate: the pollen and ovum of a thousand year old tree combine to produce a vibrant seedling. The sperm of an eighty year old man and the egg of a forty five year old woman unite to create a newborn infant. Yes, the clock of time ticks within each of us. But that clock is reset to zero as each child is born, to be reset once again with each new generation.

We know at the heart of each cell lies DNA, the molecule that carries the instructions to build our body. I have studied DNA for many years, first as a student of the great James D. Watson, then as a scientist at Harvard Medical School and now as founder and CEO of Human Genome Sciences. I have watched DNA as it ages, breaks apart and reassembles, repairing damage sustained from some internal or external insult.

I can tell you with certainty that the solution to the mystery of life lies in understanding how, with each new generation, the structure of DNA returns to its original form. We know from the work of British embryologist John Gurdon that replacing the nucleus of a fertilized egg with the nucleus of an older cell returns the transplanted nucleus to its newborn state. Therefore, I conclude there must be substances in the fertilized egg that restore DNA to its primal state. I predict we will soon discover the key to reversing the biological clock. That discovery will open a new vista of medicine, one in which our own cells can be used to build a new, younger version of our bodies, if not our minds.

We are not far from the day when that is possible. Even now we have the ability to pluck one cell from the inner mass of a five day embryo and nurture it to grow indefinitely, each daughter a faithful copy of the parent. These are the so called pluripotent stem cells. Each pluripotent cell is fully capable of being nudged into producing the vast variety of cells that comprise our bodies. Indeed, each can—on its own—yield an entire living animal. This is the parentage of Dolly the Sheep, born just three years ago. You will be pleased to know that Dolly is thriving.

Our goal is not to produce new human offspring but rather to replace aged tissue with young vibrant cells. This is not a pipe dream. We do this even today. For some blood cancers, we first kill all blood forming cells and replace them with healthy tissue. Replacement is possible because we know that cells exist with the ability to reproduce the entire blood cell. These are hematopoietic stem cells. Stem cells from a healthy donor do reconstitute all the blood forming tissues. The typical donor is much younger than the recipient. Voila! An age hybrid. An older person with younger blood.

Most of our tissues and organs undergo constant replacement, each seeded by its own specialized stem cells.

Scientists are deciphering the signal that directs the formation of each type of stem cell, from the fertilized egg to the fully functional specialized stem cell. In other words, we are mapping the process by which our bodies are formed and by which they are maintained. With each discovery will come the ability to restore you to younger tissues, to create a younger organ. We are limited today in matching donor to recipient. If my prediction is correct, the day is not far off when we can turn back the clock on our own cells to become stem cell donors to ourselves.

The wait was not long. In 2006, a scientist trained in the U.S. then working in Japan solved the mystery. Shinya Yamanaka discovered that four genes active in the fertilized egg produce proteins that work together to turn back the genetic clock. These genes are so powerful that they return even highly differentiated adult cells, skin cells, for example, to the equivalent of a fertilized ovum.

Yamanaka[156] called these cells *induced pluripotent stem cells*, or iPS cells, for short. One of these iPS cells, implanted into a receptive womb, will give rise to a normal fetus and eventually an adult. They have been used to create many different types of mammals, including primates.

Scientists around the world are teasing out the signals mature cells need to create specialized stem cells for each tissue in our body. There is progress in other ways as well. For example, in the first months of 2020, scientists affiliated with the Institute for Stem Cell Biology and Regenerative Medicine at Stanford University Medical School found that aged cartilage cells no longer secreted inflammatory factors when the cells were dosed for a short period in cultures of Yamanaka factors after being removed from osteoarthritis patients.[157]

The Stanford team also found that human muscle stem cells impaired by muscle disease could be restored to a youthful state. The headline on the *New York Times* report on the breakthrough summed up well my vision from years ago, "Turning Back the Clock on Aging Cells."[158]

I have a name for this new medicine: Regenerative Medicine. My definition includes all interventions that restore to normal function organs, tissues and cells that have been injured through trauma, damaged by disease or worn by time. For me, any intervention that restores our bodies or minds to normal function is regenerative medicine. Regenerative medicine is not limited to the use of stem cells.

Let's explore some of the frontiers of this new view of what medicine can be.

MECHANICAL ASSISTS

Most of us may need a replacement part at some point in our lives. For the athletes among us, many of those parts are for worn joints in knees, elbows, hips and shoulders. For others, it is a clouded lens. For still others, it may be an entire organ: a kidney, liver, lung or heart; or a leg or ligament. Whatever the need, our common wish is to be restored to near normal as much as possible.

We have made great advances over the past century. Joints of bone and cartilage are replaced with finely engineered metallic substitutes. Interocular lenses made of flexible silicon and acrylic glass restore clear vision. Steel rods reinforce damaged bone. Metal plates and screws reinforce our spine. Surgeons are ever inventive, on the lookout for new materials and new techniques. We all benefit from their success. My guess is that at least half of us in this room carry one or more replacement parts.

XENO-TRANSPLANTATION

But our needs exceed what can be done with metal and plastic. Despite heroic efforts, the search for a durable artificial heart, lung or kidney continues. We need living organs and tissues to replace ones that fail.

Organ transplants are one solution. Heart, lung, liver and kidney transplants are possible today. But we all know the problem: scarcity of donor organs. Many people die waiting for an organ that never arrives. Regenerative medicine offers two solutions: genetically engineered animal organs, and laboratory grown human organs. Both are on the horizon.

The concept of replacing human parts with animal parts is not new. Today we routinely replace faulty heart values with those from pigs, cows and sheep. These are non living substitutes. Although functionally similar, our bodies reject as foreign all living organs from other animals.

Stem cell technologies hold the key to a solution. A new species of pig with organs suitable for human transplant can be created using combinations of stem cell technology and genetic engineering. We have the technology now to modify the DNA in pluripotent pig stem cells grown in laboratories.

We can identify and replace the genes of the pig that induce rejection with their human equivalents. These modified cells can be used to build human-pig hybrid cells. The prospect is real. I believe it will be achieved within the next twenty to thirty years. What we can do today, we can improve upon tomorrow to speed that happy day.

> Pigs indeed soon may be a major source of transplant organs. Technology has eliminated at least one major hurdle known as endogenous pig retrovirus. All vertebrates have retrovirus in their genomes. Most have no function, but some are capable of activation and infection, most notably for patients whose immune systems are suppressed.

Strains of pigs have been bred that are free of these virus genomes. Moreover, genes have been deleted that produced the most reactive substances that trigger organ rejection. Some pig strains have been bred to carry human genes that facilitate transplantation. Monkeys that have received donor organs from these strains of pigs have survived for more than one year.

Pig to human kidney and heart transplants are likely to begin in the early 2020s. A biotech startup, eGenesis, is cloning pigs with the goal to harvest organs that can be safely accepted by the human immune system. "It is not a question if this will work but when and how," eGenesis president Paul Sekhri told the *Financial Times* late in 2019.[159] George Church, the famed Harvard geneticist, molecular engineer and chemist, is a company cofounder.

The second method, known as tissue engineering, grows new human tissues and organs in the laboratory. The idea is straightforward. Create a framework, or scaffold, with materials compatible with our cells and tissues. Derive cells from the patient using stem cell technology to populate the organ. Incubate the cells and scaffold in fluid containing nutrients the cells need to flourish. Surgically insert the new organ and restore the patient to health.

Can this be done? Absolutely yes—but so far only with limited success. My friend and fellow Harvard professor Anthony Atala has used a similar method to create the urethra, the small tube leading from the bladder to the exit. He also has grown bladder tissue for implantation. In both cases, the source was mature cells derived from the patient, not modified stem cells.[160] Scientists and surgeons around the world are searching for new biomaterials to use as scaffolding and new sources of stem cells to grow organs as complex as a heart or lung.

Time has not been kind to this second approach. When I spoke that fall I was among those who believed that replacement of relatively simple tissues, blood vessels, trachea and skin was coming soon. Not so.

Attempts to create functioning organs have failed, some even in scandals that tarnished the reputations of entire universities. Evidently, the information our bodies use to build our organs is far more complex than we realized in 1998.

Unlike human proteins and antibodies, human cells are specific to individuals, and likely to remain so for many years. This means that tissue engineering is likely to be performed at hospitals where the patients are. Tissue samples will be harvested from patients and worked on by technicians at a regional hospital.[161]

A HUMAN MEDICINE

There is yet a third, more gentle approach to repair damaged and worn tissues. Our bodies have at least a limited capacity to repair damage. We have all witnessed scraped and sliced skin and muscle knit together. Many of us have endured the discomfort as broken bones heal. Those who have suffered severe injuries with nerve damage know that sensation gradually returns.

Many of you may not realize that at least one part of the brain, our olfactory bulbs, regenerate even if destroyed by surgery or accident. Our primary sensory organs—eyes, ears and olfactory bulbs—are best thought of as parts of the brain extended outside of the brain case to sense the world around us.

Modern science reveals the secret behind regrowth. Each type of cell responds to signals from the environment. These signals trigger pre-programmed responses. Think of them as binary on-off switches. One set signals the cell to live or die (yes, cells commit suicide, a process called apoptosis). Another set instructs cells to divide and proliferate or remain quiescent. A third very important set signals the cell to remain in its current state or transform itself to a cell with different capabilities. A final set commands the cell to remain stationary or to move.

These signals are conveyed by substances made in one type of cell that acts on a second type of cell. We have a good idea of what these signals are: proteins, each the product of a single gene. These signaling proteins leave the cell of origin and bind to a second protein, called a receptor, on the target cell. Signals and receptors are paired: one protein, one receptor.

A pre-programmed response in the receptor is triggered when the signal protein attaches. You already know what some of these signals are. For example, human growth hormone is a protein that signals many different types of cells in our body to grow. This single protein, when used as a drug, restores normal growth and stature to a person who lacks this gene.

Thanks to genomics, the study of a complete set of an organism's genes, we now have access to nearly complete sets of these signaling and receptor proteins. To function, the signals leave the interior of a cell to interact with a receptor on the surface of another. At Human Genome Sciences, we have isolated a virtually complete set of these signaling molecules, more than two thousand in all. We currently are testing them systematically to determine their function, and plan to develop as drugs either ourselves or with partners any signaling molecules that we determine have a medical function.

For example, we found three proteins that activate white blood cells (known as B cells) to produce antibodies. One, which we called B lymphocyte stimulator, or BLyS for short, was much more potent. We believe it has several possible uses:

- Restore normal immune function to patients incapable of making antibodies because they lack the protein

- Attach a poison to the protein to kill B cell tumors that uniquely carry the receptor

- Treat people with B cell mediated autoimmunity (such as lupus) with drugs that block the action of too much BLyS, an error that causes the immune system to go awry and attack healthy cells

In another case, we identified a protein with a signal that initiates the growth of new blood vessels, confirmed when we injected it into normal or injured muscle in a mouse, rat or rabbit. We believe this protein, which we call vascular endothelial growth factor 3 (VEGF-3), has at least two promising uses:

- Restore circulation of a damaged heart by injecting VEGF-3, instead of conducting bypass surgery

- Create new arteries to bypass those in our arms or legs that are blocked

And, in a third case, we found a signal that stimulates rapid tissue growth in wounds as well as wound healing in animals. To our surprise, the protein, epidermal growth factor-3, also stimulates hair growth. Possible medical uses include:

- Rapid repair of surgical incisions, speeding healing of burn victims by stimulating growth of skin grafts

- Treating male pattern baldness

To summarize, the discovery of a complete set of human genes puts us on the threshold of a new human form of medicine. The new drugs are products of our own body. They may be delivered as genes, proteins or chemicals that mimic proteins. They can be used to augment functions we lack entirely to supplement our natural healing ability. They may also block signals in cells that go awry as treatments for cancer, autoimmune disease and growth abnormalities.

It has been challenging to find ways for growth proteins such as VEGF-3 to work well in solid organs such as the heart or liver. Those organs are dense, with many cells. We were sure that by now we would have functioning blood vessels and maybe even functioning hearts. We do not even have a blood vessel.

It has turned out to be far more difficult to create organs than we thought. It is not going to be impossible. It is like immunotherapy. You have to keep trying and trying and trying. Ultimately, it will work.

A new method developed by Anthony Atala shows promise in growing blood vessels. A small piece of tissue half the size of a postage stamp is coated on the outside with growth muscle cells, then on the inside with lining cells, "cooked" in an oven like device, or incubator, and allowed to mature before the tissue is reinserted.

Dr. Atala established the Wake Forest Institute for Regenerative Medicine nearly twenty years ago after leaving his post as a urologist at Harvard Medical School. His institute now has four hundred physicians, scientists and staff working on replacement tissues and organs to cure patients.

MIND-MACHINE INTERFACE

Let me end with a few comments about what seems like science fiction: mind-machine interface.

Accidents that sever the spinal cord leave the brain intact but powerless to prompt muscles into action. The body cannot move on its own. One approach is for the body to learn to repair and regrow vital connections. I believe that will be possible one day, directing nerve fibers to grow and reconnect in specific parts of our injured bodies.

A second approach may deliver faster cures: connecting signals directly from the brain to artificial limbs. Neuroscientists have mapped two regions of the brain responsible for intentional motion, for example moving an arm or leg. One region signals intent. Another issues signals that travel along nerves to activate muscle contraction. Microchips implanted in the brains of monkeys can read these signals. Computers can interpret them. The result: signals generated directly by the brain pass through a computer... and move artificial limbs in real time.

Here is a specific example I witnessed a few months ago, starting first with a quick summary of the experiment:

- Implant chips at the proper location of a monkey's brain

- Train the monkey to track a moving dot on a video screen by manipulating a joy stick

- Reward the monkey's success with a shot of orange juice

- Restrain the arms and connect signals from the chip to a mechanical arm

There, before my eyes, I saw the monkey manipulate the mechanical arm and track the moving dot by using only signals from the brain. The monkey was faster and more accurate than any human. This was mind-machine fusion... achieved!

The next step will be linking brain signals to an array of mechanical support systems. They may include total body suits that allow a paraplegic to move normally. Body suits already exist to help people partially paralyzed to walk again. Contraction of muscles in the upper body is used to activate walking motions. Again, mind-machine fusion... achieved!

What will the future bring? We know computers will be faster, programs more sophisticated and chips denser and more powerful. One day we may even fashion a cap that reads signals of thoughts through the scalp.

What I have described so far is one-way communication between the brain and a mechanical device. But this is not how our bodies work. We receive real time feedback from our sensory nerves. This is how we know the position of our limbs, the pressure on any part of our body as well as surface properties of objects we touch: hot or cold, soft or hard, rough or smooth. Microsensors exist that measure each of these properties. Can such microsensors embedded in prosthetic devices such as mechanical hands and feet be directly linked to our nervous system? Preliminary work in advanced biomechanical labs suggests the answer is yes.

Mind-machine interface is progressing rapidly. Paraplegics with implanted chips are able to control mechanical arms and wheelchairs. Electric signals picked up on the scalp can decipher silent speech with up to seventy percent accuracy. Chips with as many as two hundred sensors implanted in a monkey's visual cortex can recreate highly accurate images of what the monkey sees.

You may be able to put an artificial retina in the eye of a blind person, take signals from the outside and send them straight into the optic centers as if they were coming from the retina. This will allow the blind to see.

Mind-machine interface may soon transcend medical use and permit brain-to-brain communication. An engineered 21st century mirroring of telepathy, with no words spoken, that is accessible to thousands.

We are going to have micro prosthetics that become progressively smaller and smaller as we do better bioengineering. Already we engineer things almost at the level of molecules. Computer chips and quantum devices will be at the level of individual atoms. Medical devices and devices to substitute in our failing systems will follow along. It is a predictable path, but you cannot plot the timescale.

FINAL THOUGHTS

The future of regenerative medicine is in your hands, not mine or my fellow scientists or physicians. We can explore the limits of the possible but without your help the possible will never be practical.

You need to fund the research. You need to hold open and honest debates on the limits of the ethical. Just as we here are discussing the future of the euro, let us also find the time to discuss the future of medicine.

AUDIENCE QUESTIONS

Questions following my remarks were thoughtful and animated. Three topics stood out: extending human life span, electronic thought transmission and pig to human transplants. Here are my edited replies:

Extending human life span. I do believe it someday will be possible to renew and repair most of our body... indefinitely. How far into the future will that be? I cannot say. I also am far less certain about our ability to renew and repair the brain. If we are able regrow parts of the aged or damaged brain, will the new functioning parts know what the old brain knew? All memory is encoded in an array of literally countless neuron connections. Will the new tissue reconnect with that network? (Twenty years later, we still are not able to answer that question.)

What about the ethics of achieving much longer lived, if not immortal, generations? We do not question the set of technologies that allowed the average lifespan around the world to double in the past century. I doubt that we will question the ethics of technologies that allow us to double lifespan yet again in the century to come. (Currently, a natural healthy lifespan is estimated to be one hundred twenty five years.) Extended lifespans will arise slowly across the centuries, one millennium at a time. I cannot speak for what future generations will judge to be ethical. For myself, I believe it ethical to extend healthy aging as long as possible.

Reading thoughts, interpreting electrical brain signals. If we can decipher intention and action, which we can, then I do believe it is feasible to decode our thoughts, spoken or unspoken. It may even be possible without penetrating the skull.

Pig to human tissue or organ transplants. Today someone dies every minute for want of a replacement organ. That number will only rise over time with our aging global population. The longer we live, the more likely various parts will wear out. The barriers likely will be more regulatory than technical. I am confident our science is up to the challenge. Your challenge is to develop support for enabling legislation and direct donors to fund the research.

LAUNCHING THE FIELD

The informal reactions to my presentation that night and the following day were gratifying. Several participants asked what they could do to help; others, how I intended to develop this new field.[162]

Back in the States I quickly recruited Tony Atala to organize the first Society for Regenerative Medicine and join me in editing a new online journal for the field, *e-Biomed: The Journal of Regenerative Medicine.* We co-chaired several annual conferences for scientists, physicians, journalists and bioethicists.

Today arrays of societies advance new knowledge through conferences and journals for various branches of the field. Many if not most medical schools, institutes and universities around the world now include departments of regenerative medicine.

The providential leitmotif that flashed into my mind along the shore of Lake Como gave voice—arising from decades of research, teaching and discovery—to a new field of medicine that is changing our understanding of the possible.

PART VI

31

THINK TANK, ADVISORY IN GLOBAL HEALTH

THAT FIRST YEAR AFTER STEPPING DOWN at Human Genome Sciences I traveled to many countries to visit what were reputed to be the best health-care systems—specifically, outstanding medical departments and operations within those systems. I was looking for novel methods combining high quality and low cost that I could bring back to the United States.

What I discovered in a city on the southeastern tip of India amazed me: one hospital conducting hundreds of thousands of cataract operations annually with outstanding results, the vast majority for free.

Actual cost per operation, including materials and supplies, physician time and overhead, was about thirty U.S. dollars.

How could that be? A relentless focus on efficiency and cost control. For example, operating rooms had two tables, not one. As a physician operates on a patient at one table, the next patient is prepped on the other. When the first operation is finished, the physician turns around to begin the next one.[163] One physician might perform as many as fifty cataract operations each day!

At the time, Aravind Eye Hospital's small network of facilities in Madurai had nearly fifteen hundred beds. Twelve hundred were provided at no cost for people with no means to pay and another three hundred for patients who could afford rates that matched other nearby hospitals.

ONE PHYSICIAN, A THOUSAND EYE SURGERIES A YEAR

All this began in 1976 when the retiring head of ophthalmology at the local medical college, Pamasree, Dr. G. Venkataswamy, combined his savings with some government funds to pursue his dream to eliminate blindness in his home state, Tamil Nadu, if not all of India. At the time, nine million people in India were sightless.

I first heard the inspiring Aravind story from David Green, a health technology entrepreneur whose activity over several years in Nepal and India had brought him to Madurai and Dr. V, as Aravind's founder was known. David worked closely with the Aravind team, coaching on manufacturing methods for intraocular lenses (cost: about two dollars), surgical needles (cost: about ten dollars) and antibiotics and other supplies that they produced in house.[164]

One afternoon David and I went hiking together along the beautiful Maroon Bells trail just west of Aspen, Colorado. I had helped organize science and health sessions for this first Ideas Festival of the Aspen Institute, and had met David after our session that morning, a year after he had been named a MacArthur Fellow.

As we rested for a moment along the trail, David turned to me. "Bill, have you read C.K. Prahalad's *The Fortune at the Bottom of the Pyramid*?" he asked. The book, with the subtitle *Eradicating Poverty Through Profits*[165], had been out for a year or so. I had not read it.

A prominent management professor and author at the University of Michigan, C.K. later was introduced to me by David. C.K. had keen insights for business strategy as well as commitment to the idea that profitable services and products could be developed for low income populations. We saw each other regularly during the next five years when we both served as advisors to India's massive multi-industry enterprise, Reliance Industries, at the invitation of the chairman and managing director, Mukesh Ambani. (We will return shortly to Reliance, a striking example of India's modern business initiative and strategic management skills—entirely focused within India.)

This most recent of C.K.'s books included several pages on Aravind Eye Hospital. It was one of a dozen examples demonstrating C.K.'s belief that businesses can reduce poverty when they create a market around the needs of the poor, markets that can make good economic sense. David's question to me, then soon reading *The Fortune*, set me on the path in global health that I continue to follow... fifteen years on, and counting.

During my first trip to the Aravind Eye Hospital, one of the leading surgeons and administrators, Aravind Srinivasan, suggested I visit a few of India's leading hospitals for cardiac surgery. There, he said, to my muted disbelief, I would discover surgeons typically perform more than *a thousand* surgeries a year, averaging several thousand U.S. dollars each. In the United States, in contrast, surgeons might do *one hundred* open heart procedures a year, each costing many tens of thousands of dollars.

What Aravind said was true. At Narayana Hrudayalaya Hospital in Bangalore and Hyderabad's Care Hospital, most coronary bypass operations were performed on beating hearts without the aid of a heart lung machine. This surgery without a heart lung machine is more difficult, but ultimately safer.

Each of these visits—in Madurai, Bangalore and Hyderabad—was eye opening. I knew India was advancing rapidly, lifting three hundred million from abject poverty into the economic middle class over the past three decades. My roles advising government and industry had given me a front row seat there to the changing ways of life. These remarkably advanced medical facilities and procedures more than confirmed my hunches. They energized me.

I now could visualize specifically how my global health ambitions might take shape. Learn about the most cost efficient medical practices in India, and bring them back to the U.S. Surely, I thought, that will be a way to lower costs and improve access and affordability wherever we could arouse interest in the U.S. healthcare system.[166]

After an academic career devoted to discovery research and a second career as a biopharmaceutical executive, I realized that the sharply rising cost of healthcare in the U.S. was a threat to both of those endeavors: scientific discovery and biomedical innovation. Moreover, it was clear that the discoveries and products of biomedical science were not benefiting most people.

In my farewell remarks to fifteen hundred colleagues at Human Genome Sciences, I posed this question, "If access and quality healthcare is not what it should and could be, how much longer will our fellow citizens be willing to write the checks, drawn upon their hard earned tax dollars?" (The full text of my Human Genome Sciences valedictory is in the Appendices section.)

I had seen a similar problem, a specific example of striking inefficiency, in India. An antibiotic, puromycin, was proven by a nonprofit group to be an effective cure for visceral leishmaniasis, a debilitating disease transmitted by sand flies. The drug was made available at no cost yet virtually no one benefited. Why? A poorly functioning health system could not deliver the drug to people suffering from the disease.

AS MANY PEOPLE AS POSSIBLE

Why is she suffering? Will she die? What can I do to help?

You recall how those thoughts shook me deeply, standing next to my mother's bed when I was not quite four years old. I never forgot.

So too in Calcutta, picking my way through crowds of people miserable with leprosy, no hands, no eye, no nose, or bodies horribly twisted—or dead. You remember as well how I vowed then to do whatever I could to heal the sick of the world. I never forgot.

Now was the time, the time for me to focus directly on global health.

I had been invited before leaving Human Genome Sciences to consider roles as a university president, a medical sciences professor and a consultant and partner at a biotech venture fund. But these were too far afield for what I knew I wanted: bringing high quality, affordable healthcare to as many people as possible.

To do this, I teamed with an attorney and seasoned business adviser based in India, John Michael Lind. We established a not-for-profit foundation based in the U.S., ACCESS Health International. Our mission was to become a think tank, studying best practices in healthcare services, and an advisory service for people in government or the private sector who shared our objective.

Hyderabad was our choice for headquarters. A founder and leader there of CARE Hospitals,[167] Dr. Krishna Reddy, an outstanding cardiologist, was excited by our plans. We appeared at a time when he was struggling for ways to treat poor people in his for profit hospitals. Krishna believed the profitability discipline would keep his operations efficient, innovative, affordable and sustainable. He was right! By 2020, CARE Hospitals Group numbered fourteen hospitals in five states of India.[168] Krishna welcomed us with open arms, providing space in his hospital for our initial base of operations in the largest urban area of south central India.

To lead that office, we brought on a recent graduate of Sweden's Stockholm School of Economics. Sofi Bergkvist had worked on health issues in India and Malawi, and at the United Nations in New York. She was eager and committed, willing to move to Hyderabad and organize the office. It was a wise choice. For ten years, as an ACCESS Health executive director, Sofi helped us build offices in India and Singapore and conducted studies in Bangladesh, Brazil, Sweden and eventually China and the Philippines.

Our approach had two parts. The first was to find the best examples of healthcare service in the world, try to understand them deeply, rigorously, then describe them in reports that could become an effective tool to help people around the world interested in replicating these models. We worked hard to capture knowledge. The second was to identify government officials who genuinely wanted to improve healthcare delivery and encourage them to adopt these proven models.

Why focus on governments? Policy precedes money. Consider: the U.S. spends more than three trillion dollars annually on healthcare; the pharmaceutical industry budgets roughly ninety billion dollars annually for research; and the largest foundation dedicated to global health, the Bill & Melinda Gates Foundation, commits roughly five billion dollars a year. Why focus on governments? That is where the money is.

We believe that government is the strongest tool available for improving global health. If we can influence government policy to do various things— to spend money a little bit better—we have done something. A little bit of science can solve a problem for hundreds of millions of people. You can do the same thing, improve the lives of hundreds of millions of people, if you hit the policy right. This is harder than science; you need both patience and resources to work with and through legions of people with varying opinions, motivations and influence.

BROOKINGS, LASKER

The first approach was modeled on the Brookings Institution, the venerable, centrist public policy research organization in Washington, D.C. The second was modeled on the Lasker Foundation that changed the course of cancer research by convincing Congress to accelerate funding in the '50s, '60s and '70s. I have been a trustee, admirer and occasional author and commentator of Brookings for many years. My campaign urging Congress to accelerate AIDS research funding was inspired in part by the Lasker Foundation's earlier campaign for cancer research. As I noted earlier, I was a direct beneficiary of that campaign. Before the AIDS crisis, government grants were the major source of funds for my Dana-Farber cancer research.

Years before, I concluded after trying to organize a global AIDS response that I would not be effective in large bureaucracies such as the World Health Organization, UNICEF or the World Bank. These organizations often do good work but my view was that international politics usually prevailed over scientific merits in policy and project development.

ACCESS Health began as an experiment, an initial investment with the idea that if early projects worked, they would become self sustaining and continue. We viewed each project internally as an experiment with many uncertainties, and looked for talented people willing to take a chance. This is the venture capitalist's approach. Each project depends upon circumstance and funding, but the main task is finding talented young people and giving them freedom to pursue their dreams.

My concept also was analogous to leading a university research department. You hire talented scientists. They support themselves and their overhead from government or private funding. You judge people by performance. If they do not get grants, they lose the part of their salary coming from the grants. Professors may have tenure but there is no guarantee they will keep the same salary or the same office and laboratory space.

Not everything will work out as planned. When it does not, just as with a laboratory research hypothesis or a startup company's initial product strategy, you adapt. And adapt I did.

I had to. I found little interest at all in the United States or Europe in learning from India's health systems innovations. A typical reaction: "That is an impressive story but will never work here. Everything they do, we know how to do." After some probing, I concluded that this was a coded message, another indictment in my view against the U.S. health system: "We have no need to be more efficient. We are making plenty of money doing what we do. Why should we change?"

This resistance went beyond the U.S. My friend from Villa d'Este conferences, Guilio Tremonti, then Italy's deputy prime minister, candidly described his hesitation about introducing any of India's cost saving practices after acknowledging many were impressive.

"My problem is that healthcare is the only source of job growth in my country," he said. "I suspect that is true in many other advanced economies as well. If we become more efficient, we will destroy the only source of job growth we have... a political and economic disaster."

For the first five years, I spent half of my time in different countries, absorbing their culture, their healthcare issues and working with people. I would develop a view about the issues, share that with colleagues and partners and test it in real situations. We always looked for people in government, nonprofits or the private sector who already were eager to make changes we would advocate. I realized years before it was a waste of time attempting to persuade people who were skeptics or otherwise passive about my ideas. You can never implant motive in another human being.

"HEALTH FOR ALL" IN ANDHRA PRADESH

A few months after we opened in Hyderabad, waiting rooms in Dr. Krishna Reddy's Care Hospitals suddenly were overflowing with low income patients. The chief minister of the state, Andhra Pradesh, had declared that everyone below the poverty line was entitled to free medical care in hospitals. Eighty percent of the state's eighty million people qualified... *sixty four million people.*

Here was a golden opportunity, right outside our doors, to study a health system transitioning as fast as humanly possible to serving the poor. Most of these patients had never before been evaluated by a nurse or physician. Patients needed only to present identification papers to be admitted at hospital.

The program, Aarogyasri, covered nearly a thousand medical and surgical procedures for ailments affecting the heart, liver, kidney, lung and pancreas as well as burns or birth defects. The state would pay full costs, generating revenues to cover the costs from an increase in liquor sales taxes. All public and private hospitals were enrolled as care providers if they met minimum requirements of quality. These public and private care providers were reimbursed at the same rates. The funds flowed back from the government typically within weeks of filings, in contrast to what often had taken a year or more before the policy change.

In English, Aarogyasri translates as "health for all," an uncanny expression of my purpose to improve human health and our belief at ACCESS Health that all people no matter where they live, no matter what their age or income, have a right to affordable high quality healthcare and to lead healthy and productive lives.

Foundations in the United Kingdom, Germany, Canada and Sweden wanted to know how Aarogyasri worked. So did the Gates and Rockefeller foundations in the United States and the World Bank. Each provided funding for reports we developed. We were in the right place at the right time, another illustration of how taking initiative to achieve your vision creates unforeseen opportunity. The optimist's dividend.

Many neighboring states in India were interested as well. As you can appreciate, political leaders across the world's largest democracy quickly assessed Aarogyasri as a landmark policy innovation. The program was enormously popular in Andhra Pradesh.[169]

We soon built capabilities to transfer the progress of health systems in Andhra Pradesh to others in central and southern India. We gained experience and expertise to advise in healthcare finance, governance, quality assurance, supply chain management, medical audit and management. Kerala, Karnataka and Tamil Nadu were quick to follow, but not so for others further north.

Millions of people in India, mostly in remote or rural areas, still have no option for primary care except to turn to so called unlicensed practitioners, charlatans who charge exorbitant fees. In 2018, the national government set a goal to provide five hundred million poor or vulnerable people with health insurance.

A DELICATELY ENGINEERED AMBULANCE SERVICE

Around the same time, one of the leaders in Hyderabad's fast growing global outsourcing industry in information technology was marshaling resources to provide vastly improved ambulance service in all parts of Andhra Pradesh.[170]

The need for an integrated approach to handling emergencies and providing prehospitalization or paramedical care was acute. Thousands of patients lost their lives because they did not receive adequate care within the first hour of an emergency. Of the three hundred thousand emergencies *occurring daily* in India, eighty percent involved people at the bottom of the economic pyramid. The absence of a reliable, affordable emergency response network serving the vast majority of citizens was a huge gap in India's system for healthcare delivery.

Studies showed that four hundred thousand Indian people died each year from untreated or tardily treated injuries... ten percent of total deaths. The number of ambulances was disproportionately low. Coordination among emergency response agencies was poor. Ambulances were rarely available in remote areas. Two thirds of women who died in childbirth did seek some form of care but were in crisis by the time they received any; three quarters of maternal deaths were clustered in rural areas of poorer states. Private hospitals and medical practitioners often refused to provide emergency care because of legal complications.

In urban areas, passersby were hesitant to help victims of road accidents, fearing police persecution. (The rate of road accidents in India broadly is one of the world's highest.) Steep payments to private ambulance services often created crushing financial burdens for patients and their families. Hospitals often refused admission to patients who could not pay upfront.

A trial program started in 2005 with seventy five ambulances serving five cities and thirty major towns in Andhra Pradesh was the beginning of what became an astounding success. Within the next decade, India created a world class emergency response system, drawing from its home grown expertise in information management systems and collaborating with emergency medical experts at Stanford University.

The program, known as Call 108, now reaches eight hundred million people. Each day in 2018, on average, this network processed one hundred and fifty thousand calls and provided twenty four thousand emergency responses. The program is administered by a public private partnership, the Emergency Management and Research Institute (EMRI). The service costs less than fifteen U.S. dollars per emergency, *less than one percent of a 911 emergency response in the U.S.* It has saved nearly three million lives.

The role of effective ambulance systems is often neglected in the roadmap for achieving sustainable development goals. No system of universal health coverage is complete or even effective without careful integration of the ambulance service with other medical services and facilities.

Most of this material about EMRI and similar emergency response organizations in India is covered in my book *Every Second Counts: Savings Lives with India's Emergency Response System.*[171] It is the story of an outstanding example of a public private partnership in global health, an innovation that emerged in one of the most complicated and resource-constrained environments in the world.[172]

THE MARVEL OF RELIANCE

India has extraordinary capabilities. I came to appreciate this through my varied roles there over the past quarter century: advisor on biomedical science, health systems and innovation to state and national government officials and for several companies.

The best board I have ever participated on might well be Reliance Industry's innovation council. Once a year, five of us would meet with the chairman and managing director, Mukesh Ambani, and his senior managers. They reviewed their business plans with us and asked for advice. The next year, they described how they had implemented our advice. It was remarkable. They usually implemented everything!

Reliance recently became India's largest corporation, as measured by revenues and market capitalization, by wisely executing a strategy focused entirely within India. "We do not have to do things outside of India," Mukesh believed. "We are focusing on India." During my ten years there, Reliance invested seventy billion dollars in India's infrastructure. Their core strength—"core competence," as C.K. Prahalad would say[173]—was executing major projects in industrial innovation.

They built an oil refinery half the size of Manhattan (twelve square miles) along with an entire city to support it. Created the mobile phone giant Jio, with many apps the rest of the world has not yet matched. Transformed how information technology infrastructure and operations work in India. Became one of the world's largest makers of industrial fibers and synthetic materials for clothing. Built a major retail presence in clothing and groceries.

By any measure, this was corporate performance at the highest level. Mukesh Ambani is one of the most capable executives I have ever met, certainly among the world's top ten business leaders. His management team impressed me as rock solid. All were Indians educated in India, careers developed in India; not "return" Indians, a colloquial term for an Indian national educated or experienced in businesses in the U.S. or western Europe before returning to India.

Over the years I was involved, Reliance's profits grew at an annual rate of seventeen percent. Phenomenal. Yes, India has many structural and governance problems, which any visitor quickly perceives. For foreign investors, it also presents many challenges. Yet, with its comparatively young population—more than sixty five percent below the age of thirty five—and expanding middle class, India's prospects for economic growth far exceed those of the United States and China.

One of our tenets is to share information freely and collaborate with other foundations. We also take on projects with the private sector. The problems in global health are too big to work on alone. Over time, various groups have requested our help. In one case, we collaborated with a British charity, the Children's Investment Fund, in India to address one of the U.N.'s Millennium Development Goals: reducing infant deaths.

For five years, we coached staff of neonatal intensive care units in several hospitals in Andhra Pradesh and neighboring Telangana. Our goal was a thirty percent reduction of infant deaths. A few hospitals showed improvement but results overall were disappointing. Why? Our review showed that neither hospital managers nor staff were held accountable for measuring the number of infant deaths or rewarded in any way for reducing the number of deaths.

When government agencies or insurers paying for these services could not understand who is responsible, what processes are being used or how many babies died, improvements were not possible regardless of how well people were trained. Hospitals with the best performance in reducing infant deaths had the highest levels of transparency and accountability.

Those themes, transparency and accountability, were two vital elements in the remarkable rise of NYU Langone Health from mediocrity in medical care, research and education. We will take a close look in chapter 33 at NYU Langone Health's transformation and the lessons it offers for improving quality and reducing costs in any healthcare system.

HEALTH POLICIES FOR ALL OF INDIA

One of our first ventures into international advisory work was establishing the Center for Health Market Innovations. The concept came through one of our partners, the U.S.-based nonprofit Results for Development. Our teams studied and described more than three hundred programs on maternal health, and summarized them in the book *Improving the Health of Mother and Child: Solutions from India*, and on the Center's website: www. healthmarketinnovations.org. Funding was provided by the British government's Department for International Development, the Gates Foundation and Rockefeller Foundation.

Years later, teaming again with Results for Development and supported by the Rockefeller Foundation, we developed a resource center for best practices in health system management to help low income countries. Two reports we produced described how to conduct medical audits and price various services.

The Joint Learning Network, as our resource center was called, began with six participating countries in Africa and southeast Asia and expanded to thirty four, including several in central America, Mexico, more in Africa and two with more advanced economies, China and South Korea. At last count, more than thirty reports with practical guidance on specific challenges were drafted. All are available at www.jointlearningnetwork.org/resources. (To access, please paste the URL into your browser.) Implementation remains a challenge because turnover among officials in participating countries' governments often is high. Incoming officials can face a steep learning curve on many fronts.

When I reflect now on our many projects in India, none may be more significant than the report we helped organize and draft in 2019 for the central policy think tank of India's national government, NITI Aayog. Prime Minister Narendra Modi chairs the group, which was established in 2015 to advise the nation in pursuing sustainable development goals.

Health Systems for a New India: Building Blocks, Potential Pathways to Reform far exceeds what I had hoped to achieve when I first thought decades ago about how I might improve access to high quality affordable care in the world. The report is an apotheosis of our work in India. (NITI is an acronym for National Institute for Transforming India.) It draws from our experience and knowledge to help shape the health policy of a country with one billion three hundred and eighty million people.

ACCESS HEALTH TODAY

ACCESS Health has codified granular, detailed knowledge from people in healthcare delivery in many local environments now for more than a decade, and matched it with global knowledge of what has worked best. Our local and global knowledge are continuously evolving, and integrated. When invited, we help health system leaders implement our recommendations.

Our largest operations are in India and China followed by the Philippines, Singapore and the United States. We also conduct studies in northern Europe.

We recently had a team working in an area of the Philippines so remote, and inflamed occasionally by militia attacks, we needed military clearance to move our people in for interviews with the local population. Our hope is to coach for profit clinics in that remote area on best practices for controlling tuberculosis, practices that we identified in Pakistan. This is practical, detailed knowledge.

Our goal now is to become a global thought leader and preferred partner for leaders of healthcare systems. Our purpose is to advise these leaders, coaching them on these best practices so they can elevate their systems further toward higher quality and lower cost.

We recently organized a specialized center of expertise within our broader ACCESS Health think tank to codify best practices for leading this change to stronger health systems in regions where we operate: South Asia, the Middle East, Southeast Asia, China, Africa and the United States. Our Institute for Health Systems Strengthening is the first of several steps to encourage these transitions. Its research and publishing focus has five building blocks: governance, finance, healthcare provision, digital health and community health. Each is described here:

FIVE BUILDING BLOCKS

Governance. How health systems are governed determines in large measure both health outcomes and efficiency. Policies cover government finance, audits, management and oversight of public private partnership.

We are developing policy recommendations to increase healthcare investments needed to meet rising demand from the recent rollout of the national public health insurance program. ACCESS Health also is part of a consortium studying FinTech solutions for financing cancer care and consumer health.

Finance. Sustainable finance is key to the success of all health systems, public and private. We focus on efficient use of government and private funds. Our subspecialty in FinTech for health will expand and strengthen this work in India and elsewhere in Asia.

Healthcare provision. The health of a population depends upon access to high quality, affordable healthcare. The provision of healthcare services is the responsibility of governments (national, state and local) as well as healthcare providers themselves.

The Institute will advise both the public and private sectors on improving healthcare delivery. Our focus is integrated care, seamless integration of home care, community care, out-patient care and tertiary care as well as integration of health and social services.

Digital health. The Institute has developed deep expertise in digital health solutions for national and state governments as well as for hospital networks that provide integrated health and social services. Digital health is central to modern management of efficient health systems.

Community health. Strong community health services are the backbone of a healthy population. The Institute will focus on how to improve community health services as well as on coordinating and blending community health services with one another. Integrating local hospital services also will be addressed.

DIAMOND CUTTERS

Archimedes said, give me a lever long enough and I can move the earth. Well, we are not privileged to have such levers. But it is not by chance that I am using my skills and accumulated knowledge to be the small lever through our global health think tank and advisory service to make big change.

The best thing you can do with a small foundation is conduct excellent studies, draw precise conclusions about best practices and influence policy in government or the private sector to support those best practices.

Our approach at ACCESS Health is to be like a diamond cutter. If you can find the flat point to make a little tap, you can break apart the toughest diamond. This now is my answer to the riddle: What can you do to make the biggest difference for human life?

32

FROM
SINGAPORE TO CHINA

By THE YEAR 2000, Singapore's economy was on firm footing. Thinking about what they could do next for future growth, leaders looked to biotechnology.

The government was about to open an expansive research center futuristically named Biopolis, had lured many outstanding scientists to head laboratories there and was planning more investments. "Would you be willing to advise our sovereign wealth funds and our finance ministry?" Singapore's long serving ambassador to the United States and a good friend, Heng Chee Chan, asked me. "We would like to know if we are making a wise investment."

"I would be happy to," I told her.

A month later, spending a week touring Biopolis and several corporate laboratories gave me a clearer understanding of Singapore's commitments. The facilities were world class. Highly accomplished scientists tackling major problems directed the labs. Impressed, I expressed my admiration in meetings with Singapore's finance minister, Tharman Shanmugaratnam, and the chief executive of Temasek, the country's largest sovereign wealth fund, Ho Ching.

Both wanted to know: Will biotech be an important engine for our future economic and financial growth?

"You are building excellence in modern biological science," I replied. "You have hired top people, supporting them appropriately, and they are doing well. Unfortunately, that is not enough to create a new business hub. You simply are not big enough. It takes a larger community and several generations of companies to build the infrastructure and talent you need. Your research enterprise, even when fully developed, will be smaller than any of our great universities, say Stanford or MIT.

"Use the knowledge and talent you have attracted here from all over the world to advise you," I continued. "They can help you make wise investments in Europe, the United States and, more importantly, in your neighbors, China and India. China and India are on their way to becoming powerful players in biotechnology."

At the time, Singapore ranked No. 20 among the world's nations in per capita gross national product. (In 2019, it had risen further to No. 9, between the United States and Denmark.[174]) Thirty five years before, when the former British colony gained its independence in 1965 from Malaysia, it was among the world's poorest; average annual income per person barely exceeded five hundred dollars.

Meanwhile, with many ACCESS Health projects in India flourishing, I increasingly kept an eye on Singapore. Wouldn't that be a good hub for us to expand, not only in Singapore but also more widely in the region of southeast Asia? To Thailand, Cambodia, Myanmar, Laos and Vietnam?

I was primed, delighted, when an invitation came in 2010 to attend a kickoff meeting for what Singapore's government framed as its Initiative to Improve Health in Asia. That theme sounded ambitious for such a small nation, but not after I heard the longtime health minister, Khaw Boon Wan, describe spectacular results of Singapore's own health system.

Singaporeans enjoyed such high levels of quality health that the nation ranked among the world's ten best by any major measure, achieved with total spending by government and the private sector on health slightly above four percent. I could hardly believe my ears. At the time, the U.S. was spending seventeen percent of GDP on health (soon to rise to where it has remained for the past few years, at eighteen percent) with Americans receiving significantly lower overall quality of health, ranking far below all other industrialized nations.

"What a great example... proof of principle that high quality affordable healthcare is achievable," I thought, listening with amazement. "I should study this in detail. What I learn may be valuable to others, especially back home."

The president of the National University of Singapore (NUS), Dr. Tan Chor Chuan, quickly embraced my idea to write a book, aiding the cause by hiring a research assistant to pitch in. Chor Chuan, who invited me to the conference, also guaranteed a publisher, the Ridge Press imprint of the National University of Singapore Press. We immediately were off to the races. I spent the next eighteen months, traveling back and forth, interviewing dozens of political leaders, bureaucrats, hospital administrators, doctors, nurses and patients.

I encourage anyone concerned with improving their national healthcare system to read *Affordable Excellence: The Singapore Healthcare Story*, published in paperback in 2013. To give you some impressions of what I found, here are some edited excerpts.

HARD WORKING POPULATION

One of the pillars of Singaporean government and politics is that a strong society requires social harmony. All social groups should benefit, to some degree, from the country's achievements. In his memoirs, Singapore's founding father, Lee Kuan Yew, explained this approach:

A competitive, winner-take-all society, like colonial Hong Kong in the 1960s, would not be acceptable in Singapore... To even out the extreme results of free-market competition, we had to redistribute the national income through subsidies on things that improved the earning power of citizens, such as education. Housing and public health were also obviously desirable. But finding the correct solutions for personal medical care, pensions or retirement benefits was not easy.[175]

Lee had witnessed the beginning of the British welfare state when he studied at Cambridge in the 1940s. Over time, he concluded it would never succeed in Singapore. A poor, struggling country needed a motivated population that worked hard. The average person's desire to achieve and succeed should never be compromised by an overgenerous state.

The nation's legendary prime minister from 1959 to 1990, Lee led the country with a conviction that citizens must develop and retain a sense of responsibility for all aspects of their lives, including their own physical and emotional well being.

PROMOTE HEALTHY LIVING

The government took the lead in promoting healthy living in 1993 when it adopted the blueprint for Singapore's modern healthcare system, Affordable Health Care.

The five objectives were:
» Become a healthy nation by promoting good health

» Promote individual responsibility for one's own health and avoid over-reliance on state welfare or third party medical insurance

» Ensure good and affordable basic medical services for all Singaporeans

» Engage competition and market forces to improve service and raise efficiency

» Intervene directly in the healthcare sector when necessary, where the market fails to keep healthcare costs down

Policy recommendations included:
» Moderate demand

» Create incentives to keep costs down

- » Prevent an oversupply of healthcare services and other examples of government oversight and action

- » Adjust medical savings programs

- » Sponsor insurance programs

- » Subsidize hospitals and polyclinics

- » Apportion the specific number of beds per hospital

- » Fund new medical schools

- » Control the number and types of physicians who practice

- » Regulate and limit the number of private insurance programs

Health was not a top priority for the government after Singapore separated from Malaysia and became a sovereign state in 1965. National security, job creation, housing and education were ahead in the queue. Those priorities seem to me to have been apt at the time. It was vitally important to set up the defense of this small nation, and then attract investors to set in motion economic growth and tackle glaring problems in unemployment, housing and education.

Singapore's approach to the healthcare market is a kind of highly calibrated capitalism. Government intervention is sanctioned in certain circumstances to correct or redirect the market. For example, the government funds public hospitals and other care facilities but also encourages private hospitals and clinics to participate.

The government successfully executed strategies that required most ministries to work together after determining early on that ensuring people's health had to be included in every aspect of urban planning. Numerous ministries overseeing all sectors of government were expected to cooperate: housing, water and food supply, air quality, waste disposal, road traffic, parks, tree planting and more.

Then, too, since the late 1960s, people have been required to pay into a compulsory savings program for certain medical expenses. This aligns with the national ethos of self reliance, personal responsibility and family responsibility. Perhaps when people have to spend their own money, they tend to be more economical in the solutions they pursue to their medical problems. Singapore has forestalled rising healthcare costs far better than most countries. When someone else is paying—government programs, insurance companies—there is less incentive to be prudent.

By keeping costs down, this compulsory health savings program, Medisave, allowed the entire system to remain more affordable to everyone, including government. It has allowed government to focus assistance programs on the very needy who are unable to pay for their own care.

ELDERCARE, UNSOLVED CONUNDRUM

I wish I could say that is the end of the Singapore story. Unfortunately, it is not. Costs keep rising. Families keep getting smaller, which limits their ability to share Medisave dollars. People are living longer, needing more care. To its credit, the government added a new program, catastrophic insurance.

Some say Singapore is small and its healthcare solutions cannot work in larger countries. My answer as a scientist is that Singapore's healthcare system is a "proof of principle." The experiment does work. Healthcare systems can be designed that provide healthcare to all citizens in a highly developed economy at a cost the economy can afford. These costs can be controlled while delivering excellent service.

No doubt, the continuity and long term perspective that political stability provide make it easier for a government to develop such a system. The People's Action Party has been in power since independence. Yet it could not have maintained its rule without being responsive to voters. For example, after the 2011 election, the government doubled health spending to provide more care for the elderly. This included subsidies for nursing homes, for middle income families caring for older people in their homes as well as for day care, rehabilitation care and home-based care.

In recent years, moreover, the priority has been using the same cross-ministry approach to address the coming demographic crisis, an aging population. How can the current system, designed around hospitals, be adapted to provide excellent care for the elderly at a cost the country can afford? This is the central issue for all developed countries.

Many middle income countries face problems of low birth rates and an aging population. Many elderly suffer multiple chronic diseases, such as diabetes, high blood pressure, dementia and Alzheimer's. These chronic diseases cannot be treated episodically; they must be treated over long periods. The goal typically is to reduce the impact of a chronic illness in curtailing a person's physical activity and lifespan, not to eliminate the illness.

The best place for the patient, and for the healthcare system, is to make this care available in outpatient and community care centers or at home... not hospitals. Some well equipped local clinics already conduct eighty percent of surgeries in these outpatient settings. That is the future.

Thanks to their health and social problems, Singaporeans today are among the longest lived populations on earth. As early as 2011, women were living an average of eighty three years, up from sixty six in 1960, and men, seventy nine years, up from sixty two. Yet with a low birth rate, the burden of caring for the elderly is rising sharply; even as lifespans were increasing in 2011, Singapore's replacement rate was one the world's lowest, at 1.2 children per woman.

Absent immigration, a difficult political issue in Singapore as it is in many countries, the result is predictable. Growing numbers of older people supported by the taxes on declining numbers of young and middle aged workers is a recipe for social and financial disaster. Unlike many pending disasters, such as plagues, tsunamis and earthquakes, the devastating effects of demographic change are predictable decades in advance. We know how many people are born and die each year. We can predict average lifespans. Yet in most countries, leaders neglect to make effective planning for the consequences of what is to come a priority.

Singapore is not one of those countries. The Health Ministry recently established a new Office of Healthcare Transformation to actively manage the transition to a system that both addresses and balances the burdens of the elderly and those of younger generations. Its executive director is my friend, Dr. Tan Chor Chuan.

His articulated mission, posted on the office's website, demonstrates anew Singapore's aspirations to lead the world in quality health:

Look at new ways to help Singaporeans adopt behaviors promoting health that will prevent or delay the onset of chronic conditions.

Work with primary care providers to make home based management a viable and effective care model and, in the longer term, the preferred choice for patients with chronic diseases like diabetes, hypertension and high blood cholesterol.

Team with hospitals to explore new approaches to provide patients with multiple medical conditions holistic patient care.

SWEDEN, ONLY FIRST STEPS

What countries do best in responding to demographic change? I thought, What about Sweden? I traveled there regularly over the years for scientific meetings and consulting projects. After writing the Singapore book, I decided to open an ACCESS Health office in Stockholm and explore those and other questions.

To my surprise, Sweden was bedeviled by failures in caring for its elderly. Unsafe conditions in eldercare homes had contributed to a political party's defeat and fall from power years earlier. "The world looks to Sweden as a leader in healthcare best practices," I said to our local staff member, Sofia Widen. "If they are having problems it is a warning for others. Let's write a book to help people avoid the most obvious problems."

Our interviews with pioneers in Sweden's eldercare professions quickly surfaced major problems: lack of coordination between social and healthcare workers; unmet hopes of aging people to live longer in their homes, supported by home care; unsolved challenges of caring for elderly with Alzheimer's disease, dementia and related cognitive declines.

We soon broadened the study to examine best practices for eldercare and dementia care in the United States and elsewhere in Europe: Germany, the Netherlands, Norway and Finland. Sofia conducted the interviews in Europe and Jean Galiana joined me for research in the United States.

Our major findings on eldercare? Provide care wherever and when a person needs assistance; integrate care in all aspects of a person's life; and create purpose by encouraging community engagement and lifelong learning for older persons. *Aging with Dignity: Innovation and Challenge in Sweden – The Voice of Care Professionals*, written by Sofia and me, was published in in 2017 by Nordic Academic Press.

For dementia? Structure environments to encourage autonomy; make use of new technologies, including robot companions, to improve quality of life. *Voices in Dementia Care*, the book based on Sofia and Jean's interviews, and written by me and our ACCESS Health communications director, Anna Dirksen, was first published in 2018 by Tethys Books in New Delhi.[176]

The healthcare responses we chronicled are only first steps. We are at the early stages of what is becoming a panoply of darkening health crises, with fewer resources to manage long term debilitating diseases that are proliferating among our aging populations. Can the private sector play a role? Absolutely. In Sweden, we conceived of a business incubator for startups addressing problems of the elderly, especially people with declining cognitive ability. "There is even a Swedish fund, the Post Code Lottery, that will support us," said our ACCESS Health leader in Stockholm, Stephanie Treschow. "Great idea, Stephanie!" I said as she outlined the plan. "Go for it!"

Our Modern Aging Program, which Stephanie conceived and proposed, quickly took wing in Singapore as well, and then Beijing and Shanghai. Funds from the Singapore government and ACCESS Health provided seed capital for more than twenty companies, each investment spanning five years. Our office director in Singapore then, Adrienne Mendenhall, collaborated as well with a small business incubator at National University of Singapore for additional seed capital. These startups developed new technologies for care of the elderly and mentally ill.

As the program wound down in 2019, our new leader in Singapore, Sejal Mistry, breathed new life into our initial strategy, to advise and strengthen health systems across southeast Asia. Further east, we maintain an office in the Philippines, conducting research and advising the Health Ministry and local governments and private enterprises.

A MISGUIDED SYSTEM, SLOWLY CHANGING

Our signature effort across southeast Asia in those years, Modern Aging also set the tone for our programs in China. We described it as an ecosystem of innovation we curated to address the needs of the elderly. In fact, most of our activity in China is with startups and established companies, not government. We have offices now in Beijing, Shanghai and Hong Kong, working often with a community of entrepreneurs and business leaders, supporting them with deep knowledge about best practices in healthcare for the elderly.

The head of all our China programs, Chang Liu, was yet another Singapore find. Chang called me out of the blue one day from the NUS-Duke Medical School. He was a newly minted faculty member in the department of health economics. "I have been trying to learn about the health system here," he said. "Your book is the only clear and comprehensive description I could find. I am calling to thank you."

"That is very nice of you to say," I said.

He explained he also was intrigued by ACCESS Health's initiatives in the financing and health needs of aging populations. I, in turn, was intrigued by Chang's knowledge and experience in China as well as his commitment to improve the health of the elderly. After we met a few weeks later, I invited him to join me and Julio Frenk, then dean of the Harvard School of Public Health, for meetings with key government, university and hospital leaders in Beijing, Shanghai and Hong Kong.

A great trip. Those conversations made it clear China was serious about strengthening its health systems, and especially improving the quality and affordability of care for its rapidly aging population. Julio told me about an organization of healthcare professionals in the U.S. and China who for a few years had used the forum to share studies, concepts and connections, the U.S.-China Health Summit. This, we both knew, was a valuable resource to help me jump start ACCESS Health activity in China.

It certainly was! I soon joined the board of directors and in recent years, as the organization's chairman, have helped design and lead its yearly conferences. In 2019, it was Harvard's turn to host the event. More than four hundred specialists attended, representing leading institutions and enterprises in global health, biomedical research, healthcare policy and service delivery.

People who travel often to China on business or professional activities soon realize there are many Chinas. That statement requires a bit of explanation for others, so let me give you an overview.

The primary local incentives for Chinese public officials are to build, not to operate. This is unfortunate. Local mayors send taxes to Beijing, but they control local real estate. No surprise: they emphasize building massive hospitals, often with ten thousand beds, instead of getting healthcare services into neighborhoods where people live.

I caution all my Chinese audiences, "You are putting multiple heavy stones around your neck, stones which your great grandchildren are going to have to carry."

There is increasing recognition that the current system is not good. Many Chinese think seriously about this, and I do see the overall system slowly changing. When you look closely you can see people in government, nonprofits and the private sector experimenting with healthcare services in almost every imaginable way. As I said, there are many Chinas.

DENG XIAOPING'S HISTORIC MISTAKE

Even when China was still a very poor society, in the '60s and '70s and into the '80s, government policy was to give everyone primary healthcare. People were vaccinated. They had barefoot doctors. The nation's statistics in health outcomes fared relatively well in world rankings, a testament to its universal primary care.

But China policy under Deng Xiaoping dramatically shifted course on healthcare in the '80s. Deng destroyed the fundamental primary care system. His policy was to install a capitalist model, sending people to private doctors while building big hospitals for surgeries and urgent care.

That surely did not work. Nothing came in place of the barefoot doctors. Peasants by the hundreds of millions and others could not afford private care. Health conditions plummeted. Xi Jinping's government has made healthcare planning and spending a high priority now for several years. He is moving toward a mixture of public and private healthcare providers. I think it is unlikely to work.

The new paradigm for any national health policy should make prevention the priority, and deliver most medical services in communities, not hospitals—the distributed healthcare model. Care in the community, not the hospital, is much less expensive. It is patient friendly. Clinics and outpatient surgical centers located near where people live are much more accessible, and, therefore, better for patients.

Yet in most countries, including the United States, entrenched players resist the distributed care model. Preserving the status quo is their ultimate priority, and they push, even manipulate, the political system for friendly policies.

In my experience, a national health system with a single payer and private providers works best. When the government both provides and pays for healthcare, change to incorporate new best practices is difficult. Those entrenched players push back. With a public payer and private providers, you can encourage people to compete, to innovate and actually lower costs.

Price transparency is a motivator. In Singapore, where the Health Ministry posts updates on prices from common hospital bills on its website, the price of LASIK surgery to correct nearsightedness plunged to fourteen hundred Singapore dollars in 2008 (about one thousand U.S. dollars) for one eye, from twenty three hundred Singapore dollars (sixteen hundred fifty U.S. dollars) just four years earlier. The Japanese, Koreans and Taiwanese also do well with this approach.

Much of the preventive care you need does not derive from the doctor or other medical services. It is social, meaning it originates from services such as visiting nurses and physical therapists in the community. The goal of preventive care is to keep people healthy, to encourage nutritious diets, exercise and other keystones of healthy living. Then, if they do contract an illness, to manage the illness toward positive outcomes.

China has several best practices in elder care. To wit, in dense urban areas of Shanghai, people use recreation centers as a social club when they are healthy. If they fall ill, nurses in the center can arrange to get these seniors into beds in that same location. When the seniors recover and return home, nurses know to track their daily health markers, if needed.

Chinese entrepreneurs are accelerating the global revolution in information technology, innovating and adapting it for high quality care outside of hospitals. Imaging and diagnostic technologies in clinics allow disease to be diagnosed with speed and precision. Nurses can monitor remotely a patient's status before and after surgeries, and any side effects from new medicines or other interventions when patients have wearable and home sensors.

Our Health Futures Program in China convenes partners from both public and private sectors to promote these and other innovations for health systems in the future. Our focus is three areas of innovation, technologies and new models for delivering and paying for health services.

ACCESS Health also operates a research center in China, documenting and analyzing best practices. Our Health Futures Academy attracts many innovators, industry leaders and policy makers determined to improve health-care services. The team also offers a consulting service for best practices.

AFRICA, UNITED STATES

My hope for the future, and my expectation, is to expand ACCESS Health's impact and activity into Africa. Egypt is the most likely location on the continent for planting our flag. Many like minded travelers in global health there are part of my network of friends and medical professionals in the region, dating from my PhD studies at Harvard.

I also remain determined to make a bigger impact on health policies in my own country. The next chapter as well as my observations, criticisms and forecasts about the COVID-19 pandemic should give you a clear idea of how I am driving toward that goal.

‖ 33 ‖

HIGHER QUALITY CARE, LOWER COST

THOSE OF US WHO HAVE TRAVELED TO MANY COUNTRIES probably know that access to high quality, affordable care even in advanced economies is neither universal nor equally available.

The United States is exceptionally peculiar in this way. We provide some of the most advanced healthcare anywhere in the world but, on average, we do not do well. Most people of privilege in our country believe they have the best healthcare in the world. They are not wrong. We have healthcare as good or better than anybody, if you have access to it. Yet we as a society are highly inequitable. Most people do not receive our high quality healthcare. We do not distribute healthcare equally.

What is more, we are inefficient. The United States spends twice as much on healthcare than other countries—more than $3.6 trillion in 2018: more than eleven thousand dollars per person annually on average and nearly eighteen percent of our total economic output.[177]

Much of the debate in Congress centers on how we pay for healthcare services—private insurance, employer sponsored insurance, federal and state payments or out of pocket payments. Should we maintain the status quo or move to single payer? But we are wrong as a nation to argue exclusively about how to pay for what we agree can be outrageously expensive healthcare.

We should look more closely at how well, or poorly, our healthcare is *delivered*. If we demand and celebrate more efficient, more effective delivery of higher quality healthcare, we can have it sooner than you might think possible.

GLOBAL EXCELLENCE, RIGHT IN MY HOME CITY

When I first organized ACCESS Health International, my hope was to help improve the quality, cost and efficiency of care in the United States by learning about and describing some of the best examples of healthcare delivery in other countries. But most American healthcare leaders were not interested.

Yet as pleasing as our success in India, China, Singapore and other countries became, I never gave up hope that we might someday include U.S. examples in our research, publishing and advisory work. Then that opportunity came, unexpectedly, right in my home city.

In Shanghai, where I was a member of an innovation council at New York University's local campus, I had encouraged the vice chancellor, Jeffrey Lehman, to consider adding a medical school. "You'll need to speak with folks at the Medical Center in New York," he said.

NYU's center had lagged badly in rankings for the quality of its patient care, medical school and medical research at the turn of the century. It was complacent, foundering. Even worse, by 2007 the financial stability of New York University itself, one of America's finest academic institutions, was threatened by the medical center's mounting losses.

Then a new dean and CEO was hired. He was an unusual choice, with none of the typical credentials for leading an academic medical center. He had no prior business experience. He had never been trained or mentored as a manager or executive. He did not sit on any outside board of directors.

In fact, Dr. Robert Grossman had never managed anything larger than his NYU radiology department.

Grossman was in his sixth year at the medical center's helm in 2013 when he agreed to meet in his New York office and hear my Shanghai proposal. He listened, then said unequivocally, "I have no interest in creating a new medical school and hospital in China. I am focused like a laser on building the best hospital and medical school in New York. That is more than a fulltime job."

That was not the end of our meeting, fortunately. It was instead for me the beginning of an eye opening discovery of how one leader with a vision for excellence and accountability at every level transformed the culture and elevated the performance of his institution.

The scale and rate of improvement during Bob Grossman's first ten years leading NYU Medical Center (later renamed NYU Langone Health) were remarkable. He catapulted a financially failing institution into one of the nation's best medical centers. Here are some of the numbers:

Quality and safety of patient care ranking rose to the top five from the bottom one third, with three consecutive years as No. 1

Medical school ranking rose to third place from thirty fourth

Research grants from the National Institutes of Health nearly doubled, to two hundred thirty million dollars

Revenues increased to more than seven billion dollars from two billion dollars

Annual charitable donations increased to an average of more than two hundred and forty million

Total square feet of hospital and research facilities increased by 1.2 million

Number of physicians on staff increased to more than thirty six hundred from two hundred fifty

An annual surplus of two hundred forty million dollars was recorded, in contrast to a deficit averaging one hundred fifty million dollars

In the summer of 2018, Grossman achieved another of his original goals, as truly audacious, even revolutionary, as it seemed in 2007.

The person most responsible for persuading trustees to hand Grossman the reigns at NYU Langone Health was Home Depot cofounder and NYU Langone Health chairman Kenneth Langone. It was Langone who proclaimed to an audience of cheering students and parents in 2018 that all current and new medical students would receive full tuition scholarships.[178] Millions more later tuned into the CBS *60 Minutes* segment about the free tuition story, a stunning development in the medical world.[179]

The detailed case study of NYU Langone's rapid ascendance is told in my book *World Class: A Story of Adversity, Transformation and Success at NYU Langone Health*. This was one of the most exciting studies of my life. Published by Fast Company Press in 2019, *World Class* is a guide to how more healthcare systems can become outstanding on their own despite the burdens and failings of our national health policies. The book quickly became an Amazon best seller in three categories: Management and Leadership, Workplace Culture and Hospital Administration.

For research spanning two years, I interviewed more than fifty people at all levels of the organization, some several times. These sessions were scheduled, with Bob Grossman's knowledge and support, entirely at my own initiative and expense and with no conflicts to shade any of my independent conclusions. They included some twenty senior executives of the medical center, senior leaders of NYU's hospitals and medical school as well as several department chairs, doctors, nurses, students and research scientists.

HOW TRUSTEES DRIVE CHANGE

In his inaugural speech, Grossman asserted that NYU Langone should not simply be satisfied to recover from crisis. Why not be the best, he proposed, and compete with "the Hopkinses, Harvards and Penns"? To get there, he said, every decision taken at every level must answer one question: Will this step improve patient care? Nursing schedules. Executive and dean hirings and promotions. Emergency department staffing. Elevator maintenance. Ambulance routes. Lighting. Everything... *Will this improve patient care?*

Backed by the board of trustees through initial episodes of resistance and even lawsuits by faculty and others threatened by his revolution, Grossman was relentless, upbeat, unflappable. In his inaugural remarks, he asserted that NYU Medical Center would not be satisfied simply to recover from an existential crisis. Instead, it would lift itself up by the bootstraps and become, "a world class, patient-centered, integrated academic medical center." The center soon was renamed NYU Langone Health in the wake of a two hundred million dollar donation by Ken Langone and his wife Elaine.

Grossman was convinced he needed to change the culture. He fired five top executives on his first day on the job and eventually replaced thirty of thirty three department heads. This was not a case of a new CEO removing existing managers so that he could install a new team that he had waiting in the wings. He simply was removing people that he thought were not doing their jobs well.

Richard Woodrow, former executive director of the Organizational Development and Learning Department at NYU Langone, told me people at the center were genuinely nice, civil and content but, at the time, "disconnected from harsh realities. If you did not want to work hard, you could find a way to appear busy."

Grossman began building a new organizational structure designed to be agile, lean, flexible and for everyone, at every level to be accountable to themselves and each other. "When we changed the system, we eliminated a whole level of management," he told me.

Bob Grossman's achievements would not have been possible without the support and hands on engagement of its trustees. Many stories of organizational transformation in business focus only on the CEO. But, as I wrote in my book, an effective board creates the conditions for success.[180]

"The board must agree to the need for fundamental change. The board must enthusiastically endorse the vision and the road map of the new leader. The board then must enable the new leader to do his or her job. The board must help wherever it can, especially financially. Boards must also run interference for the new leader.

"Very often powerful players will seek to use their connections with board members to undermine and derail changes they may view as personally threatening to their own positions of power," I continued. "Boards must protect a leader of transformational change from such backstabbing.

"What a board must not do is equally important. A board must not interfere or meddle with the daily execution. As a group the board must do what Bob Grossman did as an individual: agree to a broad outline of change, empower the changemaker, let the changemaker free to execute the plan, but measure and hold the changemaker accountable for results. NYU Langone has been and continues to be blessed with a board that meets these criteria."

Moreover, the chair of the university's trustees, my longtime friend Marty Lipton, and John Sexton, the university's president, solidly supported Ken Langone's and Bob Grossman's plans to remake the medical center. As I wrote, "Innovators face the risk of dangerous isolation from those parts of the organization that are hesitant or resistant to change; they can be undercut by appeals to other power centers. But that couldn't happen at NYU Langone."[181]

"LET ME SHOW YOU HOW I MANAGE"

Grossman knew from the start that he would need immediate access to real time data measuring the performance of his three operating units: medical education, medical research and healthcare services.

"Information is everything," Grossman told me.

With his chief information officer, Nader Mherabi, Grossman designed and implemented an information system that charted each day the performance of every physician, every manager and other employee against high standards. The system, developed with vendor Epic Health, cost several hundred million dollars. Moreover, it replaced one completed shortly before

Grossman became dean and CEO, one that he rejected as siloed by department and with essential data, such as it was, broadly inaccessible to him.

"Without solid real time information you are flying blind," he said. "You cannot improve the quality of care without the necessary data." Even more daring to some observers, he made these dashboards available to everyone in the organization. Patients could access test results as soon as they were entered in the system.

For all that NYU Langone has achieved, there was nothing unique or new in its story—with perhaps this one exception, information technology.

Many physicians are frustrated, even angered, by inefficiencies new electronic health management systems forced upon them in the past decade. That did not happen at NYU Langone Health. In practice, the system provided transparency of data on the medical center's entire operations, in real time, across all departments and both vertically and horizontally at all levels of the organization. Grossman's revealing term for the creation was "cross mission integration."

Quickly after discarding my Shanghai proposal that first day we met in his conference room, Bob offered, "Let me show you how I manage. I manage to quantifiable goals."

He motioned for me to sit beside him at his computer, then clicked a few keys. "For example, we have a goal to reduce the number of blood transfusions. Blood is expensive and a source of dangerous infections." A list of all surgeons performing hip replacements quickly appeared alongside the number of units of blood each required on average, with rankings from highest to lowest.

"Look, the variation is fourfold for the same operation!" He said. "Why? We have a group of doctors and nurses looking at the issue now. All of our surgeons can see all this data, too. Our data is horizontally as well as vertically transparent."

"Here is how we manage research," he went on. "When I became CEO, our faculty was at the lower end of NIH research dollars received per scientist. Today we rank number one by the same measure."

Another few clicks and a list of all NYU neuroscientists appeared, each ranked according to the total amount of funding they received from external sources for their research. Arrows indicated trend lines, with levels of funding support shown rising or declining. Another few clicks. The same researchers were ranked by grant totals for studies across multiple disciplines. More clicks. Now, rankings by number of papers published in respected medical journals.

"We give additional funding to researchers who demonstrate they work well with others," Bob said. "Again, our scientists can see this same data you and I are seeing." Translation: each researcher can see, at any time, how their funding and publishing totals compare with colleagues. It is like the major league baseball player, always aware—as is his manager—of how his stats compare with every other player.

Bob then showed me a series of charts tracking infection rates for patients, length of stay, returns visits following surgery and in-hospital death rates. "We are doing our best to improve quality as measured by both clinical outcomes and patient satisfaction," he said. "We intend to rank number one in quality, safety and patient satisfaction not only in New York but in the United States."

My head was spinning when I left Bob's office that day. Now, years later, I still shake my head in amazement, marveling at the sustained high performance measures each time I look at NYU Langone Health's latest stellar rankings amongst all major healthcare systems in the U.S.

WHAT WORKS IN MANHATTAN, WORKS IN BROOKLYN

When an institution is not doing well, people become complacent. Yet when they see leaders who want great results, people come out of the woodwork to help, especially in the medical world.

As we have seen, NYU Langone today ranks among the most efficient U.S. medical centers in delivering high quality care to its patients.

Its revival of a struggling four hundred fifty–bed safety net hospital in Brooklyn's Sunset Park neighborhood, Lutheran Medical Center, offers lessons for how the principles NYU Langone applied in Manhattan for a dozen years can benefit hundreds of mainstream healthcare institutions across the U.S. and the world.[182]

Lutheran Medical Center was established more than a hundred years ago. The neighborhood it serves has more people enrolled in Medicaid and uninsured than any other ZIP code in the United States. The hospital's survival has long depended on government support, a marked contrast to the main NYU Langone hospital across the East River in Manhattan, where many patients have high incomes and extensive insurance. Brooklyn has long been an important market for NYU's Manhattan hospital: approximately half of the babies born at NYU Langone's Tisch Hospital go home to Brooklyn.

When NYU Langone took over management in 2015, the hospital was confronting the same challenges facing many safety net hospitals: uneven staffing resulting in inefficient care, limited resources for improving quality and providing special services and an aging facility. It offered NYU Langone an opportunity to expand its care systems across Brooklyn and its 2.6 million residents. But, would what worked in Manhattan work in Brooklyn?

When the NYU Langone team arrived, it methodically tested each section of its playbook with Bob Grossman's same question at the heart of the Manhattan success: Will this improve patient care? The team looked at how each function in the hospital affected patient care. Several senior leaders were replaced, but the staff remained largely unchanged.

Within a few years, internal measures of patient service and quality of care matched, and sometimes exceeded, the ultra high scores at NYU Langone in Manhattan. The Lutheran Medical Center, now renamed NYU Langone Hospital – Brooklyn, was breaking even financially.

One day I learned firsthand how this transformation of a healthcare system dramatically improved the experience for its patients. An Uber driver overheard me talking on the phone about my description in *World Class* of the Brooklyn hospital's turnaround. "I need that book," he said. I was taken aback. "You do?" I replied.

He explained that he, his grandmother, mother and brother all were patients at the hospital. He was ecstatic about the changes: shorter wait times in the emergency room, friendlier staff members, better care and follow-up. He added a little story that for me spoke volumes about how small details add up to excellent patient experiences.

One day when he and his grandmother went to the emergency room, a doctor saw them within minutes. When the doctor realized the grandmother spoke only Arabic, he quickly retrieved a tablet with an app that translated what she was saying into English. A few minutes later, even better: an Arab speaking translator appeared.

"Anything we needed, everyone on staff tried to provide it," my driver said.

That genuine unsolicited testimonial should encourage every healthcare system executive to embrace the wisdom of patient-centered medicine.

NO PRIORITIES AMONG ESSENTIALS

Cadets at the U.S. Military Academy, our future Army leaders, are taught that there are no priorities among essentials. Here are five essentials from successes honed in Manhattan that NYU Langone applied in Brooklyn to rapidly improve quality of patient care and rein in costs.

Leadership. Good leaders define and support the optimal path to move their organizations toward desired goals. Most prior leaders were replaced, but the staff remained largely the same. New leaders provided more clarity on how equipment would be upgraded and maintained, the urgency to improve patient satisfaction scores and how performance would be measured and rewarded.

Quality. Treating patients with the right medicine at the right time in the right way is cost-effective. Unnecessary diagnostic tests and blood transfusions were eliminated, clinical practices redesigned and patients discharged when they were ready to leave rather than linger in the hospital, waiting for nonmedical tangles to get sorted out.

Real time data. Medical staff are able to view medical records in any of its locations for what are nearly two million patients. Any doctor can know what every other doctor has done for a patient's care and treatment and evaluate their own performance against their peers. Patients can access test results almost the minute they are in.

Ambulatory care. Before the merger, dozens of ambulatory clinics in nearby neighborhoods offered mainly primary care to schools. Few were equipped with the kind of modern medical technology that made it possible after the merger to do things once done only in hospitals. By 2019, there were sixty five of these locations, most quite sophisticated, some staffed with surgeons and state-of-the-art equipment. These facilities are less expensive to operate and provide more services where people live.

Financial discipline. Although hospital admissions fell thirty percent in 2018, revenues from hospital stays were only modestly lower. The system's billing process is more efficient in collecting payments from the government, insurers and patients for the varying levels of care provided. Bills also are calculated more accurately and consistently.

SIX OTHER PRINCIPLES

We know that effective leadership and organizational structure (form following function) are vitally important for any enterprise to achieve ambitious goals. I have discussed these two principles in detail already, so let me conclude by briefly summarizing six other principles that were foundations for Bob Grossman's achievement at NYU Langone Health. These are principles I believe all leaders of healthcare systems can, and should, embrace: culture, vision, integrated care, real time data, quality and safety and self reliance.

Culture. When I asked in my interviews for the key factor in this remarkable transformation, the words varied but everyone essentially had the same answer: the culture changed from complacency to aspiration.

NYU Medical Center had languished during the 1980s and 1990s after a long and distinguished history. People remembered being ranked at the bottom third in quality and safety in patient care and being told by the CEO at the time that this was "okay."

That culture changed quickly under new leadership. One of the most striking features to me was that it was largely the same staff, now re-energized, empowered and rewarded for delivering outstanding outcomes, that delivered outstanding results. Culture is everything.

Vision. Knowing where you are going and why is core to any organizational transformation. The vision must be uplifting as well as something everyone can understand and identify with.

The driving vision at NYU Langone was *putting the patient first.* All medical institutions should have the same motto, whether they are devoted to patient care or research. It seems obvious but unfortunately, in my experience, this is not so.

Political expediency, profit or staff comfort in many healthcare organizations prevail above the welfare of the patient. Many people resist being held accountable for their performance; they believe, without data, that they are doing what is best for the patients when it is actually best for them.

A culture demanding measurement and accountability, paired with a unifying vision of patient wellbeing, are essential. NYU Langone achieved both.

Integrated care. Bob Grossman, his leadership team and trustees realized early that hospital-centered care, the dogma of healthcare systems managers since the 1950s, was not suited for the soaring caseloads of chronic illnesses in the 21st century. As we saw in missteps in China that I strongly discouraged, large multi-specialty hospitals are best for treating acute illnesses, not chronic illnesses.

Responding to this new reality, NYU Langone made two fundamental changes. The first was expanding out-patient services. Over a period of twelve years, NYU Langone built more than four hundred out-patient clinics throughout the city. Out-patient clinics have three advantages over large hospitals. They are more convenient to patients because they are located close to where people live; they are safer because they greatly reduce the danger of infection; and they are much less costly to operate. Today eighty percent of all surgeries at NYU Langone are performed in out-patient facilities and generate ninety five percent of the system's financial surplus.

The second change was to bring almost all doctors on staff and sharply reduce the ranks of independent consulting physicians. Most physicians welcomed the opportunity because costs in their independent practices for medical equipment and other capital expenses were soaring. Costs were accelerating as well for administrative workloads to recover costs from numerous payers, such as Medicare, Medicaid and private insurance. For hospitals, it is far easier to monitor performance of physicians on staff, especially on quality and safety measures, than a loose collection of consulting physicians.

Real time data. Yes, a reprise here for what I have already underscored: the immense value of information systems tailored for transparency. What Bob Grossman showed me in his conference room was but the tip of a towering iceberg of change in the ways NYU Langone uses information.

A comprehensive, real time, interface free, user friendly information system is key to achieving the goal of value based, zero fault patient care. NYU Langone applies this capability in all aspects of its integrated academic medical center devoted to patient care, teaching and research.

Value in medical care is determined by a simple equation: medical outcome, plus safety, plus patient satisfaction: divided by fixed plus variable cost. NYU Langone has created an information system that allows measurement of all these parameters. Real measurement of all outcomes and safety, coupled with rigorous follow up, is mandatory for any healthcare system's pursuit of zero fault—a new goal and, hopefully, an attainable one for healthcare.

Quality and safety. Quality and safety of patient care come first. A smoothly functioning information system enables managers to capture all relevant data immediately. Problems can be quickly addressed and hopefully resolved.

Here is one example I observed during my NYU Langone research. A quality and safety team detected that deaths from maternal bleed out were exceeding safety targets. The team quickly staged simulations of maternal bleeds for all the birthing teams, doctors, nurses and medical technicians. A recognizable pattern appeared: birthing teams were late to recognize initial symptoms. Once birthing teams were trained to recognize these symptoms, maternal deaths from hemorrhage in NYU Langone's system dropped well below national averages.

Another goal was lowering the percentage of patient deaths in hospitals. These deaths were tracking at a troubling rate, near the national average. "We can do better!" was the motto. A case by case review revealed that patients languished long before they entered a final crisis. Then, treating physicians attempted heroic measures on their own to save them.

The solution? Create special teams to rescue patients at the first sign of failure. Change the culture to team rescue from a heroic single doctor. The result? Death rates in NYU Langone hospitals fell by fifty percent and remained low, to a level half that of other leading New York City hospitals. Data plus a commitment to excellence made the difference.

Self reliance. Much of the work we do at ACCESS Health focuses on governance and the role of national and state or provincial governments in strengthening their health systems. In this regard, specifically government relations, the NYU Langone story teaches another important lesson.

NYU Langone's leader did not ask, What can the federal government, or New York State and City government, do for us? They accepted the complex set of regulations and reimbursements as they were. Instead, they asked themselves *what can we do* to improve? As we have seen, they collectively could do a tremendous amount.

Evolution and continuous improvements are keys to success in any organization. NYU Langone demonstrated both the will to change, and the will to lead. Yes, it has a great leader and a visionary board of trustees. But it also recognized that excellence is a journey, not a destination.

NYU Langone will have to deliver new services in new ways and in new places to hold its place among the elite in providing excellent care, teaching and research. Medical science will continue to change rapidly. So will medical economics.

Americans have always believed that given the freedom to act, we will find solutions to pressing problems. If we look carefully at the details of this

My Lifelong Fight Against Disease

inspiring story, we may catch what could be first glints of sunlight on the horizon for better care and lower costs for patients and society.

Delivering high quality transforms healthcare. It frees up funds to reduce patient charges, raise salaries, invest in new services and more. GenX, Millennial and GenZ cohorts rising behind the boomers, and the boomers themselves, are not cursed with forever declining quality of care and rising costs. By sharpening basic operations, hospitals, clinics and other essential parts of how we get our healthcare can and will do better.

The stakes for everyone are immense, and especially biomedical scientists. In my farewell remarks at Human Genome Sciences in 2004, I cautioned that American taxpayers' enthusiasm for spending billions of dollars annually on biomedical research could falter if we as a society do not conquer huge inefficiencies in how we deliver healthcare.

I warned, "If the benefits of our discoveries don't reach most of the people in this country, not because the benefits don't exist, but because they are not available due to the cost and structure of our enormously complex health system, then support for biomedical will wane, budgets will shrink and the golden doors of opportunity for discovery we now enjoy will close."

My concern has not diminished over the years. It has multiplied. Some of our people who are wealthy do very well, but those are counterbalanced by the vast majority of people who are just slightly ahead of a middle income country. It is shameful. We should not tolerate it. In my view, one of the primary drivers of insecurity in modern life is healthcare. If you lose your job, you lose your healthcare benefits. If you lose your healthcare benefits you have no safety net. Imagine the desperation of a mother or father who has been working then loses their job. You lose your job. You lose your house. You can lose your family.

One adage of modern management is that which gets measured gets managed; or, conversely, you cannot manage what you do not measure. As we have seen, Bob Grossman was a believer. What he told me that day we met is what every healthcare executive should be repeating—to their boards, their communities, their leadership teams and every employee counting on their clear direction to produce the highest quality care for patients. "I manage to quantifiable goals."

I am convinced that NYU Langone's proven approach can help communities anywhere in the country accomplish what we all want and urgently need: high quality healthcare at lower cost.

34

INFLUENCE, IMPACT

"WHAT DO YOU THINK OUR MOTTO SHOULD BE? How should I position my campaign?"

Gov. Bill Clinton and I are with a few dozen other people at a private gathering in Manhattan two weeks after he had built an insurmountable lead in convention delegates to win the Democratic Party's 1992 nomination for President. He is adjusting his sights tonight, working the room, looking for ideas to lift his campaign over the next five months and defeat White House incumbent George H.W. Bush and billionaire Ross Perot, the independent candidate.

"I think your motto should be, 'A Country That Works,'" I replied. "People are worried about their jobs and government dysfunction. This phrase addresses both."

"Great idea," he replied, his eyes fixed on mine. "I understand you work on AIDS. Any ideas for me on that front?"

"Bush isn't giving AIDS the attention it deserves. Young people know that," I said. "You could say something like 'AIDS is yet another example of how Bush and his administration are missing the boat on issues key to the lives of young people. I pledge, if I am the President, to take it seriously and do whatever we can to end the epidemic here and around the world.'"

Two nights later, watching Clinton on the Hollywood set of MTV's *Choose or Lose*,[183] I saw him field questions about inhaling marijuana and boxers or briefs ("briefs, mostly"), then pivot to address HIV/ AIDS, framing the issue with my very words.[184]

BRAINSTORMING WITH THE PRESIDENT

Bill Clinton's presidency was nearly destroyed two years later by serious missteps and misjudgments on healthcare reform. The midterm elections in 1994 delivered a resounding public backlash, the "Republican Revolution." Republicans won a huge majority in Congress, controlling both houses for the first time since 1952. They added fifty four seats in the House, and eight in the Senate. They won ten governorships, and control of several state legislatures. It would take a President of rare courage, Barack Obama, to attempt and succeed later in passing healthcare legislation after that singular failure a quarter century before.

One day in the wake of the '94 midterms carnage, my secretary rushed into my office, wide eyed. "The White House is on the phone!" It was the President's close adviser and former chief of staff, Mack McLarty. Mack, a close friend of the President since their boyhood days in Arkansas, was desperate now to help the President recoup. We knew each other; Mack and his charming wife Donna were social friends.

"The President is setting up an advisory group of prominent CEOs, which we are calling the President's Leadership Council," he said. Here again, Clinton was looking for campaign ideas, this time for what many considered a real long shot: re-election in 1996. Mack added, "We would like to have you as a member."

It was not long before I found myself in the White House Map Room with four other participants and the President. Four different meetings in all, each with the same one hour format and a different cast of characters in each except for the President.

We brainstormed ideas with him, covering a whole series of issues. He was more than smart; he was brilliant. More than any other human being I have ever met, he understood our country. He had emotional connections to the poorest black in the South, to the wealthiest businessman in New York and everybody in between. It was fascinating to watch how he used that understanding to reposition himself for reelection. He asked deep questions in these meetings, pressing for information, recommendations.

At our final session, he laid out his approach. "I am going to create a centrist bridge between Republicans and Democrats." This strategy, famously known as triangulation, captured the political mood of those times; Clinton won three hundred seventy nine of the five hundred thirty eight electoral votes.[185]

For my efforts trying to help Clinton understand and navigate the issues, I was rewarded with investigations by both the FBI and the *New York Times*. Who else was in the room? What did they say? And so on. "When Clinton was in the room, no one else was really visible to me," I replied. "I can describe what I said and what the President said. But I did not pay attention to anyone else in the room." That was the end of that.

When you are a government leader, especially a President or party nominee campaigning for President, so many things are coming at you. The crises of the day, fires that have to be seen and put out quickly, along with big priorities for the long term that have to be addressed and managed. Presidents and candidates seeking the White House have to make many judgments based on imperfect information. What decisions do I make today? Which experts and advisers do I listen to? Which data and interpretations are most relevant?

Leaders in government, think tanks, business councils, lobbying associations, non profits and more came to me as they learned of my prominence in cancer and HIV research, in health and genomics, my extensive knowledge in science and health. "We have this problem." "We have this issue." "What do you think?" Each conversation was an opportunity to put into action two of my highest career priorities: leverage government policy to change people's lives for the better, and improve people's access to quality healthcare.

The question is, where can your efforts make the biggest difference in human life? No matter how big your foundation, corporation or non profit organization, you cannot do what government can do. As noted earlier, the United States government spent $1.3 trillion on healthcare in the 2018 fiscal year, through Medicare, Medicaid and veterans' medical care, dwarfing the efforts of private foundations and the pharmaceutical industry.[186] Private insurers spent roughly the same amount, $1.2 trillion. Government serves as society's board of directors, determining what can and cannot happen. Policy is extremely important. Policy *precedes* money.

The best approach you can take with a small foundation, a think tank or leading research institute is to advise governments. Help shape government policy, and policy perspectives in general—whether the institution is public or private. Better to use your influence to change government policy, to change government funding. I have to say, one of my lasting impressions from hundreds of meetings over the years with government officials in many countries is that inaction, paralysis, lack of decision making are *lethal* for citizens.

IMPORTANT KNOWLEDGE, INORDINATE INFLUENCE

If you want to change society as a scientist, you need to work through myriad powerful institutions in society—think tanks, major corporations, foreign diplomats, government agencies, military brass, the news media. You can build personal networks that over time become valuable for gaining influence and shaping government policies. Many people who take on these roles overlap in many organizations, including the arts.

Once you have this role advising governments and other institutions, you begin to realize how tightly the world is linked. A few people with important knowledge have inordinate influence and impact—sometimes for better, sometimes for worse. In time, and to my surprise, leaders from a much wider range than I anticipated—of nations, industries, professions, humanitarian causes and more—sought my advice. I traveled at their invitations around the country and around the world.

When I leapt into the breakneck AIDS funding campaign in 1985 as Rock Hudson's flight from Paris headed back to the West Coast, I already grasped many levers for influencing public policy. Marshaling key facts. Writing articles. Briefing journalists. Informing local communities. Communicating. Persuading. Convincing. All elements of the craft that I put into action during those antiwar protests and campaigns in the '60s and '70s.

I was able to convince many powerful people to think about and work on AIDS. I wasn't alone, other people helped but I think that I played a really central role in those early years, in early response, and helped speed up the whole process. It is a wonderful feeling to know that I was able to do that.

The AIDS funding campaign validated and expanded those approaches to building political alliances and lobbying Congress. But I still had a lot to learn about high impact influence after I left Harvard and Dana-Farber to build a business. The clashes, contradictions, ironies, delights and inspirations I observed behind closed doors continue to shape my approach to advising policymakers in dozens of countries.

"WE CAN'T DO IT"

Think tanks, for the most part, are havens of intellectual rigor funded by like minded advocates. Their missions are to shape policy and influence policymakers, and they reside all along the political spectrum. As we saw earlier, ACCESS Health was designed around this model.

From its founding in 1916, the Brookings Institution has maintained a university model. Its two hundred fifty policy experts are the "professors"; members of Congress, Congressional staff and the White House and federal agencies are the "students."

"Bill, we need more science. We are very light on science. We need to strengthen our knowledge and capabilities in healthcare." Steve Friedman was calling.

The former co-leader of Goldman Sachs had just taken on a new role as Brookings's co-chairman. He had heard me talk about advances in genome modeling and accelerating drug development at a recent conference. "You understand both business and science. I'd like you to help us understand how we should be advising the government on science policy and healthcare."

"Yes, I'd be delighted," I said immediately—and I *was* delighted. Brookings is among the world's most respected think tanks.[187] It has brilliant thinkers, many of whom played important roles in government. Over the years, Donna Shalala, head of Health and Human Services in the Clinton Administration, and Alice Rivlin, Clinton's federal budget director and later a Federal Reserve vice chair under Alan Greenspan, became good friends. Heads of many other Brookings research groups as well. We had intense discussions often on a range of urgent policy questions—healthcare, economics, international politics over dinners at my Georgetown home.

One of these friends, Richard Haass, left his Brookings post as head of foreign policy studies in 2001 to lead policy planning under Colin Powell in George W. Bush's State Department. But Richard departed after two years, a few months after America invaded Saddam Hussein's Iraq. Richard contended with sharp elbowed political maneuvering during that time in ways that I found instructive about personalities and processes beyond Foggy Bottom. Those were private discussions so I'll leave it at that, except to add that Richard took his expertise in diplomacy to the Council on Foreign Relations, where he has been president since leaving the State Department.[188]

I was not officially a member of the Center for Strategic and International Studies (CSIS), but that was not an obstacle for me or John Hamre when John, the Center's president, called with an appealing proposal.[189] This was in the late '90s, a time when my articles and speeches on regenerative medicine were getting more attention and my interviews about genomics and Human Genome Sciences were in the news. "We're planning a new study on demographic change and its implications for social policy," John said.

"The governments of Japan and Italy are funding it. We'd like you to chair the committee, lead it."

This was a significant opportunity, a project that I knew would deepen my growing knowledge about issues on aging populations—a major challenge facing nearly every advanced economy.

Japan? Italy? That was the tipoff. The percentage of populations aged sixty five years and older in Japan and Italy are the highest of all industrialized countries. Our analysis addressed many issues confronting aging societies; I testified about them before Congress. When I urged the CSIS to include a section in the study on immigration, I was forbidden. "The governments of Japan and Italy will withdraw funding if we include immigration," I was told. "We can't do it."

How dreadfully shortsighted those governments have been. Their societies are being hollowed out by the demographics of aging. Japan has the oldest population of any industrialized nation, with one person sixty five years or older for every two people between the ages of twenty and sixty four. Twenty six percent of the total population is sixty five or older.[190] Italy ranks second, with twenty three percent sixty five or older.

MANO A MANO

The Ambrosetti Forum in Italy is a fantastic assemblage of world leaders, bringing together leaders in science, business and government in the same venue, the Villa d'Este on Lake Como where I delivered that impromptu speech on regenerative medicine in 1998.[191]

I have attended a dozen times over the years, speaking typically about developments in science and technology. Business leaders discuss global trade. Top economists present their outlook for the world economy. Government leaders speak, and vent, about both country and cross border politics. Everyone mingles, which is when genuine, unvarnished insight happens.

I shared drinks and smoked cigars one year with Shimon Peres, the Israeli prime minister, and Mahmoud Abbas, chief negotiator for the Arab League.

My wife and I had dinner one night with three cabinet members in the interim Italian government headed by Mario Monti, a technocrat. This was at the depths of the European Union's financial crisis in 2011, with Italy's budget deficits soaring.

Each a university professor in normal times, these women talked animatedly about exercising entirely unanticipated powers. One was reforming Italy's justice system, another closing nearly half the country's post offices. At another Ambrosetti weekend, I stood nearby when the prime minister of Austria shouted into the face of Recep Tayyip Erdogan, then Turkey's prime minister and now president. "We are never, ever going to let you in." In the European Union, that is. And, for Turkey, so it remains.

On the sidelines of the 2019 meetings, specialists with the Ambrosetti consultancy advising the Italian government asked me, "What policies can help Italy deal with its aging population?"

I could barely restrain myself, aroused by memories of my CSIS study two decades before. "Without dealing with immigration, *you can't do what you need to do*. Everybody is getting old. You are not going to have the people! Your replacement rate is about 1.2"—an ominous figure, they knew. Births per woman required to maintain steady population from one generation to the next, excluding migration, is roughly 2.1 for most countries. "*Without immigration, what the heck are you going to do?*"

The U.S. Chamber of Commerce is Washington's most powerful pro business lobbying group (also the oldest and largest), flaunting a war chest continuously replenished by the country's biggest corporations. I served on the Chamber's policy setting executive committee, a group of forty CEOs, for several years. There were often eye opening clashes showing how, in our pluralistic society, organizations fight with one another.

One unforgettable confrontation pitted the CEO of General Motors against his Pfizer counterpart; the leader of America's largest auto manufacturer versus the head of America's largest pharmaceutical manufacturer.

"I am paying two hundred million dollars a year for your heart medications, your cholesterol reducing drugs," the General Motors CEO said, bristling. "It is causing me to raise the price of my cars. I am going to do everything I can to lower the price of those drugs... to make sure that you, the pharmaceutical industry, cannot have such unfair pricing."

The Pfizer CEO was unimpressed. "If you do that," he said, menacingly, "I am going to instruct all of my employees not to buy any of your cars." Pfizer's employment at the time probably exceeded eighty thousand.

I resigned abruptly from the leadership group in 2004 after Thomas Donohue, the Chamber's commanding, occasionally pugnacious president and CEO, made what in my view was a serious mistake. He poured one million dollars of Chamber money into advertisements opposing Tom Daschle's reelection to the Senate from South Dakota. Daschle, the Democrats' Senate Minority Leader, was one of the Capitol's most knowledgeable lawmakers on health and health policy. Tom was a positive force in the Senate, a compromiser who knew how to balance the interests in his rural state. His defeat that fall was a travesty, and it was a contravention of the Chamber's neutral political role to take him out.

"DO NOT GO TO PARIS"

A few years earlier organizers of an annual Congressional retreat asked me to speak about genomics and drug development. These annual affairs were at the Greenbriar, a rambling resort hotel in West Virginia once equipped with a fully functional, underground redoubt for Congress during a nuclear attack or other catastrophic national emergency.

Members of Congress were friendly, and also slightly wary, when I approached them walking around the grounds. I felt like an alien as they greeted me. "Hi, I'm a Democrat from wherever. You must be a Republican from wherever since I don't recognize you. What district do you represent?" The same from Republicans. "You must be a Democrat. What district are you from?"

That night at dinner I found my seat at a small round table of honor. There were only five of us, including Democrat Richard Gephardt, the House Minority Leader, and Republican Dennis Hastert, the House Speaker. These two paragons of American democracy, supposedly, at the time, sat the entire evening with their backs turned toward each other. *The entire evening.* Never spoke one word. This duo offered right before my eyes a stark image of Washington gridlock.

In the tense days before the Iraq invasion in 2003, I received a blunt message from President Bush's chief of staff, Andrew Card: "Do not go to Paris." I was perturbed. The U.S.–French Business Council was an important network: twenty five American and twenty five French executives meeting annually, keeping in touch about differences and agreements on trade and other vital issues. Meeting venues were reciprocal and the French, including President Jacques Chirac, were about to host the entire group.

Wall Street legend Felix Rohatyn organized the council with President Clinton's backing when Rohatyn was Clinton's ambassador to France in the late '90s. With Chirac and his government stridently opposed to U.S. war against Iraq, the Bush administration was retaliating in various ways diplomatically. I ignored the message and went to Paris anyway. But the meetings collapsed immediately, a fiasco, with only three of us Americans in the room. Our French hosts were insulted, knocked on their heels, as they should have been. The U.S.–French Business Council fell apart and was never reconstituted.

I was dismayed by this capitulation for three reasons: future opportunities lost, established relationships complicated or even dissolved and personal disappointment, the blow to my Francophile sensibilities. The future networking opportunities might have been substantial. Who knows? For example, French executives on the council had approached me in 1998 about becoming chief executive of what would become France's largest pharmaceutical company as the boards of Rhone-Poulenc and Germany's Hoechst laid plans to merge the companies as Aventis.[192] The fit was not right for me,

My Lifelong Fight Against Disease

but that overture through my contacts on the council illustrates how these opportunities can arise.

HOSTING A POLITICAL DEMILITARIZED ZONE

One of the reasons I loved living in Washington was the unmatched array of talent converging there, from across the country and around the world. No other city in the world has it. My home became a venue for frank bipartisan discussions, a demilitarized zone, politically speaking. I believe this was so at least partly because people leading or allied with Republicans or Democrats, as well as independents, were interested in my opinions and perspectives.

Ted Stevens made sure I got to know several of the nation's top military brass. Ted was my indispensable ally on Capitol Hill during the 1985 sprint for AIDS research funding. In Washington, the military brass are highly influential, powerful players in politics and economics, as well as military matters. Through Ted, I became friendly with generals such as Wesley Clark, John Ralston and Jim Jones, and members of the Senate who framed military policy debates, Republicans John McCain and Chuck Hagel and Democrat John Kerry.

Many foreign diplomats and top journalists participated in these dinners, and I attended social gatherings at embassies as well—among them France, Spain, Italy, Brazil, Singapore and Great Britain. Their ambassadors became good friends, opening my mind to how lives were lived and policies developed in other countries—and, importantly, how America was seen from other countries.

The same with journalists. Many top journalists in Washington have reported from all over the world. They give you a deep perspective on current events, grounded in the history and culture of different countries. (Kissinger's lesson at Harvard often came to mind: foreign policy is always rooted in and derivative of domestic politics.) These conversations and the ideas and insights we shared are other reasons the Washington life appealed so much to me. I lived there for twenty five years, 1992 to 2017, commuting between my homes in Georgetown and Manhattan.

A month after the 9/11 terrorist attacks, I was sitting in the backyard of my Washington home with the Moroccan ambassador, Aziz Mekour, and a famous foreign correspondent and editor in chief of the *Washington Times* and a powerful intellect at CSIS, Arnaud de Borchgrave. We were all saying this war in Iraq was going to be a disaster.

"Going after Iraq is the wrong thing," I said. "Destroying Iraq's military will destroy the bulwark that protects the Middle East, including Israel, from Iran. We're putting our head in the lion's mouth. We're never going to get out."

Arnaud added: "I have been in every war in the Middle East since the Gulf States were created. I have an Israeli officer's uniform. I have an Egyptian officer's uniform. I have been on all sides in every war. I even saw Lumumba stabbed in the Congo. But this is the worst."

Most people I soon encountered in my various networks were not having it. Many reacted to my warnings with rage, sixty and seventy year old guys about to beat me up. I had to physically back away. "You have no idea what you are talking about, Bill! We're going to be in and out of Iraq in two weeks. This is going to be a cakewalk." It was madness, a rampant war fever.

When I see these people today, it is rare when anybody concedes they were wrong about Iraq. They respond with adult excuses. "Oh well"—grumbling—"we just didn't do it right." "No, I really did not think that."

One of the few who acknowledged they were wrong in backing the war in Iraq was Richard Cohen, the *Washington Post* political columnist, now retired. "You are right, Bill. I did say that and I was wrong. I can tell you why I was wrong, but I did say it and I know how wrong I was."

We saw in the first pages of Part VI how one of my Aspen Institute outings sparked the idea for ACCESS Health. During a later two-week Aspen conference, Moral Leadership for Business, a new acquaintance gave me an insight into the Nixon-Kissinger relationship I had never heard before. This man had been a White House top aide to Kissinger. One of his tasks was taking notes for Kissinger while he spoke with Nixon.

I asked him one day, "Who had all the ideas? Was it Nixon or Kissinger?"

"It was Nixon, no question," he replied. "Nixon had all the major ideas. The China initiative? Totally Nixon. Kissinger's role was to flesh out the details." Carrying the Kissinger imprint from my first year at Harvard, I had expected the opposite answer. A good reminder for me: be cautious about your assumptions when you do not have the actual facts.

WHATEVER DIRECTIONS YOU CHOOSE

The case for advising leaders of powerful institutions was something I relayed frequently to hundreds of research colleagues at Harvard, Human Genomes Sciences and professional societies. The key point to me is simple: "Your ticket for entrée is the unique knowledge that you accumulate as a practicing scientist. That is something you have that most others do not. Joining these leadership councils and groups creates wonderful opportunities to see how the world works. You can move beyond your role as a scientist."

If I had stayed in each of the fields I helped create, I likely would have had enormous recognition today. High honors in science come about ten years after you have done the work. Many scientists, most scientists, will stick to one field, get recognized, and stay in their lane. Not that I have not had recognition.

TIME Magazine included me on its 2001 list of the world's twenty five most influential business people. Being on that list prompted several appealing invitations and inquiries. In 2015, *Scientific American* named me one of the hundred most influential leaders in biotechnology. The Biotechnology Association, Ernst & Young and other organizations honored me with their top awards. More invitations, inquiries and requests. Recognition is a tool that helps you get things done.

One day years ago one of my former PhD students who was doing important research on viruses asked me to have lunch: "What did you do to get on all these boards and councils?" she asked. "How does all of this happen, Bill? What do you think I should be doing?"

"Well, you really cannot 'apply' for these opportunities, if that is what you mean," I said. "But as you get to be better known from your research, you will be invited to become part of many decision making bodies, and often advise on and recommend policy. You inject yourself into these streams and it gives you the contacts, the people and the tools to do things you would like to do."

These people can and do include candidates and nominees for President, and even President. Bill Clinton nodded attentively, listening to my advice that night in Manhattan. I was delighted that he quickly embraced the AIDS recommendation, but for his campaign motto he did not use "A Country that Works." He chose instead "A New Covenant," a line soon forgotten. Anyone who remembers will tell you the war cry of that Clinton campaign was pinned to the wall of campaign headquarters in Little Rock: "It's the Economy, Stupid."

"What about the power structures?" my lunch partner asked. "Who are the key people? How do you get them to change their minds? Who has the real power to change policies? What are the constraints they have to navigate?"

I told her several of these stories—Clinton, think tanks, business groups, informal and formal social networks. Collectively, what I learned along the way gave me solid answers to those questions.

"The opportunities that scientists have are almost endless," I went on. "People are interested in what you have to say. Science is a big part of our world, and these people want your help to think through the issues. People who are interested in the world are interested in science.

"As a scientist, if you do it well, you have a golden key. You can use that key to open doors that will take you in whatever directions you choose."

PART VII

THE NEXT CHAPTER

EARLY IN 2020, AS I WORKED ON THE FINAL CHAPTERS of this book, the first rumblings of concern about a new pneumonia-like illness were coming from Wuhan, China. COVID-19 has gone on to infect at least twenty five million people worldwide and, as of this writing, can be tied to nearly one million deaths. Despite the breadth of damage COVID-19 has already wrought, we are only beginning to glimpse what its long term toll might be. There is no doubt though that the impact of the pandemic will be massive, indelibly imprinting and changing the behaviors of our rising generations.

My personal losses have been far fewer than what many have suffered. Yet COVID-19 has still completely upended my life. From the very beginning of the outbreak, my friends and colleagues have come to me for counsel. Some wanted to know the best way to protect their families. Some wanted to discuss the science behind the virus itself. Still others sought to commiserate over how poorly our leaders seemed to grasp the seriousness of the pandemic. In most all cases, I found I had something to offer.

Today after a lifetime spent in science, medicine and pursuing better public health, I find myself once again logging eighteen hour days battling a new and still somewhat unknown disease. I am working closely with three generations of students—my former students, their former students and those who studied under them—to understand the virus and what makes it tick. Together, and along with many in the private sector I have worked with over the years, we are doing what we can to create new diagnostic tests, new drugs and new vaccines. I have also been asked by governments all over the world – in Europe, Asia, the Middle East, Africa and here in the United States – for advice on the best policies and containment measures.

Equally important is my effort to advance the public's understanding of SARS-CoV-2 and how to defeat it. On January 22, a day after the first COVID-19 case was diagnosed in the United States, President Donald Trump declared on national television that the U.S. had the virus "totally under control." In fact, no coordinated plan was in place to contain an outbreak that by then might have been spreading within our borders for weeks. A week after that hollow declaration, I published an article in *Scientific American*, "Want to Prevent Another Coronavirus Epidemic? We need to treat it as the deadly biological threat that it is." Since then, my opinions about ongoing news, research and other developments in the pandemic have been sought regularly, many times a week, in live conversations with anchors at major cable news networks MSNBC, CNN, Fox and international networks like Bloomberg Asia and CGTV. My commentaries on COVID-19 have been published online and in print at the *Washington Post*, *Los Angeles Times*, Project Syndicate, CNN.com, Forbes.com and *Psychology Today*. I have interviewed dozens of physicians, scientists and economists as they published new research or proposed new ideas. Suggestions I offered on their approaches often enabled me to discover new details that in turn deepened my understanding of the virus, our attempts to contain it and the long term effects now unfolding.

This final chapter of my autobiography now marks the beginning of my next, the first chapter of a collection of my writings, research and interviews on COVID-19. My *COVID Commentaries: A Chronicle of a Plague* is a Living eBook, updated regularly with new information on the disease and our response as it unfolds. It is organized into four sections. The first contains my published commentaries and social media posts on the outbreak, providing a quick, spur of the moment glimpse into my thinking day to day. The second section includes my interviews with scientists, economists, parents, grandparents and children that have informed my thinking and understanding of the virus and its disease. The third section provides links to my media interviews and mentions in news articles. The final section is a robust assemblage of links to COVID-related news, medical and scientific research papers, webinars and online resources from other organizations.

I first coined the term Living eBook when I published *A Family Guide to Covid: Questions & Answers for Parents, Grandparents and Children* in June 2020. At the time, I was acutely aware of how frustrated, confused and frightened many people were over what was happening in the world, their world. My goal in writing the book was to simplify the science and make as much information as possible available to anyone looking for answers to those questions and others like them. I also wanted to make sure that the information in the book was as accurate as possible. I knew that as the science and our understanding of the virus evolved, so too would my recommendations of how best to protect ourselves and those we love against infection.

I soon found that no publishing house would be able to deliver a book as quickly as we needed or update it as regularly as I wanted so I created a new genre of books. *The Family Guide* and my subsequent book, *A Covid Back to School Guide: Questions and Answers for Parents and Students,* were the first books published as Living eBooks. They are free on the ACCESS Health website and available in print on Amazon. Each time new discoveries happen, we update the books immediately on our website and within a few days through the major retailers. The *Commentaries* will follow the same format.

When this pandemic is finally over, as it no doubt will be one day, my hope is that my *Commentaries* will provide the historical perspective to help us reckon with mistakes we have made, especially in the United States, and provide insights into how we might better contain the next contagion and reduce the number of lives ultimately, needlessly lost—a modern day version of Samuel Pepys's *Plague Diary*.

Once more, just as in that summer of 1985, my sense of purpose flashes red. A continuous loop runs through my thoughts, "This is it!"... a second imperative to capture the world's attention, to be heard, to push our leaders to deliver the resources and respect for scientists, doctors and public health professionals required to control this pandemic—and prepare for future biological threats.

Nature is coming for us. Allow me, if you will, to put a new time stamp, August 2020, on the science based warning with which I ended my September 1985 testimony to the U.S. Senate, and now conclude my autobiography: "This may be the worst epidemic to emerge from our ancestral past for many generations, but it is unlikely, given current conditions, that it will be the last one."

ACKNOWLEDGMENTS

I AM DEEPLY GRATEFUL FOR THE ESTEEMED MENTORS IN MY LIFE: George Pimentel at UC Berkeley, James Watson and Walter Gilbert at Harvard, Emil Frei and Baruj Benacerraf at the Dana-Farber Cancer Institute and Wallace Steinberg at HealthCare Ventures.

I thank the many colleagues, partners and associates I have worked with over the years in classrooms, laboratories and offices around the world. In particular, my admiration is deep for former Harvard colleagues in the department of HIV/AIDS research and the department of human retrovirology research, many of whom continue to find solutions for some of the most daunting infectious disease and public health challenges facing the world today. I thank them not only for the work they have done and continue to do, but also for their efforts to preserve and expand upon the knowledge they have gained by cultivating and training new generations of young scientists.

I express my sincere appreciation to my colleagues at ACCESS Health International, including Anna Dirksen, and to Thomas C. Hayes for his research and editorial support during our two years collaborating on this book. My thanks also to Jessica Murphy and her staff in the Center for the History of Medicine of Harvard Medical School's Francis A. Countway Library of Medicine for guiding Tom through my papers in the Countway archives, which span some thirty years. I also thank Brian Stauffer for designing the cover of this book, as well as my two Living eBooks, *A Family Guide to Covid: Questions & Answers for Parents, Grandparents and Children* and *A Covid Back to School Guide: Questions and Answers for Parents and Students.*

Finally, to my children, stepchildren and grandchildren—Mara, Alexander, Karina, Manuela, Camila, Pedro Agustin, Enrique Matias and Carlos Eduardo—I thank each of you for the lessons you teach me each day about resilience, responsibility and loving kindness. Above all, I thank my wife, Maria Eugenia, for her love, patience and tireless efforts to care for us all.

APPENDICES

FULL TEXTS AVAILABLE AT WWW.WILLIAMHASELTINE.COM/AUTOBIOGRAPHY

1) "What We Learned from AIDS: Lessons from another pandemic for fighting COVID-19," by William A. Haseltine, *Scientific American*, October 2020.

Like all viruses, coronaviruses are expert code crackers. SARS-CoV-2 has certainly cracked ours. Think of this virus as an intelligent biological machine continuously running DNA experiments to adapt to the ecological niche it inhabits. This virus has caused a pandemic in large part because it acted on three of our most human vulnerabilities: our biological defenses, our clustering patterns of social behavior and our simmering political divides.

2) "What AIDS Taught Us About Fighting Pandemics," by William A. Haseltine. *Project Syndicate*, May 15, 2020.

Just as it is impossible for us to control tsunamis, earthquakes and volcanic eruptions, our ability to subdue contagious outbreaks is more limited than we like to admit. Despite what we often tell ourselves, we cannot always impose our will upon the natural world.

3) Valedictory Speech to Human Genome Sciences, by William A. Haseltine, PhD; founder, chairman & chief executive officer. October 2004.

From the beginning I saw my job as creating and shaping the genomics tools you use so well. My intent was to demonstrate by our success that genomics was the key to unlock new generations of medicines to cure the diseases of our world.

4) Testimony of William A. Haseltine, PhD, to the Presidential Commission on the HIV Epidemic. February 18, 1988.

It may never prove possible to fully reverse the damage done by the AIDS virus, but it may very well prove possible to prevent the damage from ever occurring. I look forward to the day when diagnosis of infection of HIV is similar to a diagnosis of diabetes—with proper and continual medical care, those infected can look forward to a normal, full term life.

5) "AIDS: The Darkening Shadow." Testimony of William A. Haseltine, PhD, before the United States Senate Subcommittee on Appropriations. September 26, 1985.

This is today's reality: Adequate funds are simply not available to attract the best minds in our country to the problem of AIDS. As the solution to the AIDS problem is likely to require innovative, multidisciplinary approaches, the current situation is intolerable. We have the best biomedical apparatus in the world; much of it is lying idle with respect to the AIDS problem as a result of inadequate funding and shortsighted programmatic efforts.

BIBLIOGRAPHY

BY WILLIAM A. HASELTINE

A Covid Back to School Guide: Questions and Answers for Parents and Students. New York: ACCESS Health Press, 2020.

A Family Guide to Covid: Questions & Answers for Parents, Grandparents and Children. New York: ACCESS Health Press, 2020.

Stay Young Navigators: The Pursuit of Active Aging and Seniors Caring for Seniors. New York: ACCESS Health Press, 2020.

Voices in Dementia Care: Reimagining the Culture of Care. Anna Dirksen and William A. Haseltine. Based on Interviews by Jean Galiana and Sofia Widén. Austin: Greenleaf Book Group Press, 2020.

World Class: A Story of Adversity, Transformation, and Success at NYU Langone Health. New York: Fast Company Press, 2019.

Every Second Counts: Saving Lives with India's Emergency Response System. Washington, DC: Brookings Institution Press, 2019.

Aging Well: Solutions to the Most Pressing Global Health Challenges of Aging. Jean Galiana and William A. Haseltine. London: Palgrave Macmillan, 2019.

Aging with Dignity: Innovation and Challenge in Sweden – the Voice of Care Professionals. Sofia Widén and William A. Haseltine. Lund: Nordic Academic Press, 2017.

Affordable Excellence: The Singapore Healthcare Story. Washington, DC: Brookings Institution Press, 2013.

Improving the Health of Mother and Child: Solutions from India. Priya Anant, Prabal Vikram Singh, Sofi Bergkvist, William A. Haseltine and Anita George. New York: ACCESS Health International, 2012.

ADDITIONAL TITLES

Ammann, Arthur J., MD. *Lethal Decisions: The Unnecessary Deaths of Women and Children from HIV/AIDS.* Nashville: Vanderbilt University Press, 2017.

Bernal, J.D. *The Social Function of Science.* Cambridge, London: The MIT Press. Paperback edition, 1967.

Camus, Albert. *The Plague,* Paris: Gallimard (French). 1947. London: Hamish Hamilton (English), 1948.

Church, George and Ed Regis. *Regenesis: How Synthetic Biology Will Reinvent Nature and Ourselves.* New York: Basic Books, 2012.

The Committee of Concerned Asian Scholars. *The Indochina Story: A Fully Documented Account.* New York: Pantheon Books, 1970.

Crile, George. *Charlie Wilson's War: The Extraordinary Story of How the Wildest Man in Congress and a Rogue CIA Agent Changed the History of Our Times.* Grove Press, 2003.

Diamond, Jared. *Guns, Germs, and Steel: The Fates of Human Societies.* New York: W. W. Norton & Company, 1997.

Doudna, Jennifer A. and Samuel H. Sternberg. *A Crack in Creation: Gene Editing and the Unthinkable Power to Control Evolution.* Boston, New York: Mariner Books. Houghton Mifflin Harcourt, 2018.

Dow, Unity and Max Essex. *Saturday is for Funerals*. Cambridge, London: Harvard University Press, 2010.

Emanuel, Ezekiel J. *Reinventing American Health Care: How the Affordable Care Act Will Improve our Terribly Complex, Blatantly Unjust, Outrageously Expensive, Grossly Inefficient, Error Prone System*. New York: Public Affairs, 2014.

Frankl, Viktor. *Man's Search for Meaning*. Fourth edition. Boston: Beacon Press, 1992.

Fumento, Michael. *The Myth of Heterosexual AIDS: How a Tragedy Has Been Distorted by the Media and Partisan Politics*. New York: Basic Books, 1990.

Galbraith, John Kenneth. *The New Industrial State*. Subsequent edition. Boston: Harcourt Mifflin Harcourt,1985.

Galea, Sandro. *Well: What We Need to Talk About When We Talk about Health*. New York: Oxford University Press, 2019.

Harden, Victoria A. *AIDS at 30: A History*. Dulles, Va.: Potomac Books, 2012.

Ibsen, Henrik. *An Enemy of the People*. London: William Heinemann, 1907.

Isaacson, Walter. *Leonardo da Vinci*. New York: Simon & Schuster, 2017.

Kissinger, Henry. Diplomacy, New York: Simon & Schuster, 1994.

Kroeber, Theodora. *Ishi in Two Worlds: The Biography of the Last Wild Indian in North America*. Berkeley: University of California Press, 1961.

Le Fanu, James. *The Rise and Fall of Modern Medicine*. New York: Basic Books, 1999.

Lewis, Oscar. *Life in a Mexican Village, Tepoztlán Restudied*. Paperback. Urbana: University of Illinois Press, 1963.

McNeill, William H. *Plagues and Peoples.* New York: Anchor Books, 1998.

Mukherjee, Siddhartha. *The Gene: An Intimate History.* New York: Scribner, 2016.

Mukherjee, Siddhartha. *The Emperor of All Maladies: A Biography of Cancer.* New York: Scribner, 2010.

Packer, George. *Our Man: Richard Holbrooke and the End of the American Century.* New York: Alfred A. Knopf, 2019.

Powers, Richard. *The Overstory*, A Novel. New York: W. W. Norton & Company, 2018.

Prahalad, C.K. *The Fortune at the Bottom of the Pyramid: Eradicating Poverty Through Profits.* Upper Saddle River: Wharton School Publishing, 2004.

Rand, Christopher. *Cambridge U.S.A.: Hub of a New World.* New York: Oxford University Press, 1964.

Reich, David. *Who We are and How We Got Here: Ancient DNA and the New Science of the Human Past.* New York: Pantheon Books, 2018.

de Saint Phalle, Niki. *AIDS: You Can't Catch It Holding Hands.* San Francisco: Lapis Press, 1986.

Shilts, Randy. *And the Band Played On: Politics, People, and the AIDS Epidemic.* 20th Anniversary Edition. New York: St. Martin's Press, 2007.

Starr, Paul. *The Social Transformation of American Medicine: The rise of a sovereign profession and the making of a vast industry.* New York: Basic Books, 1982.

Thomas, Lewis. *The Lives of a Cell: Notes of a Biology Watcher.* New York: Viking Press, 1974.

Warren, Rick. *The Purpose-Driven Life: What on Earth Am I Here For? Nashville:* Zondervan, 2002.

Watson, James D., Tania A. Baker, Stephen P. Bell, Alexander Gann, Michael Levine, and Richard Losick, with Stephen C. Harrison. *The Molecular Biology of the Gene*. 7th edition. Glenview, Ill.: Pearson Education Inc., 2014.

Watson, James D. *The Double Helix: A Personal Account of the Discovery of the Structure of DNA*. New York: Scribner, 1968.

Woolf, Steven H. and Laudan Aron, editors. *U.S. Health in International Perspective: Shorter Lives, Poorer Health*. The National Research Council and Institute of Medicine. Washington, DC: The National Academies Press, 2013.

Yong, Ed. *I Contain Multitudes: The Microbes Within Us and a Grander View of Life*. New York: HarperCollins Publishers, 2016.

NOTES

1 Anna Casselman. "20 Years Ago in *Discover*: Misunderstanding AIDS." *Discover* Magazine. April 28, 2005. Excerpt: "The magazine did find one scientist whose decidedly minority views turned out to be correct. William Haseltine, then a pathologist at Harvard University, argued that the virus was fast becoming a heterosexual disease. 'To think that we're so different from people in the Congo is a nice, comfortable position, but it probably isn't so,' Haseltine told *Discover*. "It's heterosexual promiscuity. The more lovers, the better the chance of being infected." See, https://www.discovermagazine.com/health/20-years-ago-in-discover-misunderstanding-aids#.XBFIEmDrN50.email; accessed February 21, 2020.

2 Bob Redfield cofounded the HIV research department at the University of Maryland after retiring from the military. An outstanding virologist, he became director of the Centers for Disease Control and Prevention in 2018.

3 Safi Bahcall, "The History of Pfizer and Penicillin, and Lessons for Coronavirus: A 'scientist general' to coordinate private and public efforts can lead the medical response." *Wall Street Journal*, March 20, 2020. See, https://www.wsj.com/articles/the-history-of-pfizer-and-penicillin-and-lessons-for-coronavirus-11584723787?mod=searchresults&page=1&pos=1; accessed, March 30, 2020.

4 The War Department was created by Congress in 1789, the first year of George Washington's administration. The name ultimately was changed to the Department of Defense in 1949, when operations of the Department of the Army, Department of the Navy, and Department of the Air Force, each established in 1947, were consolidated.

5 The official name later was changed to the Naval Air Weapons Station at China Lake.

6 The Poseidon missile became the capstone to the Cold War doctrine of mutually assured destruction. Deployed in every active submarine beneath the waves, the Poseidon and its Soviet Union counterpart assured that a nuclear attack by either nation would result in its own destruction. Two types of weapons used today, precision guided bombs (the early version was the Rockeye) and Tomahawk cruise missiles launched from warships, also were developed at China Lake.

7 William McLean, Navy physicist and father of one of my scouting buddies, Donnie McLean, conceived and developed the heat-seeking short-range Sidewinder, aptly named for the desert snake that senses prey from heat detecting nerve receptors. One garage invention I watched him putter with was an underwater bicycle. If you are an inventor, you just cannot stop. Frank Bothwell, a neighbor, invented the concept for a submarine launched nuclear missile.

8 When your goal in life is to have an impact in health for the population of the entire world, and you have an opportunity to do so, you have a responsibility to speak up. Debate team was a great confidence builder. I benefited in each of my roles later as a medical sciences professor, antiwar activist, science funding advocate in Washington and leader in research laboratories, businesses and nonprofit organizations. We would argue both sides of a question and had to

be prepared: presentation, counter presentation and cross examination. You learn to stand up and make an argument supported by fact, to understand other people's arguments. We worked on impromptu speaking as well. Many years later I told Ann Cierley how valuable her debate training had been for all aspects of my professional life. Ann's students were important to her as well. Just before she died in 2019, she sent me clippings of newspaper and magazine articles she had about various aspects of my career.

9 An Army MP in the closing days of the war in Europe, Mr. Reisser was lucky to survive. An escaping convict, himself an Army soldier, turned and shot him as they raced into an alley. The .45 caliber slug passed straight through Mr. Reisser's chest. An Army thoracic surgeon, minutes away, arrived in time to save his life.

10 My experiments were tightly focused. Step one: Measure how dark the same amount of each chemical turned when exposed to the same amount of light. To do this I measured how much light could pass through one centimeter of liquid when the color was at its darkest. Step 2: Measure the time it took for each of the different molecules to reach maximum darkness. Step 3: Measure the time it took for the color to vanish. Step 4: Repeat these measurements in bright sunlight. Step 5: Repeat these experiments with different types of light, including non-visible ultraviolet and infrared light. Ultraviolet light worked best.

11 A twenty seven-minute video of Kennedy's visit to China Lake on June 7, 1963 is accessible from the archives of the John F. Kennedy Presidential Library. Kennedy was there primarily to be briefed privately about strategies to defeat peasant rebellions ostensibly backed by the Soviet Union, including in Vietnam. See https://www.jfklibrary.org/asset-viewer/archives/USG/USG-03-H/USG-03-H; accessed February 28, 2020.

12 My habit as a teenager was falling asleep to classic music playing on a turntable near the bed. The first time I went through Toscanini's recordings of all Beethoven symphonies, I awoke one night with a start. What is this boisterous chorus in the fourth movement of Beethoven's Ninth? In my stupor, I checked the label to make sure I had not played some different recording by mistake.

13 I began attending the Great Artists series when I was eight. I can still smell the cigarette smoke and feel on my legs the itchy wool in suits I had to wear. During intermissions my little friends and I would weave through a forest of legs in the lobby. As a teenager, I was privileged to join my parents and others a few times a year at dinners honoring guest performers.

14 My own instrument, not of choice, was the Sousaphone. My preference was to play the trumpet or clarinet, but the bandleader asked me to fill a hole in the lineup, the Sousaphone. I played in marching band in sixth, seventh and eighth grades. I was too small to carry the fifty pound instrument, so they made a cart to hold the instrument upright. As I marched and played, someone else pulled the cart. A Sousaphone is big. We had to disassemble it to fit in the family car. "Why didn't you pick up the piccolo?" my mom complained. My best memory from junior high band was a Disneyland trip four years after the park opened in 1955. As long as we wore our green and white uniforms all rides were free. My favorite was the Jungle Cruise. I repeated it so many times that I memorized the guide's script. He shot that same hippo every time. It was pretty exciting. I eventually realized the guide was not steering the boat; it was pulled along underwater by a chain.

15 I learned the secret of making cherry cordials: surround the fruit with a fondant paste infused with liquor and with enzyme invertase added, dip in chocolate, cool on a marble slab. The invertase slowly liquefies the sugar, which is why you sometimes see bits of white undigested fondant at the center of some cordials.

16 My first wife, the mother of my two children, learned of an eerily similar family secret that mirrored my mother's story, in reverse. My first wife was raised in a Jewish family. When she was fifteen, she learned for the first time that her mother, an orphan, had been raised by nuns in a Catholic convent. Her mother converted to Judaism just before the war to marry my first

wife's father. These two reciprocal religious conversations are powerful testament to the social pressures that religious identify stirred in the Depression and World War II eras.

17 After he retired, Dad set up his garage to continue experiments on vision and perception. For Christmas one year, I gave him a set of twenty one monographs on the eye. After reading the entire collection, he said drily, "It taught me more about the eye than I needed to know." It was the only time I ever witnessed his thirst for knowledge slaked on any subject that fascinated him.

18 The First English Civil Wars soon followed, spanning 1642 to 1647.

19 Have you ever heard the 18th century Scottish ditty "Jock o' Hazeldean"? This is a ballad of two young lovers, developed into a poem from ancient Scottish lore by Sir Walter Scott. The repeating chorus: "But aye she loot the tears down fa', For Jock o' Hazeldean.". If you are truly endlessly curious, you can retrieve the four stanzas online.

20 Historical articles about Soapy Smith and Frank Reid's gunshot to the heart that killed Smith are abundant. For a credible summary citing several sources, see the Wikipedia entry: https://en.wikipedia.org/wiki/Shootout_on_Juneau_Wharf; accessed November 12, 2018.

21 My grandfather grew up in a house, owned by his father, near where locals claim the Republican Party was founded in 1854. The last I heard that house was owned by Chinese immigrants, with a Chinese take-out restaurant operating on the first floor.

22 The name is anomalous. You will not see any ridges and certainly no ridge crests near Ridgecrest, California. The U.S. Postal Service rejected the name originally submitted by locals, Mountainview; too many Mountainviews with zip codes already on the California map. Use Ridgecrest. Residents shook their heads at the bureaucratic miscue, and carried on.

23 The news brought to mind the jarring 1952 Tehachapi earthquake not far from China Lake. That one notched 7.5 on the Richter scale. Our house rolled and shook. Picture frames fell from the walls. Tableware scattered on the floor. Later we all drove out to see deep fissures in the scarred earth along White Wolf Fault twenty five miles away.

24 When I was sixteen, I received a spontaneous lesson in measuring earthquake intensity in real time from an expert. When the table where I was sitting began shaking, the world famous seismologist directly across from me, Pierre Saint-Amand, started tapping rhythmically with his forefinger. A wondrous smile lit his face, his eyes intensely tracking the second hand as it ticked around his wristwatch. The moment the shaking stopped, I asked what he had been doing. "Timing the intervals between the rolling surface wave and the vertical shocks," he replied, happily. Then, the lesson. "The first shock to hit are surface waves. The vertical shocks follow after they bounce off the core beneath the mantle. The time between tells your distance from the epicenter, and therefore the strength (of the quake). That was a small quake. The epicenter is no more than a mile from here."

With a hat tip to Saint-Amand and that fortuitous encounter, no matter where I travel, I pay attention to the surrounding geology. For example, I am writing these words in southern Tanzania's Selous Game Reserve, a UNESCO World Heritage Site. The Reserve lies just below the Great Escarpment on the coastal plain of southern Africa, stretching five hundred kilometers eastward toward the Indian Ocean. The plain is a mixture of sandstone and limestone. Earthquakes here are rare.

25 See https://news.usni.org/2019/08/21/navy-facing-billion-dollar-tab-years-to-get-china-lake-fully-operational-after-quake; accessed March 4, 2020.

26 The Navy League of the United States today numbers some fifty thousand members whose mission is supporting men and women of the nation's sea services—Navy, Marines, Coast Guard and U.S. flag Merchant Marine—and their families.

27 Planted in 1875 by her biracial parents to honor newborn Princess Ka'iulani, the tree was memorialized by Robert Louis Stevenson in his poem about the beautiful princess, then a teenager heading to Scotland, her father's (and Stevenson's) homeland, for schooling.

Forth from her land to mine she goes,
The island maid, the island rose,
Light of heart and bright of face:
The daughter of a double race.

Her islands here, in Southern sun,
Shall mourn their Kaiulani gone,
And I, in her dear banyan shade,
Look vainly for my little maid.

But our Scots islands far away
Shall glitter with unwonted day,
And cast for once their tempests by
To smile in Kaiulani's eye.

28 *The World of Suzie Wong* was a popular 1960 American-British film drama set in the back streets and brothels of Hong Kong during the 1950s.

29 The Navy Department estimated by 1945 that an American invasion of Japan's home islands would cause between 1.7 million and four million American casualties, with four hundred thousand deaths. Japanese casualties could reach ten million. See https://www.historylearningsite.co.uk/world-war-two/the-pacific-war-1941-to-1945/operation-downfall/#:~:text=Admiral%20Leahy%20estimated%20that%20the,to%2010%20million%20Japanese%20casualties; accessed March 14, 2020.

30 My mother coached me on this speech, as she did on my treatise the prior year about my ambitions to experience Navy life at sea. From memory, key lines from my Odd Fellows and Rebekahs speech were as follows:

Each of us belongs to several communities. Imagine a letter addressed to a foreign country. Each line in the address represents a different level of community involvement. The first line... represents each unique human being. Our individual actions reverberate around the world, first to those closest to us, then to our community, our nation and the world.

To quote John Donne, "No man is an island," each is part of the whole.

The effect of each life is that of a pebble dropped into a pond. Ripples of each action go outward, affecting a wider and wider pool of our fellow men and women... Your actions reverberate throughout the world. Collectively, we are the world.

31 The first nationwide youth trip to the U.N. was initiated by the Odd Fellows and Rebekahs in 1949.

32 Listening to other students, I made mental notes about how they structured their talks, and how they used body language, voice inflections, humor and timing to emphasize important points.

33 We traveled a more southerly route on the eastbound journey to New York City: Nevada, Utah, Colorado, Texas, Arkansas, Tennessee, the Carolinas, then angling northward through Washington, D.C., Maryland, Delaware, Pennsylvania and New Jersey. The northern route for the return trip spanned upstate New York, Ohio, Indiana, Illinois, South Dakota, Wyoming, Montana, Washington, Oregon and finally southward to home in California's Indian Wells Valley.

34 As I write these words, my wife and I are heading to a two week drive through the vineyards and chateaux of southwest France, taking suggestions in *Michelin* guides *rouge* and *vert* for appealing places to dine and visit.

35 To avoid confusion possibly suggested by this close linkage of *Grote Beer* with "party" in that sentence, I am compelled to note that the English translation for *Grote Beer* is great bear, not great beer.

36 In the 2020 fiscal year, the National Science Foundation budget amounted to $8.3 billion, supporting twenty seven percent of all federally funded scientific research in U.S. colleges and universities. In mathematics, computer science and the social sciences, and other fields, NSF is the major source of federal funding. See, https://www.nsf.gov/about/glance.jsp; accessed April 5, 2020.

37 C. Bradley Moore, "George Claude Pimentel, 1922–1989, A Biographical Memoir." National Academy of Sciences, Washington, D.C. 2007.

38 Wallace Turner, "Joel Hildebrand, 101, Chemist; Joined U of California in 1913," *New York Times*. May 3, 1983. Page D27. See, https://www.nytimes.com/1983/05/03/obituaries/joel-hildebrand-101-chemist-joined-u-of-california-in-1913.html; accessed, April 5, 2020.

39 James S. Shirk, William A. Haseltine and George C. Pimentel, "Sinton Bands: Evidence for Deuterated Water on Mars," Science. 01 Jan 1965: Vol. 147, Issue 3653, pp. 48–49.

40 Erwin Schrodinger, *What is Life? The Physical Aspect of the Living Cell*. Cambridge University Press. London. 1944. Schrodinger, one of the fathers of quantum mechanics, wrote this book for lay readers to describe the stability of genetic structures. He had won the Nobel Prize for Physics in 1933.

41 John C. Stephenson, William A. Haseltine, C. Bradley Moore, "Atmospheric Absorption of CO2 Laser Radiation." *Applied Physics Letters*, volume 11, September 1, 1967. Pages 164–166.

42 The first Telluride house was established at Cornell University early in the 20th century, with Berkeley added later. The Berkeley program ended after I graduated but another was established at the University of Michigan in 2000. Telluride alumni from the three campuses include Nobel Prize winners Steven Weinberg, Linus Pauling and Richard Feynman, as well as former World Bank President and U.S. Deputy Defense Secretary Paul Wolfowitz, President Franklin D. Roosevelt's Labor Secretary, Frances Perkins, and philosophers Michael Foucault and Francis Fukuyama. The founding industrialist, Lucien L. Nunn, made his fortune bringing electrical power generation to mining fields near Telluride, Colorado, in the late 19th century. His goal was to promote intellectual life and social responsibility on campus. See https://www.tellurideassociation.org/about-us/history/; accessed April 6, 2020.

43 In his 2015 summary of Gandhara civilization on the website of the *Ancient History Encyclopedia*, Muhammad Bin Naveed writes, "Alexander left sizeable populations of Greeks in every region he conquered and Gandhara was no exception, with craftsmen, soldiers and other followers encouraged to inter-marry and blend with the locals and bring to them the fruits of Greek civilization. When Alexander died in June 323 BCE, his occupying Greek force, desperate to return home, started the journey back regardless of the orders to stay in the region and this left a large vacuum in the already thinly spread Greek occupation force in Gandhara. Nonetheless, enough Greek centers were created in the region to affect its history for centuries to come." See, https://www.ancient.eu/Gandhara_Civilization/; accessed April 6, 2020.

44 Robert Redfield, *Tepoztlán: A Mexican Village—A Study of Folk Life*. University of Chicago Press. Chicago. 1973. (First published 1930.)

45 Oscar Lewis, *Life in a Mexican Village: Tepoztlán Restudied*. University of Illinois Press. Urbana, Ill. 1951.

46 The two hour film, *Berkeley in the Sixties*, has many scenes and interviews with key leaders of the Free Speech Movement. The soundtrack is memorable as well, including Jefferson Airplane, Jimi Hendrix, Joan Baez and the Grateful Dead.

Nominated for an Academy Award as Best Documentary Feature in 1990, the film won the National Society of Film Critics Award in 1991. I am in some scenes, typically one of a few or the only one in a white shirt and wearing black horn rimmed spectacles. The entire film can be accessed online on Amazon Prime, at https://www.amazon.com/gp/video/detail/amzn1. dv.gti.10a9f702-2ac9-9b39-b409-fae34107f379?autoplay=1.

47 Savio's "body upon the gears" speech was ranked among the top one hundred political speeches of the 20th century by *American Rhetoric*. To read the full speech, see, https://americanrhetoric.com/speeches/mariosaviosproulhallsitin.htm.

48 For an absorbing even handed summary of Mario Savio's life and influence in the Free Speech Movement, see this review of the Savio biography, *Freedom's Orator*, in *The Nation*: https://www.thenation.com/article/archive/body-gears/.

49 Kali temples abound in several regions of India. Believers revere Kali as the most powerful Hindu goddess, devourer of demons, conqueror of evil, and benign motherly figure for the faithful. Kali also is the goddess of blood and gore. Her statues beneath high temple domes show her in a fierce expression, with three eyes—to see your past, present and future—multiple arms and an extended red tongue.

50 See, https://www.infoplease.com/world/population-statistics/total-population-world-decade-1950–2050; accessed April 15, 2020.

51 Concerns about rapid population growth in 1960 are explored in a 2011 article by University of Michigan economist David Lam, "How the World Survived the Population Bomb: Lessons from 50 Years of Extraordinary Demographic History." See, https://www.ncbi.nlm.nih.gov/pmc/articles/PMC3777609/; accessed April 15, 2020.

52 Khajuraho, as I discovered in my pre-travel research, features several erotic stone figures among many others depicted in small scenes along many levels of twenty two structures that remain from the original eighty. Many regard Khajuraho as the most exquisite ancient temples in India, each dedicated to a Hindu god or goddess and evoking various facets of human experience, including procreation. The UNESCO World Heritage site draws more than three hundred thousand visitors a year, mostly foreigners. It was discovered, overgrown by date trees, by the British army in the 1850s. India's central government has worked to preserve the ruins since the late 1950s and develop a local tourism economy.

53 The journey took us through rural lands where people lived in tiny huts with mud floors, near dirt roads. I gazed out, observing their medieval farming techniques and oxen to plow their fields, before the train headed into mountains.

54 Absinthe is about 100 proof, with a heavy licorice flavor similar to Pernod. It is blended from several botanicals, primarily green anise, Florence fennel seed and grand wormwood.

55 Absinthe was not legal in Europe either. It had been banned in the U.S. since 1912 after health officials raised alarms about illicit toxic concoctions.

56 The Angkor Wat temples were carved from stone by Hindus a thousand years ago during the Khmer Empire to honor the god Vishnu. The site later was expanded by Buddhists. Declared a UNESCO World Heritage site in 1992, Angkor Wat today draws more than a million tourists annually, four decades since the collapse of the genocidal Khmer Rouge regime of Pol Pot that killed an estimated two million countrymen and women.

57 Excavated by German archaeologists in the late 1800s, followed by decades of restorations by Lebanon, the temples at Baalbek originally stood more than thirty feet high with enormous stone pillars at least four meters in diameter. Fantastic feats of engineering that would become a UNESCO World Heritage site in 1984.

58 The metropolitan topography of Damascus is bizarre, a shape you never see in Europe or North America. Centuries of accumulated detritus have left an expansive mound on the landscape, formed from layer upon layer of garbage, old houses, and buildings left by each generation. New generations cover it and keep going.

59 In June 1967, triumphant after the Six-Day War against Egypt, Jordan and Syria, Israel would annex all of Jerusalem, the Golan Heights bordering Syria to the north, and some of Egypt's and Jordan's lands to the south. When I was in east Jerusalem and Damascus, though, I had no inkling the leaders of those three countries would soon conspire, and have their armies humiliated in sudden complete defeat.

60 Built by Romans under King Herod a few years before Christ's birth, the wall is an extension of the temple, known as the Second Temple, erected by Jews returning to Jerusalem. They had been exiled by Babylonian rulers for more than a half-century until Cyrus, the empire-building Persian king, welcomed them back. His army routed the Babylonians in Jerusalem years before.

61 *Isaac Asimov's Guide to the Bible*, I discovered later, is a fantastic book for explaining the history, geography, culture and biography behind Biblical stories. Those stories, of course, are a deep part of western history. I was surprised to read in Asimov's guide, for example, that Jews never had a kingdom in ancient times. At best, they prevailed periodically in constant warfare with people around them. As Asimov explains, Jews never controlled the Mediterranean coast before the twentieth century.

62 Ramesses II lived to age ninety or ninety one; his original red hair turned ginger-colored by his death. Some years after my 1965 visit, Egyptologists were alarmed to discover that his mummy was infested by mites. High-energy X-ray treatments by French specialists in synchrotron radiation cured that malady in Grenoble. In 1975 Ramesses II was returned in his sealed glass coffin to the Egyptian Museum where visitors continue to throng for a glimpse. Ramesses's skeleton, accompanied by his beating heart or not, may well have traveled more than that of any other Pharaoh. He lived during Egypt's New Kingdom, which by Egyptian history is fairly recent. Scholars estimate construction of the pyramids in Saqqara began about 2600 BC.

63 An English biochemist and crystallographer at Cambridge University, John Kendrew shared the 1962 Nobel Prize in chemistry with a Cambridge colleague, Max Perutz, for describing the atomic structure of myoglobin, a muscle protein. Jim Watson not only was one of Kendrew's PhD students, he lived in a small room in Kendrew's house. See, https://www.nobelprize.org/prizes/chemistry/1962/ceremony-speech/; accessed April 19, 2020.

64 Henry Kissinger, *Diplomacy*. Simon & Schuster. New York, 1994.

65 We learned a few years later that Kissinger's "Fellows" luncheon program was funded privately by Nelson Rockefeller—the Rockefeller fortune heir then governor of New York State—and the U.S. Central Intelligence Agency.

66 Helmut Schmidt was West Germany's chancellor from 1974 to 1982.

67 John Kenneth Galbraith, *The New Industrial State*, Houghton Mifflin & Company, Boston, 1967.

68 Fairbank and Reischauer coauthored two survey textbooks: *East Asia: The Great Tradition, A History of East Asian Civilization*, published by Houghton Mifflin Co., Boston, 1960; and *East Asia: The Modern Tradition*, published by Houghton Mifflin Co., Boston, 1966.

69 In just a few years, Jon and some colleagues were the first to isolate a gene from the chromosome of a living organism. He warned at the time of the public announcement in 1969 that this discovery could, in the wrong hands, lead to many dangers from genetically engineering any life form. Jon's memoir, *Making Genes, Making Waves*, is a lively examination of the scientist's responsibilities in research and to the wider society. The book was published by Harvard University Press in 2002.

70 Well into his 80s, Jon was still teaching and leading research projects at Harvard Medical School in 2020.

71 The book remains the defining survey of the field. *The Molecular Biology of the Gene*, 7th edition, by James D. Watson, Tania A. Baker, Stephen P. Bell, Alexander Gann, Michael Levine and Richard Losick, with Stephen C. Harrison. Pearson Education Inc., Glenview, Ill. 2014.

72 Kornberg, a biochemist, had shared the Nobel Prize in Physiology or Medicine in 1959 for his discovery. For a lively explanation of the research and significance, see the speech conferring the Nobel award, https://www.nobelprize.org/prizes/medicine/1959/ceremony-speech/; accessed, April 21, 2020.

73 For a compelling summary of Tsuneko Okazaki's life and her contributions to molecular biology, see https://thebumblingbiochemist.com/wisewednesday/tsuneko-okazaki/; accessed, April 21, 2020.

74 The Nobel Prize speech honoring Monod, Jacob and Lwoff at the 1965 award ceremony in Stockholm is available here: https://www.nobelprize.org/prizes/medicine/1965/ceremony-speech/; accessed, April 21, 2020.

75 The impact of these articles, three especially in *The New Republic*, one in 1970 and two in 1971, caught the attention of prominent journalists. Some encouraged me to move from science into investigative journalism, a career path that would have appealed if my PhD studies had for any reason gone haywire.

76 Haseltine, W.A.; Block, R.; Gilbert, W; Weber, K. (1972). "MSI and MSII Made on the Ribosome in Idling Step of Protein Synthesis." *Nature* 238 (5364); 381-284.

77 Haseltine, W.A.; Block R. "Synthesis of Guanosine Tetra- and Penta-phosphate Requires the Presence of Codon Specific Uncharged Transfer Ribonucleic Acid in the Acceptor Site of Ribosomes." Proceedings of the National Academy of Sciences. 1974. 70: 1564–1568.

78 The grim annual toll of American soldier corpses ferried back across the Pacific peaked in 1968 at more than sixteen thousand. Meanwhile, in 1967, some three hundred thousand men opened Defense Department notices ordering their induction into the Army. See, https://www.nytimes.com/2017/10/06/opinion/vietnam-draft.html; accessed, December 14, 2019.

79 One friend from junior high and high school, a photographer, died when the military plane he was on was shot down leaving Khe Sanh. He had just made a series of images on the ground of a bomb shell exploding in front of him. He survived that, but not the plane crash. One of those images from his recovered camera made the cover of *Newsweek*.

80 The audio recording of President Kennedy's 1962 graduation remarks at West Point, in full, at seventeen minutes, thirty three seconds, is available from the archives of the John F. Kennedy Presidential Library. The quotation cited begins at eight minutes, twenty two seconds from the beginning of the recording. https://www.jfklibrary.org/asset-viewer/archives/JFK-WHA/1962/JFKWHA-103-001/JFKWHA-103-001.

81 J.D. Bernal, *The Social Function of Science*. Routledge & Kegan Paul Ltd., London, 1939, p. 387. Reprinted by the MIT Press, 1964.

82 Bernal, teaching at Cambridge in England, naïvely admired aspects of Marxism in the Soviet system. "In its endeavor, science is communism," he once wrote. "In science men have learned consciously to subordinate themselves to a common purpose without losing the individuality of their achievements." See this essay, published in *The Modern Quarterly* a year before his book with the same title, https://www.marxists.org/archive/bernal/works/1930s/social-science.html; accessed, April 27, 2020.

83 This 2018 *Jacobin Magazine* interview with a longtime NARMIC staffer, Diana Roose, "Understanding the Vietnam War Machine," is an excellent primer on NARMIC's history and impact. See, https://www.jacobinmag.com/2018/06/namric-antiwar-research-vietnam-war; accessed April 28, 2020.

84 Michael T. Klare became a professor of peace and world security studies, and an author of more than fifteen books on U.S. military policy, international peace and security affairs, the

global arms trade and global resource politics. He contributed regularly to *Foreign Affairs*, *The Nation*, the *Los Angeles Times* and many other publications. A professor emeritus at Hampshire College in Massachusetts, his most recent book, published in 2019 by Metropolitan/Henry Holt, is *All Hell Breaking Loose: The Pentagon's Perspective on Climate Change*. See, https://www.hampshire.edu/faculty/michael-klare; accessed, April 27, 2020.

85 *Harvard Magazine* published an extensive retrospective on these events, "Echoes of 1969: Recalling a time of trial, and its continuing resonances," in its March-April 2019 issue. See, https://www.harvardmagazine.com/2019/03/1969-student-protests-vietnam; accessed December 14, 2019.

86 A book about the March 4 Movement and its lasting impact on the public debate about the role of science in American society was published in 2019 by MIT Press, entitled *March 4 Scientists, Students, and Society*. Jonathan Allen was the editor. *Science Magazine* published Audra J. Wolfe's review of this book, "Speaking truth to power: Fifty years after MIT's memorable protest, a key question remains: Should scientists ask for change or should they demand it?" See https://blogs.sciencemag.org/books/2019/02/28/march-4/; accessed April 28. 2020.

87 A recent book, *Science for the People: Documents from America's Movement of Radical Scientists*, asserts that Science for the People was "the most important radical science movement in U.S. history." The organization was shuttered for various reasons in 1989 after twenty years of impact in the public square on vital issues such as nuclear proliferation, industrial pollution, health risks and racial and gender equality. The Union of Concerned Scientists after fifty years remains highly respected and influential, with studies to prevent U.S. nuclear plant uranium from being stolen and channeled into the black market for weapons and examining how false science damages U.S. leadership in climate change research.

88 Fotis Kafatos was appointed professor of biology in 1969, at age twenty nine, the youngest to achieve that position at Harvard. A native of Crete, Greece, he became widely admired as a science administrator, most notably as founding president of the European Research Council. His continuing research, begun in the Watson-Gilbert lab, was sequencing genomes. In his final post, professor of immunogenics at Imperial College London, he "was still focusing on the genomes of the insect vectors of malaria," according to his obituary in *The Lancet*, published two months after Fotis's death in 2017. See, https://www.thelancet.com/journals/lancet/article/PIIS0140-6736(18)30112-0/fulltext; accessed April 27, 2020.

89 The name changed to *Boston Phoenix* in 1972 when a new owner merged *Boston After Dark* with the *Cambridge Phoenix*. The final issue of *Boston Phoenix* was published in 2013.

90 Author Max Boot's biography, *The Road Not Taken: Edward Lansdale and the American Tragedy in Vietnam*, was a finalist in that category for the 2018 Pulitzer Prize. The publisher was Liveright Publishing Corporation, a division of W.W. Norton & Company. New York, 2018. See, https://wwnorton.com/books/9780871409416; accessed April 28, 2020.

91 Nader's Raiders was a group of consumer advocates, many of them progressive young professionals or graduate students who uncovered and challenged a range of government failures in nuclear safety, regulation of insecticides, land use and other areas. They were led by Ralph Nader, a young lawyer who sparked a surge in activism around public safety with his 1966 book, *Unsafe at Any Speed*. The best-selling exposé documented willful neglect at General Motors, Ford and Chrysler in the design and manufacture of their automobiles. Nader likely will be remembered more for his delusional run for the Presidency in 2000. He won enough votes in New Hampshire and Florida that, if they had been cast instead for Democrat Al Gore, as was likely, Gore would have won the election, not Republican George W. Bush.

92 Robert E. Cook, William Haseltine and Arthur W. Galston, "What Have We Done to Vietnam? Deliberate Destruction of the Environment," *The New Republic*. January 10, 1970. Pp. 18–21.

93 William Haseltine, "The Automated Air War: The Illusion of Withdrawal—II," *The New Republic*. October 16, 1971. Pp. 15–17.

94 William Haseltine and Arthur H. Westing, "The Wasteland: Beating Plowshares into Swords," *The New Republic*. October 30, 1971. Pp. 13–15.

95 Outbreaks in the U.S. caused an average of more than fifteen thousand cases of paralysis in young children and peaked in 1952 at more than twenty thousand before the Salk vaccine was developed in 1955. The last polio case in the U.S. was reported in 1979.

96 Baltimore identified six ways that messenger RNA encodes protein, how these viral proteins can take over a cell and make more particles of virus. These six paths "are the essence of the virus infection process," he explained in an excellent nineteen-minute video lecture: https://www.youtube.com/watch?v=skC7XgkpAD8; accessed December 24, 2019.

The six different kinds of viruses resulting from these six paths became known as the Baltimore classification, beginning in 1970. Many textbooks still use the six different instructions for making viral proteins as a way to differentiate the six kinds of viruses. However, Baltimore says, the six sets of instructions are "not a classification; it is a statement of how viruses fit their style of handling genetic information into the needs of the central dogma" of DNA to RNA to protein.

97 David's findings were published in two articles in *Nature*: Baltimore, D., "Viral RNA-dependent DNA Polymerase: RNA-dependent DNA Polymerase in Virions of RNA Tumour Viruses"; *Nature* 226, 1209–1211 (27 June 1970). See, https://www.nature.com/articles/2261209a0; accessed, May 4, 2020; and, Altaner, C. and H.M. Temin, "Carcinogenesis by RA Sarcoma Viruses," Virology 40, 118–134 (1970).

98 Matt Meselson, at Harvard, also discovered a restriction endonuclease. This variation cut the DNA at random locations, a finding that proved to have limited value in genetic engineering.

99 Insulin injections for people with diabetes help move sugars from the blood to body tissues that convert sugar to energy. Human growth hormone is essential for body growth, and often is prescribed to help maintain, build or repair tissue in the brain and other organs.

100 Daniel Nathans, Werner Arber and another molecular biologist, Hamilton Smith, shared the 1978 Nobel Prize for Physiology or Medicine. Paul Berg, Wally Gilbert and Frederick Sanger shared the 1980 Nobel Prize in Chemistry for their contributions to basic research related to nucleic acids. See, https://www.nobelprize.org/prizes/medicine/1978/ceremony-speech/; accessed May 5, 2020.

101 See, https://www.nobelprize.org/prizes/medicine/1993/ceremony-speech/; accessed December 14, 2019.

102 James Dahlberg, biomolecular chemist and protégé of Howard Temin, was at the time a young professor. A DNA and RNA researcher his entire career at the University of Wisconsin, Jim also cofounded a company based on his discovery of an enzymatic reaction that helped identify genetic mutations. See, https://morgridge.org/story/james-dahlberg-scientific-successes-enhanced-by-chance/; accessed, May 5, 2020.

103 Dolly the Sheep was born at Scotland's Roslin Institute in 1996. She died six years later. This *Scientific American* article is one of several in recent years summarizing the significance of the Institute's cloning work, and avenues for new discoveries it opened in stem cell research. https://www.scientificamerican.com/article/20-years-after-dolly-the-sheep-led-the-way-where-is-cloning-now/.

104 The Leukemia Society of American later was renamed the Leukemia & Lymphoma Society.

105 Frei's accomplishments in medical laboratories, unheralded for decades, saved the lives of millions of cancer patients. Tom Frei and Emil Freirich observed that attacking cancer with

only one drug yielded only temporary remissions; a cancer might disappear but then return, adapting to, then defying the one drug treatment. Death, not cures, loomed as inevitable.

Combination chemotherapy remains, sixty years since their pathbreaking research, standard protocol for treating many adult and childhood cancers. Edward M. Kennedy Jr. may have been Tom's most famous patient. Kennedy credited Tom with saving his life. The classic textbook Tom coauthored with James F. Holland, *Holland-Frei Cancer Medicine*, continues to introduce thousands of future physicians to the subject. This 2000-page reference is now in its ninth edition.

106 My previous course, Biology and Social Issues, had been ably orchestrated by another professor during my three years at MIT. Now a member of the Harvard Medical School faculty, I had sufficient academic rank to oversee a General Studies course on my own. Cancer and Society was structured the same way as Biology and Social Issues. This new course explored the history, politics and biology of cancer research. I and other faculty lectured on biology science and modern life, such as how the FDA approved certain drugs and whether these drugs might be carcinogenic. Experts in the community led sections or volunteered on panels covering a range of issues—nuclear power, radiation, smoking, cyclamates in sodas, red dye number two in foods, carcinogens in Scotch whiskey and cooked bacon, ultraviolet ray exposure and more. We examined the 1976 moratorium in Cambridge on recombinant DNA research as well.

107 The paper described what became known as the Maxam-Gilbert method of DNA sequencing. I was aware that Allan Maxam and Wally Gilbert had finished documenting all their experiments and writing the paper some time before. I needed that paper. As soon as I could, I took the shuttle from my Farber lab back to the Harvard campus and obtained a mimeograph copy at my old haunts in the BioLabs.

108 Alan and I published two papers on the experiment results as quickly as possible. They were accepted by the journal *Biochemistry*. Here are the citations: Alan D. D'Andrea and William A. Haseltine, "Sequence specific cleavage of DNA by the antitumor antibiotics neocarzinostatin and bleomycin." *Biochemistry*. Vol. 75, No. 8, pp. 3608–3612, August 1978. And, Alan D. D'Andrea and William A. Haseltine, "Modification of DNA by aflatoxin B1 creates alkali-labile lesions in DNA at positions of guanine and adenine." *Biochemistry*. Vol. 75, No. 9, pp. 4120–4124, September 1978.

109 Mustard gas agents, a whole series of alkylating agents, bind to and damage DNA. Cis-platinum binds to DNA. Our experiments showed how these agents, although they appeared to have similar biochemistry, reacted differently on different parts of the DNA.

110 When those chemotherapy trials were in the first years, new combinations of drugs were administered to patients at gradually higher and higher levels. How much could patients tolerate? How rapidly would the cancers recede? No one knew. One week when high dosage levels were given, four patients died. Those were sobering days. Tom Frei counseled, "These four people died more quickly than they would have if nothing had been done. What they have done is show us the limits of this approach. The heroes in cancer research are the patients, not the clinical team, not the scientists in the labs. Patients put their lives on the line. Many people, thousands of people, will benefit from what these four people have enabled us to learn."

111 A 1979 global conference on virus and cancer included one hundred twenty five presentations entirely on animal viruses and cancers. As John Coffin, my colleague at Tufts, later observed, not one of the scientists at the "Viral Oncogenes" gathering at Jim Watson's revitalized Cold Spring Harbor Laboratory discussed viruses and human cancer. See, https://www.ncbi.nlm.nih.gov/pmc/articles/PMC4697431/; accessed May 11, 2020.

112 Gallo's team by the mid-'70s had established irrefutable fundamentals for comparing normal and leukemic (cancerous) blood cells in animals and humans. They also had found evidence of reverse transcriptase in the cells of adult lymphocytic leukemia patients that indicated the same characteristics of reverse transcriptase in a retrovirus.

Writing about this years later, Bob Gallo said, "I believed then and I believe now that this was indeed a 'footprint' of a human retrovirus, but we failed to isolate virus from this patient; that is, we failed to perpetuate virus in cell culture." Gallo, Robert C., "History of the discoveries of the first human retroviruses: HTLV-1 and HTLV-2." *Oncogene*, volume 24, pp. 5926–5930 (2005). See, https://www.nature.com/articles/1208980; accessed May 11, 2020.

113 Source: Centers for Disease Control and Prevention. See, https://www.cdc.gov/mmwr/preview/mmwrhtml/mm5021a2.htm#fig1; accessed July 21, 2020.

114 At the time, feline leukemia cancer killed an estimated three to five percent of the fifty million domestic cats in the U.S. annually.

115 Dendreon and its original cell therapy for prostate cancer, Provenge, is now owned by a larger Chinese retailer with a significant stake in healthcare services, Nanjing Cenbest. A subsidiary of the company acquired Dendreon assets, then owned by Valeant Pharmaceuticals, in 2017 for $820 million.

116 How big is that microbial universe? In his book *I Contain Multitudes*, science writer Ed Yong estimated the human body has thirty trillion cells of its own making while another thirty nine trillion or so foreign microbial cells lurk somewhere inside. See, Ed Yong, *I Contain Multitudes: The Microbes Within Us and a Grander View of Life*. HarperCollins Publishers. New York. 2016.

117 The prize committee's tradition is to honor only living men and women.

118 Robert W. Redfield was named director of the Centers for Disease Control and Prevention in 2018.

119 Presentation to the Cambridge Forum, "AIDS: The Battle Ahead," by William A. Haseltine, PhD. February 19, 1986.

120 *Frontline*, "The AIDS Quarterly: The Trial of Compound Q," PBS. Produced by WGBH/Boston and hosted by Peter Jennings. January 31, 1990. See, https://www.pbs.org/wgbh/pages/frontline/aids/docs/compoundq.html; accessed May 20, 2020.

121 Alan Riding, "Scandal Over Tainted Blood Widens in France." *New York Times*, February 13, 1994. See, https://www.nytimes.com/1994/02/13/world/scandal-over-tainted-blood-widens-in-france.html; accessed, May 16, 2020.

122 "Fact Sheet: The President's Emergency Plan for AIDS Relief," White House Press Announcement, January 29, 2003. See https://georgewbush-whitehouse.archives.gov/news/releases/2003/01/20030129-1.html; accessed May 25, 2020.

123 *Frontline*, "The Age of AIDS; Interview: Richard Holbrooke." PBS. Posted May 30, 2006. See, https://www.pbs.org/wgbh/pages/frontline/aids/interviews/holbrooke.html; accessed May 26, 2020.

124 Dr. Anthony Fauci, "The HIV/AIDS pandemic is #Solvable." An interview uploaded to YouTube by the Rockefeller Foundation, December 1, 2019. See, https://www.youtube.com/watch?v=zjeuujJV2PA; accessed May 25, 2020.

125 Ibid.

126 "The United States President's Emergency Plan for AIDS Relief," 2019 Annual Report to Congress. See, https://www.state.gov/wp-content/uploads/2019/09/PEPFAR2019ARC.pdf; accessed May 25, 2020.

127 For 2019, Biogen reported $14.4 billion in revenues and $4.9 billion in net income. Nearly two thirds of revenues were generated by treatments for multiple sclerosis.

128 Chiron acquired Cetus in 1991 for $700 million; the FDA soon after approved interleukin-2 for cancer treatments. The drug now is considered one of the most successful immunotherapy treatments for kidney and skin cancers.

129 Genetic Systems was acquired in 1986 by Bristol-Myers for $294 million.

130 In the summer of 1978, Genentech successfully expressed human insulin in bacteria; essentially, synthetic insulin that could be manufactured in high volume. A licensing agreement with Eli Lilly soon followed and in 1980 Genentech completed its initial public offering, valued at $85 million. By 1995, Lilly's Humulin, trade name for its synthetic insulin, accounted for more than sixty percent of total U.S. insulin sales, $300 million.

In 2009, Roche acquired Genentech for $47 billion. For a detailed report and analysis, see "Incentives and Focus in University and Industrial Research: The Case of Synthetic Insulin," by Scott Stern, in *Sources of Medical Technology: Universities and Industry*, National Academy of Sciences. 1995. https://www.ncbi.nlm.nih.gov/books/NBK232052/ accessed, June 1, 2020.

131 During Richard Lerner's twenty years as president, beginning ten years later in 1991, he established the Scripps Research Institute as one of the largest nonprofit biomedical research organizations in the world.

132 Dr. Bernard N. Fields, a physician and virologist, was responsible for multiple advances in applying genetics to understand how viral infections damage cells in animals and humans. His textbook first published in 1985 and since updated frequently, *Fields Virology*, remains the authoritative reference.

133 David Blech's four year jail sentence started in 2013 after he pleaded guilty to securities fraud. His wealth, estimated by *Forbes* magazine in the early '90s at nearly $300 million, evaporated when biotech stocks plummeted a few years later. He describes himself on LinkedIn now as a private investor in New York.

134 LeukoSite acquired ProScript and Velcade, and in turn was acquired by Millennium Pharmaceuticals in 1999 for more than $600 million. Millennium took Velcade all the way to market, an effective treatment for a very difficult cancer that became a blockbuster drug. Velcade and related technology are owned by Takeda Pharmaceutical, which acquired Millennium in 2009. Velcade revenues in 2019 amounted to more than $1 billion.

135 One of Wally's rejected recommendations, to license Amgen's foundational drug discovery through recombinant DNA, erythropoietin, certainly made Amgen. The drug, which generates production of red blood cells, is commonly used for treating chronic kidney disease, Crohn's disease and ulcerative colitis and certain cancers. For years now, Amgen has been the world's largest biotech company.

136 To some scientists the quest to sequence the human genome was undertaken in the spirit of pure inquiry... knowledge for knowledge's sake. Others saw the genome project as purely a technical challenge. I once asked the leader of the Japanese Human Genome Project why he was sequencing the genome. He replied, "I like to sequence DNA." I persisted. "To what purpose?" He became agitated. "Don't you understand? I have no purpose. I sequence DNA to sequence DNA!" To him and many others, my focus on only one part of the genome made no sense.

137 The Human Genome Project was the largest international collaboration ever undertaken for an experiment in biology. Thousands of scientists around the world participated over the course of thirteen years until the "finished" sequence of nearly the entire genome was completed in 2003. Total government funding through 2003 was $2.7 billon (in 1991 dollars), slightly less than the $3 billion projected at the outset for a timeline anticipated to end in 2005. Researchers continue to fill in "gaps" in the sequence and report new data as it becomes available. For the U.S. government's comprehensive description of the project, see https://www.genome.gov/about-genomics; accessed June 15, 2020.

138 The Bristol-Myers grant for scientific research was one of the most generous of that period. It was unrestricted, meaning we could use the money however we chose. Retrovirus discoveries we had published, as we saw in chapters 18 and 19, were significant for understanding cancer, and Bristol-Myers wanted to support our work. My only obligation was to meet with

other top medical scientists in my field for three or four relaxing days near Kennebunkport, Maine. There was no pressure. Bristol-Myers research scientists just wanted to get to know us and for us to know them.

When an executive first called me out of the blue to explain the award, "We would like to give you five hundred thousand dollars for unrestricted research," and congratulate me, I found it hard to believe. "Well, if this is not a joke, please give me your number. I am going to call you back."

139 Julia Flynn, "Is SmithKline's Future in its Genes?" *Business Week*, March 4, 1996. See, https://www.bloomberg.com/news/articles/1996-03-03/is-smithklines-future-in-its-genes; accessed December 14, 2018.

140 Gene Bylinsky, "Genetics – The Money Rush is On: The final decoding of the secrets of life is opening a new era in the treatment of disease and has set drug giants rushing for alliances with biotech startups." *Fortune,* May 30, 1994. See, https://money.cnn.com/magazines/fortune/fortune_archive/1994/05/30/79350/index.htm; accessed, December 14, 2018.

141 John Carey, "The Gene Kings," *Business Week.* May 8, 1995, pp. 72–78. See https://www.bloomberg.com/news/articles/1995-05-07/the-gene-kings; accessed, December 14, 2018.

142 Those Roche Institute positions were prized. Staff scientists could work on any project they desired, with guaranteed funding and no pressure to produce results leading to marketable products. "It was a scientific Camelot," wrote authors of the Institute's history. The Roche Institute endured until closing in 1997, "a victim of the biotech revolution that resulted in numerous entrepreneurial startups funded by Wall Street dollars."

The history by Herbert Weissbach, a cofounder of the Institute, and David Fisher is *A Camelot of the Biomedical Sciences: The Story of the Roche Institute of Molecular Biology*. RIMB Adventures. October 2016. See, https://www.amazon.com/Camelot-Biomedical-Sciences-Institute-Molecular/dp/0998278408; accessed June 22, 2020

143 According to Google Scholar Citations, Bert Vogelstein's published research, encompassing more than five hundred scientific papers, has been cited more often than those of "any other scientist, in any discipline, in recorded history."

144 Bert Vogelstein went on to explain that the body's inability to repair these mismatch mistakes during DNA replication causes random changes in the genome every time the cell divides. More growth of cells with mismatched genes, more risk of cancerous outbreaks. Cells in the colon divide all the time. So do ovarian and endometrial cells. (Endometrial cancer starts in cells of the uterus's inner lining.)

145 The mismatch repair defects Bert Vogelstein identified in our gene samples ultimately were found in about two percent of all cancer patients, not only those with hereditary colorectal cancers. The significance of further studies of mismatch repair defects was underscored when the 2015 Nobel Prize for Chemistry was awarded for discoveries in that field.

146 A founder of Cambridge Antibody Technology, Gregory Winter, was a superb scientist whom I knew was easy to work with. In 2018, Winter shared the Nobel Prize in Chemistry for his advances in evolving antibodies to produce new pharmaceuticals. One of the most commercially successful antibody drugs, adalimubab (brand name Humira, annual sales approaching twenty billion dollars), was discovered by his company.

147 In 2006, Human Genome Sciences and GlaxoSmithKline agreed to co-develop the BLyS antibody, then known as belimumab, through Phase III and Phase IV trials. More than fifteen hundred patients participated in two Phase III clinical trials. A high percentage showed reduced levels of the disease and severe episodic flare-ups, without damaging side effects. Unfortunately, African American and African patients in the trials did not show much improvement.

148 William A. Haseltine, "The Case for Gene Patents: Drug development cannot thrive without them, argues the CEO of Human Genome Sciences." *MIT Technology Review*. September

1, 2000. See https://www.technologyreview.com/2000/09/01/236177/the-case-for-gene-patents/; accessed December 14, 2018

149 Scott Shane, "U.S. Settles Suits Over Anthrax Attacks," *New York Times*. November 29, 2011. Section A, page 19. See https://www.nytimes.com/2011/11/30/us/anthrax-victims-family-to-receive-2-5-million-in-settlement.html; accessed, June 25, 2020.

150 Centers for Disease Control and Prevention, "Anthrax: The Threat." See https://www.cdc.gov/anthrax/bioterrorism/threat.html; accessed June 24, 2020.

151 David Willman, "Selling the Threat of Bioterrorism," *Los Angeles Times*. July 1, 2007; and Annie Jacobsen, *The Pentagon's Brain: An Uncensored History of DARPA, America's Top Secret Military Research Agency*. Little, Brown & Company. 2015. Page 293.

152 Ken Alibek and Stephen Handelman, *Biohazard: The Chilling True Story of the Largest Covert Biological Weapons Program in the World*. Random House. New York. 1999.

153 "Dr. Anthony Fauci hosts Ask the White House." May 19, 2004. See https://georgewbush-whitehouse.archives.gov/ask/20040519.html; accessed June 26, 2020.

154 Scott Shane and Eric Lichtblau, "F.B.I. Presents Anthrax Case, Saying Scientist Acted Alone." *New York Times*. August 6, 2008. See, https://www.nytimes.com/2008/08/07/washington/07anthrax.html; accessed June 24, 2020.

155 The conference was convened by the Aspen Institute of Italy.

156 Shinya Yamanaka shared the Nobel Prize for Physiology or Medicine in 2012 with John Gurdon for the discovery that mature cells could be converted to stem cells. Yamanaka built on Gurdon's original work in the 1960s establishing the potential for mature cells, or differentiated cell nuclei, to return to stem cell status, by demonstrating how intact mature cells in mice could be reprogrammed to become immature cells that are able to develop into all types of cells in the body. See, https://www.nobelprize.org/prizes/medicine/2012/press-release/; accessed June 30, 2020.

157 Tapash Jay Sarkar, Dr. Thomas A. Rando and Vittorio Sebastiano, "Transient non-integrative expression of nuclear reprogramming factors promotes multifaceted amelioration of aging in human cells," *Nature Communications*. March 24, 2020. See, https://www.nature.com/articles/s41467-020-15174-3; accessed, June 30, 2020.

158 Nicholas Wade, "Turning Back the Clock on Aging Cells: Researchers report that they can rejuvenate human cells by reprogramming them to a youthful state," *New York Times*. March 24, 2020. See, https://www.nytimes.com/2020/03/24/science/aging-dna-epigenetics-cells.html; accessed June 30, 2020.

159 Hannah Kuchler, "Gene editing success heralds era of animal-to-human transplants: Biotechs race to serve patients stuck on waiting lists for organs," *Financial Times*. December 8, 2019.

160 Tony Atala presented a vivid overview of his current work at the Singularity University Summit in Jalisco, Mexico in 2018. The thirty minute presentation is available on YouTube. See, https://www.youtube.com/watch?v=SNwHASw1VJ8; accessed, June 29, 2020.

161 I discussed tissue engineering and other topics covered in my 1998 speech in Italy in an interview published in *Life Extension Magazine* in July, 2002. See, https://www.lifeextension.com/magazine/2002/7/report_haseltine; accessed, January 15, 2019. The Brookings Institution published my more complete discussion of regenerative medicine, "Regenerative Medicine: A Future Healing Art," on December 1, 2003. See, https://www.brookings.edu/articles/regenerative-medicine-a-future-healing-art/; accessed, April 16, 2019.

162 *New York Times* columnist William Safire requested a copy of my speech text. "I collect great speeches," he said that night. "That was a great speech." Alas, I had no text then and re-

grettably did not follow up with Bill. Until I pulled them from memory to write this chapter, I had never before typed out those remarks.

163 By chance I later met a prominent cataract surgeon from Johns Hopkins Medicine who was visiting the same hospital in Madurai. He was there to learn, not advise. "I pity the poor patient that has me as a surgeon," he said. "At home I may do five to ten operations a week at most. They are excellent, with far fewer failures and infections than we do!"

164 David Green continues his phenomenal activity as a social entrepreneur, creating low cost technologies that have helped hundreds of thousands of poor people restore their sight and hearing. As NPR reported in 2013, he "sets up for profit companies, or nonprofits that run operating surpluses, so the firms have the ability to invest and grow." See, "One Man's Quest to Make Medical Technology Affordable to All," by John Ydstie, as heard on *Morning Edition*, July 3, 2013; https://www.npr.org/sections/health-shots/2013/07/03/198065436/one-mans-quest-to-make-health-care-accessible-and-affordable; accessed July 4, 2020.

165 C.K. Prahalad, *The Fortune at the Bottom of the Pyramid: Eradicating Poverty Through Profits*, Wharton School Publishing, Upper Saddle River, N.J. 2004.

166 India is incredibly diverse, and that includes healthcare policies and approaches. The country is not a microcosm of anything. Think of a region that encompasses the same landmass, multiple cultures and languages as Europe and northern Africa, from the Atlantic Ocean, the southern Mediterranean Sea and Ural Mountains to the east. If that were one country, you would have more than a billion people. India has nearly 1.4 billion people, with twenty six official languages, including eleven languages on its currency. China's population in 2020 was sixty million more than India, at 1.44 billion.

167 A top cardiologist who still sees patients, Krishna also is a talented administrator and executive. I was excited to have him join ACCESS Health fulltime in 2019 to lead all our projects in India and pursue his passion to create a think tank on transforming health systems.

168 CARE Hospitals Group is part of a healthcare organization, the Evercare Group. Based in Dubai, the group operates a clinical network of twenty six hospitals, eighteen clinics and forty diagnostic centers in Sub-Saharan Africa and South Asia. Evercore was established through a one billion dollar impact fund. TPG Group of the U.S. is general managing partner of the fund, formerly known as the Abraaj Growth Markets Health Fund. See, https://carehospitals.com/about-care/the-story-of-care/; accessed, July 23, 2020.

169 Even so, Aarogyasri as designed was not a comprehensive long term health system solution. It created its own problem. People with minor ailments flocked as well to hospitals. When they learned that these most common health problems were not covered by the program, they became angry.

170 Outsourcing companies fueled India's breakthrough into the modern global economy, providing low cost information technology services to an array of large corporations, primarily in the United States. Several outsourcing firms were based in Hyderabad; IBM and Accenture also established large operations there.

171 William A. Haseltine, *Every Second Counts: Savings Lives with India's Emergency Response System*. Brookings Institution Press. Washington D.C. 2019.

172 Highlights of India's emergency response system were the topic of my blog post, "What the U.S. Can Learn from India's Emergency Response System." The post had been accessed by midyear 2020 more than twenty thousand times. See, https://www.forbes.com/sites/williamhaseltine/2019/01/23/what-the-u-s-can-learn-from-indias-emergency-response-system/#93f28663b274.

173 C.K. Prahalad was co-author, with Gary Hamel, of two popular *Harvard Business Review* articles, "Strategic Intent" and "The Core Competence of the Corporation." The articles led to their best-selling business book, *Competing for the Future: Breakthrough Strategies for Seizing*

Control of Your Industry and Creating the Markets of Tomorrow, published by Harvard Business School Press in 1994.

174 For global GDP per capita rankings, see, http://statisticstimes.com/economy/projected-world-gdp-ranking.php; accessed July 23, 2020.

175 Lee Kuan Yew, *From Third World to First: The Singapore Story 1965–2000*. HarperCollins Publishers. New York, 2000. p. 95.

176 Greenleaf Book Group Press published *Aging with Dignity* and *Voices in Dementia Care* in the United States in 2020.

177 For the Centers for Medicare and Medicaid Service's most current statistics on U.S. healthcare spending, see, https://www.cms.gov/Research-Statistics-Data-and-Systems/Statistics-Trends-and-Reports/NationalHealthExpendData/NationalHealthAccountsHistorical#:~:-text=U.S.%20health%20care%20spending%20grew,spending%20accounted%20for%2017.7%20percent.; accessed, July 8, 2020

178 Langone, who earlier with his wife Elaine donated two hundred million dollars to the medical center, contributed one hundred million dollars of six hundred million dollars targeted to establish the fund for these scholarships.

179 The CBS *60 Minutes* segment on the free tuition announcement can be viewed here: https://www.cbs.com/shows/60_minutes/video/wm_ydR60LLE2bLYRZVdexzYTZpQ8rHtk/how-the-nyu-school-of-medicine-is-going-tuition-free/.

180 William A. Haseltine, *World Class: A Story of Adversity, Transformation, and Success at NYU Langone Health*. Fast Company Press, New York. 2019. p. 74.

181 Ibid. p. 90.

182 Much of the material describing NYU Langone Health's transformation of Lutheran Medical Center was adapted from my previous commentaries. These include an April 5, 2019 piece in STAT News's *First Opinion*, "High-quality care can lower U.S. health care costs: a case study from Brooklyn." See, https://www.statnews.com/2019/04/05/high-quality-care-lower-costs/; accessed April 5, 2019. Also, from four commentaries on my Forbes.com blog:

"Delivering High Quality Care at a Price Everyone Can Afford: A Case Study," posted August 2, 2019; see, https://www.forbes.com/sites/williamhaseltine/2019/08/02/delivering-high-quality-care-at-a-price-everyone-can-afford-a-case-study/#2eb9606f7c82; accessed, July 8, 2020;

"Changing the Culture of an Organization: The NYU Langone Case Study," posted August 28, 2019; ; see, https://www.forbes.com/sites/williamhaseltine/2019/08/28/changing-the-culture-of-an-organization-the-nyu-langone-health-case-study/#1f057645516a; accessed, July 8, 2020;

"How Do You Transform a Healthcare Organization? With Vision," posted September 20, 2019; see, https://www.forbes.com/sites/williamhaseltine/2019/09/20/how-do-you-transform-a-healthcare-organization-with-vision/#37465ec654be; accessed July 8, 2020;

"A Health Information System That Puts People First," posted October 21, 2019; see, https://www.forbes.com/sites/williamhaseltine/2019/10/21/a-health-information-system-that-puts-people-first/#73c6e9cb24c3; accessed July 8, 2020.

183 Gwen Ifill, "THE 1992 CAMPAIGN: Youth Vote; Clinton Goes Eye to Eye with MTV Generation," *New York Times. June 17, 1992. See,* https://www.nytimes.com/1992/06/17/us/the-1992-campaign-youth-vote-clinton-goes-eye-to-eye-with-mtv-generation.html; accessed, April 3, 2020.

184 Eric Ditzian, "Bill Clinton to Barack Obama: MTV's History with Politics," MTV News. October 12, 2010. See, http://www.mtv.com/news/1649854/bill-clinton-to-barack-obama-mtvs-history-with-politics/; accessed April 3, 2020.

185 Ronald Brownstein, "Will Trump Triangulate?" *Atlantic*, April 6, 2017. See, https://www.theatlantic.com/politics/archive/2017/04/will-trump-triangulate/521973/; accessed April 2, 2020. Brownstein's summation of Clinton's strategy was this: "Nimble and nuanced, Clinton simultaneously energized Democratic partisans and restored his reputation with independents as a fresh thinking centrist. Two years after his midterm rejection, he cruised to reelection."

186 The official U.S. budget statistics for healthcare are available from the Centers for Medicare and Medicaid Services. For the fiscal 2018 figures, see, https://www.cms.gov/Research-Statistics-Data-and-Systems/Statistics-Trends-and-Reports/NationalHealthExpend-Data/NHE-Fact-Sheet; accessed, April 1, 2020.

187 It was Brookings that created much of the Marshall Plan that put western Europe back on its feet after World War II.

188 In an NPR interview in 2009 about his new book, *War of Necessity, War of Choice: A Memoir of Two Iraq Wars*, Richard Haass said, "I believed in diplomacy, I believe in multilateralism, I believe in institutions... I did not believe in the Iraq war. I thought the United States did have viable alternative policy options, and I feared by going to war, it would—to use the phrase that Colin Powell and I bandied about—'Take the oxygen out of the room on American foreign policy.' So yes, on virtually every foreign policy issue, I found myself on a very different page from my colleagues." See https://www.npr.org/templates/story/story.php?storyId=104088144; accessed, April 13, 2020.

189 The Center for Strategic and International Studies is best known for authoritative analyses of global security issues, but its policy research mandate, expertise and influence extend much wider, to economics, energy, trade, international affairs, global health and more. https://www.csis.org/programs/about-us; accessed April 14, 2020.

190 See, https://www.weforum.org/agenda/2019/09/elderly-oldest-population-world-japan/; accessed, April 13, 2020.

191 More than four hundred journalists, representing the BBC, CNN, CNBC, *Financial Times* and dozens of other news outlets cover the sessions at high level, meaning they can report on ideas and opinions but not attribute anything to specific participants.

192 Aventis later merged with Sanofi-Synthélabo, in 2004, to form Sanofi-Aventis, now the world's third largest pharmaceutical firm after Pfizer and GlaxoSmithKlilne.

PHOTO CREDITS

INDEX

Ruprecht, Ruth, 234
Rwanda, 278–279, 280–281

S

Sachs, Goldman, 428
Safai, Bijan, 217
Sallin, Steven, 200
Sandoz, 228
Sanger, Carol Bayer, 249
SARS-CoV-2, 440
Savio, Mario, 96, 97, 98
Scharff, Matty, 190
Schering-Plough, 320
Schirra, Wally, 26
Schlief, Bob, 189
Schlossman, Stuart, 220
Schmidt, Helmut, 118
Schrodinger, Erwin, 79
science, 23–32
    advanced coursework, 116–117
    begins with observation, 71–72
    dissecting frog, 27
    Eric's career in, 31–32
    field theory, 116
    first independent experiments, 28
    Florence's career in, 30–31
    and humanity, 87
    launch of Sputnik, 32
    lover for, 23–32
    material science, 117
    naval weapons research base, 25–27
    as part of life, 244–248
    and photochemistry intern, 29–30
    preventing war, role in, 153–154
    reading books, 24–25
    statistical mechanics, 116
    structural biology, 116
    world of microbes, fascination
        towards, 28–29
Science (journal), 78–79, 84, 136, 185
Science fair, 27
Scientific American (journal), 435
Scott, Walter, Sir, 24
Scottish Puritans, 36, 38
Scripps Research Institute, 288
Seaman's life, 54–57

Securities and Exchange Commission,
    298, 326, 327
Sekhri, Paul, 366
Sent, Gunter, 122
Sexton, John, 412
Sexually transmitted diseases
    (STDs), 55–56
Shalala, Donna, 428
Shanmugaratnam, Tharman, 393
Sharp, Philip, 180
Shearer, Derek, 159, 160
Shirk, Jim, 77, 78
SHIV. *See* SIV-HIV hybrid virus
Sidney Farber Cancer Institute, 184, 192
sigma factor, 138
sigma protein, 136
Sihanouk, Prince Norodom, 105
Simian Immune Deficiency Virus
    (SIV), 232, 234
Singapore
    absent immigration, 399
    Affordable Health Care, 396–397
    Biopolis, 393
    eldercare and unsolved
        conundrum, 398–400
    hard working population of, 395–398
    healthcare market, approach
        to, 397–398
    Medisave, 398
    Office of Healthcare
        Transformation, 399–400
    price transparency in, 405
    promoting healthy living, 396–397
Sinton (scientist), 77, 78–79, 80
SIV. *See* Simian Immune Deficiency Virus
SIV-HIV hybrid virus (SHIV), 232
Skagway, 41
Sloan Kettering Memorial Cancer
    Hospital, 190
Smith, Soapy, 41, 52
SmithKline Beecham, 228, 316, 318
The Social Function of Science (Bernal), 153
social injustice flares, at Berkeley
    campus, 94–95
Sodroski, Joe, 211, 212, 221, 224, 232